DUNS SCOTUS ON
TIME & EXISTENCE

DUNS SCOTUS ON TIME & EXISTENCE
The Questions on Aristotle's *"De interpretatione"*

Translated with introduction and commentary
by Edward Buckner and Jack Zupko

The Catholic University of America Press
Washington, D.C.

Copyright © 2014
The Catholic University of America Press
All rights reserved

Library of Congress Cataloging-in-Publication Data
Duns Scotus, John, approximately 1266–1308.
[Quaestiones in Aristotelis libros I-II Perihermenias. English]
Duns Scotus on time and existence : the questions on Aristotle's On
interpretation / translated with introduction and commentary by
Edward Buckner and Jack Zupko.
pages cm
Includes bibliographical references and index.
ISBN 978-0-8132-3638-4 (pbk)   1. Aristotle. De interpretatione.
2. Logic—Early works to 1800.   3. Language and languages—
Philosophy—Early works to 1800.   I. Buckner, Edward, 1955–
translator.   II. Title.
B439.D8613 2014
160—dc23   2014016451

CONTENTS

Acknowledgments	ix
Abbreviations	xi
Introduction	1

TRANSLATION

Opus I	25
Question 1. What Is the Subject of *On Interpretation*?	25
Question 2. Do Names Signify Things, or Species in the Mind?	28
Question 3. Does a Change Occur in the Signification of an Utterance Given That a Change Has Occurred in the Thing Signified?	39
Question 4. Does Aristotle Designate an Appropriate Difference between Inscriptions and Utterances, and Affections and Things?	43
Questions 5. Is a Common Term Said Univocally of Existing Things and Non-Existing Things?	45
Question 6. Are There Any *Supposita* Belonging *Simpliciter* to a Common Term Signifying a True Nature, apart from Things That Exist?	47
Question 7. Are the Propositions 'Caesar is a man' and 'Caesar is an animal' True When Caesar Does Not Exist?	49
Question 8. Are the Propositions 'A man is a man' and 'Caesar is Caesar' True When Neither of Them Exists?	52
Question 9. Does a Common Term Suppositing with a Present-Tense Verb Supposit Only for Presently Existing Things?	67
Question 10. In a Past-Tense Proposition, Does the Subject Stand Only for Things That Were, and in a Future-Tense Proposition, Only for Things That Will Be?	70
Question 11. Is a Common Term Distributed for Any of Its *Supposita Simpliciter* in Every Proposition in Which Some Immediate Contracting Term Is Not Added to It?	71
Question 12. Is 'Caesar is a man' True When Caesar Does Not Exist?	83
Question 13. Can a Common Term Be Restricted?	87

Contents

Opus II. Questions on the Two Books of *Perihermenias*:
On Book I   96
    Prologue   96
    Question 1. Does a Name Signify a Thing or an Affection?   98
    Question 2. Does a Name Signify a Thing Univocally When the Thing Is Existing and When It Is Not?   106
    Question 3. Do Truth and Falsity Only Concern Composition and Division?   110
    Question 4. Does an Indefinite Name Posit Something, Such That the Predication of the Being of That Thing Is Required?   113
    Questions 5. Is the Verb 'Is' Only a Copula of the Predicate with the Subject?   119
    Question 6. Is a Present-Tense Verb a Copula for the Present 'Now' or Indifferently for Anything Present?   121
    Question 7. Is a Proposition about the Future Determinately True or False?   131
    Question 8. Is '*a* will be' Now Determinately True?   132
    Question 9. Is It Possible That Neither Part of a Contradiction Is True?   133

Opus II. Questions on the Two Books of *Perihermenias*:
On Book II   142
    Question 1. Does an Indefinite Verb Remain Indefinite in a Sentence?   142
    Question 2. Does 'This is not just; therefore, this is non-just' Follow?   147
    Question 3. Does a Consequence of This Sort Hold for Relational Terms?   149
    Question 4. [Does a Consequence of This Sort] Hold with Past-Tense Verbs: First, Would 'It was non-white; therefore, it was not white' Follow?   149
    Question 5. Conversely, [Does a Consequence of This Sort] Follow, Assuming the Constant Existence of the Subject?   150
    Questions 6. Is 'A white man runs' One?   153
    Question 7. Is 'A white thing is musical' One?   155
    Question 8. Is 'A white man is a musical man' One?   156
    Question 9. Is 'A man, who is white, runs' One?   157

COMMENTARY

Opus I   169
    Question 1. What Is the Subject of *On Interpretation*?   169
    Question 2. Do Names Signify Things, or Species in the Mind?   172
    Question 3. Does a Change Occur in the Signification of an Utterance Given That a Change Has Occurred in the Thing Signified?   187

Question 4. Does Aristotle Designate a Proper Difference between
Inscriptions and Utterances, and Affections and Things? 194
Questions 5–8. Summary Outline 197
Question 5. Is a Common Term Said Univocally of Existing Things
and Non-Existing Things? 197
Question 6. Are There Any *Supposita* Belonging *Simpliciter* to a
Common Term Signifying a True Nature, apart from Things
That Exist? 202
Question 7. Are the Propositions 'Caesar is a man' and 'Caesar is
an animal' True When Caesar Does Not Exist? 206
Question 8. Are the Propositions 'A man is a man' and 'Caesar is
Caesar' True When Neither of Them Exists? 213
Questions 9–11. Summary Outline 230
Question 9. Does a Common Term Suppositing with a Present-Tense
Verb Supposit Only for Presently Existing Things? 231
Question 10. In a Past-Tense Proposition, Does the Subject Stand
Only for Things That Were, and in a Future-Tense Proposition, Only
for Things That Will Be? 238
Question 11. Is a Common Term Distributed for Any of Its *Supposita*
without Qualification in Every Proposition in Which Some Immediate
Contracting Term Is Not Added to It? 241
Question 12. Is 'Caesar is a man' True When Caesar Does Not Exist? 254
Question 13. Can a Common Term Be Restricted? 260

Opus II. Questions on the Two Books of *Perihermenias*:
On Book I 274
Prologue 274
Question 1. Does a Name Signify a Thing or an Affection? 276
Question 2. Does a Name Signify a Thing Univocally When the
Thing Is Existing and When It Is Not? 283
Question 3. Do Truth and Falsity Only Concern Composition
and Division? 288
Question 4. Does an Indefinite Name Posit Something, Such That
the Predication of the Being of That Thing Is Required? 292
Question 5. Is the Verb 'Is' Only a Copula of the Predicate with
the Subject? 299
Question 6. Is a Present-Tense Verb a Copula for the Present 'Now,'
or Indifferently, for Anything Present? 302
Questions 7–9: Future Propositions and Truth 317
Question 7. Is a Proposition about the Future Determinately
True or False? 320
Question 8. Is '*A* will be' Now Determinately True? 321
Question 9. Is It Possible That Neither Part of a Contradiction
Is True? 323

Opus II. Questions on the Two Books of *Perihermenias*:
On Book II — 331
    Question 1. Does an Indefinite Verb Remain Indefinite in a Sentence? — 331
    Questions 2–5: On Inferential Relations between Propositions Containing Definite versus Indefinite Terms — 335
    Question 2. Does 'This is not just; therefore, this is non-just' Follow? — 340
    Question 3. Does a Consequence of This Sort Hold for Relational Terms? — 343
    Question 4. [Does a Consequence of This Sort] Hold with Past-Tense Verbs: First, Would 'It was non-white; therefore, it was not white' Follow? — 344
    Question 5. Conversely, [Does a Consequence of This Sort] Follow, Assuming the Constant Existence of the Subject? — 345
    Questions 6–9. The Unity and Complexity of Propositions — 349
    Question 6. Is 'A white man runs' One? — 350
    Question 7. Is 'A white thing is musical' One? — 352
    Question 8. Is 'A white man is a musical man' One? — 353
    Question 9. Is 'A man, who is white, runs' One? — 354

Bibliography — 365
Index of Names — 377
General Index — 381

ACKNOWLEDGMENTS

The present translation was made possible by the appearance in 2004 of the critical edition of Scotus's *Quaestiones in Libros Perihermenias Aristotelis*—edited by Robert Andrews, Girard Etzkorn, the late Fr. Gedeon Gál, OFM, Romuald Green, OFM, Timothy Noone, Roberto Plevano, Andrew Traver, and Rega Wood—in volume II of the *Opera Philosophica* of Blessed John Duns Scotus, jointly published by the Franciscan Institute of St. Bonaventure University and the Catholic University of America. Along with the entire scholarly community, we owe a debt of gratitude to the editorial team for making available to present and future Scotus scholars a reliable, modern edition of the *Perihermenias* along with other important writings. We are also grateful to the publishers for permitting us to use the critical edition as the basis for our translation.

We began translating Scotus's commentaries on *De interpretatione* separately, but were alerted to each other's efforts early on thanks to the intervention of Tim Noone. The difficulty of the text made it advisable to work together, which is what we did, to the point where it is now no longer easy to identify who wrote what. Our procedure was for one of us to translate and the other to revise the translation, alternating our roles for each question. But the revisions inevitably prompted discussion, which led to further revisions and further discussion until we were confident we had the text right, or at least that we had provided our best rendition of what we took Scotus to be saying. Any remaining uncertainties are flagged and discussed in the translation.

During the five years that we worked on the translation, we encountered many passages that were challenging not only linguistically, but also in terms of their underlying historical and doctrinal context. Here we freely availed ourselves of the scholarship of others, especially concerning the Oxford logic scene in the

1290s. The generous advice of Sten Ebbesen and Tim Noone helped us out of several difficult spots. Finally, we are grateful to our two referees for the Catholic University of America Press, Mary Beth Ingham and Simo Knuuttila, for very helpful comments and suggestions that led to many improvements in the text. Our CUAP editor, Paul Higgins, read a complicated manuscript with great care and saved us from many mistakes our authors' eyes prevented us from seeing. Of course, we are responsible for any errors that remain.

In terms of institutional support, Jack Zupko received a semester's leave sponsored by the Emory University Research Council, which greatly facilitated our work in its early stages.

We would both like to thank our families for their patience and support during the years it took to complete this project.

This volume is dedicated to the memory of our teachers, C. J. F. Williams (1930–1997) and Norman Kretzmann (1928–1998).

ABBREVIATIONS

AA   *Les Auctoritates Aristotelis*. Edited by J. Hamesse. Louvain-Paris: Publications Universitaires-Béatrice Nauwelaerts, 1974.

AL   *Aristoteles Latinus*, Corpus philosophorum medii aevi, Academiarum consociatarum auspiciis et consilio editum (1939–). (II^1 5 = *De interpretatio vel Periermenias translatio Boethiii, specimina translationum recentiorum*. Edited by Laurentius Minio-Paluello. Bruges: Desclée de Brouwer, 1965.)

n., nn.   Standing alone, refer to numbered paragraphs in the translated text.

OPh   *B. Ioannis Duns Scoti Opera Philosophica*, 5 vols. St. Bonaventure, N.Y.-Washington, D.C.: 1997–2006.

PL   *Patrologiae cursus completus*, series latina, accurante J. P. Migne. Paris: 1844, sqq.

DUNS SCOTUS ON
TIME & EXISTENCE

INTRODUCTION

Life and Key Dates

John Duns Scotus was born between 1265 and 1266, mostly likely in the village of Duns, Scotland.[1] However, like most of his biography, this is based on conjecture from the mere handful of events in his clerical and academic career that have been recorded for posterity. In this case, we know that he was ordained to the priesthood in Northampton, England, as a member of the Franciscans, or Order of Friars Minor, on March 17, 1291. Assuming he was ordained as early as the Franciscans permitted, he would have been about 25 years old, placing his birth around 1266. His place of birth is inferred from the fact that he was known as 'John Duns' (*Johannes Duns*) during his lifetime, following the medieval practice of referring to people by their Christian or given name and place of origin.[2] The 'Scotus' designation is also contemporary. In a document of 1304, the Franciscan Minister-General mentions 'John the Scot' as most worthy of promotion to Master of Theology at Paris, an event which occurred the following year.

Tradition has John Duns studying at the Franciscan convent in Oxford as a boy, perhaps in the late 1270s or early 1280s. There he would have begun his studies of grammar and dialectic, though this is not known for certain.[3] In the absence

---

1. For a concise discussion of the available evidence on Scotus's life, see Thomas Williams, "The Life and Works of John Duns the Scot" in *The Cambridge Companion to Duns Scotus* (Cambridge: Cambridge University Press, 2002), 1–14. For a superbly detailed discussion of the manuscript and historical evidence, see Antonie Vos, *The Philosophy of John Duns Scotus* (Edinburgh: Edinburgh University Press, 2006).

2. Vos argues that 'Duns' must have been John's family name, as someone from Duns would have been known as 'de Duns,' a name attested in the fourteenth century (*Duns Scotus*, 23). Be that as it may, all the available evidence points to John having been a Scotsman.

3. The colophon of Merton 66 states that Scotus flourished at Cambridge as well as Oxford and

Introduction

of datable evidence, we are hampered in constructing an educational chronology for him because members of mendicant orders such as the Franciscans were exempt from the undergraduate degree requirements that applied to secular masters (much to the consternation of the latter, it should be added). Likewise, Franciscans and Dominicans tended to receive their arts training at schools belonging to their respective orders rather than in the arts faculties of the universities. This is significant where Scotus's commentary on Aristotle's *De interpretatione* is concerned because it suggests that he would have first studied this text, and subsequently lectured on it himself, in the company of other Franciscans at a Franciscan custodial school. Unlike his theological works, these logical writings were probably not intended for delivery to the broader university community.

Our knowledge of Scotus's career as a theologian is more wide-ranging, but only slightly. He appears to have been in Oxford in 1300 and 1301, taking part in a disputation under the regent master, Philip of Bridlington. By 1302 he was in Paris, lecturing on the *Sentences* of Peter Lombard. Along with other Franciscans, he was expelled from Paris in 1303 for opposing King Philip the Fair's efforts to depose Pope Boniface VIII; thence, he likely went back to Oxford, though he was permitted to return to Paris the following year, where he incepted as Master of Theology in 1305. He conducted the disputation which has come down to us as the *Quaestiones Quodlibetales* in Advent 1306 or Lent 1307.[4] For reasons unknown, he left Paris in 1307, reappearing later that year as a lecturer at the Franciscan school in Cologne. He died there on November 8, 1308.

Major Works

Owing to his itinerant career and early death, there are only a few (relatively) finished works among Scotus's literary remains; the rest are in various stages of completion, including some texts, such as his Paris lectures on the latter books of the *Sentences*, which are really lecture notes taken by a secretary or student. Scotus lectured on the *Sentences* more than once, first at Oxford and then at Paris,

---

Paris, but we do not know if this is true, or if it was, when he was there: "Haec de ordinatione ven. Fratris J. duns de ordine fratrum Minorum, qui floruit Cant Oxon et Parisius et obiit in Colonia," quoted in A. G. Little, "Chronological Notes on the Life of Duns Scotus," *English Historical Review* 47 (1932): 571, citing A. Callebaut, "Le bx. Duns Scot a Cambridge vers 1297–1300," *Archivum Franciscanum Historicum* 21 (1928): 608–11.

4. Felix Alluntis and Allan B. Wolter (eds. and trans.), *John Duns Scotus, The Quodlibetal Questions: God and Creatures* (Princeton, N.J.: Princeton University Press, 1975).

and revised his Oxford lectures over a number of years, inserting updated material from his Paris lectures. Likewise, he lectured on Aristotle's *De interpretatione* on two separate occasions (*Opus I* and *Opus II* below), although these works are more difficult to relate to each other chronologically and also doctrinally.

Scotus's major work is his *Ordinatio*, or revised version of his Oxford lectures on the *Sentences*. The *Sentences* commentary was the main genre of theological writing in the later Middle Ages, and in it Scotus presents his most famous teachings, such as the univocity of being, the formal versus real distinction, less-than-numerical unity, individual nature or 'thisness [*haecceitas*],' and the synchronic theory of contingency. However, as noted above, even this work was subject to later revisions and additions by Scotus himself on multiple occasions, at times with material from his Paris lectures. It is also incomplete, meaning that we know from the *Lectura*, Scotus's notes for his earliest Oxford lectures on the *Sentences*, that he treated some questions which were never dictated in revised form in the *Ordinatio*. From his Paris lectures we have several *reportationes*, or student notes. Of these versions, we know that Scotus examined one himself, and the Vatican editors have dubbed this '*Reportatio examinata*' or '*Reportatio* 1A.'[5] Finally, to complicate matters even further, we have the *Additiones magnae*, a set of notes on the Oxford and Paris lectures compiled and published a few years after Scotus's death by his secretary, William of Alnwick (c. 1275–1333). This text is important to Scotus scholars because it appears to fill in, quite faithfully, material that is missing from the *Ordinatio*.

Scotus's theological writings also include a number of disputations (the *Collationes* and *Quaestiones Quodlibetales*) in which he participated at Oxford and Paris, and an independent treatise on natural theology, *De primo principio*, a late work which Scotus may have overseen rather than composed on his own. Scotus's philosophical writings are all commentaries on individual works of Aristotle, which was the main genre of philosophical writing in later medieval universities. These were in two forms: *expositiones*, or literal commentaries, which offered a line-by-line analysis of the Aristotelian text under discussion; and *quaestiones*, or question commentaries, which considered a philosophical question or difficulty raised by the text (usually in a lemma from the text, quoted at the beginning of

---

5. Oleg V. Bychkov and Allan B. Wolter (eds. and trans.), *John Duns Scotus, The Examined Report of the Paris Lecture (Reportatio I-A)*, vol. 1 (St. Bonaventure, N.Y.: The Franciscan Institute, 2004).

the question). We have one *expositio* by Scotus, on Aristotle's *Metaphysics*, recently discovered by Giorgio Pini,[6] and seven question commentaries: one each on Porphyry's *Isagoge* (or *Introduction* to Aristotle's *Categories*), the *Categories* itself, *De sophisticis elenchis*, *De anima*, and *Metaphysics*, plus two on *De interpretatione*, which are the works translated here. There are a few other commentaries on Aristotle that appear in the Wadding (sixteenth century) and Vivès (nineteenth century) editions of Scotus's collected works, but these are now believed to be inauthentic.[7]

The logical works—that is, Scotus's question commentaries on the *Isagoge*, *Categories*, *De interpretatione*, and *De sophisticis elenchis*—are together known as the *parva logicalia* ('little logicals'). They are believed to have been written early in Scotus's career, perhaps between 1290 and 1295, when he was most likely teaching at Oxford,[8] though it is possible that they were written later. According to C. K. Brampton, "during the year 1301–2, Scotus probably lectured on the *Porphyry*, the *Predicaments*, the *Perihermenias* and the *Elenchi*, just as William of Ockham (c. 1287–1347) did in similar circumstances."[9] Allan B. Wolter also suggested that they were completed during Scotus's years in Paris, on the evidence of Antonius Andreas, an early Scotist who said his own logical writings are based on what Scotus taught him at Paris.[10] Vos, however, argues that this is unlikely.[11] The fact that Antonius Andreas witnessed him lecturing on such questions in Paris, however, does not necessarily mean that he wrote them during that period. For a more on the dating of the logical works, see the editorial introduction to *Opera Philosophica* I.[12]

---

6. See Giorgio Pini, "Critical Study: Duns Scotus's Metaphysics," *Recherches de théologie et philosophie médiévale* 65 (1998): 353–68.

7. These include sets of questions on Aristotle's *Prior* and *Posterior Analytics*, *Meteorology*, and *Physics*, as well as a treatise on speculative grammar by Thomas of Erfurt famously misidentified as a work of Scotus by Martin Heidegger. For more on this work by Thomas of Erfurt, see Jack Zupko, "Thomas of Erfurt," *The Stanford Encyclopedia of Philosophy* (Spring 2011 Edition), ed. Edward N. Zalta; http://plato.stanford.edu/archives/spr2011/entries/erfurt/. See also the section on "Authenticity" below.

8. See Vos, *Duns Scotus*, 124.

9. C. K. Brampton, "Duns Scotus at Oxford, 1288–1301," *Franciscan Studies* 24 (1946): 17.

10. Andreas is quoted in William A. Frank and Allan B. Wolter (eds. and trans.), *Duns Scotus, Metaphysician* (West Lafayette, Ind.: Purdue University Press, 1995), 3: "Haec de dictis magistri fratris Ioannis Duns, natione Scoti, sedentis super cathedram magistralem, ut potui, colligens, in unum compilavi." Frank and Wolter are citing Pius Sagüés-Azcona, "Apuntes para la historia del escotismo en España en el siglo XIV," in *De doctrina Ioannis Duns Scoti*, ed. Camille Berubé, Vol. 4: *Scotismus decursu saeculorum* (Rome: Societas Internationalis Scotistica, 1968), 3–19.

11. Vos, *Duns Scotus*, 35.

12. *B. Ioannis Duns Scoti Opera Philosophica*, 5 vols. (St. Bonaventure, N.Y.-Washington, D.C.:

Until the mid-twentieth century, Scotus scholars had to rely on the aforementioned Wadding or Vivès editions of Scotus's writings, which, besides containing spurious works, did not always provide reliable readings because they were not prepared according to modern editorial principles. Since 1950, the Scotus Commission in Rome has published fourteen volumes of the *Opera Omnia* of Scotus's theological writings in a critical edition ('critical' in the sense that the Latin text is arrived at through careful study and analysis of the interrelationships of all known manuscripts), covering Books I–II of the *Ordinatio* and the entire *Lectura*. But there is still a long way to go: the texts are difficult and the manuscript tradition is many-faceted, to say the least. As Antonie Vos observes, "in terms of the present speed, the *Commissio Scotistica* will need a century to complete the *Ordinatio*."[13]

The situation is much better with Scotus's philosophical writings. Editorial teams based at St. Bonaventure University and the Catholic University of America, as well as in Bonn, have recently completed critical editions of all of Scotus's philosophical works.[14] With a critical Latin text available for the first time, English translations of these works could finally be undertaken.

The present translation covers roughly the first half of Volume II of the *Opera Philosophica*, published in 2004. Volume II contains both commentaries on *De interpretatione*, the commentary on *De sophisticis elenchis*, and the *Theoremata*, a late work on faith and natural theology of questionable authenticity. Only the two commentaries on *De interpretatione* are translated here.

Scotus's Significance in the History of Philosophy

Duns Scotus is one of a handful of figures in the history of philosophy whose significance is difficult to overestimate. Despite an academic career lasting barely two decades and the sorry state of his literary remains, Scotus's thought exerted a profound influence on the history of western philosophy. Indeed, this influence began to be felt in his own lifetime among his students and younger Franciscan contemporaries, such as William of Alnwick, Antonius Andreas (c. 1280–1320), and Peter Aureol (c. 1280–1322). His theological views occasioned comment almost immediately, challenging both sympathizers and opponents, most notably

---

1997–2006), I, xxvi–xxxi; hereafter "*OPh*." For full citation information, which varies by volume, see bibliography.

13. Vos, *Duns Scotus*, 147.
14. See Scotus, *OPh*.

William of Ockham (c. 1288–1347), who was influenced by Scotus's notion of an intuitive mode of knowing, but who rejected Scotus's realist metaphysics and defense of theology as a science.

To later medieval theology, Scotus contributed a rigorous and philosophically sophisticated Augustinianism which proved a worthy competitor to the Aristotelianism of Thomas Aquinas and the Dominicans, thereby enriching both the Franciscan and Dominican theological traditions. His writings also helped to bring more Neoplatonic ideas and sources into mainstream theological argumentation, providing new perspectives on everything from the problem of universals to the nature of human freedom.

In the fifteenth century, Scotism evolved into a school of thought competing with other scholastic systems such as nominalism and Thomism. With the demise of scholasticism in the early modern period, however, it becomes much more difficult to document Scotus's influence with any precision. Partly this is a problem of not knowing who was reading what, though there were some who continued to read and admire Scotus in the modern period, including the American philosopher Charles Sanders Peirce in the nineteenth century. There are certainly modern philosophical theories that look Scotistic, or exhibit what look to be Scotistic elements; for example, Scotus and Immanuel Kant appear to be fellow travelers, at the very least, on the question of the autonomy of the will vis-à-vis the intellect. But even if Kant was innocent of Scotus's account of the will, it is interesting to compare the two theories in term of their philosophical strengths, and to evaluate as well their implications and background assumptions.

The Questions on the *Perihermenias* (*De interpretatione*)

As indicated above, the two works translated here belong to Scotus's *parva logicalia* and probably date from early in his career. Question commentaries emerged as a popular genre in the mid-thirteenth century as a way of studying the authoritative works of 'the Philosopher,' Aristotle, which were required reading for the Bachelor of Arts degree. The genre seems odd to modern readers who are unfamiliar with it, but this impression is easily dispelled when it is remembered that these works originated in the classroom, and still bear the marks of a text that was meant to be heard rather than silently read.

Medieval *Questions* on the *Perihermenias* were loosely based on problems arising from Aristotle's text (now more popularly known by its Latin name, *De interpretatione*), although many of the same topics were also discussed in other genres, such as *sophismata* literature, during the second half of the thirteenth century. This is especially true of questions pertaining to the semantics of time, existence, and quantification. Scotus himself covers three general topics in the *Questions* translated here: the signification of empty terms (*Opus I*, qq. 2–3, 5–8, 12; *Opus II.I*, qq. 2, 4; *Opus II.II*, qq. 2–5); the semantics of terms signifying past and future objects (*Opus I*, qq. 9–11, 13; *Opus II.I*, qq. 7–9); and the semantics of the verb 'is' (*Opus II.I*, qq. 3, 5–6; *Opus II.II*, qq. 6–9).

Scotus's *Questions* on the *Perihermenias* comes down to us in two versions. *Opus I* consists of thirteen questions on topics from Book I of the *Perihermenias*.[15] *Opus II* consists of two books, *Opus II.I* and *Opus II.II*, covering *Perihermenias* Books I and II respectively. There is some overlap in the topics covered by the two versions, but mostly they are distinct. For example, the questions on empty names (*Opus I*, qq. 5–8) and reference to objects in the past (*Opus I*, qq. 9–11) do not occur in *Opus II.I*. Conversely, the questions about the copula and reference to objects in the discrete present (*Opus II.I*, qq. 5–6) and about Aristotle's famous 'sea battle' problem (*Opus II.I*, qq. 7–9) do not occur in *Opus I*. We do not know which set of *Questions* came first.

Authenticity

There were doubts about the authenticity of Scotus's *Questions* on the *Perihermenias* even among its pre-modern readers. We will briefly discuss the attribution problem here in order to identify the main questions that need to be asked. We believe the work is authentic, though we do not pretend to base this on any new textual research; rather, we have relied on existing scholarship, together with our own experience in working with the text.

We know that early attributions of certain logical and metaphysical works to Duns Scotus are mistaken. There were already concerns about this within two centuries of his death, when the sixteenth-century logician Jacobus Naveros found inconsistencies between these texts and Scotus's commentary on the *Sentences*, leading him to doubt whether Scotus had written any logical works at all.[16]

---

15. Medieval commentators understood Aristotle's *Perihermenias* to contain two books: Book I, which covers our modern chapters 1–9, and Book II, beginning at 19b5, which covers our modern chapters 10–14.

16. See E. J. Ashworth, "Jacobus Naveros (fl. ca. 1533) on the Question, 'Do Spoken Words Signify

8   Introduction

In 1922 the logical work *De modis significandi* was shown by Martin Grabmann actually to have been written by Thomas of Erfurt, a fourteenth-century logician belonging to the Modist school. Thus, the oft-repeated claim that Martin Heidegger wrote his *Habilitationsschrift* on Scotus is only partly true, for the second part of that work (*die Bedeutungslehre*) is based the *De modis significandi* of Thomas of Erfurt. The first part, however, *die Kategorienlehre*, is based on Scotus's commentary on the *Categories* or *Praedicamenta* of Aristotle, which is authentic.[17]

The authenticity of Scotus's *Questions* on the *Prior Analytics* was called into doubt in the 1930s.[18] It is almost certainly not by Scotus, as the notion of the object of knowledge being what is "complexly signifiable [*complexe significabile*]," which is mentioned in the commentary, was first introduced in 1331 in the *Sentences* commentary of Adam Wodeham (c. 1300–1358).[19] Its true author remains unknown.

The two books on the *Posterior Analytics* (*In librum primum et secundum Posteriorum Analyticorum Aristotelis Quaestiones*) are also inauthentic.[20] It is thought that they were written by John of Cornwall, as the work is attributed to him in an Oxford manuscript. John studied at Oxford around 1300 and taught theology at Paris from 1310 to 1315.[21]

There is also controversy over the authenticity of Scotus's *Questions* on *De sophisticis elenchis*.[22] A. C. S. McDermott and Allan Bäck have argued that they, too,

---

Concepts or Things?'" in L. M. de Rijk and H. A. G. Braakhuis (eds.), *Logos and Pragma: Essays on the Philosophy of Language in Honour of Professor Gabriel Nuchelmans* (Nijmegen: Ingenium, 1987), 189–214.

17. Heidegger actually corresponded with Grabmann about his misattribution of *De modis significandis*, but, incredibly, made no effort to correct it in his lifetime. See Zupko, "Thomas of Erfurt."

18. B. Gölz, "Die echten und unechten Werke des Duns Scotus nach dem gegenwärtigen Stand der Forschung," *Lektorenkonferenz der deutschen Franziskaner für Philosophie und Theologie* 6–7 (1931–33): 56.

19. See *Ioannis Duns Scoti Doctoris Subtilis Ordinis Minorum Opera Omnia*, ed. L. Vivès (Paris: 1891–95), q. 8, 98b–101b; this is a reprint, with corrections, of *Ioannis Duns Scoti Doctoris Subtilis Ordinis Minorum Opera Omnia*, ed. L. Wadding, 12 vols. (Lyon: 1639). See also Gedeon Gál, "Adam of Wodeham's Question on the *Complexe significabile* as the Immediate Object of Scientific Knowledge," *Franciscan Studies* 37 (1977): 66–102, and Jack Zupko, "How It Played in the *rue de Fouarre*: The Reception of Adam Wodeham's Theory of the *Complexe Significabile* in the Arts Faculty at Paris in the Mid-Fourteenth Century," *Franciscan Studies* 54 (1994–97): 211–25.

20. Wadding, *Opera Omnia* I, 342–430, and Vivès, *Opera Omnia* II, 199–347.

21. See P. Parthenius Minges, *Ioannis Duns Scoti doctrina philosophica et theologica*, 2 vols. (Quaracchi: 1930), and Uriël Smeets, *Lineamenta Bibliographiae Scotisticae* (Rome: Commissio Scotistica, 1942), 8–9.

22. See Wadding, *Opera Omnia* II, 1–80, and Scotus, *Oph* II.

were written by John of Cornwall, as were Scotus's *Questions* on the *Prior Analytics* and *Posterior Analytics*.[23] However, Stephen Read has pointed out that both extant manuscripts of the *Questions* on *De sophisticis elenchis*, unlike those of the other two commentaries, explicitly ascribe them to Scotus.[24]

The remaining logical works—the *Questions* on the *Categories*, both sets of *Questions* on the *Perihermenias*, and the *Questions* on *De sophisticis elenchis*—are still thought to be authentic. However, some doubts remain. These logical works differ from other works written by Scotus in two fairly substantial respects. First, Scotus posits a complete equivocation among being in the different categories in his *Questions* on the *Categories*, whereas, as is well known, the mature Scotus was a proponent of the univocity of being.[25] Second, there is no suggestion of the 'synchronic' conception of modality, which allows for alternative possibilities at a given time and which Scotus may have been the first in the Middle Ages to advance in his *Lectura* and in the corresponding discussion in the *Questions* on the *Perihermenias* (*Opus II.I*, qq. 7–9).[26]

More generally (although perhaps unsurprisingly), there also is a lack of interest in theology in the *Questions*, whereas theology suffuses Scotus's mature work. Perhaps this is simply due to genre differences between the two kinds of commentary: one Aristotelian and the other theological. However, God ('the divine') is mentioned only once in the *Questions*, in a question which is a closely-worded imitation of Thomas Aquinas's discussion of truth and falsity in his commentary on the *Perihermenias* (Book I.3). Likewise, there are only two references to God in Scotus's *Questions* on the *Categories*, and none in his *Questions* on the *Isagoge*.

On the other hand, we have positive evidence that the work is authentic. The manuscript tradition consistently attributes these texts to Scotus. According to the editors of the *Questions* on the *Perihermenias*, eight of the thirteen manu-

---

23. A. C. S. McDermott, "Notes on the Assertoric and Modal Propositional Logic of the Pseudo-Scotus," *Journal of the History of Philosophy* 10 (1972): 274, and Allan Bäck, *On Reduplication* (Köln: Brill, 1996), 205–7 and 274–78.

24. Stephen Read, "Self-reference and Validity Revisited," in Mikko Yrjönsuuri (ed.), *Medieval Formal Logic. Obligations, Insolubles and Consequences* (Dordrecht: Kluwer, 2001), 183–96.

25. See Robert Andrews, "Andrew of Cornwall and the Reception of Modism in England," in *Medieval Analyses in Language and Cognition*, eds. Sten Ebbesen and Russell L. Friedman (Copenhagen: Royal Danish Academy of Sciences and Letters, 1996), 113.

26. For discussion of the relation between Scotus's early and later views on modality, see Vos, *Duns Scotus*, 34, and Calvin Normore, "Duns Scotus' Modal Theory," in Williams, *Cambridge Companion to Duns Scotus*, 129–60.

scripts of *Opus I* and five of the six manuscripts of *Opus II* attribute the works to Scotus. There are also several early references by Adam Wodeham, who explicitly mentions q. 2 of *Opus I*.[27] Further evidence comes from Antonius Andreas's own commentary on the *Perihermenias*, written no later than 1333.[28] This is a commentary on Aristotle's text which is shuffled together with a redaction of Scotus's *Questions*. These are not mere summaries of the *Questions* (as the introduction to the critical edition suggests),[29] but selective arrangements of Scotus's *Questions* reproduced practically verbatim. Antonius only omits passages which are prolix, confused, or rambling. He also changes the section order frequently, usually (in the style of Thomas Aquinas) by including the main arguments that agree with the reply in the reply itself. The order of questions is also changed to better reflect Aristotle's presentation. Finally, Antonius entirely omits the anomalous 'duplicate' questions, viz., *Opus I*, qq. 12–13 and *Opus II.I*, qq. 1–2.

We do not have the manuscript(s) that Antonius used. The evidence that Antonius was redacting our text, or something closely resembling it, is that whenever he changes the section or question order, he also removes cross-references suggestive of the original order and adds cross-references consistent with his new order. In one case, he adds explanatory material to a question which occurred much later in the original, but much earlier in the revised version.

Whether the text he was using was in all respects the same as the one that has come down to us is a more difficult question to answer. The main contrary evidence is that, whereas Scotus does not include Antonius's q. 9 ("Whether a sign [of quantity] can be given on the side of the predicate"), a fragment of it appears verbatim in *Opus I*, q. 12, nn. 17–18. This means that either Antonius took this fragment and turned it into a whole question, which seems unlikely for the reasons given in our commentary below, or else he was working from a different source which included the whole question, or most of it. Another two questions not appearing in Scotus are Antonius's q. 17 ("Whether the mode is predicated in

27. Adam de Wodeham, *Lectura secunda in primum librum Sententiarum*, eds. Rega Wood and Gedeon Gál, 3 vols. (St. Bonaventure, N.Y.: The Franciscan Institute, 1990), I, d. 1, q. 14 (187): "Item, hoc idem, scilicet quod res extra est extremum propositionis, licet non ut extra, tenet ipse [Scotus] super I Perihermenias, quaestione 2"; ibid., I, d. 22, qu. Unica (283): "Aliter respondet Scotus, quaestione 2 Super primum Hermenias"; qu. Unica (287): "Sic enim exponit Scotus illas auctoritates, quaestione 2 super I Perihermenias."

28. See Antonius Andreas, *Scriptum Antonii Andreae in Perihermenias Aristotelis*, in *Scriptum Antonii Andreae in arte veteri*, 63r–88r (Venice: 1508).

29. Scotus, *OPh* II, 32.

modal propositions") and q. 18 ("Whether modal and assertoric propositions are of distinct species"). No fragments of these are found in the Scotus text, and it is possible that they were an attempt by Antonius to complete the discussion.

Aristotle's *Perihermenias*

According to the Kneales,[30] the *Perihermenias* is one of Aristotle's earlier logical works. The Greek name means 'On Exposition' or 'On Interpretation.' It was called by that name by most, but not all, medieval authors, and was also known by its Latin name, *De interpretatione*, the most common designation today.

The *Perihermenias* is about the proposition or statement (*enuntiatio*), which, according to Scotus, "is not an act of understanding itself, but is more what is done by the understanding."[31] The proposition is the second of the three "operations of the understanding" which concern composition and division. The objects of the first operation are terms which are combined into propositional form by affirmation or negation. The third operation is the argument or syllogism that combines propositions into arguments with premises and conclusions.

Aristotle's *Perihermenias* dominated the study of logic in the Latin West from the sixth through the twelfth centuries, and for much of the later scholastic period as well. This is partly a historical accident. Many of the logical and philosophical works of Aristotle—what medieval authors called the 'new logic' (*logica nova*), consisting of the *Prior Analytics, Posterior Analytics, Topics,* and *De sophisticis elenchis*—did not become available again until the late twelfth and early thirteenth centuries. The 'old logic' (*logica vetus* or *ars vetus*), consisting of Aristotle's *Categories* and *De interpretatione*, Porphyry's *Isagoge*, and (somewhat later) the *Liber sex principiorum* associated with Gilbert of Poitiers (c. 1070–1154), was available in the West from the early medieval period onward, and by the thirteenth century there was an established tradition of commentary on these texts. The *logica vetus* is concerned with the first two operations of the understanding, and hence with questions of logic and language such as the meaning and properties of simple terms, the nature of assertion, and the semantics of modality and time, rather than with argumentation and formal reasoning, which are proper to the third operation.

30. William C. Kneale and Martha Kneale, *The Development of Logic* (Oxford: Clarendon Press, 1962), 24.
31. Duns Scotus, *'Quaestiones in libros Perihermenias Aristoteli,' op. prim. et sec.*, in *OPh* II.1, 135.

Like the other works in the *logica vetus*, the *Perihermenias* was known in the Latin West through the translations of Boethius (c. 472–524), a Roman Christian who wrote extensively on logic, philosophy, and mathematics. His Latin versions of Aristotle's *Categories* and *De interpretatione* were probably the only texts of Aristotle available to philosophers during the early medieval period.[32] He also wrote two influential commentaries on *De interpretatione* (from which Scotus quotes extensively). The survival of these works was assisted by their inclusion in Alcuin's program for the revival of classical scholarship in the ninth-century court schools of Charlemagne.

There was also a substantial literature on the *Perihermenias* by Greek commentators, some of which was known to the scholastics. These included Ammonius Hermiae (c. 440–520), who was a source for Stephanus and others.[33] In a translation by William of Moerbeke, the commentary of Ammonius influenced Thomas Aquinas and other authors of the late thirteenth century.[34]

In the Latin West, Peter Abelard (c. 1079–1142) wrote one of the earliest and most original commentaries on the *Perihermenias*, a penetrating work which wanders in interesting ways from Aristotle's text. Most scholastic writers of any reputation would have written at least one such commentary. Notable commentators of the thirteenth century were Albert the Great (c. 1193–1280), Thomas Aquinas (whose commentary was left unfinished),[35] Duns Scotus, and William of Ockham.

---

32. See L. Minio-Paluello, "Note sull 'Aristotele latino medievale," *Rivista di filosofia neo-scolastico* 44 (1952): 398–401, and "Les traductions et les commentaires Aristoteliciens de Boece," *Studia Patristica* 2 (1957): 358–65.

33. See David Blank, "Ammonius," in *The Stanford Encyclopedia of Philosophy* (Fall 2011 Edition), ed. Edward N. Zalta; http://plato.stanford.edu/archives/fall2011/entries/ammonius/.

34. See *Ammonius in Aristotelis De Interpretatione Commentarius*, ed. A. Busse (Berlin: 1897). French translation: *Commentaire sur le Peri hermeneias d'Aristote (opus a Guillelmo de Moerbeke translatum)*, ed. G. Verbeke (Louvain: Institut supérieur de philosophie, 1961). English translations: *On Aristotle's 'On Interpretation' 1–8*, trans. D. Blank (Ithaca, N.Y.: Cornell University Press, 1996) and *On Aristotle's 'On Interpretation' 9*, trans. D. Blank (Ammonius) and N. Kretzmann (Boethius) (Ithaca, N.Y.: Cornell University Press, 1998). Blank's translation (slightly revised by G. Seel and J.-P. Schneider) is also found in Gerhard Seel, *Ammonius and the Seabattle: Texts, Commentary, and Essays* (Berlin: De Gruyter, 2000).

35. Thomas's commentary ends at the second lecture on Book II, which corresponds to *De interpretatione* I.10.19b30. The rest was completed more than two centuries later by Thomas Cajetan (1469–1534).

Scotus's *Perihermenias*

Both sets of Scotus's *Questions* deal with topics we would now consider as belonging to the intersection between metaphysics and the philosophy of language: reference and signification, existence and essence, and truth and its connection with reality. After an introductory discussion (*Opus I*, q. 1), Scotus begins with the question of whether a name signifies a thing (q. 2), arguing that it signifies a thing, although not a thing signified as it exists in reality, but as it is conceived by our understanding, which, as becomes clear, is the essence of the thing as signified by the definition of the name which signifies it.[36] This was the position held by the Parisian Modists, who believed that between existence in reality and existence in the understanding there must be some nature which remains the same, and which underlies the essence of reality, our understanding of that reality, and the signification of the language expressing that reality.

Scotus then turns to the question of whether the meaning of a name depends on the existence of the objects falling under it, that is, named by it. Next he addresses (q. 3) whether, given a substantial transformation in the thing signified, there is a transformation in the meaning of name that signified it. Scholastic doctrine holds that in a substantial change, something changes into something else of an entirely different kind, such that the original thing simply ceases to exist. For example, when Caesar dies, his soul is separated from his body and his body becomes a corpse. Finally, q. 5 asks whether a name can apply in the same sense to an object which does not exist as to an existing object.

In keeping with virtually all other authors of the period, Scotus takes the position that empty terms have meaning and that they mean the same regardless of whether there are any objects falling under them. Meaning and existence are independent. This view commits him to a specific theory of existence (and later, to a specific theory of truth). In reply to q. 3, he says that when the thing signified is destroyed, so is the sign (n. 13). But even so, the thing is not destroyed as it is understood; thus, the significate of the utterance is not destroyed.[37]

---

36. This is in his second reply to q. 2 (n. 39), which, as we argue in the commentary below, is consistent with his later replies to qq. 3 and 5–8.

37. There are some similarities here with the contemporary debate about whether language has a 'semantic dependency' or 'object-dependency' on external reality. Authors such as Nathan Salmon have argued that the semantic contribution of a proper name or demonstrative term is simply the

14   Introduction

Next is the question of whether non-existing things can fall under a term (q. 6). Scotus replies that they can (n. 43) in a passage that perhaps anticipates his later views on individuation insofar as he talks about a nature in the understanding that is not common or predicable of many. Both natures (common and individual) are attributed to a thing as it is conceived in the understanding, not as it exists.

This leads Scotus to questions about the nature of truth (qq. 7–8); in particular, the question of whether propositions in which the predicate is said to 'belong essentially' to the subject (that is, where the predicate is 'of the essence' of the subject or belongs to it per se) are true when the subject does not exist. Is 'man is an animal' true when there are no men? It seems to be essentially and eternally true: 'man,' after all, belongs to the genus 'animal.' Yet orthodox Aristotelianism maintains that an affirmative proposition is true only when there is a union of the terms (or rather, of objects falling under the terms) in reality, and that would not happen if nothing fell under the subject.[38]

Scotus discusses this problem in relation to the propositions 'Caesar is Caesar' and 'Caesar is a man,' outlining a theory of truth consistent with the position he has taken on existence and essence (n. 49). According to this theory, these propositions are true even when the terms do not exist, for the union of terms is sufficient for the truth of an affirmative proposition, and in such propositions the understanding of the predicate is included in the understanding of the subject.[39] Again, a common nature is not attributed to a thing as it exists, but as it is conceived in the understanding. To the objection that the subject 'Caesar' and the predicate 'man' are not actually united, since Caesar does not exist (n. 54), he replies that the predication is incidental (*per accidens*).[40]

---

referent of the term—see Salmon, "Reflexivity," in Nathan Salmon and Scott Soames (eds.), *Propositions and Attitudes* (Oxford: Oxford University Press, 1988), 240–74. Thus, a term's signification is intrinsically linked to the existence of the objects it signifies or denotes, so that when the objects are destroyed, the signification is changed or destroyed. The position is known as 'direct reference' or 'Millianism,' although it applies only to proper names, whereas in the thirteenth century it applied to both common and proper names. This is the view that Scotus, along with most of his contemporaries, opposed. A name, including a proper name, retains its significance even when the object falling under it is destroyed and thus it cannot have 'semantic dependency' in our modern sense.

38. A significant area of the medieval *sophisma* literature was devoted to this difficult question at Paris and Oxford from the 1250s to the early 1300s.

39. This view was also taken by other authors of the period, including possibly Robert Kilwardby.

40. See the more detailed discussion in the comments on n. 58 below.

A similar problem is discussed by the early modern philosopher John Locke.[41] If truth is nothing more than the joining or separating of words in propositions, according as the ideas they stand for agree or disagree in our minds, then their truth is trivial and worthless. For 'all centaurs are animals' is just as true as 'all men are animals.' In both, words are put together according to the agreement of ideas in our minds, and 'centaur' agrees with 'animal' just as much as 'man' agrees with 'animal.' Locke avoids the problem by distinguishing between 'real' and 'verbal' truth.[42] However, Locke would have rejected Scotus's understanding of the nature of the ideas which are said to agree or disagree here. For Locke, ideas are in the mind only. For Scotus and most other authors of the late thirteenth century, what we understand is not just an idea but rather the essence of a thing, which is something real. When we grasp a proposition by composing a subject and predicate, we compose not ideas (*species*) but things, and not as they exist but as they are understood.[43] An affirmative proposition signifies the union of subject and predicate in reality, and this is so when the understanding of the subject is included per se in the understanding of the predicate.[44]

This 'essentialist' view contrasts with the position of those belonging the terminist school a generation later, including Ockham and John Buridan (c. 1300–1361), but also with earlier authors such as Roger Bacon (c. 1214–94) and Boethius of Dacia (fl. third quarter of the thirteenth century), as well as Scotus's contemporary Walter Burley (c. 1275–1344),[45] who sought an explanation of truth in terms of *supposition*. These authors held that the universal proposition 'every a is b' is true if and only if every object falling under a also falls under b.[46] Thus, when no as exist, the predicate supposits or stands for nothing the subject stands for, and the proposition is false.

Scotus clearly would have disagreed with this position. Behind his view is a distinction between 'natural' and 'accidental' supposition shared by many philos-

---

41. John Locke, *An Essay Concerning Human Understanding* IV.v, §§1–5.
42. Ibid., IV.v, §8.
43. Scotus, *Opus I*, q. 2, n. 41 (*OPh* II, 56–57).
44. Ibid., q. 8, n. 49 (*OPh* II, 84–85).
45. See q. 4 of Walter Burley's *Questions on the Perhermenias*, where he denies that essential propositions are necessarily and eternally true. See Stephen Brown (ed.), "Walter Burley, Questions on the Perihermenias," *Franciscan Studies* 34 (1974): 274.
46. See *William of Ockham, 'Summa Logicae.'* (*Opera Philosophica, vol. 1*), eds. P. Boehner, G. Gál, and S. Brown (St. Bonaventure, N.Y.: The Franciscan Institute, 1974), II.4.

ophers of the period.[47] Natural supposition is what belongs to a term per se, that is, naturally and intrinsically; it has this supposition when it is not joined to any other term or word qualifying it. Accidental supposition, on the other hand, is the supposition a term has when it is restricted by an adjoining term, such as a verb having temporal reference, so that its supposition is consistent with the adjoining term.[48] Accordingly, propositions that are essentially true are explained by natural supposition. Every proposition whose subject has natural supposition is universally true for every time and all *supposita*. Furthermore, no proposition whose subject has natural supposition carries existential import, such that 'every *a* is *b*' implies 'an *a* exists.' Thus 'rain falls in droplets' does not imply 'rain exists.' By characterizing rain in this way, we are not implying that it is raining now. Similarly, no proposition whose subject has natural supposition requires the existence of its terms in order to be true.

Various attempts were made to provide a theory of truth consistent with the essentialist thesis. One of these, which Scotus appears to endorse in his reply to q. 8 (n. 80) is that there does not have to be a union between subject and predicate in reality for a proposition to be true so long as there is composition in the understanding, as is clear from the presumed truth of 'a chimera is a chimera.' Another is the distinction between the use of 'is' as a second element, which predicates being or existence of the subject, and its use as a 'third element,' where it only predicates the union of subject and predicate, which can take place without either representing existing things.[49]

The next questions (qq. 9–11) concern the range of a quantified term. For example, can 'every man' include objects in the past or future (Caesar and the Antichrist, respectively, were the standard medieval examples here)? If so, can its reference be 'restricted' in a proposition by the verb whose subject it is? This question is also related to natural supposition. As an anonymous Parisian writer of the 1260s points out, a term is not said to be restricted (or the opposite, 'ampliated') except by reason of its natural supposition, for if it did not have or could not have

---

47. Natural supposition had advocates in later years. In fact, the most detailed articulation of the theory was given by Vincent Ferrer (1350–1429).

48. See *Ps.-Lambert of Auxerre* (Lambert of Lagny) in Norman Kretzmann and Eleonore Stump (trans.), *The Cambridge Translations of Medieval Philosophical Texts, Volume 1: Logic and the Philosophy of Language* (Cambridge, Mass.: Cambridge University Press, 1988), 208.

49. *Opus I*, q. 8, n. 63 (*OPh* II, 88).

natural supposition, how could it be restricted, that is, restrained from what is natural to it?[50] Note that medieval logicians in general held that only things in the present truly exist. Accordingly, present-tense propositions with subject terms such as 'Caesar' and 'the Antichrist' are, at least in their unanalyzed form, false.

These questions are closely connected with the issues discussed in qq. 5–8. If 'Caesar is a man' is true, then 'some men do not exist' must be true, and so the range of 'men' includes men who existed in the past and the term is not restricted by the tense of the verb; but if it is false, it is restricted. Therefore, those who disagree with restriction (as Scotus does in q. 9) generally hold that 'Caesar is a man' is true (as Scotus does in q. 7), and that 'every man exists' is false.

Opus II.I, q. 4 and *Opus II.II*, qq. 2–5 likewise concern the topic of existential import. *Opus II.I*, q. 4 asks whether a negative name such as 'non-man' posits the existence of something. Scotus argues that the word 'something' has two senses. In the first sense, a 'thing' is something having a particular nature, such as a man or a horse. In this sense, 'non-man' does not signify a thing. In the second sense, a 'thing' is anything that can be signified, a 'signifiable being.' *Opus II.II*, qq. 2–5 continue in the same vein, asking whether a sentence affirming a negative name follows from a sentence denying the positive name. Does 'it is not the case that Socrates is white' imply 'Socrates is a non-white thing'?

Opus II.I, qq. 7–9 are about future contingents, that is, the problems raised by Aristotle's famous example of the sea battle in Book IX of the *Perihermenias*. If it is true that there will be a sea battle tomorrow, then it is true now that there will be a battle. But if it is true now, it is already true, and since we cannot change what is already true, we cannot change what is going to happen. But then, as Aristotle observes, "there would be no need to deliberate or to take trouble (thinking that if we do this, this will happen, but if we do not, it will not)."[51]

Scotus's solution to the problem is interesting. He replies that a singular future contingent proposition is neither true nor false without qualification, nor is it determinately true or false. A future-tense proposition may signify something 'in the future' in two senses: either so that it is true now that something will happen,

---

50. "*Album fuit disputaturum*," q. 2, in *César et le Phénix: Distinctiones et sophismata parisiens du XIIIe siècle*, ed. Alain de Libera (Pisa: Scuola Normale Superiore, 1991), NL 16135, 12vb–14vb: "Whether a common term is restricted to suppositing for things in the present."

51. Aristotle, *De interpretatione* I.9.18b30–32, in Jonathan Barnes (ed.), *The Complete Works of Aristotle: The Revised Oxford Translation*, 2 vols. (Princeton, N.J.: Princeton University Press, 1984), 1:29.

or so that it signifies now that something will happen. And these are different, for to signify that it is now true that *a* is going to happen signifies more than to signify (now) that *a* will happen. Any proposition signifying that a state of affairs is true now is related differently to being than one signifying (albeit signifying now) that a state of affairs exists in the future. Scotus denies, in effect, that there is any presently existing truth-maker for a proposition about the future. The state of affairs which would make it true (or false) is not in existence yet, although it will be.[52]

Scotus's Sources

The early work of an author is often interesting insofar as it reveals the influence of teachers and received ideas of the time, sometimes even providing clues about the direction and development of an author's mature thinking. Even the most original thinkers cannot help but be influenced by teachers and tutors, by what they find in libraries, and by their exposure to popular topics of debate among their peers. In the case of Scotus, unfortunately, we have little information about the first two.

We do not know who taught Scotus in his early period at Oxford. The names of his masters would be useful evidence, but there is no comprehensive list of the masters who taught at Oxford in the late thirteenth century and may have been an influence on the young Scotus. Part of the problem is that student-teacher relationships in the later Middle Ages were much more varied and fleeting than the more institutionalized modes of instruction typical since the modern period. In all likelihood, several different masters would have taught Scotus over a period of time, while he himself taught some of the younger students at the convent school.[53] Virtually all of his teachers and students would have been Franciscans, however.

We also do not know what Scotus studied in logic apart from the texts of Aristotle, which were required reading for all students in the scholastic period. If Scotus studied at the Oxford convent (popularly known as 'Greyfriars'), he would have been familiar with the library there. However, we know little about its con-

---

52. Scotus's solution is similar to Ockham's discussion of time in *Summa Logicae* I.59, where he denies the existence of any concrete thing in the present determining the existence of something in the future.
53. The picture is a little clearer in theology—but only a little. See Vos, *Duns Scotus*, 51–53.

tents. According to Little,[54] by the fifteenth century there were two libraries: the convent library itself and the library of the student friars. The convent's first large collection of books probably came from Adam Marsh, who received it upon the death of his uncle, Richard Marsh, in 1226. According to John Twyne,[55] Roger Bacon's writings were in these libraries. Unfortunately, the library was dispersed after the Reformation, and very few of its books, some of which probably ended up in other college libraries such as Caius, can now be identified, if they survived at all.

Likewise, very little survives in other college libraries dating to before the 1270s.[56] Merton was the most significant of the later medieval Oxford colleges, but it not founded until the 1260s. Most of the masters taught in smaller halls where manuscripts had a lower chance of surviving. The best witness to the material taught and studied at Oxford in the late thirteenth century is the manuscript 'Worcester 13,' a book of lecture notes and copies of other source material compiled by John of Aston, probably in 1294–95. It contains the *Summa Grammatica* of Roger Bacon (probably written before 1250),[57] two collections of *sophismata*, a discussion of terminist logic together with a section of William of Sherwood's *Introduction to Logic*,[58] and Richard Clive's *Questions* on Aristotle's *Metaphysics*. The latter texts look like a series of notes, for teacher or student use, produced in connection with lectures on fifth treatise of Sherwood's *Introduction*. According to Ebbesen, Worcester 13 is a witness to an Oxford tradition of interest in old-fashioned terminist logic throughout the latter half of the thirteenth century and the continuous use of elementary textbooks by British writers.[59] Their evident interest in supposition theory and terminist logic is also demonstrated by other works in the manuscript, such as an anonymous set of *Questions* on the *Prior Analytics*.

54. A. G. Little, *The Grey Friars in Oxford. Part 1: A History of Convent. Part 2: Biographical Notices of the Friars, Together with Appendices of Original Documents* (Oxford: Clarendon Press, 1892), 57–59.

55. Ibid., 58.

56. P. Osmund Lewry, "The Oxford Condemnations of 1277 in Grammar and Logic," in H. A. G. Braakhuis, C. H. Kneepkens, and L. M. de Rijk (eds.), *English Logic and Semantics from the End of the Twelfth Century to the Time of Ockham and Burleigh, Acts of the Fourth European Symposium on Mediaeval Logic and Semantics, Leiden/Nijmegen 23–27 April 1979* (Nijmegen: Ingenium, 1981), 236.

57. See Irène Rosier-Catach, "Roger Bacon and Grammar," in Jeremiah Hackett (ed.), *Roger Bacon and the Sciences: Commemorative Essays* (Leiden: Brill, 1997), 68–69.

58. Transcribed with an introduction in Jan Pinborg and Sten Ebbesen, "Thirteenth-Century Notes on William of Sherwood's Treatise on Properties of Terms. An Edition of *Anonymi Dubitationes et Notabilia circa Guilelmi de Shyreswode 'Introductionum logicalium Tractatum V'* from ms. Worcester Cath. Q.13." *Cahiers de l'Institut du Moyen-Age grec et latin* 47 (1984): 103–41.

59. Ibid., 106.

As for other details of scholarly life in late-thirteenth century Oxford, such as curricula, reading lists, student rosters, financial records, and so on, we have almost no information. We can be certain that masters and students would have been familiar with well-known textbooks such as Sherwood's treatises on logic (especially his *Introduction* and *Treatise on Syncategorematic Words*), and with the logical textbook of Peter of Spain, the *Summa de Dialectica* or *Tractatus*. English students would have been acquainted with the *Abstractiones* attributed to Ricardus Sophista ('Richard the Sophister,' also known as the *Magister Abstractionum* or 'Master of Abstractions'), who may have been Richard Rufus of Cornwall. However, the material Scotus refers to is far more detailed and comprehensive than anything in those works, and it is clear that he is using other commonly available sources.

There are sources which can be identified from the text itself, including works by Scotus known to be from the same period, such as the questions on the *Categories* and on Porphyry's *Isagoge* or *Introduction* to the *Categories*. However, another problem for understanding the background to medieval texts is that except in cases of great authority, such as Aristotle ('the Philosopher'), Averroes ('the Commentator'), or the church fathers, it was not the practice of medieval authors to acknowledge their sources. Students at modern universities are taught to provide an unambiguous reference for any idea arising from someone else, and to adhere to a more or less standard system of citing sources which includes author, publication date, page number, and so on. But this is possible because we enjoy a stable material culture of printed books and, more recently, electronic sources. In the best case, medieval authors used manuscripts that were copied by scribes from other handwritten manuscripts, with all of the errors and omissions such a system might produce. More often than not, they worked from memory, or from abridged collections of remarks such as *florilegia* and glosses of authoritative texts, prepared with the student lecture in mind. Contemporary authors are not usually named, but simply referred to formulaically—'certain persons say [*quidam dicunt*]'—leaving modern scholars to guess their identity. Of course, the reference would have been clear enough to masters and students of the period, who would have known the context of the debate, and, often enough, been personally acquainted with the disputants. But even passages deriving from standard medieval authorities such as Thomas Aquinas and Albert the Great must be checked, since the common understanding of their views evolved separately from their texts, with the result that the two were not always the same.

Introduction   21

Scotus's *Questions* on the *Perhermenias* emerged from a vibrant culture of academic debate, the details of which lie hidden behind his words. We understand this debate in only its broadest outlines.[60] Filling in the details is a task that awaits historians of medieval logic, as more texts from the period are edited and brought to light.

Principles of Translation

Translating Scotus is never an easy task; this is doubly true for his commentaries on the *Perihermenias* due to the relatively unfinished state in which these works have come down to us, as well as Scotus's own (perhaps youthful) deficiencies as a philosophical stylist.[61] His native tongue was unrelated to Latin, unlike the case of Thomas Aquinas, who at least grew up speaking a Romance vernacular. As a result, there are numerous inconsistencies of expression and infelicities of style. Perhaps this is the sort of thing we might expect to find in a work written by a 'foreigner' less accustomed to classical Latin idiom. In any event, Scotus's Latin is less polished than that found in other medieval commentaries on the *Perihermenias* from the same period, and this can cause interpretive problems when the idea being conveyed is complicated or especially difficult. Needless to say, Scotus's thought abounds in such ideas.

We are helped, however, by the fact that medieval logic texts employ many standard idioms, as well as by the sheer technical nature of much of the discussion, which invokes common distinctions in medieval logic and semantics. Our strategy throughout has been to keep as closely as possible to the literal meaning of Scotus's text, explaining certain technical expressions and finer points of doctrine in the accompanying commentary. Of course, the literal approach (some-

---

60. For example, there is the question of the influence of the so-called Parisian 'Modist' school on Scotus's thinking. Jan Pinborg argued that Scotus's logical works are modist; see "Der Logik der Modistae," *Studia Mediewistyczne* 16 (1975): 39–97. But as Sten Ebbesen has pointed out more recently, "there never was a period in which all theoretical work in grammar followed 'modist' principles ... [and] there are also problems with defining clearly what is meant by 'Modism' in logic" ("The Copenhagen School of Medieval Philosophy," in *Medieval Analyses in Language and Cognition*, eds. Sten Ebbesen and Russell L. Friedman [Copenhagen: Royal Danish Academy of Sciences and Letters, 1996], 11–12). Certainly there are many passages in Scotus which invoke the technical concepts and expressions associated with Modist authors, but we cannot be sure to what extent he was merely writing in the conventions accepted in his day, or deliberately following the doctrines of a particular school.

61. Again, whether these deficiencies are 'youthful' depends on the assumption that the commentaries on the *Perihermenias* were written early in Scotus's career, which is something we cannot determine.

times even the 'grindingly literal' approach) is generally a good idea in translating medieval logic because medieval logicians worked in natural rather than symbolic language, so that the exact word order of the target proposition is usually important as far as which distinction is being represented. But we have not hesitated to depart from the literal sense where cleaving to it would obscure rather than clarify the point we take Scotus to be making. In such cases, and also where we felt it important to indicate Scotus's precise phraseology, we have included the Latin text in square brackets.

There are several places in both commentaries where we remain uncertain about what Scotus is saying, or why he is saying it (for example, because it appears to contradict something he says elsewhere in the commentaries). Here we tried to offer our best hypothesis about the meaning of the passage in question. We fully expect more satisfactory readings of these passages to be developed by others in the future as we learn more about the background and figures involved in what was a very exciting period in the history of medieval logic.

TRANSLATION

OPUS I

[Question 1. What Is the Subject of *On Interpretation*?]

First we must settle, etc.[1]

With regard to the subject of this book,[2] it should be noted that Boethius[3] proposes that interpretation is what the interpretation of the name 'Perihermenias' also indicates.

[1] But if the definition of interpretation is "articulated utterance, uttered with the idea of signifying,"[4] then interpretation is said of both complex and and non-complex utterances, and interpretation is thus not the proper subject of this book, which occupies a position midway between the *Categories* and *Prior Analytics*, the former of which concerns what pertains to the first operation of the

---

1. Aristotle, *De interpretatione* I.1.16a1: "First we must settle what a name is and what a verb is" [hereafter *"De interpr."*]; Latin edition is *Aristoteles Latinus*, Corpus philosophorum medii aevi, Academiarum consociatarum auspiciis et consilio editum (1939–), II¹ 5 = *De interpretatio vel Periermenias translatio Boethiii*, specimina translationum recentiorum, edidit Laurentius Minio-Paluello (Bruges: Desclée de Brouwer, 1965) [hereafter "AL," by volume/part number].
2. Cf. Scotus, *Opus* II, Prologue and nn. 1–2.
3. Boethius, *Anicii Manlii Severini Boethii Commentaria in Librum Aristotelis Peri Hermenias*, ed. C. Meiser (Leipzig: Teubner, 1877 and 1880), I.6 [hereafter *"De Interpr."*] = *Patrologiae cursus completus*, series latina, accurante J. P. Migne (Paris 1844, sqq.) [hereafter "PL"], 64:395A: "That is why this book of Aristotle deals not only with speech, but also of the noun and the verb, and not of expression alone, but of meaningful expression, which is interpretation."
4. Cf. Boethius, *De interpr.* I.6 (PL 64:394B): "Interpretation is produced by three things occurring together: the striking of the tongue [upon the teeth], the articulation of a vocal sound, and some idea of expressing. For an interpretation is an articulate sound signifying through itself."

25

intellect,[5] and the latter of which what pertains to the third. Therefore, this book will be about what pertains to the middle operation of the intellect. But whether the aforementioned definition is the definition of interpretation, or whether it is—according to others[6]—more specialized than that, viz., "articulate sound, uttered with the idea of signifying something being the case [*esse*] or not being the case," the subject in this case will not be 'interpretation,' since no part of logic concerns sound considered as a subject, as is stated at the beginning of my *Questions on Aristotle's 'Categories,'* in the first question.[7] That is because in logic, all of the affections are equally present in its subjects, without any sound existing.

[2] Therefore, 'assertion' can be aptly proposed here as the subject, and by this we mean 'the mental assertion,' since it is caused by the second operation of the intellect, and since what is determined here is determined in accordance with it. Consider, for instance, first what is determined as regards the integral parts of an assertion, e.g., the noun and the verb; second, its genus, which is speech; next, what it is [both] essentially and as regards its division into its primary species; and finally, its properties, viz., opposition, form, and other things of this kind. And if these properties are present in a spoken assertion, this is not per se and primarily, but only insofar as it is a sign of a mental assertion.

[3] Against this: a subject should be common to all things that are determined

---

5. Cf. Aristotle, *De anima* III.6.430a26–28 [hereafter "*De an.*"]; Thomas Aquinas, *Sent. De an.* III.11 (XLV^1 224–28) [all works of Thomas Aquinas cited in this translation are from *Opera* (Rome: Leonine Commission, 1882–)]. See also *Les Auctoritates Aristotelis*, ed. J. Hamesse (Louvain-Paris: Publications Universitaires-Béatrice Nauwelaerts, 1974), 187 [hereafter "AA"]: "The activity of the intellect is twofold: one [sort of operation] is said to be the apprehension of simple terms; another is the composition and division of apprehended simple terms. Included in the latter is a third operation, viz., speculative reasoning." Translators' note: We have included the translation of this passage from the *Auctoritates Aristotelis* because it appears in the footnotes of the critical edition. The Auctoritates Aristotelis was a *florilegium*, or popular collection of authoritative passages from Aristotle (and a few others) in wide circulation during the later Middle Ages. Its editor, Jacqueline Hamesse, believes it was composed between 1267 and 1325 (ibid., 38). However, we do not know if Scotus actually used this collection, or one like it, in writing his commentaries on the *Perihermenias*.

6. Cf. Thomas Aquinas, *De interpr.* I (I^1 6): "For evidently, what is interpreted is what expounds something as being true or false."

7. Duns Scotus, '*Quaestiones in librum Porphyrii Isagoge*' *et* '*Quaestiones super Praedicamenta Aristotelis*,' in *OPh* II, q. 1, n. 11 [hereafter "*Quaest. in librum Porph.*" and "*Praedic.*"]: "To the question, it can be said that this book is not about 'the ten utterances,' as in '[the ten things you can say] about a primary subject.' No part of logic concerns utterance, because all of the properties of the syllogism and all of its parts can be in it according to the mode of being they have in the mind, even if they are not expressed."

in a science. But the assertion is not like this, since it is determined here as regards the noun and the verb, and an assertion is not predicated of these.

[4] Again, the authority of Boethius,[8] stating that this book is about interpretation, is against it.

[5] Again, an assertion is not in the mind. Proof: the noun and the verb are not parts of [a mental assertion], since they are both utterances. But those are the parts of an assertion that are under discussion here.

[I. Reply to the Counter-Arguments]

[6] To the first:[9] if the major premise is understood as regards the universality of predication, as of the universal whole in relation to its parts, then it is false. For in every science with a composite subject, it is necessary to make a determination about the parts of that subject—parts of which the subject is nevertheless not predicated. But if the major is true in some way, it should be understood that [its] subject is common because its cognition is what is principally inquired about in the cognition of everything else in the science, insofar as those other things are all determined according to the cognition of the principal subject.

[7] To the second:[10] we say that there is a science of many things that have no principal subject, as is stated in [my *Questions on*] *Porphyry*, in the third question.[11]

[8] As for the third:[12] I say that just as the spoken noun and verb are parts of the spoken assertion, so also are the parts of the mental assertion in the mind itself. For those things that are conceived by the intellect in its first operation are compounded in the second, even though neither the one nor the other is expressed.

---

8. Boethius, *De interpr.* I.6-7 (PL 64:395A): "Therefore, since the name 'interpretation' is suited to words as well as to names and significant speech, all of which this book will treat, i.e., by interpretation, this book draws its title from their common name, 'On Interpretation.'"
9. Cf. n. 3 above.
10. Cf. n. 4 above.
11. Duns Scotus, *Quaest. in librum Porph.*, q. 3, n. 17 (*OPh* I, 15): "To the argument for the third position, I say that they [i.e., the metaphysician, the dialectician, and the sophist—cf. Aristotle, *Metaphysics* IV.5.1004b22–23, hereafter "*Metaph.*"] are working on the same thing, not because the subject is the same, but because in logic, something is considered through which our work happens to be about everything. For many things are the subject of our work in the sciences, nevertheless, not on account of this is each of them the principal subject of a science"; cf. ibid., nn. 20, 24.
12. Cf. n. 5 above.

And when it is said that noun and verb alike are utterances, either [i] this is true in view of the fact that they become more known to us, because we should fix their descriptions so that through them their descriptions are as clear as they are in the mind; or [ii] it is a different thing to say that a noun is an utterance and that a noun is spoken, perhaps because an utterance can be essentially unspoken, i.e., unexpressed, just as it can also be expressed. And we propose the first way as the definition of a noun.

[Question 2. Do Names Signify Things, or Species in the Mind?]

And so there are [spoken sounds], etc.[13]

[1] Aristotle provides a brief account here of significant utterances. Accordingly, we can ask whether names signify things or species in the mind. And this is in no way to be understood as applying to names imposed for signifying likenesses or species. But of any name imposed on any other thing, e.g., the names 'man,' 'animal,' and others of this sort, we ask whether 'man' signifies the human nature or the species. But I call an intelligible species or likeness that which is in the understanding as in a subject, just as the sensible species or likeness of the sensible thing is what is in the power of sense as in a subject.

[The First Way: That Names Signify Species]

[2] That it would signify a species is evident here in the text. For Aristotle states, "spoken sounds are symbols," i.e., signs, "of affections in the soul." Those affections are not things, because there are no things in the soul.

[3] Again, a little further on:[14] "The affections of the soul, the primary [objects] of which the utterances are marks, are the same for all, as are the things of which these affections are the likenesses." This passage clearly expresses what he means by 'affection,' [i.e.,] that it is a likeness. And he says that it is primarily

---

13. Aristotle, *De interpr.* I.1.16a3–4 (AL II[1] 5): "And so there are spoken sounds, which are signs of affections in the soul, and written marks, which are signs of spoken sounds."

14. Ibid., 16a5–8: "And just as written marks are not the same for all, so spoken sounds are not the same for all. But the primary things of which these are marks—affections of the soul—are the same for all, as are the things [themselves] of which these affections are the likenesses."

signified by an utterance, which is a likeness of the thing, and the thing is not a likeness of itself. Therefore, etc.

[4] Again, truth and falsity only exist in an expression as in a sign of something; therefore, a spoken assertion signifies that in which there is truth and falsity. That is the composition and division of the act of understanding, as Aristotle says a little further on in the text.[15] Therefore, a composite assertion signifies only what is in a composite understanding. And so as well, the parts of an assertion signify those things that are in a simple understanding. Species are of this [latter] sort.

[5] Again, Boethius clearly states quite often in his commentary on this text that utterances signify likenesses, and he says that this is Aristotle's opinion.[16]

[6] Again, Priscian says that each part of speech signifies a concept in the mind; this concept is not a thing but a likeness, as is evident.[17] Therefore, etc.

[7] Again, what is primarily signified by an utterance is [also] what is primarily understood; [but] things are not like this. Therefore, etc. Proof of the minor: everything capable of being understood exists in the understanding; [but] things do not exist in the understanding, because according to Aristotle in *De anima* III, "a stone is not in the soul, but its likeness or species."[18] Therefore, etc. Proof of the ultimate major: according to what is held in *De anima* III, "something more truly one is made from understanding and understandable than from matter and form," but from what is outside the soul, nothing is made more truly one with the understanding than from matter and form.[19] Therefore, etc.

---

15. Ibid., 16a13–14: "For truth and falsity concern composition and division."

16. Boethius, *De interpr.* I.1 (35; PL 64:410B): "That is why the affections of the soul, which he called acts of understanding, are a kind of likeness of things. Therefore, Aristotle, when he speaks a little later about affections of the soul, switched in the next line to 'likenesses,' since it makes no difference whether one says 'affections' or 'likenesses.'"

17. Priscian, *Institutiones grammaticae*, in M. Hertz (ed.), *Prisciani Caesarensis Grammatici institutionum grammaticarum libri XVIII* (Leipzig: 1855–60), XI.2, 1:552: "For what is a part of speech other than an utterance indicating a concept in the mind, in other words, a cognition?"

18. Aristotle, *De an.* III.8 (AL 12² 235.1.12; III.8.431b29–432a1): "For there is not a stone in the soul, but the species of a stone."

19. Something similar is found in AA 194: "In what is understandable there is something of the act of understanding itself; both the act of understanding and the thing understood are in every way the same." Cf. Averroes's commentary on *De an.*, found in F. Stuart Crawford (ed.), *Averrois Cordubensis, Commentarium Magnum in Aristotelis De Anima Libros* (Cambridge, Mass.: Medieval Academy of America, 1953), III, com. 5 (404): "Let us say, then, that it is clear that a man does not actually understand except by contact between the intellect and what is actual. It is also clear that matter and form

[8] Again, nothing is understood except through a species; therefore, nothing is signified by any utterance except through a species; therefore, the species is signified more, because "that on account of which each and every thing [exists] is greater."[20]

[The Second Way: That Names Signify Things]

[9] On the opposing side: below, at the end of the chapter 'On Verbs,' Aristotle remarks, "verbs signify something, for the one who speaks establishes the understanding [of a thing in the mind of the hearer]." From this, we take it that "to signify is to establish the understanding [of a thing]."[21] Therefore, that thing whose understanding is established is signified by an utterance. But it is the understanding of the thing, not the concept, that is established by the utterance, as is obvious to anyone hearing a significant utterance.

[10] Again, in the first chapter of *De sophisticis elenchis*, Aristotle says, "because we cannot bring things with us into the discussion, we use names as symbols of things."[22] Therefore, utterances are not signs of those symbols,[23] but of things.

[11] Again, a little further on in the same place, [Aristotle says] that "things are infinite in number, but names are finite."[24] Therefore, it is necessary for one name and one expression to signify several things.

[12] Again, in *Metaphysics* IV, Aristotle says, "the nature which the name signifies is the definition."[25] But a definition points to the true essence of a thing. Therefore, that essence is signified by a name.

---

are joined to each other such that their combination makes something one and that this holds even more as regards the material intellect and the intention that is actually understood. For what is joined together from them is not some third thing different from them, as is the case with other composites of matter and form." Cf. also Thomas Aquinas, *Sent. De an.* III.3 (XLV^1 216b).

20. Aristotle, *Analytica Posteriora* I.2 (AL IV^1 9; I.2.72a29–30) [hereafter "*Anal. post.*"]: "For in all cases, that on account of which each and every thing exists is greater."

21. Aristotle, *De interpr.* I.1, c. 'On Verbs' (AL II^1 7; I.3.16b19–21): "When said by itself, a verb is a name and it signifies something—for the one who speaks establishes an understanding and the one who hears pauses [in order to hear it]"; see AA 305: "To signify is to establish understanding."

22. Aristotle, *De sophisticis elenchis* I.1 (AL VI^1 6; I.1.165a5–6) [hereafter "*De soph. elench.*"]: "But since there is no way of bringing the things themselves to the discussion, we use names as symbols of things."

23. Implicitly, "of those affections."

24. Aristotle, *De soph. elench.* I.1 (AL VI^1 6; I.1.165a11–12): "For names are finite and there is a multitude of expressions; things, however, are infinite in number."

25. Aristotle, *Metaph.* IV.28 (AL XXV^1 90; III.7.1012a24–25): "The nature of which the name is the sign is the definition."

[That Names Do Not Signify Species]

[13] It seems, however, that a species would not be signified.

[14] Because in that case, every name would signify some accident, since the species is in the soul as in a subject, just like the visible species in the eye.

[15] Because in that case, every affirmative proposition would be false in which the subject and predicate are cognized through different species, as in 'a man is an animal,' since the species of man through which that proposition is understood is one thing and that of animal is another. And in general, every proposition would be false in which a real actuality is asserted of some subject, as in 'a man is running,' etc.

[16] Because in that case, the following proposition of Aristotle from *De anima* III, viz., "A stone is not in the soul, but the species of a stone," would contain a contradiction.[26] That is because 'being in the soul' is first removed from the species of a stone, which is signified by the name 'stone' by the first part of the proposition, 'a stone is not in the soul,' and yet in the second part the same predicate would be attributed to the same subject.

[17] Because in that case, every proposition would be true in which the verb 'is' is predicated as a second element, as in 'Socrates is,' 'Antichrist is,' because the species of any subject of which [the verb] 'to be' is asserted, is.

[18] Because in that case, no syllogism would be perfect, because if a species in the soul is signified by the middle term, then, whether a thing or a species is subsumed, what is subsumed will not be a *suppositum* of the middle term.

[19] Because in that case, only what is understood would be signified. The intelligible species is not understood. This is shown [i] because by a similar case, the visible species is not seen; [ii] because the intelligible species is that by which what is intelligible is understood, but in all things short of the first, there is, according to Boethius, a difference between 'that which is' and 'that by which it is';[27] and [iii] because if it is understood, it would be understood by another species, for since it is a passive power, the understanding understands nothing except actual beings through the species of their objects.

---

26. Cf. n. 7 above.

27. Boethius, in R. Peiper (ed.), *Anicii Manlii Severini Boethii De hebdomadibus* (Leipzig: Teubner, 1871), c. 2 (169; PL 64:1311B) [hereafter "*De hebdom.*"]: "Being and that which is are different, for being itself is not yet, but that which is, is and exists when it has taken on the form of being." The edition mistakenly gives the reference here as being to c. 3 of *De hebdom.*

[I. Reply to the Question]

[20] To the question it is said[28] that an intelligible species is immediately signified by the utterance. But this is considered in two ways: either insofar as it is what it is in itself, viz., an accident informing the soul, or insofar as it represents a thing. It is not signified in the first way for the reasons given on the opposing side, but in the second way. But since every sign of a sign insofar as it is a sign is a sign of what is signified, it follows that an utterance signifying a likeness insofar as it is a sign of the thing also signifies the thing itself, though indirectly, viz., because it directly signifies that which is the sign of the thing insofar as it is a sign.

[21] Against this: no substantial nature of substance and accident would be the same since they would not belong to the same most general genus. But to the thing that is the substance, its likeness is an accident. Therefore, if the thing and its likeness were signified by some name, for them it will be [true] that they have 'only the name in common and distinct definitions of substance,' and so every name will be equivocal.

[22] The reasoning is confirmed by Aristotle at the beginning of the *Categories*, where he gives the example of equivocal terms, e.g., 'both a man and a picture of a man are animals,'[29] understanding by this that if any name were to signify a thing and its likeness, it would be equivocal.

---

28. Boethius, *De interpr.* I.1 (40; PL 64:298D–299A) [this citation is taken from 'ed. prima' of Boethius's text; all other references to his *De interpr.* in this work are taken from 'ed. secunda']: "For example, when I say 'stone,' it designates both the concept of the stone and the stone itself, i.e., the substance itself; but primarily it signifies the understanding, in the second place the thing. Therefore, not everything that the utterance signifies is an affection of the soul, but only those that are first; for it signifies understandings first, but in the second place, things"; Ammonius, in Adolf Busse (ed.), *Ammonius, in Aristotelis De Interpretatione Commentarius, Corpus latinum commentarium in Aristotelem graecorum* (Leuven: De Wulf-Mansion Centre, 1971), c. 1 (II, 45) [hereafter "*De interpr.*"]: "For [Aristotle] says, 'but what these are signs of in the first place,' these meaning those things that are in the utterance, i.e., names and verbs, of which they are primarily the signs (but he is speaking of concepts: through these, things are also signified, though not immediately but by intermediary concepts. Concepts, however, are not signified through any further intermediaries, but primarily and immediately)"; Albert the Great, in A. Borgnet and A. Borgnet (eds.), *Alberti Magni Opera Omnia*, 38 vols. (Paris: 1890–99; Köln: Institutum Alberti Magni, 1951–), I.2 (1:381a) [all texts by Albert the Great cited in this work are taken from this edition]: "But by the fact that signs are of affections caused in the soul by the intentions of things, it is held that they are not primarily signs of things, but rather, they are primarily signs of likenesses that are in the soul, and by means of these likenesses they are related to things"; Thomas Aquinas, *De interpr.* I.2 (I^1 11a): "Therefore it was necessary for Aristotle to say that utterances signify conceptions of the understanding immediately, and things by means of them."

29. Aristotle, *Praedicamenta*, c. 1 (AL I^2 47; 1.1a1–2) [hereafter "*Praedic.*"]: "Things having only a

[23] To this,[30] it is said that an equivocal term signifies many things in diverse acts of signifying. But the utterance is something signifying the thing and the likeness by the same act because by the same act, the utterance is the sign of a sign insofar as it is a sign and also [a sign] of its significate.

[24] We can use this against the confirmation:[31] Aristotle's understanding is that 'animal' would signify both the picture and the man by diverse acts of signifying and a diverse imposition. It is clear in like manner that not every written expression is equivocal, and yet, as Aristotle says,[32] the written expression signifies an uttered expression and thereby a thing. But there is no equivocation in that case because the spoken expression is signified insofar as it is a sign of the significate.

[II. Reply to the Arguments on the Opposing Side]

[25] As for the main arguments against this position,[33] all the arguments proving that the thing is signified are conceded.

[A. Reply to the Arguments Proving That Names Do Not Signify Species]

[26] As for the arguments proving that the species is not signified: to the first,[34] we reply that there is no inconsistency in every name signifying an accident directly, not insofar as it is what it is in itself, but as a sign of the thing. And so some utterances signify a substance as an ultimate significate, and are thus said to signify a substance absolutely. For something can signify *simpliciter*, but not directly, as is obvious in the case of written expressions. Some of those expressions are said to signify substance *simpliciter*, even though every one of them would signify an utterance directly, according to Aristotle in the text.[35]

[27] To the second proof:[36] it must be understood that truth and falsity are only in a sign by what is signified. For truth is conformity of a sign with what is signified, and falsity the lack of conformity. But the combination of species with each other, insofar as they are signs of things, is true or false only by virtue of what

---

name in common and different definitions [in the category] of substance corresponding to that name are called equivocals, as a man and a picture [of a man] are animals."

30. Cf. n. 21 above. 31. Cf. n. 22 above.
32. See n. 1 above. 33. Cf. nn. 9–19 above.
34. Cf. n. 14 above. 35. See n. 1 above.
36. Cf. n. 15 above.

is signified, i.e., by virtue of things, when we speak of species as signs. Therefore, every truth of any proposition must be related to things because it is things rather than signs that are the ultimate significates. This is clear in this example: the written proposition, 'man is an animal,' is not said to be false even though the utterance 'man' is not the utterance 'animal.' And this is because the letters do not signify utterances as what they are in themselves, but as signs of other things. And so in all these cases, one must always have recourse to the ultimate significate.

[28] In the same way, it is clear how one replies to all the proofs about the truth and falsity of propositions,[37] because truth is only to be judged as belonging to the ultimate significates, which are things.

[29] If one argues against this here, 'man is an animal,'[38] the primary significates are denoted to be the same because the utterance places its primary significate in the expression; therefore, the species are denoted here to be the same, and yet they are not the same; therefore, the proposition is false as regards its primary significate.

[30] Having conceded that species are joined insofar as they are signs of things and that they are not the same, it does not follow that the proposition is false, because neither truth nor falsity is naturally suited to concern the sign qua sign except in relation to its significate. But if something like this should be said, the composite should even more be said to be true because the composition of significates is true.

[31] Against this: this species insofar as it is the likeness of a thing is not that species insofar as it is the likeness of a thing, and yet according to you they are denoted to be the same by the verb 'is.' Therefore, in every affirmative proposition, things that are not the same are primarily denoted to be the same, and every proposition with respect to that composite is said to be true or false, since it is a composite *simpliciter*. And this is not true, because it is not as the proposition signifies. Therefore, it is false.

[32] Although this argument seems difficult to resolve,[39] it still does not reach its conclusion of necessity because in other areas where there is the same form

---

37. Cf. nn. 15–17 above.

38. This is a repunctuation of the edition, which places the demonstrative inside the mentioned proposition: "Si arguitur contra hoc 'hic homo est animal.'"

39. Scotus's text in nn. 32–33 is referenced by Adam Wodeham, in Rega Wood and Gedeon Gál (eds.), *Adam de Wodeham, Lectura secunda in primum librum Sententiarum*, 3 vols. (St. Bonaventure, N.Y.: The Franciscan Institute, 1990), I, d. 22, q. un., n. 5 (3:285).

of argumentation, it is not difficult [to resolve]. That is because in the written expression, 'man is an animal,' the utterances are joined first because they are signified first. But the written expression is not false on account of this.

[33] It seems, then, that it must be said that no matter how many things are signified by the same thing, of which one is signified insofar as it is the sign of the other, if it is compounded in an expression with the other, there is no composition of signs but of ultimate significates, which are not signs. And by the spoken assertion there is signified not the composition of species but of things, just as the composition of utterances is not signified by the written expression, but rather, the composition of things.

[34] As for the proof of the syllogism,[40] it can be said that the *supposita* must be taken in a perfect syllogism under the middle term with respect to its ultimate significate, and so the thing as it is considered by reason is the *suppositum* of the thing.

[35] As for the final proof,[41] it is said that the species is understood, although not in the first instance, but by reflection. And because imposition is conventional, an utterance can be imposed for signifying it by reflection through the mediation of the intellect, just as it was understood in the first instance.

[36] As for the arguments proving that the intelligible species is not understood: as for the first,[42] the likeness is denied. For sense cannot reflect on its own act or go beyond what it cognizes because it is a material power, and so the sensible species is not sensed. But because of its immateriality, the understanding can reflect on its own act and go beyond the species it cognizes, and even beyond itself. And all things other than its first object it can understand by reflection and cognition.

[37] As for the other proof,[43] I concede that the species differs from what is cognized through it, i.e., from its first object, because it is its species. But along with this it remains true that the species itself is something intelligible that differs from the primary object.

[38] To the third,[44] I say that the species is not cognized through another species because only what is cognized in the first instance by the understanding, i.e., the first object of the understanding—which is the what-it-is of a material

---

40. Cf. n. 18 above.
42. Cf. n. 19 above.
44. Cf. n. 19 above.
41. Cf. n. 19 above.
43. Cf. n. 19 above.

thing—produces a species in the understanding. All other things cognized by reflection and discursive thought are cognized without[45] a proper species.

[B. Reply to the Arguments Proving That Names Signify Things]

[39] To the opposite side of the question,[46] it is said that a thing is primarily signified, but not as it exists, because it is not understood in this way. But it is signified as conceived per se by the understanding, i.e., the very essence of the thing signified by the definition that is the first object of the intellect, which is the intention of the authoritative passage from *Metaphysics* IV cited above.[47] Nor is the entire composite signified, which is 'the thing as it is understood,' because that is a being *per accidens*. All names that signify a thing belonging to some genus signify a being per se, for only a being per se is in a genus.

[III. Reply to the Main Arguments]

[40] As for all the authorities on the other side,[48] it is said that 'the thing as it is *understood*' is signified by 'species' or 'affection' or 'concept' or any other term in the other authorities, in order to denote that 'the thing as it *exists*' is not signified. But if anyone were to say something more obvious on behalf of this text of Aristotle, it is said that in this he is not expounding Aristotle.

[41] As for the one about composition and division,[49] I say that there is composition not of the species themselves but of the things—not yet as *existing* but as *understood*. And therefore truth and falsity are said to concern the composition and division of the understanding, because that composition is caused by the act of understanding and it is in the understanding as what is cognized exists in the one cognizing it, and not as an accident in a subject. And so I concede as regards the parts of a composition that they are in a simple understanding, as what is cognized in the one cognizing it, and in this way there are things in the intellect, not just species.

[42] As for the other,[50] I say that a thing is understood primarily and a species

---

45. Reading *sine* with mss. Rome Coll. S. Isidori (= L), Oxford Merton 260 (= O), and Vat. Lat. 9402 (= R).
46. Cf. nn. 9–12 above.   47. See n. 12 above.
48. Cf. nn. 2–8 above.
49. See n. 3 above. Scotus's text in n. 41 is referenced by Adam Wodeham, *Lectura secunda* I, d. 1, q. 1, n. 4 (1:187–88).
50. Cf. n. 7 above.

only reflexively. As for the other passage about understanding and understandable, etc., I say how this should be interpreted in my commentary on Porphyry.[51]

[43] As for the other,[52] the consequence, 'nothing is *understood* except by the species; therefore, nothing is *signified* except by the species,' can be denied if the word 'by [*per*]' is taken in both places causally. That is because signifying and understanding are not ordered to each other as necessary cause and effect, but signifying presupposes understanding as its *sine qua non*. But the cause of what is presupposed in this way does not have to be the cause of what is presupposing, but it is only presupposed in relation to it as that of which it is the cause; in this way, the species is presupposed with regard to the signification.

[44] But having conceded the proposition, 'nothing is signified except by the species' (whether the 'by [*per*]' is taken causally or presuppositively), it does not follow further that the species is signified, because the proposition, "that on account of which each and every thing," etc.,[53] is understood as regards the efficient and univocal, per se and total, cause—and the species with respect to its signification is not of this kind.

[IV. Returning to the Question]

[45] Of these different ways,[54] we choose what seems more probable.

[On Behalf of the First Way]

[46] On behalf of the first way and against the second, we have most notably the authority here in the text and the arguments about the truth and falsity of propositions.[55]

[On Behalf of the Second Way]

[47] On behalf of the second way and against the first, we have most notably this line of reasoning: that a thing is understood in time and nature prior to its

---

51. Duns Scotus, *Quaest. in librum Porph.* qq. 9–11, n. 20 (*OPh* I, 47–48): "That remark by the Commentator cannot be understood [as saying] that a single composite is made from them, because then the understanding would be composed of the quiddities of all sensible things. But it should be understood as saying that the understanding in act more truly receives the predication of [being] one with the understandable in act, than matter with form, because the understanding in act is the same as what is capable of being understood in act, since it can understand itself reflexively, by the species of what is capable of being understood in act."
52. Cf. n. 8 above.
53. See n. 8 above.
54. That is, in nn. 2–8 and 9–19 above.
55. See n. 1 above and n. 4 above.

species being understood reflexively, and so in virtue of that priority, the understanding can impose a name on it that only signifies the thing. Therefore, it is not necessary that every name signify a species.

[Against Both Ways]

[48] But against both ways, though more against the first, is the force of names imposed to signify singulars. For although this could be preserved in the second way, viz., because singulars are understood in some way although not in the first instance, it could not be explained in the first way because singulars by no means produce species in the intellect. Therefore, the names imposed on them do not signify intelligible species immediately.

[49] One can argue in a similar way as regards names imposed to signify imaginary entities because they are just like singular things, although they produce species in the imaginative power and not in the understanding. That is because the understanding alone is naturally suited to receive the species of its first object, which is the what-something-is of a material thing, but not the species of other things, since a single power can only receive forms belonging to the same genus.

[Against the Second Way]

[50] Against the second way is the fact that every proposition is false where some real actuality is denoted to inhere in the subject, because if the name signifies a thing as it is understood, then such a predicate would be attributed to it as it is understood, and so it would not inhere in it; therefore, etc. That it does not inhere in it in this way I prove as follows: intentional predicates inhere in it as it is understood; and a middle term contrasting real and intentional predicates is taken under extraneous considerations—and in this way, by taking the middle term in the syllogism, the fallacy of accident would be committed if any conclusion were drawn.

[51] The first way seems more probable according to the authoritative passages; the second way seems more probable according the arguments, as is obvious.

[Question 3. Does a Change Occur in the Signification of an Utterance Given That a Change Has Occurred in the Thing Signified?]

It is asked whether a change occurs in the signification of an utterance given that a change has occurred in the thing signified.

[1] It seems that it does: Boethius says in *De divisione*, "when a thing is not the subject of an utterance, the utterance is not significative";[56] and the utterance was significative before, when the thing existed; therefore, etc.

[2] Again, "in substantial change a thing loses its name and its definition";[57] therefore, once a thing has changed, it does not have the name it had before; therefore, the name that signified it before does not signify it now.

[3] Again, according to Aristotle in the *Categories*,[58] once one of two correlatives is destroyed, the remaining one is destroyed too. But a sign and its significate are correlatives. Therefore, once the thing that is the significate is destroyed, the utterance is destroyed insofar as it is a sign of that thing.

[4] Again, what is not understood is not signified; non-being is not understood; therefore, it is not signified. Proof of the major: signifying presupposes understanding. Proof of the minor: everything capable of being understood produces a species in the intellect; a non-being does not produce a species in the intellect; therefore, etc. Proof of the minor: first, when the cause is destroyed, so is the effect; the thing is the cause of the species; therefore, the species is destroyed when the thing is destroyed. Second, when the significate is destroyed, so is the sign; the thing is the significate; therefore, when the thing is destroyed, so is the species.

[5] On the opposing side: in the *Categories*, in the chapter 'On Substance,'[59]

---

56. Boethius, in John Magee (ed.), *Anicii Manlii Severini Boethii De divisione liber: Critical Edition, Translation, Prolegomena, and Commentary* (Leiden: Brill, 1998), 44 (PL 64:889D) [hereafter "*Lib. de divisione*"]: "If no subject is the thing that the utterance signifies, it is not said to be designative."

57. Averroes, *De substantia orbis*, c. 1, in *Aristotelis opera cum Averrois commentariis, latine*, ed. Iuntina, 11 vols. (Venice: 1550–52), IX, f. 3rb; AA 229: "In individual substances there are two kinds of change. One change is substantial, which changes the thing in name and definition. This is called generation or corruption."

58. Aristotle, *Praedic.*, c. 7 (AL I^2 61; 7.7b20–21); AA 303: "Relatives are related in such a way that when one is posited, so is the other, and when one perishes, so does the other."

59. Ibid., c. 5 (AL I^2 53; 5.4a36–b2): "For the statement remains the same in that someone is sitting; but once the person has moved, the statement becomes true at one time and false at another."

Aristotle says that the same sentence is sometimes true and sometimes false. Accordingly, the words of a sentence that is sometimes true and sometimes false signify the same thing. Even so, there is a change in the thing that is signified by those words, as is clear from the sentence, 'Socrates is sitting,' which is sometimes true and sometimes false[60] when a change has been made (or not made) concerning the sitting; therefore, there is no change in signifying when a change has been made in the thing.

[6] Again, there are many actions such as sleeping, running, and things of this kind, which sometimes exist and sometimes do not; if, therefore, the utterance signifying them were changed on account of a change in them, the utterance imposed on them would oftentimes fail to be significative, and would at other times be significative again, and consequently, the utterance would have to be imposed many times.

[7] Again, when nothing is running, 'something is running' would not be false, because 'running' does not signify what it signified when there was running.

[8] Again, it is clear from this manner of speaking that a spoken utterance establishes the same understanding in us when the signified thing exists and when it does not; otherwise, we would not say that 'Socrates exists' is false when Socrates does not exist. Therefore, since "to signify is to establish an understanding,"[61] the same thing is signified by the utterance.

[9] Again, according to Aristotle in Book II of the *Posterior Analytics*,[62] it is possible to signify and to understand non-beings; therefore, the non-being of a thing does not imply the non-being of the significate of a significative utterance.

[I. Reply to the Question]

[10] It is said to the question that when a change occurs in a thing as it exists, no change occurs in the signification of the utterance. The reason for this is that a thing is not signified as it exists, but as it is understood, or as an intelligible species of it exists.

---

60. Adopting the variant reading of ms. L, which omits the conjunction *quia*.
61. Aristotle, *De interpr.* I, c. 'On Verbs' (AL II^1 7; I.3.16b19–21): "When said by itself, a verb is a name and it signifies something—for the one who speaks establishes an understanding and the one who hears pauses [in order to hear it]"; cf. AA 305: "To signify is to establish understanding."
62. Aristotle, *Anal. post.* II.7 (AL IV^1 78; II.7.92b5–7): "For of that which is not, no one knows what it is—the account or the name signifies something when I say 'goatstag,' but what a goatstag *is*, is impossible to know."

But in either case—since the thing as it is understood, as well as the species, remains unchanged when a change occurs in the thing as it exists, because we cognize the essence of a thing by means of the same species, and we have the same knowledge of it when it exists and when it does not exist, according to Aristotle in Book I of the *Posterior Analytics*: "of things that exist for the most part, we can have a demonstration,"[63] and [also] when they do not exist, and consequently the same knowledge when they exist and when they do exist—it therefore follows that a thing as signified by a name or an utterance is not changed by any kind of change occurring in the thing as it exists. Consequently, neither will the utterance be changed in signifying.

[II. Reply to the Main Arguments]

[11] To the first authority,[64] the actual words of Boethius are as follows: "If no thing *is* the subject that the utterance signifies, it is not said to be significative," where 'is' is predicated not as a second but a third element, as follows: "If no thing is signified by the utterance," etc.; and 'thing' is taken there not only for existing things, but also for the thing as understood, as if one were to say, "If nothing is signified by the utterance, the utterance is not said to be significative."

[12] To the second,[65] the authority can be understood as follows: in the substantial change of a singular thing, viz., a change in which the substantial form is discarded, the singular thing that is changed loses its name and species definition because it does not remain in the species in which it was before. It does not follow that 'the name of the species therefore loses its significate,' because that name signified no one *suppositum*; nor does the name of the *suppositum*, insofar as it was properly imposed on it, lose its proper significate. But only once it has been changed by the form of a species does it lose the name of the species in which it was before.

[13] To the third argument,[66] it must be conceded that when the significate is destroyed, so is the sign. But even though the thing *as it exists* is destroyed, it is not destroyed as it is understood; thus, the significate of the utterance is not destroyed.

---

63. Aristotle, *Anal. post.* I.30 (AL IV¹ 61; I.30.87b22–26); cf. Robert Grosseteste, in P. Rossi (ed.), *Robertus Grossatesta Lincolniensis, Commentarius in Posteriorum analyticorum libros* (Firenze: Unione accademica nazionale, 1981), I.18 (265) [hereafter "*Anal. post.*"]: "But all demonstration is of a thing that is always or of a thing that is for the most part."
64. Cf. n. 1 above. 65. Cf. n. 2 above.
66. Cf. n. 3 above.

[14] To the other,[67] the major premise of the first argument can be denied. As for its proof, signifying presupposes understanding in the sense that every significate was understood before; otherwise, no utterance would have been imposed on it. But once it has been imposed, it can signify in this way that thing on which it was imposed, even though it is understood by no one.

[15] Further, it can be replied to the minor premise that it is false, because according to Aristotle in Book II of the *Posterior Analytics*,[68] it is possible to understand non-beings. As for the proof of the minor premise of that argument: the major of the minor is false as regards everything other than the primary object of understanding. Furthermore, the minor of that proof can also be denied if the expression is understood to be produced as regards what is non-existent, because a non-existent can be understood through the species—not the species that it produces but that it has produced in the understanding—since that species can remain the same as it was before.

[16] When it is shown that it does not exist because "the cause is destroyed," etc.,[69] that proposition must only be understood as regards the cause in being, and not in becoming. But a thing, insofar as it exists, is only the cause of the species in becoming.

[17] When it is shown second that "when the significate is destroyed, so is the sign," I say that the thing insofar as it exists is not what is signified by an intelligible species in the soul, but rather, the thing insofar as it is understood. In that way, it is not destroyed.

[III. A Further Objection and Its Solution]

[18] An objection to the solution of the question: if an utterance signifies the same thing existing and non-existing, then what is signified by it is the same. The consequence is obvious, because every active truth can be changed into a passive truth, and further, the thing that was signified before as existing is now non-existing; therefore, the existing and the non-existing are the same, which is false.

[19] To this there is an easy reply: an existing thing was not signified by the utterance before, nor is a non-existing thing signified now; but rather, what is signified is the thing as it is understood, to which existing or non-existing is irrelevant insofar as it is signified.

67. Cf. n. 4 above.
68. Cf. n. 9 above.
69. Cf. n. 4 above.

[Question 4. Does Aristotle Designate an Appropriate Difference between Inscriptions and Utterances, and Affections and Things?]

And just as inscriptions are not the same, etc.[70]

We ask here about the difference Aristotle designates between inscriptions and utterances on the one hand and affections and things on the other, which is that utterances and inscriptions are not the same for all whereas things and affections are the same for all.

[1] It seems that it has not been given appropriately: for if affections were the same for all, since affections lead to the cognition of things, things cognized are the same for all. Therefore, all persons are equally knowledgeable.

[2] Again, some things are for some that are not for others, nor are they the same in number or species; therefore, etc.

[3] Again, comparison by different users does not make something different in itself; therefore, inscriptions and utterances are naturally the same for anyone using them.

[4] Again, what exists according to nature is the same for all; but a significant utterance is a natural sign; therefore, it signifies the same for all. Proof of the minor: of any natural power, something is the natural instrument; but the interpretative power is natural to man, since man is naturally a social animal,[71] wanting to express to another what is in him; therefore, the significant utterance, which is the instrument of that power, is a natural sign; therefore, it signifies naturally.

[5] Aristotle is on the opposing side.

[I. Reply to the Question]

[6] It must be said that the difference is appropriate, because affections in the soul, insofar as they are signs of things for anyone conceiving them, represent the same thing. That is because the same likeness in the soul is always representative

---

70. Aristotle, *De interpr.* I.1 (AL II[1] 5; I.1.16a5–8): "And just as written marks are not the same for all, so spoken sounds are not the same for all. But the primary things of which these are marks—affections of the soul—are the same for all, as are the things of which these affections are the likenesses."

71. Cf. Thomas Aquinas, *De interpr.* I.2 (I[1] 9b): "Since man is naturally a political and social animal, it was necessary that the thoughts of one man be made known to others, and this occurs by means of utterances." Cf. also Aristotle, *Politics* III.6.1278b19–21.

of the same thing, just as the likeness of a sensible thing is representative of it in the senses.

But inscriptions and utterances in themselves are not the same for all insofar as they are signs because the same inscription does not represent the same utterance for all, but either another or none at all. Nor does the same utterance signify the same affection for all, but either another or none at all. From this it is clear that things and affections are naturally signs, because they signify and are signified uniformly for all; and that which is from nature is the same for all. But inscriptions and utterances are not signs from nature because they are not the same for all insofar as they signify and are signified. Nor does Aristotle mean here to find their difference except insofar as they are signs and things signified.

[II. Reply to the Main Arguments]

[7] To the first argument,[72] it is said that although all conceive of simples in the same way, they do not compose and divide them in the same way. This is why it is said in *De anima* III[73] that the understanding is not deceived about 'what-something-is' except incidentally, that is, according to them,[74] not in absolute apprehension, but in combining the 'what-something-is' with another thing.

[8] Against this: at least it follows that all will be equally knowledgeable insofar as the apprehension of simples is concerned, and therefore all will be equally knowing with respect to the definition because the definition is a means of cognizing simples. But this is obviously false, for many know some simples about which others apprehend nothing at all. What is cited in *De anima* III is not relevant here. For Aristotle's meaning, as is obvious at the end of *Metaphysics* IX,[75] where he speaks about the same matter, is that either the understanding conceives 'what-something-is' completely, or it conceives nothing of it; and so it is not deceived about it because deception presupposes some cognition and some error.

[9] But Aristotle does not mean that anyone's understanding conceives every 'what-something-is,' because it happens for some that they conceive nothing of any 'what-something-is.' Therefore, the reply is clear to what was said in the above response,[76] that affections are not the same for all in themselves, but insofar as

---

72. Cf. n. 1 above.
73. Cf. Aristotle, *De an.* III.21 (III.6.430b26–28); Averroes, *De an.* III, com. 36 (491–93). The edition mistakenly gives the Aristotle reference as 430a26–28 and 431b16–18; it is actually 430b26–28.
74. Thomas Aquinas, *Sent De an.* III.11 (XLV^1 224–28). Again, the edition reference here is mistaken.
75. Aristotle, *Metaph.* IX.22 (AL XXV^2 182–83; IX.10.1051b18–1052a11).
76. Cf. n. 6 above.

they are signs of things. For every affection that is the same in itself always represents the same thing in whomever's mind it was.

[10] To the other argument about things,[77] [the reply] is likewise obvious: because a thing insofar as it is signified by an affection is the same for all.

[11] To the third argument,[78] I concede that the same inscriptions remain the same in themselves in relation to anyone using them. But they do not remain signs of the same utterances for all because they do not signify the same things for all. Nor is it inappropriate for them to be so variegated [in their signification] among the different people imposing them, since signs are made by imposition, which is different for different people.

[12] To the other argument,[79] I say that a significant utterance is not the instrument of the power of interpretation in man, but the throat and lungs, which contribute to the formation of the utterance. Just as if a man naturally wanted to flee from some injury, it does not follow that everything is a natural instrument by which he flees the injury, e.g., clothing or weapons or things of this sort; but nature provided those natural instruments by which man could procure these things for himself, as when [it is said that] man can procure all those things for himself by his own handiwork.[80] So by reason, and the natural instruments for forming an utterance, a man imposes some things that are conventional signs and not natural signs or concepts.

[Question 5. Is a Common Term Said Univocally of Existing Things and Non-Existing Things?]

Therefore, a name is a spoken sound, etc.[81]

In this particular section, we ask whether a common term imposed for signifying a true nature, some of whose *supposita* exist whereas others do not, is said univocally of existing and non-existing things.

---

77. Cf. n. 2 above.   78. Cf. n. 3 above.
79. Cf. n. 4 above; Thomas Aquinas, *De interpr.* I.6 (I[1] 35ab).
80. Cf. Thomas Aquinas, *De regno* I.1 (XLII, 449b): "But man was instituted without any of those things provided by nature [i.e., food, hair, teeth, horns, claws, or speed in flight]; instead of all these, however, reason was given to him, by which he could procure all of these things for himself by the work of his hands."
81. Aristotle, *De interpr.* I.2 (AL II[1] 6; I.2.16a19–20): "Therefore, a name is a spoken sound significant by convention, without time, none of whose parts is significant separately."

[1] It seems not: because what is not said univocally in a superior [genus] is not said univocally in an inferior one. But existing and non-existing *supposita* are not said univocally in a being that is superior; therefore, they are not said univocally in a common term that signifies an inferior in respect of being. The major premise is clear, because anything said univocally of an inferior is also said univocally of a superior. The minor is clear, because existing things are beings, but the others are non-beings, or only beings in potentiality.

[2] Again, univocal predication is essential predication; otherwise, it would not be distinct from denominative predication. But a common term is not predicated essentially of existing things and non-existing things, and so it is not predicated univocally. The minor is clear because essential predication is most truly made with the verb 'is,' but it is not predicated like this of non-existing *supposita*, as will be shown later.[82] Therefore, etc.

[3] Again, no univocal expression is common to being and non-being. This is clear by the topic from the greater and the lesser, because there is not something common to all beings that is univocal. Therefore, etc.

[4] For the opposing side: a common term is said of existing things and non-existing things 'according to the same name and definition,'[83] and therefore univocally. The antecedent is clear because such a common term has only one definition, since it is univocal in itself. Therefore of all things of which it is said, it is said according to that definition.

[5] Again, what signifies apart from every *differentia* of time is not determined with respect to the *supposita* of any time. A common nominal term is like this. Therefore, etc.

[6] Again, accidental differences in the significate of a term do not make it equivocal; but existing in the present, past, and future, or existing and non-existing, or presentness and pastness, are accidental differences in the significate of a term; therefore, etc. The minor is clear, because if a term were to signify an aggregate of existing in the present or the past, it would signify a being accidentally, and so what is signified by it would not be in a genus.

---

82. Cf. n. 88 below.
83. Aristotle, *Praedic.*, c. 1 (AL I^2 47; 1.1a6–7): "Things having a name in common and the same definition of substance corresponding to that name are called univocals."

[I. Reply to the Fifth Question]

[7] To this, it must be said that a common term that is not equivocal from its imposition on diverse natures, but is imposed only to signify a single nature, is said of whatever it is said *simpliciter* and univocally.

[8] This is clear because in that case, it is a univocal[84] in itself and so it has a single definition expressing the significate upon which it is imposed. Therefore, it is said univocally of whatever it is said *simpliciter* according to that definition. For, given the opposite of the consequent, viz., that it would be said of some things rather than of others according to another definition, since every definition expresses the significate of the name (because according to Aristotle in *Metaphysics* IV, "the formula [*ratio*] which the name signifies is the definition"),[85] it follows that the same name would have two significates—which is the opposite of the antecedent.

Also, because in that case, no common term is imposed to signify some *suppositum* or *supposita*; equivocation, however, is the diversity of significates; therefore, a common term will never be equivocal on account of any kind of diversity in the *supposita*, because there will never be a variation in its per se significate. Therefore, if it is said of all *supposita simpliciter*, it follows that it is said of all *supposita* univocally.

[Question 6. Are There Any *Supposita* Belonging *Simpliciter* to a Common Term Signifying a True Nature, apart from Things That Exist?]

We ask, then, on account of its truth, and in order to resolve the arguments, whether there are any *supposita* belonging *simpliciter* to a common term signifying a true nature, apart from things that exist.

[9] It seems so: everything which a term can supposit for *simpliciter* and verify a proposition is its *suppositum simpliciter*. Such things differ from existing things,

---

84. Reading *univocus* with mss. Oxford Merton 260 (= O) and Oxford Balliol 291 (= E). Antonius Andreas also has *in se univocus*; see his *Scriptum Antonii Andreae in Perihermenias Aristotelis*, in *Scriptum Antonii Andreae in arte veteri* (Venice: 1508), 69ra, l.55 [hereafter "*Periherm.*"].

85. Aristotle, *Metaph.* IV.28 (AL XXV^2 81; IV.7.1012a23–25).

as is obvious in the propositions 'a man was' and 'a man will be,' when we take the 'was' to speak of an inchoate and terminated act. For it is not verified of anything existing in this way, especially in the proposition, 'it is contingent that a man is running,' in which Aristotle says that the subject stands for what is contingent.[86]

[10] Again, participating in a natural disposition suffices for participating in common nature; therefore, participating in a natural disposition suffices for participating in the nature of a *suppositum*. The antecedent is obvious because the universal is 'naturally suited to be predicated of many.'[87] The consequence is obvious because no greater actuality is needed, it seems, for the *suppositum* participating actively than for the common nature participating passively. But things other than what exists are naturally suited to participate in the form of what is common. Therefore, etc.

[11] Again, between the *suppositum* and what is common there is order[88]—not in the things insofar as they exist, however, but only insofar as they are compared to the understanding. Therefore, the nature [*ratio*] of the *suppositum* and of the common nature does not depend on the being of the thing, but on the consideration of the understanding. But that can be the same concerning the things, whether existing or non-existing, because it is extraneous to what is considered by reason or understanding (thus considered) to exist or not to exist. Therefore, both the *suppositum* and the common nature are related in the same way to existence and non-existence.

[12] On the opposite side: The common nature belongs to the per se understanding of any *suppositum simpliciter*; therefore, it is predicated of any of them per se in the first mode, but not of non-existing things, as will be shown later.[89] Therefore, etc.

[13] Again, it does not suffice for the *suppositum* to signify in a particular way what its universal signifies in a universal way, because then, since an utterance would signify on its own, the utterance would be the *suppositum* of the utterance, which is obviously false. It must be, then, that the *suppositum* is essentially the

---

86. Aristotle, *De interpr.* II.3 (AL II[1] 28; II.12.21b26-33).
87. Aristotle, *De interpr.* I.7 (AL II[2] 45; I.7.17a39-40): "But I call 'universal' that which by its nature is predicated of many."
88. Three mss. (L, O[3], and R) add: "according to superior and inferior [*secundum superius et inferius*]."
89. Cf. n. 88 below.

same as its common nature. But non-being is not essentially the same as that which is [its] true nature. Therefore, etc.

[14] Again, in that case, every universal affirmative assertoric proposition would be false in which a predicate does not inhere in non-existing *supposita*, because the predicate is denoted to inhere in them by [the principle] 'being said of all [*dici de omni*],' since they are *supposita simpliciter* of a common distributed term. And in particular, no assertoric [*de inesse*], as-of-now [*ut nunc*] proposition would be true, or even possible, because its predicate could not be in non-existing things; thus, no universal proposition about contingency [*de contingenti*][90] would be possible, because it would be expounded in some assertoric impossible [proposition].

[Question 7. Are the Propositions 'Caesar is a man' and 'Caesar is an animal' True When Caesar Does Not Exist?]

We ask about the truth of propositions of this sort: 'Caesar is a man,' 'Caesar is an animal,' when the subject does not exist.

[15] It seems that such propositions are false: Because being cannot be predicated of non-being; but even when Caesar does not exist, man is still a true being, at least in other *supposita*, because the other *supposita* are beings in which [true being] exists *simpliciter*; therefore, it is not predicated, etc. It is argued in the same way as regards man and animal.

[16] Again, in the book *Perihermenias*,[91] when there is no opposition in the adjunct, i.e.,[92] in the predicate, and 'to be' is not predicated as an accident, then the consequence holds from what is conjoined to what is divided. But in 'Caesar is a man,' in the case at hand, there is neither opposition in the adjunct nor is 'to be' predicated as an accident, because substantial being is predicated of a true being, which is the most true being; therefore, it follows that Caesar exists. The consequent is false; therefore, so is the antecedent.

[17] Again, in the case at hand, this proposition is true: 'Caesar is a dead man';

---

90. A *de contingenti* proposition is not one that is contingently true, but rather one that contains the expression 'it is contingent that.' See our remarks below on *de necessario*.
91. Aristotle, *De interpr.* II.2 (AL II^1 25; II.11.21a19–24).
92. Here following mss. EOR, which add *id est*.

therefore, 'he is not a man' follows, because what is predicated of something with a conflicting determination is truly denied of it.

The antecedent is demonstrated [as follows]. First, this proposition is true: 'Caesar was a man,' inasmuch as 'was' means a terminated actuality, from which it follows that he is a dead man. Second, Caesar is not a living man because he does not live; therefore, he is a dead man, because 'dead' and 'living' are opposites in man.

[18] Again, 'in substantial change, a thing loses [its] name and definition,'[93] which was stated above[94] to be true of the *suppositum* as compared with [that of] the species; therefore, in corruption, which is a substantial change, the *suppositum* loses the name of the species.

[19] Again, if the proposition, 'the Antichrist is a man,' were true, by parity of reasoning it would be necessary; therefore, the middle would be truly said of a contingent *suppositum* in the mode of necessity; therefore, the same thing could not be truly said of the same thing in the mode of contingency. Therefore, every [syllogistic] mode that is uniformly about contingency would be impossible, since it would denote a middle term being said contingently of such a *suppositum*.

[20] Again, "with primary [substances] destroyed, it is impossible for anything else to remain,"[95] because all other things are either in them or are said of them. Therefore, in the case at hand, the secondary substance signified by 'man' would not be said of Caesar.

[21] On the opposite side: this consequence is necessary—'Caesar is running; therefore, a man is running.' Therefore, the middle term by virtue of which [the consequence] holds, i.e., 'Caesar is a man,' is necessary. The necessity of the consequence is shown [as follows]: because it followed at some time, and the same understanding of the antecedent and consequent remains now which [existed] then; and the consequence depends on the understanding of these [propositions]. Therefore, it follows now.

[22] Again, in *Metaphysics* IV, Aristotle says, 'this is this, because "this" signifies this';[96] but, when Caesar does not exist, the signification of 'man' belongs

---

93. Averroes, *De substantia orbis*, c. 1 (IX, f. 3rb); AA 229: "In individual substances there are two kinds of change. One change is substantial, which changes the thing in name and definition. This is called generation or corruption."
94. Cf. n. 12 of q. 3 above.
95. Aristotle, *Praedic.*, c. 2 (AL I^2 49; 2.2b6–7).
96. Aristotle, *Metaph.* IV.10 (AL XXV^2 67; IV.4.1006a33–34): "I say, however, that this signifies one thing; if this exists, [and] if this [is] a man, this will be the being of a man."

to the signification of 'Caesar,' for 'man' signifies the same thing whether or not Caesar exists; therefore, etc.

[23] It is said that Aristotle means this of the primary significate of a term, as is inferred from 'man' and 'two-footed animal'; he does not mean it of part of the definition or significate.

[24] Against this: from the whole significate one can infer the part; therefore, if it is true to assert the whole of the subject, it is also true to assert the part. However, if the consequence, 'two-footed animal; therefore, animal' does not hold when no man exists, then neither does it hold when a man exists, because the same diminution will occur on both sides, since the diminution is from the nature of the significates, which always remain the same.

[25] Again, when Caesar does not exist, he is a man based on what is understood of him per se; therefore, it is predicated of him; therefore, by necessity; therefore, etc. All these consequences are clear from Book I of the *Posterior Analytics*.[97]

[26] It is said to this: The fact that a predicate is [part] of the understanding of a subject does not entail that a proposition is necessary, but [rather, it is necessary] because the definition or part of the definition is predicated of what is defined. But there are no definitions of singular terms,[98] nor is there a definition of man if none exist because there is no definition of a non-being.

[27] Against this: if there is no definition of a non-being, then there are no demonstrations of non-beings. The consequence is clear, because one must already grasp of the subject of a demonstration that it is and what it is.[99] The consequent is against Aristotle, who says in Book I of the *Posterior Analytics* that one can have a demonstration of beings that are for the most part when they are not.[100] This is obvious because it can be known that thunder is a terrifying sound when no thunder exists.[101]

---

97. Aristotle, *Anal. post.* I.4 (AL IV¹ 13; I.4.73b16–17).

98. Cf. Aristotle, *Metaph.* VII.53 (AL XXV² 151; VII.15.1039b27–29); AA 130: "There is no knowledge or definition of singulars."

99. Aristotle, *Anal. post.* I.1 (AL IV¹ 5; I.1.71a11–13): "However, it is necessary to have prior knowledge in two ways: for of some things, it is necessary to believe already that they are; of others, one must understand what it is that is said of them."

100. Ibid., I.30 (AL IV¹ 61; I.30.87b22–26); cf. Robert Grosseteste, *Anal. post.* I.18 (265): "Every demonstration is of a thing that is always or of a thing that is for the most part."

101. Cf. Isidorus, in W. M. Lindsay (ed.), *Isadori Hispalensis Episcopi Etymologiarum sive Originum*

[28] Again, there are definitions of non-beings, at least [definitions] indicating what is meant by the name. Such a definition of man may be given when no men exist. In that [definition] 'animal' is assumed, since it belongs per se to the significate of man; therefore, it is still predicated of him per se.

[29] Again, 'Caesar is Caesar; therefore, Caesar is a man.' The antecedent is true because the same thing is predicated of itself; therefore, the consequent is too. The consequence is clear, because the consequent is part of the understanding of the antecedent.

[Question 8. Are the Propositions 'A man is a man' and 'Caesar is Caesar' True When Neither of Them Exists?]

For this reason, we ask about the truth of the proposition, 'Caesar is Caesar,' [or] 'A man is a man,' in the case at hand.

[30] It seems that they are false: because 'Therefore Caesar is' and 'Therefore a man is' follow from them, which is shown because there is neither opposition in the adjunct nor incidental predication,[102] as it seems, because substantial being is predicated. The consequent is false; therefore so is the antecedent.

[31] Again, 'therefore Caesar is a man' and 'therefore a man is an animal' follow from these because the consequents all belong to the understanding of the antecedents. But these consequents are all false; therefore, so are the antecedents.

[32] Again, when the affirmative is true, there must be a union in reality in the way it is signified by the proposition. But with 'Caesar is Caesar,' there is no union in reality because the subject and predicate are not real things [*aliquae res*]; therefore, etc.

[33] On the opposite side: 'no proposition is truer than one in which the same thing is predicated of itself,'[103] which is what we have here.

---

libri XX., 2 vols. (Oxford: Oxford University Press, 1985), XIII.8 (PL 82:476C) [hereafter "*Etymologiae*"]: "The word 'thunder' [means] that its sound terrifies."

102. Cf. n. 16 above.

103. Cf. Albert the Great, *Liber de praedicabilis* I, 49a: "And so we understand what Boethius means [when he says] that no proposition is truer than one in which the same thing is predicated of itself"; Boethius, *De interpr.* VI.14 (480; PL 64:628BC): "That is why the [proposition] 'What is good is good' is judged to be closer to the nature of goodness than 'What is good is useful.' If this is so, then the [proposition] that is true in relation to the thing itself is truer than the proposition that appears in relation to accidents."

[34] Again, in *Metaphysics* IV, 'this is this,' just as was argued above, viz., in the preceding question in the second argument on the opposing side.[104]

[35] Again, in *Metaphysics* V, in the chapter 'On "that in virtue of which":[105] "The causes of man are many; [but] there is no reason why a man is a man."

[36] Again, in *Metaphysics* VII,[106] to ask why a man is a man is to ask nothing, because there is nothing more certain that could be assumed in that question, in which that is in doubt.

[37] Again, according to Aristotle in *De interpretatione* II,[107] every negative [proposition] is true *per accidens*, in this case because it is reduced to some prior affirmative truth, and especially because it is reduced to a proposition in which the same thing is predicated of itself, just as the truth of the proposition, 'good is not evil,' is reduced to the truth of 'good is good.' Therefore, since 'Caesar is not a donkey' is true, and in this way it is possible to remove many other things from Caesar, it follows that it is possible for Caesar to be truly to be affirmed of himself.

[38] Again, it can be deduced by reason that if 'Caesar is Caesar' is denied, 'Caesar is not Caesar' is conceded, and furthermore, 'Caesar is non-Caesar' follows. For this sort of consequence holds wherever the predicates of affirmative propositions are contradictory opposites. Simple predicates are like this—e.g., 'Caesar' and 'not-Caesar'—as will be discussed below.[108] And furthermore, [if] 'Caesar is non-Caesar,' then 'Non-Caesar is Caesar' [follows] by conversion. And furthermore, from the converting and the converse, which are conceded, it is argued syllogistically as follows: 'Non-Caesar is Caesar; Caesar is non-Caesar; therefore, Caesar is Caesar.' The premises are true based on what makes the conclusion false; therefore, the conclusion is true.

It is not an obstacle that in this syllogism from opposites, there are only two terms in reality, because it suffices if there are three terms in reason. So it is in the case at hand: 'Caesar' has the nature of two terms, viz., the nature of the major term as well as of the minor.

---

104. Cf. n. 22 above.
105. Aristotle, *Metaph.* V.23 (AL XXV² 107; V.18.1022a33–34).
106. Aristotle, *Metaph.* VII.59 (AL XXV² 154; VII.17.1041a20–24): "But someone asks why man is an animal of such-and-such a nature. Clearly, he is not asking why a man exists (that he exists must be obvious; for if it were not so, he would be asking about nothing)."
107. Aristotle, *De interpr.* II.5 (AL II¹ 35; II.14.23b16–18).
108. See nn. 51–57 below.

[39] Again, according to Aristotle in *Prior Analytics* II,[109] in every syllogism from opposites, the conclusion is impossible. But whether a thing exists or not, this is a syllogism from opposites in the third of the second:[110] 'no man is white; some man is white'; and 'some man is not a man' follows. Therefore, the conclusion is impossible whether the thing exists or not. Therefore, its opposite is necessary, i.e., 'every man is a man,' whether the thing exists or not.

[40] Again, whether the thing exists or not, 'Caesar runs' and 'Caesar does not run,' or 'every man runs' and 'not every man runs' are contradictories. Therefore, the subject in both is the same. But the same thing can be truly predicated of itself with the verb 'is.' Therefore, etc.

[41] A reply to this, and to certain arguments of Boethius and some [other arguments] given above,[111] is that when 'Caesar is Caesar' is said here, not only is 'Caesar' predicated, but also the whole 'being Caesar,' because the content of the verb 'is,' together with what specifies the verb, is predicated when it is predicated third.[112] But the subject is 'Caesar' absolutely, not 'being Caesar,' and for that reason the same thing is not predicated of itself in such propositions.

[42] Although this reply involves the difficulty of the content of the verb when it is predicated as a copula, if it is part of the predicate (of which, perhaps, we will speak of later),[113] nevertheless, one can specifically argue against what is proposed in the following way: when 'being' is predicated as a third element, it predicates what is in another, i.e., the being of what specifies it.[114] For example, in 'Caesar is Caesar,' being is predicated of Caesar; and that is the same as Caesar, whether Caesar exists or not; therefore, the affirmative is true. This reasoning is confirmed by the fact that propositions such as 'a non-being is a non-being' and 'a chimera is a chimera' are conceded as true simply because the being of the predicate is the same as the subject.

---

109. Aristotle, *Analytica Priora* II.16 (AL III¹ 126–27; II.15.64b7–10, 15–16) [hereafter "*Anal. priora*"].
110. That is, in the third mode of the second syllogistic figure.
111. Cf. nn. 33–40 above.
112. That is, as a 'third element.' Cf. Aristotle, *De interpr.* II.1 (AL II¹ 19; II.10.19b20–22).
113. Cf. nn. 32–33 of qq. 8–11 below.
114. That is, the word specifying the verb 'is.'

[I. Reply to the Sixth Question]
[A. Reply]

[43] To the first of these questions[115] it can be said that the nature of what is common or of the *suppositum* is not attributed to a thing as it exists, but as it is conceived in the understanding, because to posit something existing as the nature of what is common is attributed to it just is to posit ideas, as Plato thought.

Therefore, a common term, insofar as it has the nature of what is common, is a nature as conceived under the concept 'predicable of many'[116] and so a *suppositum* is a nature conceived in the understanding under the aspect, 'incapable of being predicated of many.' But it is possible to conceive a nature in the understanding in the same way, as predicable of many, and the same [nature], as not predicable of many, whether it exists or not, whether what is conceived as non-predicable does not exist, and what is conceived as predicable exists in other *supposita*.

For in the nature of what is commonly conceived as a 'this,' a nature conceived absolutely is always understood per se; therefore, there are other *supposita* belonging *simpliciter* to a common term besides ones that exist.

[44] The assumption (viz., that an existing thing is conceived in the same way as when it is not existing) is obvious: because according to Aristotle in Book I of the *Posterior Analytics*,[117] demonstrations can be produced 'of those things that are for the most part,' etc., even when they do not exist; therefore, they can be known definitively, because a demonstrative cognition presupposes a definitive cognition;[118] therefore, they can be conceived *simpliciter* in the understanding by the same species. There is, then, strength of reason in this: human nature conceived as a 'this' is related in the same way to human nature conceived under the aspect 'predicable of many,' whether the nature is conceived as it exists or not. Therefore, it has the nature of the *suppositum* equally when it exists and when it does not.

For if the names 'Caesar' and 'Antichrist' and others of this sort are imposed for signifying *supposita* of a man or the nature conceived as a 'this,' since they always signify the same no matter what sort of change occurs with regard to the

---

115. See nn. 9–14 above.
116. Cf. n. 10 above.
117. Cf. n. 27 above.
118. Cf. Aristotle, *Anal. post.* II.3 (AL IV^1 72; II.2.90b24–26).

existence of the thing (as was stated in the resolution of the third question),[119] it follows that they always signify the *suppositum* of a man.

If, however, [those names] have been imposed for signifying the entire whole, of which Aristotle says in *Metaphysics* VII that generation and corruption per se concern that thing,[120] then they do not signify the *supposita*[121] of man when they exist or when they do not exist. For a *suppositum* per se is the same as its common nature taken in a more determinate mode; nor is the entire whole related to the species in this way. But 'this man' signifies at least the *suppositum* of a true man.

[B. Reply to the Main Arguments of the Sixth Question]

[45] To the first argument,[122] the reply will be obvious from the solution to the following question.[123]

[46] To the second argument,[124] it is obvious that it is not the nature of a *suppositum* to signify particularly what its common [noun] signifies universally. But the nature conceived in the understanding as a 'this' (which is indeed signified by an utterance and is not a signifying utterance) is a *suppositum* of the nature conceived in the understanding as predicable of many. And this nature, conceived in this way, is essentially the same as the nature so conceived, but not such that the aspect of conceiving it falls into a union made with the verb 'is.'

[47] When it is said in the argument,[125] 'non-being is not the same as a true nature,' I say that non-being as conceived in the understanding can be the same as something that in other *supposita* is true being. But, insofar as it is in it, it is non-existing, just as that [true being] is also, which will be made clear later.[126]

[48] To the other,[127] [the reply] will be clear later,[128] when it is asked whether a common term supposits and is distributed everywhere for its *supposita*.

---

119. Cf. n. 10 of q. 3 above.
120. Aristotle, *Metaph.* VII.53 (AL XXV³ 110; VII.10.1039b20–25): "But since substance [is] of two kinds—both that which is the whole [formula and matter] together and the formula ... therefore, whatever are described [*dicuntur*] in the [former] way are [capable of] destruction, for they are also [capable of] generation."
121. Reading *supposita* for *suppositum*, as seems obvious.
122. See n. 9 above.
123. See nn. 49–50 below.
124. See n. 10 above.
125. See n. 13 above.
126. See n. 70 below.
127. See n. 11 above.
128. See qq. 9–11 below; he is referring especially to nn. 23–24.

[II. Reply to the Seventh Question]

[49] To the other question:[129] such propositions can be conceded to be true because the union of extremes suffices for the truth of an affirmative proposition. For an affirmative proposition signifies this alone; but it is so in the case at hand, for in the understanding of the subject per se there is included the understanding of the predicate.

For if 'Caesar' and names of this kind are imposed for signifying *supposita* of a man, then the truth of such propositions is clear from the solution to the preceding question,[130] and from the arguments made on behalf of this part of the question,[131] as well as from certain things touched on in the solution to the following question,[132] especially from the authority of Aristotle in Book I of the *Posterior Analytics*:[133] "Being predicated of all is," etc., [and] "as animal is predicated of every man, then if it is true to call [something] a man, it is true to call [him] an animal, and if [he is] now the one, he is the other too." On the basis of this authority, it is clear that the necessity of the attendant extremes suffices for the necessity of the proposition, so that when the one is given, the other is too, although neither exists of necessity.

[50] The same [conclusion] is clear, because otherwise no assertoric proposition would be necessary in an unqualified sense in which a common nature is predicated of a *suppositum* falling under it, because it would not always be true. And nothing else can be taken under the middle term in a major premise about necessity [*de necessario*][134] except a *suppositum* belonging to a common nature. Therefore, no minor assertoric premise could be taken under a major premise about necessity in a regular syllogism. This is contrary to Aristotle in *Prior Analytics* I.[135]

---

129. See nn. 15–29 above.
131. See nn. 21–29 above.
133. Aristotle, *Anal. post.* I.4 (AL IV^1 12; I.4.73a28–31).
130. See nn. 43–44 above.
132. See nn. 75–77 below.

134. A *de necessario* proposition is not a proposition which is necessarily true, but one which explicitly contains the expression 'it is necessary that.' We have translated it as 'a proposition about necessity.' See our remarks above about *de contingenti*.

135. Aristotle, *Anal. priora* I.15 (AL III^1 32; I.13.34a35–b6); AA 309.

[B. Reply to the Main Arguments of the Seventh Question]

[51] To the first argument,[136] I say that here—'Caesar is a man'—the existent is not predicated of the non-existent, but human nature, conceived as predicable of many, [is predicated] of the same nature conceived as a 'this.'

[52] Against this: Caesar is not existing, [but] man is existing; man as existing is predicated of Caesar; therefore, the existent is predicated of the non-existent.

[53] It must be said that this is the fallacy of accident because insofar as 'man' is predicated of Caesar, it is extraneous to the predicate 'existing [*exsistens*].' And so Caesar, to the extent that he is joined to this predicate, viz. 'being that of which man is predicated,' is extraneous to the predicate 'existing.' But there is a fallacy of accident because the middle term has been joined to the extremes for extraneous reasons [*rationes*].[137]

[54] Against this: it is at least incongruous that what is existing is predicated of what is non-existing because there is no union of them in reality [*in re*]; therefore, the sentence signifying that they are united is false.

[55] I say that 'man' insofar as it is united to 'Caesar' is non-existing incidentally [*per accidens*], just as Caesar is non-existing, because there is no existing *suppositum* in connection with which is it attributed to Caesar. For the common nature [*natura communis*] as preserved in some *suppositum* is not more truly a being [*ens*] than that *suppositum*.

[56] Against this: since some *supposita* of a man are existing and others are non-existing, 'man' is equivocal for them. That is because nothing is a common univocal [term] for being and non-being, since they are contradictories.

[57] I say that existing [*exsistere*] and not-existing [*non-exsistere*] do not produce equivocation in a term since they are extraneous to the nature as signified by the term.

[58] To the second main argument,[138] I say that in 'Caesar is a man,' 'being [*esse*]' is predicated incidentally.[139] This is understood in two ways: either such

---

136. See n. 15 above.
137. Cf. Aristotle, *De soph. elench.* I.5 (AL VI¹ 11; I.5.166b29–37); cf. Peter of Spain, in L. M. de Rijk (ed.), *Petrus Hispanus, Tractatus, called afterwards Summule logicales* (Assen: Van Gorcum, 1972), tr. 7, n. 103 (147) [hereafter "*Tractatus*"]: "But if one asks about that accident which contributes to the subject thing, I say that it is extraneous or diverse with regard to some third thing."
138. See n. 16 above.
139. Oxford Balliol 291 (= E) has *secundum adiacens*, although clearly *accidens* is meant. The con-

that it is in keeping with something extraneous, or such that it is in keeping with something whose being as regards the subject does not posit being in an unqualified sense. It is both ways in the case at hand, for the being of man as regards Caesar is extraneous to 'being' when it is predicated second.[140]

For the 'being' which states the predication of man of its *suppositum* subsists in the same way as when it is predicated second, regardless of what changes occur in being. It is also incidental [*secundum accidens*] in the second way, for 'to be a man,' as said of Caesar, does not posit being of necessity.

[59] Against this: 'Caesar is white; therefore, Caesar is' follows; therefore, by the topic 'from the greater [*a maiori*],' 'Caesar is a man; therefore, Caesar is' also follows. If the being of an accident, which is a less true being, posits being in an unqualified sense, all the more does the being of a substance, which is the truest being, posit true being in an unqualified sense.[141]

[60] Again, being either belongs to the essence, or is by necessity consequent upon the essence of anything; therefore, so [is the being] of man, since it signifies a true essence. But in both ways, being *simpliciter* follows upon being a man.

[61] Again, at the beginning of Book II of the *Posterior Analytics*,[142] it is said that 'whether it is [*si est*]' is something truly knowable because it can be a subject of inquiry. Therefore, it is necessary that 'being' be predicated of anything and also [that it be predicated] per se; therefore, it also follows upon anything.

[62] Again, in the same text:[143] it is not possible for those ignorant of 'whether it is [*si est*]' to know 'what it is [*quid est*].' But someone who knows the definition of man, or what genus is predicated of it, knows what it is. Therefore, 'if it is an animal, then it is' follows.

[63] I say that on neither of the aforementioned interpretations is being predicated here incidentally in 'Caesar is white.'[144] For a real accident, which is the kind 'white' is, only inheres in an existing subject; therefore, its being in a subject by necessity posits being absolutely.

---

fusion may have been a result of the later reference to *secundum adiacens* ('esse' quando praedicatur secundum, i.e., secundum adiacens); that is, when the verb 'to be' is predicated as a second element (*secundum adiacens*), being is predicated only incidentally (*secundum accidens*).

140. That is, when predicated as a second element.
141. The text has 'posit true being *simpliciter*,' but the 'true' here is superfluous.
142. Aristotle, *Anal. post.* II.2 (AL IV^1 69–70; II.2.89b36–90a12).
143. Ibid., II.2 (AL IV^1 71; II.2.90a25): "For if we do not perceive it, we seek (as we lack this knowledge) whether it is [or not]."
144. See n. 59 above.

When the consequence is proved that 'the being of substance is the truer being,' it is true [of] the being of a non-existing substance. But being specified by substance is not a truer being, i.e., existential being [*esse exsistere*], than being specified *per accidens*. For when being is predicated as a third [element], it predicates a union of extremes, which is necessary [for the union] of substance to substance [even] without the extremes existing, but not for [the union of] an accident to a non-existing substance.

[64] To the other:[145] the major is true of being as it exists. And so it is not assumed to be predicated of Caesar except as he is understood, and so [its] existing is extraneous to him.

[65] To the other:[146] I say that 'whether it is,' as understood in Book II of the *Posterior Analytics*, is not [to be taken] in the sense of 'existing [*exsistere*]' but in the sense of 'to be a being [*esse ens*],' i.e., 'having an essence [*habens essentiam*],' as 'being [*ens*]' is a name, because one must know that something has an essence before it is known definitely what essence [it is]. And the first pertains to the question 'whether it is'; the second to the question 'what it is.'

But if it is understood in some way as regards existing, this is only as an aptitude. For nothing has an essence except unless it is naturally suited to have existence. But it is obvious that it can be known what an utterance is, even though no utterance is actually known to exist, e.g., when someone actually hears nothing.

[66] To the third main argument,[147] I say that 'dead' and 'alive' can be understood with respect to actuality or with respect to aptitude. The accidents of the essence signified by the name 'man' are [understood] in the first way. And so it can be conceded that Caesar is not a living man, but dead, and that being 'dead' in this way does not take away from 'man,' nor imply [that Caesar is] a non-man. For the diminution of anything by another, like the opposition between them, should be by reason of the significates. For 'man' does not include in its significate the opposite of being dead, taken in this way. But if they are taken as aptitudes, perhaps in this way there are *differentiae* in the genus of substance, the same as 'animate' and 'inanimate,' and so being dead would take away from man, and 'Caesar is a dead man' is false, whereas 'Caesar is a living man' is true. Nor does 'therefore, he is alive' follow, just as 'he is able to laugh; therefore, he is laughing' does not follow.

145. See n. 60 above.
146. See nn. 61–62 above.
147. See n. 17 above.

[67] When it is proved that Caesar is a dead man because he was,[148] insofar as 'was [*fuit*]' means a complete and terminated act, I deny it, if 'was' is predicated as a third element. For being a man is not terminated in him since he is still a man. But if 'was' is predicated as a second element, it can be conceded that that man was, because existing is terminated in him; however, the use extends to the proposition, 'Caesar was a man and he does not exist [*non est*],' because usually the understanding is more readily directed to existing things than to non-existing things. And of Caesar, it is not true that he is an existing man [*homo exsistens*], but he was [*fuit*], since 'man' does not imply that its significate is an existing man. That is why the signification of a word often clashes with its use, and vice versa.

[68] To the second proof,[149] it is clear how 'he is alive; therefore, he lives' follows. The aforementioned distinction is clear in the similar [case] of 'biped,' which Aristotle frequently uses as the essential *differentia* of man. Although he says in Book V of the *Topics*:[150] not every man has two feet; therefore, it is a *differentia* of man in aptitude, or at least it is not said of every man in actuality.

[69] Against this: if Caesar is not living [*non vivit*], and [if] "for living things, to be is to live [*vivere est esse*]," according to Aristotle in Book II of *De anima*,[151] then he is not; and if he is not, he is not a being [*si non est, non est ens*]. For when 'to be' is predicated as a second element, it predicates what is in itself [*quod in se est*]; and 'if he is not a being, then he is not a man,' by the topic from the superior to the inferior in negating.

[70] [Reply] to this [objection]: the proposition 'Caesar is not living' must be conceded, and likewise the proposition, 'Caesar is not [*non est*],' when we speak of existential being; and further, 'therefore, he is non-existing,' because that being [*esse*] is predicated of existing [*pro exsistere*] when it is predicated as a second element. But 'being [*ens*]' taken for what is existing [*exsistens*] is not a superior [genus] to man. That is why in ancient times it was customarily said that being [*ens*] can be a participle or a noun.[152] Being as a participle signifies the same as existing

---

148. See n. 17 above, viz., in the first proof of the antecedent.
149. That is, to the second proof of the antecedent (see n. 17 above).
150. Aristotle, *Topica* V.1, V.5 (AL V^1 86, 101; V.1.128b26, V.5.134b6–7).
151. Aristotle, *De an.* II.37 (II.4.415b13).
152. Cf. Boethius, *Anicii Manlii Severini Boethii In Isagogen Porphyrii commenta*, ed. Samuel Brandt (Vienna: F. Tempsky, 1906), I.24 (74; PL 64:43B) [hereafter "*In Isagogen Porphyrii*"]: "But someone says that if all ten of these genera are truly subsistent, in a certain way they can be said to be beings [*entia*]. For this word flows from what it is to be [*ab eo quod est esse*], and in the participle [form] there

[*exsistens*], because it keeps the signification of the verb from which it descends. Being as a noun perhaps signifies 'having an essence [*habens essentiam*]'; and this is divided into ten genera. And it must be conceded that 'Caesar is a being [*est ens*]' when speaking of this latter being, not of the being that is a participle.

[71] To the fourth [argument]:[153] change does not befall a thing except as it exists. But in this way it does not have the nature [*ratio*] of the *suppositum*. Rather [it has the nature of the *suppositum*] as it is in the understanding in the mode of not-predicable of many.[154] Therefore, the authoritative passage would have it that the thing, insofar as it exists in a substantial change, does not have the form that it had earlier. But from this it does not follow that what was earlier a *suppositum* of something common is now not its *suppositum*, because there has been no substantial change produced in that regard. Therefore, the authority is understood only of the thing that is changed, which is the thing as it exists [*ut exsistit*].

[72] To the fifth [argument]:[155] if it is conceded that every minor [in a syllogism] that is uniformly about contingency is impossible, [this is] nothing against Aristotle, because it is not on that account any less a valid syllogistic form than what Aristotle teaches. Or if there is some *suppositum* in potentiality to the form of a term that is not a per se *suppositum* of a term, such a *suppositum* can be taken under it, and so the minor premise will be true.

[73] To the sixth [argument]:[156] how that remark from the book of the *Categories* should be understood is stated in that place.[157]

[II. Reply to the Eighth Question]
[A. Reply]

[74] To the other question,[158] all propositions like 'Caesar is Caesar' and 'Caesar is a man' must be conceded, on account of the arguments made earlier to that part of the question.[159]

[75] One of the arguments[160] is this, viz., about the syllogism from opposites:

---

is an abuse of speech due to the narrowness and compression of the Latin language. Therefore, as was stated, these could be called beings [*entia*], and 'being' [*ens*] itself, i.e., 'to be,' will perhaps seem to be called their genus."

153. See n. 18 above.
154. See n. 43 above.
155. See n. 19 above.
156. See n. 20 above.
157. See Duns Scotus, *Praedic.*, q. 13, nn. 18–21, 24–25 (*OPh* I, 369–70; 371–72).
158. See nn. 30–42 above.
159. See nn. 38–40 above.
160. The paragraph break in the edition is a mistake; n. 74 ends with *propter rationes prius factas*

it can be reduced to the solution of the preceding question.[161] Thus, in Book II of the *Prior Analytics*,[162] Aristotle says that a syllogism from opposites is not only where something is affirmed and denied of the same thing in an unqualified sense, but where something is universally affirmed of a superior and the same thing is denied of its inferior, or vice versa. And he provides an example of this in the fourth of the second,[163] as follows: 'every academic subject involves study; not every medicinal art involves study.' Therefore in the case at hand as well, this syllogism from opposites will be likewise: 'every animal is white; not every man is white'; and 'therefore, not every man is an animal' follows. Therefore, the conclusion is impossible, even with no men existing, because it is no less a syllogism from opposites by the fact [that no men exist]; therefore, its opposite is necessary.

[76] If it is said that non-existing [*non-exsistere*] removes the nature [*ratio*] of an inferior [i.e., Caesar] from man by reason of 'animal,' it follows that that nature inhered in it insofar as it existed, or at least that it depended on the thing existing, and consequently, it was not that nature in an unqualified sense by an operation of the understanding. For in its operation the understanding does not depend on the thing existing; the fact that both demonstrations and definitions are made of non-beings [*de non-entibus*][164] is all the more reason to attribute second intentions [*intentiones*] completely caused by the understanding to non-existing things.

[77] Likewise for that argument made in the first question about 'per se':[165] due to the fact that there are definitions of non-existing things, 'man' can have a definition even with no men existing; and 'animal' is given in that definition; therefore, 'animal' is predicated per se of 'man.'

At least 'man' can have a per se definition expressing what is said by the name; in that definition 'animal' would be given by necessity, since it would belong to the significate of the name, because the name always signifies the same.

('on account of the reasons given earlier'), and begins n. 75 with *Ad illam partem quaestionis, quarum una est ista*, which invites the translation 'To that part of the question, of which one is this,' although the plural *quarum* (of which) does not refer back to 'question' or 'part,' but clearly to '*rationes*' (the reasonings or arguments). The two nn. really belong together, but we maintain the format by ending n. 74 with the first four words of n. 75.

161. See nn. 49–50 above.
162. See n. 39 above.
163. That is, in the fourth mode of the second figure of the syllogism.
164. See nn. 27–28 above.
165. See nn. 25 and 27–28 above.

[B. Reply to the Main Arguments of the Eighth Question]

[78] To the first argument,[166] it was stated in the previous question how being [*esse*] is predicated incidentally.[167]

[79] To the second,[168] the propositions that were inferred are conceded, viz., 'Caesar is a man' and the like, just as they were conceded earlier.[169]

[80] To the third,[170] it can be said that 'just as a thing is related to being,'[171] so for the truth of such a proposition, there must be such a union in reality [*in re*] as is signified in discourse [*in sermone*]. But the nature signified by [the name] 'Caesar' is a being in the understanding; otherwise, the understanding would not make a composite from it. And so there is composition of the same thing existing in the intellect with itself, and such a composition suffices for truth where a thing is not existing [*non est existens*], as is clear in 'a chimera is a chimera' and 'non-being is non-being [*non-ens est non-ens*].'

[IV. Reply to the Arguments of the Fifth Question]

[81] To the first argument of that question,[172] which is about the univocity of a common term, [viz.,] that the term must not be univocal, I say that being [*ens*] as a name is not equivocal, whether as regards what exists [*exsistit*] or as regards what does not exist, although perhaps as a participle it is equivocal between them. But as a participle it is not a superior [genus] to man.[173]

[82] To the other argument:[174] it has already been conceded that what is common [*commune*] is predicated of the *suppositum* by the verb 'is [*est*].'[175]

[83] To the third argument:[176] '[no univocal expression is common] to being and non-being [*enti et non-enti*],' etc., if it is understood of them insofar as they have the nature of contradictories, perhaps no univocal expression is [common] to them.

[84] And if it is argued further, 'Robert is existing [*exsistens*]; Caesar is

---

166. See n. 30 above.
167. See nn. 58–65 above.
168. See n. 31 above.
169. See n. 74 above.
170. See n. 32 above.
171. Aristotle, *Metaph.* II.4 (AL XXV^2 37; II.1.993b30–31): "Just as each thing has being, so it is with regard to truth."
172. See n. 1 above.
173. See n. 70 above.
174. See n. 2 above.
175. See n. 43 above.
176. See n. 3 above.

non-existing; therefore, there is not something univocal between them': it is a fallacy of accident,[177] because the middle is extraneous to the one extreme insofar as it is compared to the other. The reason is that for two *supposita*, one of which is existing [*exsistens*] and the other non-existing [*non-existens*], there is something univocal per se to the extent that they include something the same per se, even though it happens that the one is existing and the other non-existing, since as those accidents inhere in them, they do not have such a common nature.

[85] But that this form of arguing is not valid is clear in a similar case. Thus it is argued that this consequence is not valid: 'There is nothing univocal [that is] common to white and non-white, since they are contradictories; this [man] is white and that [man] is not white; therefore, there is nothing univocal [that is] common to this man and that.' The reason is that the predicate, 'not having something univocal,' inheres in them perhaps by reason of affirmation and negation, just like 'being contradictories [*esse contradictoria*],' and not by reason of those things that are subsumed by the form. And in the minor premise, it is taken for those things that are subsumed under the forms.

[86] When the proposition 'nothing is univocal to being and non-being [*enti et non-enti*]' is shown by the fact that there is not something univocal to all beings,[178] the consequence must be denied because nothing the same, conceived in the understanding, is included in the concept of all beings, but there can be something the same, conceived in the intellect, as regards the understanding of what happens to exist [*exsistere*] and what happens not to exist [*non-existere*].

[V. Another Reply]
[A. Reply to the Sixth Question]

[87] Otherwise, it can be said to the second of those three questions,[179] upholding what was said in connection with the previous two questions,[180] viz., both existing and non-existing *supposita* are *supposita* of a common term *simpliciter* and univocally.

[88] Still, according to some,[181] one does not have to concede that the com-

---

177. See n. 53 above.
178. See n. 3 above.
179. See nn. 9–14 and 43–48 above.
180. That is, in qq. 7–8 above.
181. Cf. Peter of Cornwall, *Sophisma 'Omnis homo est*,' in "Oxford Logic 1250–1275: Nicholas and Peter of Cornwall on Past and Future Realities," in *The Rise of British Logic: Acts of the Sixth European Symposium on Medieval Logic and Semantics, Balliol College, Oxford, 19–24 June 1983*, ed. P. Osmund

mon [nature] is predicated of [existing and non-existing] things truly with the verb 'is [*est*],' because *supposita* are univocal *simpliciter* whenever they involve the same nature [*ratio*] of the term according to any *differentia* of time, because the significate of a common term determines no *differentia* of time for it. Therefore, it can be consistent with univocation that man is predicated of Antichrist with 'being in the future [*fore*],' and of Caesar with 'having been [*fuisse*],' because those [verbs] do not vary the signification of the term.

And this is perhaps what those [others] meant when they said that they are *supposita* of diverse appellation,[182] because they are not appellated by a common [nature] in the same way, although perhaps they participate in the same significate of the common [term].

[B. Reply to the Main Arguments of the Fifth Question Based on This Interpretation]

[89] [Reply] to the arguments against univocation.

To the first,[183] it can be said that existing [*exsistens*] and non-existing *supposita* are univocal in being [*ens*] because being [*ens*] is said of them according to a single significate, although not with the verb 'is [*est*].'

[90] To the second,[184] it is conceded that even if the predication of the com-

---

Lewry (Toronto: Pontifical Institute of Mediaeval Studies, 1983), 49: "Assuming this, you would understand that neither presentness, nor pastness, nor futurity, nor being would belong to the understanding of an utterance, because thus I say 'man [*homo*],' by way of signifying the thing, and I determine no *differentia* of time"; cf. also the anonymous *sophisma* text '*omnis homo de necessitate est animal*' (ibid., 55–56): "These [persons] speak of the nature of terms, and [say] nothing of the nature of the term 'is,' because in one sense it ['a man is an animal'] is true.... If real being is signified by the verb 'is,' as in 'a man is an animal,' it is always signified that the thing signified is present, and it is signified that those existents are really present. And thus, whatever causes [of truth] are taken, 'a white thing is black' will always be false, whatsoever causes of truth the proposition has, when what is signified by the predicate does not inhere in the subject, because any cause of truth presupposes the inherence of what is signified by the predicate in the subject. And as long as every kind of restriction is set aside, 'a past man is a past animal,' 'a future man is a future animal' are not causes of truth, because pastness and futurity do not inhere in 'man' [?] in the nature of pastness and futurity, but they do inhere in 'a man who was' and 'a man who will be.' ... But [in] 'a man who was is an animal,' 'animal' is attributed as present, and the proposition is false."

182. Cf. William of Sherwood, *Syncategoremata 'omnis,'* in J. R. O'Donnell, "William of Sherwood's *Syncategoremata*," *Mediaeval Studies* 3 (1941): 49: "But understand that when it distributes for the parts according to number, it requires three actually existing *appellata*; and when [it distributes] according to species, it requires three or several entities conditionally [*habitualiter*]."

183. See n. 1 above.

184. See n. 2 above.

mon [nature] of any *suppositum* is essential, it does not have to be that every essential predication with the verb 'is [*est*]' is true, but it suffices with any verb of any *differentia* of time.

[91] To the third [argument],[185] the reply is as was stated earlier.[186]

[C. Reply to the Opposing Arguments of the Seventh Question Based on This Interpretation]

[92] [Reply] to the arguments proving that 'Caesar is a man' is true.

To the first,[187] it is said that this consequence is not valid: 'Caesar is running; therefore, a man is running.' The reason, as is clear, is that Caesar is not now appellated by 'man' with a verb in the present tense. But [this] does follow: 'Caesar is running in the time during which he was appellated by man with a verb in the present tense; therefore, a man ran.'

[93] To the other argument:[188] Aristotle's remark must be understood as regards the composite signified by a verb of any *differentia* of time.

[94] To the other:[189] the consequence, 'Caesar is Caesar; therefore, Caesar is a man,' is denied; but it did follow when Caesar was appellated by 'man' with a verb in the present tense.

[Question 9. Does a Common Term Suppositing with a Present-Tense Verb Supposit Only for Presently Existing Things?]

We ask whether a common term suppositing with a present-tense verb supposits only for presently existing things.

[1] It seems so: because otherwise, 'a white thing is black' would be true, and 'a sitting thing can walk,' understood in the sense of composition. For it could have this cause of its truth, 'what was white is black,' if the subject can stand for things in the past; and likewise as regards the other example, 'a sitting thing walks' is possible, because what was sitting, walks. But 'a white thing is black' is false: [i] because from 'a white thing is black' there follows 'a white thing is not white,' and its con-

185. See n. 3 above.
187. See n. 21 above.
189. See n. 29 above.

186. See nn. 83–86 above.
188. See n. 22 above.

tradictory, viz., 'every white thing is white' is true because the same thing is predicated of itself; and [ii] because propositions with contrary predicates would be true at the same time, viz., 'a white thing is white' and 'a white thing is black.' As for the remaining example, Aristotle says that it is false in the sense of composition.[190]

[2] Again, the predicate in such a proposition is restricted to standing only for things that exist [*sunt*]; therefore, so is the subject.[191] Proof of the consequence: because otherwise there could not be conversion without [the fallacy of] figure of speech. Proof of the antecedent: [i] because having said '*b* is [*b est*]' in this way, the content [*res*] of the verb is the predicate; but the addition of *a* will make one thing with the content of the verb because it will be the same as '*b* is a being-that-is-an-*a* [*b est ens a*],' where the predicate is restricted by the 'being [*ens*]' specifying it; and [ii] because otherwise, 'a man is white, therefore a man is' does not follow. Proof: if 'white' on the part of the predicate can stand for what exists and what does not exist indifferently in the way it is predicated, then in the way it is predicated it is related indifferently to existing and non-existing; therefore, in the way it is predicated, it assumes neither [existence nor non-existence]. And by parity of reasoning, the consequence, 'from the conjoined to the divided,'[192] must be denied in all cases, as is apparent because in both cases, 'being' would be predicated incidentally. Therefore, it would be taught pointlessly in Book II of *De interpretatione*.

[3] Again, composition is not understood without the extremes, according to Aristotle at the end of the chapter [of *De interpretatione*] 'On the Verb.'[193] Therefore, the composition and the extremes are understood in connection with the same time. Therefore both extremes are restricted to the same time that measures the composition.

[4] Again, composition is the form of the extremes. Form is the principle of understanding something according to its nature [*ratio*]. Therefore, the extremes are understood in keeping with the nature of composition.

---

190. Aristotle, *De soph. elench.* I.4 (AL VI^1 9; I.4.166a23–26).
191. Cf. Roger Bacon, *Summulae dialecticae*, in "Les Summulae dialectices de Roger Bacon, 1–2: De termino, De enuntiatione. 3: De argumentatione," ed. Alain de Libera, *Archives d'histoire doctrinale et littéraire du Moyen Age* 53 (1986), n. 2 (278) [hereafter "*Summulae*"]: "But on the side of the predicate, a term stands within the scope of the verb [*secundum exigentiam verbi*], so that if the verb is present tense, the term stands for presently-existing things, as in 'Socrates is a man.'"
192. See n. 16 of qq. 5–8 above.
193. Aristotle, *De interpr.* I.3.16b24–25 (AL II^1 7): "But it additionally signifies some combination, which is not understood without the components."

[5] On the opposite side: if in that present-tense [proposition] [the subject] stood only for presently existing things, two contradictories would be false at the same time. Proof of the consequence: let us assume that no man exists; if the subject stands for presently existing things only, then 'every man exists' is false, as well as 'something that is a man does not exist,' because 'some man who exists does not exist' is signified.

[6] Again, if the subject stood only for presently existing things, it would follow that all these would be false: 'a house is made,' 'a man is generated,' [etc.,] because 'something that exists, is made [*illud quod est, fit*]' is signified, which is false, because 'being made [*fieri*]' is a path from non-being to being [*via a non-esse ad esse*],[194] and consequently, if it exists now, it is not made. But if all such [propositions] were false, it would follow that all such [propositions] as 'a house is made,' 'a man is generated,' [etc.,] would be false too, because 'is made [*fit*]' and 'is something-made [*factum est*]' are the same, and so the proposition, 'whatever exists, is not something-made [*quidquid est, est non-factum*],' would be true.

[7] Again, 'the Antichrist runs, therefore a man runs' follows, because the implicit minor premise, by virtue of which the consequence holds, is necessary, as was stated;[195] therefore, 'man' in the consequent can stand for Caesar; therefore; [it can stand] for that which does not exist [*non existit*].

[8] Again, a common term primarily supposits for its significate in every proposition, and does not supposit for a *suppositum* unless because the *suppositum* is the same as the significate; otherwise, no universal [proposition] would be true. Therefore, [it supposits] equally for the *supposita* that are equally related to the significate of the common [term]. But existing things as well as non-existing things are of this sort, as was shown before.[196] Therefore, it supposits equally for all.

[9] Again, it is not restricted by virtue of the verb. Proof: because [i] what stands apart from something in an expression does not introduce anything real concerning the something that stands apart from it, since every real contracting thing gives way [*cedit*] in the same extreme with what is contracted—otherwise, 'a man is dead' could be true. For if what is on the side of the predicate could contract a subject in reality [*realiter*], then what is on the side of the predicate

---

194. Aristotle, *Physics* II.15 (AL VII^1 49; II.1.193b12–13): "But further, nature in the sense of generation is a path to nature."
195. See n. 21 of qq. 5–8 above.
196. See nn. 43–44 of qq. 5–8 above.

could diminish the subject. With respect to what is proposed, there would be no difference between a contracting and a diminishing determination.

Therefore 'man' would stand in the subject position for a man diminished by 'dead,' and so 'a man is dead' would be true, from which 'therefore, a man is a non-man [*ergo homo est non-homo*]' follows according to Aristotle, because 'dead' (from what he says in Book II of *De interpretatione*) includes the opposite of 'man,' from which a contradiction follows.[197] Therefore, two contradictories absolutely and without determination, as are signified by the names 'man' and 'non-man,' would be predicated of each other. But if these are absurdities, it follows that what is on the side of one extreme cannot contract what is on the side of the other extreme. But composition holds on the side of the predicate, as will be discussed later;[198] therefore, the time that is [introduced] concerning the composition cannot restrict the subject.

[10] Because [ii] it is possible to understand the actuality measured by the present time to inhere in the subject for all *supposita* that were, are, and will be, although it would be false in the understanding. Therefore, it is also possible to signify this. But it would be impossible to signify this if the present time concerning the predicate were to cause the subject to stand only for *supposita* that exist [now]. Therefore, that hypothesis destroys the point of discourse, which exists 'so that through it, every mental concept could be signified.'[199]

[Question 10. In a Past-Tense Proposition, Does the Subject Stand Only for Things That Were, and in a Future-Tense Proposition, Only for Things That Will Be?]

We ask whether, in a past-tense proposition, the subject stands only for things that were, and in a future-tense proposition, only for things that will be.

---

197. Aristotle, *De interpr.* II.2 (AL II[1] 25; II.11.21a21–23): "But when in what is added some opposite is contained that gives rise to a contradiction, it is not true but false (e.g., to call a dead man a 'man')."
198. See nn. 24–35 below.
199. Cf. Albert the Great, *Perihermenias* I.2 (1:318b) [hereafter "*Periherm.*"]: "But [an expression signifying by convention is considered] a cause of institution when we cannot produce the thing, so that we may communicate with each other by the presentation of the things: articulate sounds were invented by which we express the things themselves or the intentions of the things, in order to communicate with each other in words."

[11] That it is so is shown by the arguments made in connection with the previous question concerning composition.[200]

[12] Again, 'a man who was, was, therefore a man was' follows, because the opposite of the consequent, which is 'no man was,' cannot stand with the antecedent, since it conflicts with the implication. It is argued in the same way in the case of the future.

[13] Again, unless the subject stood in that past-tense proposition for things that existed, the proposition 'a man was' would be false, given that all men existing now were in the first instant of their being and many others had preceded them. And if that proposition were false, then 'no man was' would be true. Therefore 'no man who was, was' follows, because the opposite of the consequent cannot stand with the antecedent. But the consequent of that consequence is false, namely 'no man who was, was,' because its contradictory is true; therefore, so is the antecedent from which it follows.

[14] The two final arguments prove only that the subject may stand for past and future things, not only for past and future things. And to the same [effect] is the second argument made in connection with the first part of the preceding question.[201]

[15] On the opposing side: the 'not only'[202] of the two final arguments works against the opposite of the preceding question.[203]

[16] Again, if it were possible for that past tense proposition to stand for past things, 'a white object was black' would be true; therefore, its corresponding present-tense proposition would sometimes be true, which is false, since opposite would be predicated of opposite.

[Question 11. Is a Common Term Distributed for Any of Its *Supposita Simpliciter* in Every Proposition in Which Some Immediate Contracting Term Is Not Added to It?]

We ask whether a common term is distributed for any of its *supposita simpliciter* in every proposition in which some immediate contracting term is not added to it.

---

200. See nn. 1–4 of q. 9 above.   201. See n. 2 above.
202. That is, that the subject of a future-tense proposition stands 'not only' for things that were.
203. See n. 9 above.

[17] It seems not: because in that case, with the major being assertoric as-of-now and the minor about contingency, the syllogism would be valid [*utilis*]—indeed, it seems, a regular syllogism. For regardless of which *suppositum* the middle is taken for in the minor premise in virtue of contingency, it would be distributed for the same in the major. The consequent is contrary to Aristotle (in *Prior Analytics* I).[204]

[18] Again, in the sense [*acceptio*] of 'which is *b* [*quod est b*],' either [i] the subject stands in it for all of its per se *supposita*, in which case any assertoric proposition and any proposition about contingency in which it is posited would be impossible since the same actuality could not inhere contingently in *supposita* belonging to any *differentia* of time; or [ii] it stands only for existing things, and then if in that assertoric proposition it stands for all of its per se *supposita*, a universal proposition about contingency would be true, and yet its assertoric equivalent would be impossible.

[19] Again, with a major about necessity and a minor about contingency, there would be a regular syllogism,[205] because whatever things were subsumed by the minor, a distribution would be made for them in the major.

[20] Again, relevant here are all the arguments proving that in any proposition, a common term stands only for the *supposita* of a single *differentia* of time,[206] because it is not distributed except for those things for which it supposits.

[21] On the opposing side: 'every man runs; therefore, Caesar runs' follows, and likewise, 'every man will run; therefore, Caesar will run,' and so for any *suppositum* of any *differentia* of time. Therefore, what is common in respect of any predicate is distributed for any *supposita*. All these consequences are clear, because all the present-tense minor premises through which consequences are reduced to syllogisms are necessary, as is clear from what was previously said.[207]

[22] Again, a univocal term suppositing for many things with a sign [of quantity] added to it supposits for the entire multitude [*pro omnibus multis*]. But a univocal common term is [common] to any *supposita*, as is clear from what was said above.[208]

[23] Again, in a universal proposition, a distribution is made for everything

---

204. Aristotle, *Anal. priora* I.15 (AL III^1 32–33; I.15.34a24–b19).
205. This refers to a 'perfect' syllogism regulated by *dici de omni*.
206. See nn. 1–4 and 11–13 above. 207. See n. 7 above.
208. See nn. 7–8 of qq. 5–8 above.

that can be taken under it, via [the principle] 'being said of all [*dici de omni*].'[209] Any and all *supposita* are like this,[210] as was stated, because all things are *supposita* of a term *simpliciter*.

[I. Reply to Questions 9 and 10]

[24] To the first two questions,[211] it must be said that a common term in any proposition, whether of the present, past, or future, supposits for any [of its] *supposita*, whether existing or non-existing, when there is not immediately added to it some determination contracting [it] to the *supposita* of a single *differentia* of time.

[II. First Reply to Question 11]

[25] In this connection, it must be said, consequent to the third question,[212] that it [a term] is distributed for all in any proposition in which it is taken absolutely. This is clear because any *suppositum* implies its common term [*suum commune*] with respect to any predicate, and is implied by its common term as distributed. That is because in both cases, the implicit minor (viz., in which the common term is predicated of its *suppositum* by the verb 'is') is necessary. Therefore, the common term supposits for any of its *supposita*, and is distributed.

The reason, however, is chiefly that when it is not specified by something directly added to it, the common term supposits for its significate absolutely, and therefore supposits equally for all its *supposita* which are equally related to its significate.[213] Included here are existing and non-existing things alike. Therefore, it supposits equally for all [its *supposita*], and consequently, it is distributed. Nor does some predicate contract it, as was shown in the opposing argument,[214] because the contracting term and the contracted term give way [*cedunt*] in the same extreme. And because it is possible to understand the predicate under any aspect as inhering in the subject for *supposita* belonging to any *differentia* of time, or for

---

209. Aristotle, *Anal. post.* I.4 (AL IV[1] 12; I.4.73a28–31); cf. Duns Scotus, *Quaestiones super libros Elenchorum Aristotelis*, q. 52, n. 9 (*OPh* II, 507). See also n. 14 of q. 6 above.
210. See n. 7 of qq. 5–8 above. 211. See nn. 1–16 above.
212. See nn. 17–23 above.
213. Reading "ergo aequaliter pro omnibus quae aequaliter *se habent* ad suum significatum" and ignoring "participant" as a scribal error. This is consistent with n. 8 above, and with mss. Rome Coll. S. Isidori 1/14 (= L) and Vat. Lat. 870 (= N).
214. See n. 9 above.

all at once, it is also possible for the predicate to signify in this way. Therefore, the predicate confers no aspect of suppositing upon the subject.

[III. Reply to the Main Arguments of Both Parts of Question 9]
[A. Reply to the Affirmative Arguments]
[I. Reply to the First Main Argument]

[26] To the first argument of the first question,[215] we should note that of an accidental form signified in the concrete, the *suppositum* is one thing, the subject is another. For the common term is the same essentially as its *suppositum*, but not the same as its subject. Therefore, if it is conceded that a common term can stand for existing and non-existing *supposita*, it is not conceded along with this that the subject sometimes had a form. Consequently, 'a white object is black' is not true. For although a subject that once was white may now be black, yet it is not true of the *suppositum* of white, that the *suppositum* once was black,[216] because as regards the *suppositum*, even when it does not exist, its common term is always predicated with the verb 'is,' and consequently, the opposite of its common term is truly predicated of it at no time.

Through this argument as well it is clear what should be said to the other example.[217] For those who say that the sort of propositions in which concrete terms are the subject must be distinguished according to composition and division do not mean that the significate of a common term—or its per se *suppositum*—could be taken for the same time or a different time with the predicate; but rather, they understand them to be about the subject of an accidental form. And so 'a sitting thing can walk' is false in the sense of composition, regardless of which *suppositum* 'sitting' supposits for per se, and likewise for the subject, when it is understood to be informed by the form of sitting for the time in which the predicate is united to it.

[27] Against this: 'black [*nigrum*]' and 'a white thing that was [*album quod fuit*]'—speaking of a past *suppositum* of white—can be said of the same subject, and so one can be predicated of the other *per accidens*. The antecedent is clear,

---

215. See n. 1 above.
216. Here Antonius Andreas has, "For although a subject which once was white may now be black, yet it is not true of the *suppositum* of white, that the *suppositum* which was once white, is [now] black" (*Periherm.* I, f. 73vb); other possible readings are listed in the variants.
217. Viz., 'a sitting thing is walking'; cf. n. 1 above.

because it is true to say of this that it is a white thing that was, and that it is black. The first argument is clear, because 'Socrates was white; therefore, he is a white thing that was' follows, and that 'he is black.'

[28] To that objection it can be said that a white thing that was, speaking of the per se *suppositum* of white, is not said now of what yesterday was white, but it is said of it for the past. And from one proposition of the past and another of the present, a conclusion about the present does not follow. Therefore, that this previously white thing is black does not follow.

As for the proof, the consequence, 'this was white; therefore this is a white thing that was,' is denied, for if a *suppositum* of white is said of a subject with [the verb] 'to have been [*fuisse*],' it does not follow that it would be said of the same thing with [the verb] 'to be [*esse*].' For that past *suppositum* is non-existent, and the subject is existent; but a non-existent cannot be predicated of an existent. If it is argued, however, that 'what was white is black; therefore, a white thing is black,' the antecedent must be distinguished. For 'what [*quod*]' either refers to the subject of white, and then the consequence is not valid because 'white' does not stand for the past subject, but is more a figure of speech, changing a 'what [*quid*]' into a 'what kind [*quale*].' But if 'what' refers to the *suppositum* of white then the consequence is valid and the antecedent false.

[29] Against this: it seems at least that in this case, '[what] was white, is black [*album fuit, est nigrum*],' a contrary is not predicated of a contrary, because the white thing that was and the black thing that is are not contraries; nor, by parity of reasoning, is it ever possible for a contrary to be predicated of a contrary.

[30] To this reply it is said that the white thing that was—speaking of a per se *suppositum* of white insofar as it includes in itself the form of its common term—is contrary to black, and under that aspect it is supposited for by its common term. And there is as much contrariety in that case as between a white thing that is and a black thing. Likewise for 'a sitting thing is walking,' it is clear that it is not true, because a past or future *suppositum* of sitting is never walking. But those who propose that a proposition such as 'a sitting thing can walk' must be distinguished in composition and division do not propose this on the side of the *suppositum*, but of the subject. For no matter which *suppositum* the extremes are taken for, there is a composite and false sense, because the *suppositum* of any time from one part cannot be united to any *suppositum* from the other part.

[II. Reply to the Second Main Argument of Question 9]

[31] To the second argument,[218] it can be said that the predicate stands equally indifferently in a proposition as does the subject, because a similar reasoning proves both. For it is possible to understand the predicate for any [of its] *supposita* (whether for all or for some) to be attributed to the subject for any of the subject's *supposita* (whether to all or to several), and to do so by any mediating [act of] composition; therefore, it is possible to signify. Therefore, when opposite is predicated of opposite, no composition posits any determination for the *supposita* regarding the extremes, either concerning the predicate or the subject.

[32] It must be said to the first proof[219] that the content [*res*] of the verb, given that it would be part of the predicate when predicated as a third element, still does not specify what follows upon it, but conversely. For example, in 'every man is an animal [*omnis homo est animal*],' although 'being [*ens*]' is the part of the predicate, it does not specify 'animal' so that it stands for existing things only, but 'animal' specifies 'being' because when 'is [*est*]' is predicated as a third element, it predicates what is in another. But now 'being,' specified by 'animal,' is in this way indifferent to its *supposita*, just like 'animal.' Or perhaps (as will be seen later),[220] the content [*res*] of the verb is not part of the predicate.

[33] To the second proof:[221] given that 'being [*esse*]' predicated as a second element never follows from 'being' predicated as a third element (at least when 'being' is specified by a nominal term in the antecedent), it does not follow that Aristotle pointlessly specifies in *De interpretatione* II the conjuncts from which a consequence to the divided [proposition] holds, and those from which it does not.

For in other conjuncts, sometimes the divided [proposition] follows, as in 'that man is running; therefore, that man is [*ille homo est currens, ergo ille homo est*]'; in others it does not, as in 'that person is a good guitarist; therefore, that person is good [*ille est bonus citharaedus, ergo ille est bonus*].' And this seems more relevant to Aristotle's proposal there than [what was said] about 'being [*esse*].' For it is said there in the text:[222] "in however many categories, where there is no

---

218. See n. 2 above.
219. See n. 2 above.
220. Cf. Duns Scotus, *Periherm.*; *Opus II.I*, qq. 5–6, nn. 21–25 and 29–34.
221. See n. 2 above.
222. Aristotle, *De interpr.* II.2 (AL II^1 25–26; II.11.21a29–31).

opposition in them, and they are predicated per se and not incidentally," i.e., not according to something extraneous to their proper aspect, "in these it will be true to predicate them *simpliciter*," where no specific mention is made of 'being,' and of its specification, more than of other composite predicates.

[Reply to the Rest of the Main Arguments of Question 9]

[34] To the third,[223] it must be granted that the extremes are understood for the same time for which the composition is understood, but from this it does not follow that they are understood only for the *supposita* of a single time.

[35] To the fourth,[224] it can be conceded that form is the principle of understanding the extremes with respect to any mode concerning the extremes, but not of [their] actual sense in relation to the *supposita*, because it is possible to understand a term for any of the *supposita* under the aspect of presentness or pastness. And this is what is customarily said, [viz.,] that 'a modal restriction must be granted, but not a real restriction.'

[B. Reply to the Arguments in Opposition of Question 9]
[I. Reply to the First Argument in Opposition]
[a. The Replies of Others]

[36] To the first argument in opposition,[225] it is said that what it assumes is impossible, viz., that no man exists.

[37] Alternatively, if the subject has some existing *supposita*, it stands only for them. If it has none, then it stands for non-existing things, and then 'some man does not exist [*aliquis homo non est*]' will be true, and not in the sense that 'some man who exists, does not exist [*aliquis homo qui est, non est*].'

[b. Arguments against the Replies of Others]

[38] Against the first reply:[226] the assumption including impossible things is not impossible, because it can be conceived without conflicting understandings. Therefore, it does not follow on account of that assumption that contradictories can be true together, because what is more impossible does not follow from what is less impossible, just as a lesser impossible does not follow from a proposition

---

223. See n. 3 above.
225. See n. 5 above.
224. See n. 4 above.
226. See n. 36 above.

that happens to be false. For a conflict of understandings does not follow from the fact that [such a thing] can be conceived. Therefore, contradictories being true together follows from something else, viz., that the subject can stand only for presently-existing things. The same goes for the argument regarding the singular proposition, that it is possible not to be [the case].

[39] Against the second reply:[227] if, with a man not existing [*homine non-exsistente*], 'a man does not exist [*homo non est*]' is true, and 'a man' stands for a non-existent, then the consequence, 'a man who does not exist, does not exist; therefore, a man does not exist [*homo qui non est, non est, ergo homo non est*],' is good because the common term is inferred with respect to the predicate from that *suppositum* for which it supposits with respect to the predicate. Therefore, by the same reasoning it will hold with a man existing, because the understanding of the antecedent and the consequent will be the same, or else the understanding of propositions will be changed on account of a change in the existence of things. And then the same sentence will not change from truth to falsity and conversely, which is contrary to Aristotle in the *Categories*, in the chapter 'On Substance.'[228]

[II. Reply to the Fifth Argument in Opposition of Question 9]
[a. The Replies of Others]

[40] To the fifth argument on the contrary side,[229] it is replied that the first proof only proves that the subject is not restricted by anything having to do with composition because they are apart from one another, but it proves only that the predicate is restricted because it gives way [*cedit*] in the same extreme as the subject.

[41] To the second proof,[230] it is said that it is possible to signify a predicate to be in a subject for all *supposita* of any time through the composition of present, past, and future, as follows: 'every man who is, or was, or will be, is white [*omnis homo qui est, vel fuit, vel erit, est albus*],' understanding the entire disjunction as the subject. And so through a descriptive phrase of this sort, there is said to be a concept expressing when it cannot [be said] by a term absolutely.

---

227. See n. 37 above.
228. Aristotle, *Praedic.*, c. 5 (AL I^2 53; 5.4a36–b2).
229. See n. 10 above.
230. See n. 9 above.

[b. Arguments against the Replies of Others]

[42] Against [this]: it is possible to understand a predicate to be in its subject on behalf of its per se *supposita*, or to be in anything insofar as it participates in a common form, beyond whose nature (as these things are understood) there is time, and disjunction, and anything outside the understanding of its common [term]; and therefore it is possible to signify a predicate to be in a subject in this way. But it is not signified by a descriptive phrase of this sort, for more is signified in the disjunction and on the part of the times than was understood.

[43] Again, in such a proposition there remains a composition of the present, just as in the others. Therefore, if a composition of the present always restricts the extremes to supposition for presently-existing things, the entire [expression] 'a man who is [*homo qui est*]' etc., will still be taken only for presently existing things, and the sense will be 'every man who is, or was, or will be, is white [*omnis homo qui est, vel fuit, vel erit, est albus*],' and there will be an infinite regress. The first consequence is clear, because the subject, which is, or was, or will be, is equally indifferent, and the composition of the present is equally indifferent.

[IV. Another Reply to Question 11]
[a. The Position of Scotus]

[44] To the other question,[231] it must consequently be said that when something immediate contracting it is not added, in every proposition a common term is distributed for any of its per se *supposita* because any of them can be taken under [the principle] 'being said of all [*dici de omni*],' and any follows upon what has been distributed on account of the arguments made above.[232] It also follows from the resolution of the previous question.[233] For a sign added to a term denotes its being taken universally of all things to which it is common, as it supposits in that indefinite [term], 'any [*quaecumque*].'

[Reply to the Main Arguments of Question 11]

[45] To the first argument on the contrary side,[234] I say that a syllogism is invalid when the major premise is assertoric and as-of-now,[235] because then the

---

231. See nn. 17–24 above.
233. See n. 24 above.
235. Add 'and the minor is of contingency'; see n. 17 above.
232. See nn. 21–23 above.
234. See n. 17 above.

middle is united to a minor extreme in the minor premise for a different time than that for which the major is true. For a minor about contingency can be taken as true for the future, in connection with which it does not have to be [the case] that the major is true, since it is sufficient that it be true for a single time. But when the major is absolutely assertoric, then for whichever time the minor is true, the major is true for the same time because it is always true. For that reason, it is necessary that the extremes be united in the middle term for the same time, but not when the major is assertoric and as-of-now. And there is no defect in the variety of *supposita* for which the middle term is taken in the major and minor premises.

[46] To the second argument,[236] it can be said that no per se *suppositum* is contingently joined to that of which it is the per se *suppositum*, but necessarily. Therefore, in the sense of 'that which is *b* [*quod est b*],' the subject is taken for all per se *supposita* insofar as they are per se *supposita*. When it is said 'therefore, every universal proposition about contingency in that sense[237] is false, and every assertoric proposition corresponding to it will be impossible' ...

[47] ... this can be conceded.[238] Nor on account of this is something lacking in the art of syllogizing, because a syllogism does not depend on the truth or possibility of propositions but on the necessary relation of the premises to the conclusion.

[48] Alternatively, it can be said that although it is impossible for something to inhere contingently in past things insofar as they are past, because there is no potentiality in relation to something past, yet it is not impossible for something to inhere contingently in any *supposita* of a common term insofar as they share the form of something common. That is because pastness is extraneous to them and to other *differentia* of time insofar as they are per se *supposita* of a common term.

But in the other sense, viz., 'what contingently is *b* [*quod contingit esse b*],' it is not taken for other things in reality, since in 'what is *b* [*quod est b*],' it is taken for all things, whereas in 'what contingently is *b*,' it is taken for other things under an-

---

236. See n. 18 above.
237. That is, in sense [ii] of n. 18 above.
238. The section headings and quotation marks in the critical edition are mistaken here. The scope of 'this can be conceded [*hoc potest concedi*]' includes everything indicated in the quotation marks, not just from 'therefore' to 'contingency'; accordingly nn. 46–47 really belong together. We have used an ellipsis here to keep our numbering in line with the edition.

other aspect. For things that are taken per se necessarily are joined to a common term according to existence; taken contingently, [however,] they are joined to the same thing, because contingency is accidental to a per se *suppositum*, and perhaps in keeping with that aspect, it is taken for some *supposita* in the sense, 'what contingently is *b*.'

[49] Nor is it to be wondered that what is taken absolutely per se as the *suppositum* of some common term—if it is taken under the aspect of something extraneous to it, insofar as it is a *suppositum*—is *per accidens* and contingently under a common term, e.g., this man is a per se and necessary *suppositum* of man and this white man is a contingent *suppositum* that happens to exist per se in this way for a *suppositum* of a man, just like a white thing. But the proposition must be assumed to have the sense, 'what is [*quod est*],' from the nature of the term in itself, which is taken of itself for all per se *supposita*, just as it is taken in that sense.

But the proposition from the contingent mode has another sense, viz., 'what contingently is [*quod contingit esse*],' in which it is taken for the same things, but under another aspect; although this mode could not confer a sense on the term for some determinate *supposita*, it can still confer a sense on it for those things for which it would stand as taken per se, though under another aspect. For all composition can leave behind its mode of understanding concerning the extremes, although without any real restriction of the *supposita*. Assuming this, it can be granted that these senses are antecedents to a proposition about contingency, i.e., they are related to the universal just as they are to the indefinite. For although a term is distributed by a unique actuality for all per se *supposita*, yet it is not distributed for all by a unique actuality insofar as they are per se *supposita* and insofar as they are taken under an extraneous aspect.

[50] Against this: in the sense that 'what is [*quod est*]' is contingency about composition, then, there remains a similar mode of understanding concerning the extremes. Therefore if, in another sense—viz., 'what contingently is [*quod contingit*]'—there is nothing except such a mode of understanding concerning the extremes, it follows that there is no difference between the senses because the term is taken in both cases for all per se *supposita*, although under the aspect of the understanding of contingency.

[51] Again, the mode of contingency cannot leave behind a sense concerning the subject for *supposita* taken under an extraneous aspect, [i] because then it would be taken for the same things under the same aspect as in the sense of

'what is [*quod est*],' since that is a contingency concerning composition; and [ii] because the mode of composition would posit a real determination concerning the extremes, for the *supposita* per se are not *supposita per accidens* unless they are understood under some real superadded determination. But composition does not convey anything real concerning the extremes, as was said previously.[239]

[52] Therefore, it can be said that the sense, 'to be what is [*esse quod est*],' in which the term stands for any per se *supposita* (although such an aspect concerns those things that are understood to be present in the composition), has [supposition] by virtue of discourse in a proposition about contingency. In another sense, viz., 'to be what it is possible to be [*esse quod contingit esse*],' it does not from signification, nor as an accident, but only from our pre-determination. For this reason it is called 'sense [*acceptio*],' i.e., it is possible to take the understanding of a proposition under such a determination. But it can just as well be called the 'sense' of any proposition, unless that conforms more to the mode of composition than in other propositions. Yet, with the proposition taken in that understanding, the syllogism holds formally.

[53] To the third main argument,[240] it can be said that for the perfection of a syllogism, it is not sufficient that what is taken under the minor premise is that for which distribution is made in the major premise, but it must be taken under that aspect for which the distribution is made for it—just as the syllogism, 'every man necessarily is an animal; that white man is a man; therefore, etc. [*omnis homo necessario est animal; ille homo albus est homo; ergo, etc.*]' is not perfect, although distribution is made for the man in the major premise. But this is because distribution is made for it insofar as it participates in the form of man and is taken under the aspect of white. So it is in the case at hand. If the per se *suppositum* is the same as what is contingent, the distribution is made for it in a major premise about necessity insofar as it is a per se *suppositum*, and it is not taken as such in a minor premise about contingency, but under an extraneous aspect.

[54] Alternatively, it can be said that a contingent *suppositum* is not a per se *suppositum* because any per se *suppositum* is necessarily joined to a common term.

---

239. See n. 9 above.
240. See n. 19 above.

[Question 12. Is 'Caesar is a man' True When Caesar Does Not Exist?]

We ask whether 'Caesar is a man' is true when Caesar does not exist,[241] assuming that a term signifies the same whether the thing is existing or not, as was stated above.[242]

[1] And it seems so: because in *Metaphysics* IV, Aristotle says that a term signifies 'this is [*hoc est*]';[243] but Caesar signifies a man; therefore, etc.

[2] Again, what is included in the predicate is true of that of which the predicate is predicated; but man is included in Caesar and is part of what we understand by him; therefore, just as 'Caesar is Caesar' is true, so also 'Caesar is a man' is true. But that 'Caesar is Caesar' is true I prove because 'a chimera is a chimera' is true, and likewise, 'a non-being is a non-being [*non-ens est non-ens*]'; and so it [i.e., the proposition, 'Caesar is Caesar'] is true as well.

[3] Furthermore, 'nothing is truer of something than what is the same as it';[244] but here, the same thing is predicated of itself.

[4] Again, from opposites, the impossible follows;[245] but from 'Caesar is a man' and 'Caesar is not a man,' 'Caesar is not Caesar' follows; but this is impossible. Therefore, the opposite is true.

[5] To the opposing part of the main [argument]: When 'is [*est*]' is posited as a copula, it is posited as of now, according to Aristotle;[246] therefore, if Caesar is a man, he is a man now.

[6] Again, since living accompanies man by necessity, [and] sensing and un-

---

241. See nn. 15–29, 49–73, and 92–94 of qq. 5–8 above.
242. See n. 42 of qq. 5–8 above.
243. Aristotle, *Metaph.* IV.10 (AL XXV² 67; IV.4.1006a32–34): "But I say that this has one meaning [*unum significare*]; if this is, and if it is indeed a man, then this will be the being of a man [*homini esse*]." Cf. n. 22 of q. 7 above.
244. Albert the Great, *Liber de praedicabilibus* I, 49a: "Thus we understand what Boethius says: no proposition is truer than one in which the same thing is predicated of itself"; Boethius, *De interpr.* VI.14 (480; PL 64:628BC): "For this reason the [proposition] 'What is good is good' is judged to be closer to the nature of goodness than 'What is good is useful.' If this is so, then what is true in relation to the thing itself is truer than what appears [to be true] in relation to accidents." Cf. n. 33 of qq. 5–8 above.
245. Aristotle, *De interpr.* II.10.
246. Aristotle, *De interpr.* I.3 (AL II¹ 7; I.3.16b9–10): "'Running [*cursus*]' is a noun, but 'runs [*currit*]' is a verb, for it also signifies [something's] holding now [*consignificat enim nunc esse*]."

derstanding [do] as well, if Caesar is a man, he lives, understands, and senses; all these are all false and impossible, since Caesar is now corrupted.

[I. Reply to the Question]
[A. First Opinion]

[7] Reply: it is said[247] that the first [argument][248] is absolutely false because of the arguments already presented[249] and others as well. For no one is a man unless he is a man now; this is not applicable to Caesar.

[B. Reply to the Main Arguments in the First Opinion]

[8] To the first argument:[250] when it is said regarding Aristotle that [a term] "signifies 'this is [*hoc est*],'" it is not his intention to say that whatever is signified by something is predicated of it; but wishing to prove the first principle, he is speaking there of contradictories, saying 'if that which is signified by one member of a pair of contradictories is the case [*est*], then the other contradictory is not the case,'[251] since he has affirmed it to be that which is not the case.

Or perhaps if he does not say this (though it is true), it can be said that by the word he meant only what is signified by the expression, i.e., its significate. Or if by chance he meant [this] as regards the predication, viz., that if it signifies 'this is predicated of that,' it is true if it exists in the present; in the past, however, 'man' is rightly predicated of Caesar.

---

247. Cf. Roger Bacon, *Compendium studii theologiae*, in *Roger Bacon, Compendium of the Study of Theology*, ed. and trans. Thomas S. Maloney (Leiden: Brill, 1988), c. 5, nn. 122–28 (102–8); Ps.-Boethius of Dacia, *Quaestiones super libros Elenchorum*, in Jan Pinborg and Sten Ebbesen, "Studies in the Logical Writings Attributed to Boethius of Dacia," *Cahiers de l'Institut du Moyen-Age grec et latin* 3 (1970), q. 94 (34): "On this question [viz., whether 'Caesar is a man' when Caesar does not exist] there is controversy among the moderns. Some say, as I believe, that it is false, [arguing] along these lines: according to Aristotle in *Metaphysics* V, 'Caesar is a man' is true per se in the first mode, and this is because the subject in its substance is the cause of the inherence of the predicate in the substance. Now what removes the per se cause of any effect also removes the effect of that cause, because if Socrates is similar to Plato in whiteness, what removes the whiteness removes the similarity. Now death removes Caesar's substance, which was the cause of the truth of the proposition [*causa verificationis huius locutionis*]; therefore, it removes the truth of that proposition; therefore, it is false."

248. See n. 1 above.
249. See nn. 5–6 above.
250. See n. 1 above.
251. Aristotle, *Metaph*. IV.9 (AL XXV^2 66; IV.3.1005b19–20): "It is impossible for the same thing at the same time to inhere and not inhere in the same subject and in the same respect."

[9] To the second argument,[252] some[253] deny the consequence [i.e., 'Caesar is Caesar, therefore Caesar is a man'] because when 'Caesar' signifies one *suppositum*, and that *suppositum* does not exist, it is required that what is predicated be something non-existing; so then 'Caesar' in both [cases] would stand for something non-existing. Since it has existing *supposita* of itself, however, 'man' stands for existing things when it is uttered *simpliciter* in the present; but 'existing man' is not part of the understanding of Caesar, and therefore it does not follow; but it certainly does follow at the appropriate time.

[II. Second Opinion]
[A. Exposition of the Opinion]

[10] Others[254] say that 'Caesar is Caesar' is false, just like 'Caesar is a man.' This can be shown as follows: since 'Caesar' signifies a true reality (because it signifies univocally now and earlier), to say that 'Caesar is Caesar' is to say that earlier he was a true reality [and] he is a true reality now, which is false.

[11] It can also be shown by a similar [argument]: this living ox is to be sacrificed immediately; it is not true to say, 'this ox tomorrow will be an ox,' because tomorrow

---

252. See n. 2 above.
253. Cf. Peter of Cornwall, *Sophisma 'Omnis homo est,'* 49: "With this assumption, you would understand that neither presentness, nor pastness, nor futurity, nor being [*entitas*] belongs to the understanding of the word, because I say 'man' in this way, [i.e.,] in signifying the thing, and I determine no *differentia* of time, and in this respect names differ essentially from verbs. For this reason, if the thing that is signified vocally exists, I can truly attribute present being [*esse de praesenti*] to it; but if it does not exist, I could not truly attribute present being to it. That is why I posit that 'Caesar is a man' is false: because being is attributed to this thing, which was at some time and now is not, although it is not in him but was in him. But if 'Caesar' signified its reality [*significaret rem suam*] sometimes as a being and sometimes as a non-being [*non ens*], it would be an equivocal utterance." Cf. Simon of Faversham, *Quaestiones antiquae super libros Post.*, q. 21 (ed. J. Longeway, in http://longeway.files.wordpress.com/2014/01/qq-vet.pdf, 140–41): "And if you say, 'If in actuality the Antichrist always is a man, the Antichrist always is in possession of his essence, and he does not have his essence except because he has a form in matter,' I say that this must not be, but that this certainly follows: 'If in actuality the Antichrist always is a man, then he is actually in possession of the form of Antichrist in matter, [and] as long as he is possessing it in actuality, he always is a man.' And likewise in considering Caesar with respect to what he was before his corruption, in actuality Caesar always is a man ... and this could not be unless in actuality Caesar, considered as he would exist at any time [*ut sit pro quolibet tempore*], were a man and a *suppositum* of 'man.'"
254. Cf. *Ps.*-Boethius of Dacia, *Quaestiones super librum Elenchorum*, q. 94 (33): "By this it is clear in connection with another [argument] that it is true that Caesar is Caesar, although '"Caesar is Caesar" therefore Caesar is a man' does not follow except for the time in which he is a *suppositum* of 'man.'"

it will be dead, according to the assumption; therefore, when that future has come and is present, 'this ox is an ox' is not true. The same conclusion applies to 'Caesar is Caesar,' because this [proposition] is singular, just like the other proposition.

[12] Again, change is twofold, viz., substantial and accidental.[255] Accidental change is [change] in quality, quantity, and place; this type of change does not destroy the subject. But substantial change destroys the subject, and it does not happen except by destruction of the subject. For this reason, in substantial change the subject ceases to be itself; if the opposite were assumed, it would not be corrupted, because if it does not cease to be itself, it does not cease to be.

[B. Reply to the Main Arguments according to the Second Opinion]

[13] [Reply] to the initial arguments: first, to those adduced on the basis of what is similar,[256] it must be said that there is no similarity because what is signified by 'chimera' or by 'non-being' is uniformly related to all times, and so it is true at every time. But it is not so as regards Caesar. For the thing that 'Caesar' signifies is not now, nor does it have its being at every time.

[14] To the other,[257] it must be said that 'nothing' is not said to be the same as itself. For this reason, when Aristotle[258] says 'a predication is truer when the same thing is predicated of itself,' etc., it is true when the same thing, i.e., something, is predicated of itself. Because 'nothing' is not said [to be] the same as itself and because Caesar is now nothing, therefore he is not said to be the same as himself.

[15] To the other:[259] that rule of Aristotle's regarding the conclusion from opposites must be understood [as applying] when something is actually subject to a term, because then it follows that the same thing would be denied of itself, which is impossible to be true.

[III. Some Noteworthy Points]

[16] Note that on the part of the predicate, the sign is included in the identity of the predicate, just as 'being [*ens*]' in every proposition is the primary predicate and what is added is a specification of the thing itself; and whatever specifies it is

---

255. Averroes, *De substantia orbis*, c. 1 (IX, f. 3rb); AA 229: "In individual substances there are two kinds of change. One change is substantial, which changes a thing in name and definition, and which is called generation or corruption. The other is accidental change, which does not change a thing in name or definition, but only in accidental dispositions, i.e., quality, quantity, and so on."

256. See n. 2 above.
257. See n. 3 above.
258. Actually, Boethius. See n. 3 above.
259. See n. 4 above.

predicated with the verb itself. On the part of the subject, however, it is not the case that something must be specified by it; therefore, it does not fall into identity with the subject.

[17] And if it is objected that every proposition that is single is converted, and in that case what is the predicate becomes the subject: if it is part of the predicate, it will also be part of the subject.

[18] It must be replied that it is true, not in the nature of the sign but as it would hold materially: e.g., 'every man is every man' is converted to 'every being-that-is-a-man is every man [*omne ens homo est omnis homo*].'

[19] Again, note that the universal negative is not converted *per accidens*, because for a true conversion it is required that the one converting only grasp the truth of the converse insofar as that is possible in transposed terms; but it is not like this if a universal negative is converted to a particular negative, because there is more to grasp in the transposed terms; nevertheless, the consequence holds through middle [term] conversion *simpliciter*.

[Question 13. Can a Common Term Be Restricted?]

We ask whether a common term can be restricted; it must be said that it can.

[I. First Opinion]
[A. Exposition of the Opinion]

[1] The argument of some[260] is that the composition by which a thing verbally signified is composed with a subject is measured by the present time because it is necessary for the extremes to be measured by the same measure by which the composition is measured. And therefore in suppositing, the subject, which is one of the extremes, does not exceed in suppositing the *supposita* of the time by which it is measured.

[B. Against the First Opinion]

[2] Against this: those things that do not follow upon themselves in the understanding do not follow upon themselves in signifying. But for someone who now understands the present composition of some extremes, it is not necessary

---

260. The 'some' in question have not been identified.

that he also understand the extremes of the composition to be present at the same time, since we can compose things that are in the future in the present time. Therefore, the presentness of the composition is not necessarily related to the extremes.

[3] Again, what is not a principle for understanding a term is not a principle for restricting it. But time is not treated as a principle of understanding the subject. For that which is a principle of understanding another falls under the same extreme as the subject. For what is on the side of the predicate does not restrict the subject, as when it is said, 'a man is white,' for if it did, then 'every man is white' would be true. For a term supposits for the same things in indefinite and universal propositions.

[4] Again, time is an unqualified accident of a verb;[261] therefore, it does not restrict a substance on the side of the subject under the conformity of time.

[5] Again, when '*b* can be *a*' has been said in this way, *b* is restricted to suppositing for presently-existing things, which is false; it is not restricted when it is said in this way.

[II. Second Opinion]
[A. Exposition of the Opinion]

[6] Others[262] say that the cause of restriction is taken on the side of the purpose of speech; for words were invented 'so that what we conceive, we can express to others,'[263] e.g., if I understand this thing presently to inhere in that thing, I am able to signify it to others, but only through a present-tense verb. Therefore, it is necessary for a term to be restricted in this way.

[B. Against the Second Opinion]

[7] Against this: if the purpose of a word is nothing other than its signification, then to say that a term is restricted because this needs to be its purpose is to say that

---

261. Priscian, *Institutiones grammaticae* VIII.8 (1:404): "Time accrues to the verb for the signification of different acts appropriate [to it]."

262. The 'others' in question have not been identified.

263. Cf. Albert the Great, *Periherm.* I.2 (1:318b): "But [an expression signifying by convention is considered] a cause of institution when we cannot produce the thing, so that we may communicate with each other by the presentation of the things: articulate sounds were invented by which we express the things themselves or the intentions of the things, in order to communicate with each other in words."

a term is restricted because it signifies this. But it does not signify this unless because the term is restricted; nor is it restricted unless because it signifies this. Therefore, the term is restricted because it is restricted, and so the question is begged.

[8] Again, although words were invented so that we might express our concepts to others, we do not express any concept indifferently by any word, but [express] a determinate concept with a determinate word—just as, though an axe was made for chopping, [axe-making] is not said to be pointless if this one [axe] cannot chop. Likewise, even though a subject term with a present-tense verb does not signify that the predicate inheres in a subject relative to those things that exist at present, it is not thereby frustrated in its purpose (since I can understand the subject), because this can be signified by another word.

[9] Again, if for this reason it is said to be restricted so that we might signify our concepts to others, the end would be pointless because I can understand a subject as abstracted from every time. And as I understand it in this way, I intend to signify something presently inhering in it. But if it were restricted to the presently-existing *supposita* that I understand, I cannot signify, because the understanding is established in the significate of any thing.

[10] Again, the purpose of speech is to establish an understanding of the things signified; but the things signified by a noun do not concern any *differentia* of time; therefore, it constitutes such an understanding.

[III. Third Opinion]
[A. Exposition of the Opinion]

[11] Therefore, it is said[264] otherwise that a term is thus restricted because there are no *supposita* besides presently-existing *supposita* under a term, because in suppositing, a term only supposits for its *supposita*.

[B. Against the Third Opinion]

[12] Against this: no more is needed for the *suppositum* than that of which it is the *suppositum*; but that of which it is the *suppositum* does not include being, since it abstracts from being. Therefore, being does not belong to the nature of the *suppositum* because then the *suppositum* would include more than that of which it is the *suppositum*.

264. The reference here has not been found.

[13] Again, that-which-is and that-which-is-not are related to the understanding under the same aspect because the understanding can abstract the nature of man from what is signified by the name of Socrates, as it can also do from what is signified by a similar name. Therefore, the nature, thus abstracted from both, when it is abstracted, exists as undivided in the intellect. Therefore, the term signifies something common to those two univocally; therefore, through one and the same aspect there will be a *suppositum* and a remainder.[265]

[IV. Author's Reply]

[14] Therefore, in reply to the question it must be said that a term suppositing with a present-tense verb is restricted. And the reason is the actual inherence of the predicate in the subject. For the actuality of inherence requires the term to supposit for such things as are capable of terminating this actuality. But a term suppositing for *supposita* cannot terminate actual inherence in relation to other things, but only in those that exist. For example, what can be heated is related to heating; the terminus of heating applies only to those things in which a disposition remains that is generated by heating; and so what can be heated, as related to heating, supposits only for what has been made hot. And so 'what can be heated' is not said in itself in relation to heating, as Averroes intends in Book V of his *Metaphysics*;[266] but actually, it is said in relation to actual heating in connection with what has been made hot; but for other things, it is [said] only potentially.

[15] In the case at hand, we must reply on that side in the same way. If we consider the subject as being the terminus of the actual inherence (and in keeping with the fact that the actual inherence is adjacent to it, such that it is considered under its aspect), it does not supposit for things other than those that can terminate this inherence. And it is quite possible to consider a term in this way, because actual inherence begins in the predicate and terminates in the subject, and because it is possible to consider a term under the aspect of what is terminated by

---

265. Interpolated addition, which, according to Wadding-Vivès, "is not found in the old printed editions and manuscripts" (Wadding, *Opera Omnia* I, 202b). "But it is different for non-being repugnant to being, as in the case of a chimera; for the *same* common nature [*ratio communis*] cannot be understood and abstracted from a non-being and a being; there does not appear to be anyone who would abstract the nature of an animal from a donkey and a chimera" (ibid.).

266. Averroes, *Averrois Cordubensis, Metaphysica V*, ed. R. Ponzalli (Berne: Edizioni Francke, 1971), com. 20 (172): "Just like heating: for one only acquires this disposition with respect to what is made hot."

it (because if it is considered in this way, it would be taken under its aspect), and so under a term suppositing in this way it is not possible to subsume anything except what the term can actually be predicated of; and then the supposition of the subject is cognized by subsumption. From the fact that it cannot be subsumed with respect to such an inherence, except with respect to what the term is actually predicated of, [this] is an evident sign that a term with respect to such an inherence does not supposit for others.

And so regarding this, Aristotle says in the *Prior Analytics* that with an existing major premise that is assertoric, it cannot, as a rule [i.e., via the principle *dici de omni*], be taken under a minor premise about contingency.[267] For when I take a minor premise about contingency, something is taken for which the term does not supposit in its actual inherence regarding the assertoric [premise].

And this can be made clear in another way: for in the same way, when something is signified as potentially inhering in a subject, we do not require the subject to supposit—with respect to such inherence—for those things that exist in actuality. And this [is so] because it can terminate that inherence indifferently for things that actually exist and things that are contingent. For example, '*b* can be *a*': this is the potential and non-actual inherence of something in something, and so the subject terminating this inherence can equally supposit for those things that are and those things that will be; and therefore, '*b* can be *a*' is said in two ways.

[16] Against this: actual inherence depends on what actually inheres; but the inhering act cannot restrict a term; therefore, neither can its actual inherence.

[17] Again, if 'an animal talks' is said, the inherence of this act in the animal restricts 'animal' to the animal that is talking; and so this is true: 'every animal talks.'

[18] Again, the actual composition of extremes does not restrict the extremes; therefore, by the same reasoning, neither does the actual inherence.

[19] To the first argument,[268] it must be said that the actual and present act, without the actual inherence, cannot restrict the subject; nor can the actual inherence without that act. Nevertheless, the subject is more immediately restricted by the actual inherence than by the act. The reason for this is that it is the act of what does not inhere in the subject as immediately as the actual inherence, because the actual inherence is in the subject in the way that paternity is in a son. And just as a fire without heat cannot make something hot, so an actual act with-

267. Aristotle, *Anal. priora* I.15 (AL III^1 32; I.13.34a35–b6); cf. n. 50 of qq. 5–8 above.
268. See n. 16 above.

out actual inherence cannot restrict anything; and just as heat without fire does not make anything hot, so actual inherence in a suppositing term, without the act, does not restrict anything.

[20] To the other,[269] it must be said that the actual inherence of the act of anything inherent requires in the suppositing term only actually existing *supposita*; and because under 'animal' there are many *supposita*, it is restricted only to an actual animal to the extent that it is on the part of the actual inherence. And because an actual animal can be indifferently talking and non-talking, therefore it is not more restricted with respect to talking than with respect to non-talking. Therefore, when said in this way, the proposition, 'every animal talks,' is false.

[21] To the third argument,[270] it must be said that there can be actuality of composition without actuality of extremes, and this is because the presentness of composition is about the composition and not the extremes; for a composition whose extremes are in the future can be in the present. But there cannot be actual inherence without the actuality of the inherent, because, from its being, inherence is denominated as actual or potential. Therefore, there is no likeness in the one case and the other.

[22] Still, if one objects to the main argument that it may supposit for non-existing things[271] because a term supposits for that on which it follows, but it follows on non-being, because 'the Antichrist runs; therefore, a man runs' follows.

[23] I say [in reply] that it does not follow unless he is a man, which is clear when we reduce that consequence to syllogistic form, because then, according to the assumption, the Antichrist is a being. And so 'man' supposits for him, because it does not follow unless he is a being.

[24] Again, it can be said that if something follows from something else by a reason proper to it, as man follows on man, the major premise is true in this way. But if because of an addition, which requires that it exists (even though it does not in truth exist), it does not follow that the consequent term supposits for it under the same predicate.

[25] Again, when it is said, 'if a term is restricted on the part of the subject,' this would be a valid consequence: 'Homer is something, say, a poet; therefore, Homer exists.' But Aristotle denies this consequence.[272]

---

269. Cf. n. 17 above.
270. See n. 18 above.
271. See nn. 14–15 above.
272. Aristotle, *De interpr.* II.2 (AL II^1 25; II.11.21a25–28).

[26] It is said that from the actual inherence being of something in relation to something else that has being of itself, there follows the actual existence of that in which such being inheres. For example, when it is said, 'Caesar exists [*Caesar est*],' 'being [*esse*]' is joined to Caesar—the being that Caesar has of himself, not from any other thing; and so the being of Caesar is required so that the proposition is true.

But when being is joined as inhering in another, which does not have being in itself but in another, the actual inherence of such being does not require that that to which it is presently joined exist, but that that in which it has such being presently exist. For example, when it is said, 'the father lives in the son,' it is not necessary for the truth of this sentence that the father be alive, just the son. So when it is said, 'Homer is a poet,' it means only that he exists in his poetry, and so it suffices for the truth of the proposition that his poetry exists. This is because being is not joined to Homer in connection with him, but in connection with something else that is left behind by him; and so the being of the verb 'is [*est*]' requires something else through the actual inherence.

[27] Again, when it is said "to signify something as presently inhering in something,"[273] this is not to signify that to which this inhering is signified as being present, because if 'a man is going to run [*homo est cursurus*]' is said, here the predicate is presently united to the subject, and yet it is not necessary that that to which it is united be present, because it can be true as regards the Antichrist, who does not exist.

[28] For this reason, it is said that there is a difference between the actual inherence of some act and the actual composition of extremes, because something can be actually composed along with something else and yet not actually inhere in it; but only by a proposition of the present is no more signified than extreme inhering in extreme—here one can question how the inherence that is the cause of the restriction is signified.

[V. Some Noteworthy Points]

[29] Note that a common term on the part of the subject can be taken in three ways: [i] for the nature signified by the term as it falls under the act of reason, leaving aside all relation to *supposita*; and in this way, 'man is a species' is true and

---

273. Probably referring to n. 9 above.

'animal is a genus' is true; [ii] for the nature signified by the term as it is found in any *suppositum*; and in this way, propositions such as these are true: 'pepper is sold here and in Rome' and 'man is the most dignified of creatures,' for the sense is: the nature signified by the term 'man,' which is preserved in any *suppositum*, is the most dignified of creatures; or [iii] for *supposita*, as in 'a man runs'; this is true *simpliciter* if Socrates is running. Indeed, 'no pepper is sold here and in Rome' and 'pepper is sold here and in Rome' stand [as true] together: the first is true in relation to the *supposita*, the second in relation to the nature universally signified by the term.[274]

[30] Note that when 'pepper is sold here and in Rome' is said, 'pepper' has personal supposition; this is clear through the predicate, since it looks to the *suppositum*, not to the nature. Therefore, it is said that if it is from a copulated predicate, it is false. If copulative, it is true as follows: pepper is sold here and pepper is sold in Rome.[275]

[31] Note that supposition is said relative to a *suppositum*, and so strictly speaking, a term supposits on the part of the subject. But if it is said that the supposition is on the part of the predicate, this is improper; but the copulation should be said, not the supposition.

[32] And there is a threefold aspect of the supposition of a common term, viz., with respect to [i] the predicate for which it supposits; [ii] the things contained under it, for which it supposits; and [iii] that predicate belonging to the things contained under it themselves (but this not signified by the name 'supposition'). When a common term is said to supposit, it is noted in the first aspect. But when it is said 'for some things,' the second aspect is noted there with regard to the things contained under it; and that is properly called 'appellation.' And from this the third aspect follows, viz., of the contents themselves in relation to the predicate in which the common term supposits for them, because the things contained under that common term supposit for the same thing.

---

274. Cf. William of Sherwood, *Introductiones in logicam*, in Charles H. Lohr, P. Kunze, and B. Mussler (eds.), "William of Sherwood, *Introductiones in logicam*," Traditio 39 (1983): 268 (n. 5.1.9–11).

275. Roger Bacon, *Summulae*, n. 2 (288): "And it must be said that if a conjunction is made between two propositions, then it must be made of the individuals of which I say 'pepper' taken twice, and then it will have a twofold personal determinate, in this sense: 'pepper is sold here and pepper is sold in Rome' ... but if the copulation is made between terms, and there is a proposition with a copulated predicate, then it can have a simple or personal [determinate]. If personal, it is false; if simple, it is true."

[33] This threefold aspect is clear in this syllogism in keeping with the order of propositions: 'every man is running; Caesar is a man; therefore, Caesar is running,' because from the first two, the third follows. For 'man' supposits for that which is 'running' and appellates Caesar (or is taken for him); therefore, it follows that Caesar supposits for the same. Nevertheless, a common term can supposit under a twofold status: in one way such that it follows upon anything for which it supposits, as in an indefinite proposition, and it is called potential supposition for what actually implies nothing; in another way such that anything follows upon it, as it does in a proposition in which it is distributed, as in 'every man is running.'

OPUS II ❧ QUESTIONS ON THE TWO BOOKS OF *PERIHERMENIAS:* ON BOOK I

[Prologue]

[1] As[1] Aristotle states in *De anima* III,[2] the activity of the understanding is threefold: there is one called the thinking of indivisibles, where the understanding is said to form simple concepts; another is the activity of the intellect in which it composes and divides, called composition or division; to these two activities is added a third, which is to reason discursively from one thing to another, e.g., from what is known to what is unknown.[3]

[2] The book *Categories* is about things that fall under the first activity of the understanding, not about the activity itself, because to make a determination about this is proper to the mode of inquiry in *De anima*, since to what it belongs to investigate its substance, it belongs [also] to investigate its activity. For the *Categories* is

---

1. Cf. the exposition of Thomas Aquinas in the Prologue to his *De interpr.* commentary (I[1] 5a–8b), where one can find many similarities to Scotus's Prologue here.
2. Aristotle, *De an.* III.21 (III.6.430a27–30); Thomas Aquinas, *Sent. De an.* III.11 (XLV[1] 224–28); AA 187: "The activity of the intellect is twofold: one [sort of operation] is said to be the apprehension of simple terms; another is the composition and division of apprehended simple terms. Included in the latter is a third operation, viz., speculative reasoning [*ratiocinatio remota*]."
3. Cf. Avicenna, *Metaph.* I.2: "But the subject of logic, as you know, are second intentions [*intentiones intellectae secundo;* lit. 'intentions understood second'], which are based on first intentions in that through them, one arrives at what is unknown from what is known"; Thomas Aquinas, *Anal. post.* Prologue (I[2] 4b–5a): "But the third act of reason is in keeping with the *proprium* of reason, viz., to reason discursively from one thing to another such that one arrives at a cognition of what is unknown through what is known."

generally about simple concepts, or about concepts [the intellect] forms or understands insofar as they are predicable and capable of being ordered in a genus per se.

The *Perihermenias*, however, is about those things that fall under the second activity of the understanding, and not about the operation of the understanding itself; for the composing and dividing intellect makes an assertion, which is what this book is meant to be about, and an assertion is not an act of understanding itself, but is more what is done by the understanding. The books of the new logic concern what falls under the third activity of the understanding, however, in which it is taught when one should proceed from what is known to possessing a cognition of what is unknown.

[3] This book, which is called *Perihermenias*, is strictly speaking called *On Interpretation*, for "interpretation," as Boethius understands it at the beginning of his commentary, "is articulate speech signifying something per se [*vox articulata significans aliquid per se*]" to be or not to be.[4] Nevertheless, if in the definition of interpretation 'articulate speech signifying something per se' is assumed, then interpretation is common to complex and incomplex utterances.

But since someone interpreting wants to expound something and nothing can be expounded in a simple expression, therefore nouns and verbs should be considered more as parts of an interpretation rather than as interpretations themselves. And syncategorematic words do not have a nature [subject to] interpretation because they are not substantive words signifying per se. For the book that is called *Perihermenias* is about interpretation, as it expresses 'something being the case or not being the case [*aliquid esse vel non esse*],' i.e., as regards simple assertion; for other statements do not express being the case or not being the case.

Since, then, those things falling under the first act of understanding are parts of those things acted upon by the second act, therefore, the *Categories* is ordered to this book [that is, *De interpretatione*] per se. But those things falling under the second act are parts of those things falling under the third, and so this book [that is, *De interpretatione*] is ordered to the books of the new logic, though primarily to the *Prior Analytics* and indirectly to the others, because a syllogism is [made] from propositions.

[4] From these remarks it is clear what the subject [of logic] is, and the order

---

4. Boethius, *De interpr.* I.6 (6; PL 64:394B): "For interpretation is articulate sound signifying through itself [*per se ipsam*]."

that holds between the books of logic, and on account of what necessity: it is on account of the necessity of having the art of the syllogism.

[Question 1. Does a Name Signify a Thing or an Affection?]

It is asked whether a name signifies a thing or an affection in the soul.

[1] That it signifies an affection is seen from Aristotle, who says, "spoken sounds are signs of those affections that are in the soul,"[5] etc.

[2] Again, Aristotle says, "they are the likenesses of things, of which spoken sounds are the signs, and they are the same for all just as the things are."[6]

[3] Again, Boethius says that vocal expressions are signs of expressions that are in the mind; and his words are, "an expression that is in speech is the sign of an expression that is composed silently in thought [*tacita cognitione conficitur*]."[7]

[4] Again, after much discussion, Boethius says[8] that Aristotle does not think that nouns and verbs signify the things themselves, but affections of the soul. Therefore, it is clear from Aristotle and Boethius that spoken sounds are signs of affections in the mind (and not of things).

[5] Again, Priscian says, "a part of speech signifies a concept in the mind";[9] but a thing is not a concept in the mind; therefore, etc.

[6] On the opposing side is Aristotle in *Metaphysics* IV: he says, "a name signifies the proper concept that the definition expresses";[10] but that proper concept belongs to the things; therefore, etc.

---

5. Aristotle, *De interpr.* I.1 (AL II^1 5; I.1.16a3–4): "And so there are spoken sounds that are signs of affections in the soul, and written marks that are signs of spoken sounds."

6. Ibid.,16a7–8: "But the primary things of which these are marks—affections of the soul—are the same for all, as are the things [themselves] of which these affections are the likenesses."

7. Boethius, *De interpr.* I.1 (30; PL 64:407BC): "That is why the noun and the verb are principally parts of speech: there will be some verbs and nouns which are written, some which are spoken, others considered silently in the mind [*tacita mente tractentur*]."

8. Ibid., I.1 (35; PL 64:410B): "That is why the affections of the soul, which he called acts of understanding, are certain likenesses of things. Therefore, Aristotle, when he speaks a little later about the affections of the soul, switched in the next line to 'likenesses,' since it makes no difference whether one says 'affections' or 'likenesses.'" Cf. Thomas Aquinas, *De interpr.* I.2 (1^1 12b): "To this, Boethius replies that Aristotle here names affections of the soul as conceptions of the understanding [*hic nominat passiones animae conceptiones intellectus*]."

9. Pricianus, *Institutiones grammaticae* XI.2 (I.552): "For what is a part of speech other than an utterance indicating a concept in the mind, in other words, that is, a thought?"

10. Cf. Aristotle, *Metaph.* IV.28 (AL XXV^1 90; III.7.1012a24–25): "The nature of which the name is the sign is the definition." This reference is omitted in the edition.

[7] Again, what is signified by a name is what the one who is asserting something primarily means to signify; but when someone says 'a man runs,' he primarily means to assert running: not of an intention of the soul, but of a thing.

[8] Again, signifying follows upon understanding; therefore, what is primarily understood is what is primarily signified; but we primarily understand the thing and not the affection; therefore, the name primarily signifies the thing.

[I. The Opinion of Some]
[A. Exposition of This Opinion]

[9] On account of these arguments, it is said that a name signifies the affection of a thing and the thing, but it signifies the thing by what comes later; the affection, however, is signified by what comes earlier.[11]

[B. Against This Opinion]

[10] This is not valid, for the understanding composes names with each other relative to their primary significates; therefore, if names primarily signify affections in the soul, it follows that the primary signification of any sentence would be false, for otherwise, saying 'a man is an animal [*homo est animal*]' would be the same as saying 'this affection is that affection [*haec passio est illa*].'[12]

---

11. Cf. Thomas Aquinas, *De interpr.* I.2 (I¹ 11a): "For the name 'man' signifies human nature in abstraction from singulars, which is why it cannot be that it signifies a singular human directly. For this reason, the Platonists held that it signifies the idea of man itself, separated [from singulars]. However, because on Aristotle's view this does not really subsist, in its abstraction, but exists in the understanding alone, it was necessary for Aristotle to say that spoken sounds signify conceptions of the understanding directly, and things by their mediation"; Albert the Great, *Periherm.* I.2 (1:381a–382b): "However, by the fact that signs are of affections caused in the soul by the intentions of things, we hold that they are not primarily marks of things, but rather, that they are primarily marks of likenesses in the soul, and through those likenesses they are referred to things.... Now then, having made the assumption that spoken sounds are like this: [viz.,] both that they are significative utterances and that they are primarily significative of affections (and consequently that they are significative of things)"; and *Dubitationes et notabilia circa Guilelmi de Shyrewode Introductionum logicalium tractatum quantum*, in Jan Pinborg and Sten Ebbesen (eds.), "Thirteenth-Century Notes on William of Sherwood's Treatise on Properties of Terms. An Edition of *Anonymi Dubitationes et Notabilia circa Guilelmi de Shyreswode 'Introductionum logicalium Tractatum V'* from ms. Worcester Cath. Q.13," *Cahiers de l'Institut du Moyen-Age grec et latin* 47 (1984), n. 4 (121): "It can be said that a spoken sound always presents [*praesentat*] an affection in the soul directly and an external thing indirectly, which is what Aristotle means in *De interpretatione* I [when he says] that spoken sounds are signs of acts of understanding [*intellectuum*] and acts of understanding [are signs] of external things."

12. Cf. Radulphus Brito, *Periherm.* q. 3 (Cod. Bruxell. Bibl. Reg., 3540, f. 104ra): "Because if spoken

[11] Again, just as intentions extended in the air are disposed to moving the organ of sight, so are species disposed to moving the understanding; but those species are not sensed, because then they would be the primary object of sight, which is false; but rather, they are the medium through which [sight occurs].

[12] Again, what are signified later are signified only [insofar] as they have an attribution to a primary significate; therefore, if 'man' signified a thing only insofar as it has an attribution to a species, 'a stone is not in the soul [*lapis non est in anima*]' would not be true,[13] because what is primarily signified by the name 'stone' has being in the soul.

[13] Again, if a name were to signify an affection primarily, 'Socrates is [*Socrates est*]' would be true even though Socrates does not exist outside the soul because the being of a thing outside the soul is not required in relation to what is primarily signified by the name.

[II. The First Way]
[A. Exposition of the First Way]

[14] It must be said, just as Aristotle says,[14] that a name primarily signifies affections of the soul, i.e., conceptions of the understanding. For evidence of this, you should know that three things are related in [a certain] order. First is the intelligible species, which is the understanding in act; this species is in the understanding just like a proper act in its proper matter. For, just as Averroes states in connection with Book III of *De anima*,[15] understanding is related to intelligible species just as prime matter is related to the individual forms it receives. Second is that which is the proper concept of a thing, which is the 'what-it-is [*quod quid est*]' of a thing, and which is made into the object of an intellective power in which there is an act, which is the intelligible species, and in keeping with which the cognizing power is brought to the 'what-it-is-to-be [*quod quid est esse*]' of a thing. Third is the thing as it exists particularly, under individuating conditions.

---

sounds were to signify affections or concepts of things, then all propositions in which such predicates are predicated would be false, and every per se proposition would be *per accidens*, as when we say 'man is an animal.'"

13. Aristotle, *De an.* III.38 (III.8.431b29–432a1): "For there is not a stone in the soul, but the species of stone"; Simon of Faversham, *Periherm.*, q. 5 (ed. P. Mazarella, 154): "Again, Aristotle says that a stone is not in the soul, but the species of stone. Now if 'stone' did not signify a thing outside the soul but only the species of stone, then a stone would be in the soul."

14. See n. 1 above.

15. Averroes, *De an.* III, com. 5 (404).

[15] The first thing [that is, the intelligible species] is not signified primarily by an utterance because the what-it-is is understood before the species of the thing is understood, and what is primarily understood is what is primarily signified. The assumption is clear, because the understanding only understands intelligible species by reflection, just as it understands its own act. The third thing, viz., the thing existing indifferently according to its proper nature, cannot be signified, because the understanding is primarily in act through its proper object, which is the what-it-is of a thing. For the understanding does not understand what is singular primarily. But without material conditions, the what-it-is does not exist, though it can be considered without them. And so a name is imposed on it as it is understood. That is why a name signifies an affection of the understanding, i.e., a thing as it is conceived. Nevertheless, Plato held that a name signifies a thing as it exists, because he said that a thing exists in the same way as it is understood.[16] But Aristotle held otherwise.

[B. Reply to the Main Arguments according to the First Way]

[16] To all the authorities,[17] I say that by 'affection' Aristotle and Boethius understand not the likeness that is in the soul but the thing as considered by the understanding, i.e., that into the knowledge of which the understanding is led by the species.

[17] To the other,[18] I say that by taking a name absolutely, an act is primarily asserted of a sensible thing as that thing is signified; nevertheless, it is primarily verified as regards what is singular.

[18] To one of the arguments[19] against a certain argument from analogy,[20] I say that it is possible to exhibit likeness in two ways: either according to the being it has in the soul, or as leading to the thought of a thing. If it is considered in the first way, then the name signifies[21] the likeness of the thing, and it signifies the thing itself not only analogically, but equivocally. But if it is considered insofar as it leads to the thought of a thing, then it is not primarily signified, but is that through which another is signified, just as it is not primarily understood, but is that through which what is first able to be understood is understood.

---

16. See n. 9 above; Boethius, *De interpr.* I.1 (26–27; PL 64:405D–406A).
17. See nn. 1–4 above.   18. See n. 7 above.
19. See nn. 12–13 above.   20. See n. 9 above.
21. Reading *significans* with mss. NR, rather than the edition's *significat*.

[19] To the other,[22] when it is said that every sentence would be false, I say that if the species were primarily affirmed of species in the understanding, that proposition would affirm what is false, as when we say, 'the species of man is the species of a white thing [*species hominis est species albi*]'; but it is affirmed that what is primarily understood by one name is said of what is primarily understood by the other[23]—[both of] which are nevertheless understood by those mediating species.

[20] To the other,[24] I say that in the same way, being is not affirmed of the species, but of what is understood by mediation of the species.

[III. The Second Way]
[A. Exposition of the Second Way]

[21] If someone wanted to maintain that names signify likenesses of things that exist in the understanding, it must be said that a name immediately signifies the species that is in the soul primarily, and afterwards signifies the thing.

[B. Reply to the Main Arguments of the Second Way]

[22] To the first argument,[25] I say that because the likeness of a thing is natural to the thing itself, it therefore signifies the thing; consequently, the name signifying the species [signifies the thing]. For the authority [of Aristotle] seems to echo this in many ways. The first is, "spoken sounds are signs of affections,"[26] or likenesses in the soul, and the spoken sound signifies what the speaker establishes in the hearer by it. But in the chapter, 'On Verbs,' it is said that "the person who utters a verb establishes an understanding in the hearer, whence the hearer pauses [in order to hear it]."[27] And in the previous chapter, 'On Names': "names are like thoughts,"[28] because sometimes an utterance is without truth or falsity, some-

---

22. See n. 10 above.
23. Here reading '*alia*' with ms. E (= Oxford, Balliol Coll. 291) for the edition's '*aliud.*'
24. See n. 11 above.   25. See n. 7 above.
26. See n. 1 above.
27. Aristotle, *De interpr.* I, 'On Verbs' (AL II^1 7; I.3.16b19–21): "When said by itself, a verb is a name and it signifies something—for the one who speaks establishes an understanding and the one who hears pauses [in order to hear it]"; cf. AA 305: "To signify is to establish an understanding."
28. Aristotle, *De interpr.* I.1 (AL II^1 5; I.1.16a14–15): "Thus, names and verbs by themselves are like thoughts without composition or division." Scotus's reference here is a little off; the chapter 'On Names' does not actually begin until 16a19.

times with another [utterance], for it is so in the understanding; also, "of what these are signs of in the first place—affections of the soul—are the same for all."[29]

[23] But it must be recognized that although an affection is the likeness of a thing, it can be considered in two ways: either insofar as it is a likeness, and in this way it is a sign of the thing in the mind; or insofar as it exists in the mind, just like some accident in a subject. For example, this statue can be considered in two ways: either as that to which shape is accidental, or insofar as it is the likeness of Hercules.[30] If the species is considered in the first way, then the species is signified by the name. If it is considered in the second way, it is only [signified] equivocally.

But as it is considered in the first way, the name signifying the species is a sign of the thing, just as the letters in an inscription are signs of intentions. For just as a letter primarily signifies an utterance because an utterance is the sign of a species and so signifies a species, so an utterance is primarily the sign of a species, and indirectly the sign of a thing, and so it is a sign of things.

[24] But on behalf of the [other] arguments,[31] it must be understood that just as someone ordering written words in relation to each other—such as 'a man is an animal [*homo est animal*]'—is not saying that the utterance 'man' is the utterance 'animal,' so also someone ordering the utterance 'man' together with the utterance 'animal' is not saying that the species signified by the [utterance] 'man' is the species signified by the utterance 'animal.'

The reason is that these are not ordered in relation to each other by affirming one of the other insofar as they are things, but insofar as they are signs of other things: just as letters signify utterances insofar as utterances are the signs of species, so utterances signify species insofar as species are the signs of things. Therefore, there is absolutely no affirmation or negation without first having recourse to the thing, because before that, anything is asserted of anything else only as a sign of a sign. But a sign insofar as it is a sign is said to be neither true nor false except in relation to a significate.

[25] To the first argument,[32] I say that a sentence is said to be neither true

---

29. Ibid., 16a7.
30. Thomas Aquinas, *De interpr.* I.3 (I^1 15a): "But it should be said that the conceptions of the understanding are likenesses of things, and so the things that are in the intellect can be conceived of and named in two ways. In one way, according to themselves; in another way, according to the concepts [*considerationes*] of the things of which they are likenesses. For example, a statue of Hercules in itself is said to be, and is, bronze; but insofar as it is a likeness of Hercules, it is named 'man.'"
31. See nn. 7–8 above.   32. See n. 10 above.

nor false in relation to its primary significate, because in saying 'man is an animal [*homo est animal*]' in relation to its more primary significate, it does not primarily signify man in reality being an animal, but it is primarily a sign of the thing that is a sign of a man being an animal in reality, i.e., of the understanding itself.

But what is primarily signified is the sign of another. Therefore, the utterance does not primarily signify the species of man being the species of animal, as is clear from the case of an inscription that is not a sign that the utterance 'man' is the utterance 'animal,' but only the sign of a sign. For this reason, just as a piece of writing is not said to be false even though the utterance 'man' is not the utterance 'animal,' so 'man is an animal' is not false even though one species is not the other.

[26] To the other,[33] when it is argued about analogies, I say that an analogous name signifies both analogates, and it is not prior or posterior by reason of signifying because the name signifies both by imposition; rather, priority and posteriority inhere by reason of the significates; however, this is priority and posteriority in the act of signifying, for a name only signifies a thing outside the soul because the affection that is signified by the utterance is the sign of a thing outside the soul.

For this reason, only one is signified per se; the other is signified insofar as it is the significate of what is primarily signified. But in this way, there is no inconsistency in an utterance signifying two things, just like a piece of writing. But because of this there will be no equivocation, unless the utterance could be taken for both as for its per se significate.

[27] To the final argument,[34] I say that the being of the thing outside the soul is required for the truth of a sentence, because the thing itself is the measure of the understanding. For an understanding is not said to be true unless because it is so in reality; for if a sentence were to signify what is in the understanding, e.g., one affection being [the same as] another, the argument would proceed. And it does not signify in this way because being belongs to what is real, but rather, it signifies the sign of this, which is 'this being this [*hoc esse hoc*].'[35] Therefore, for the truth and falsity of speech, it must be so (or not so) in reality.

[28] To a certain argument [based on the notion that] 'a stone is not in the soul,'[36] I say that the proposition, 'a stone is not in the soul,' is true even though

---

33. See n. 12 above.
34. See n. 13 above.
35. See Aristotle, *Metaph.* IV.10 (AL XXV^2 67; IV.4.1006a33–34).
36. See n. 12 above.

the utterance 'stone' is the sign of a likeness of a stone in the soul. The reason is that when I say 'a stone is not in the soul,' I do not signify something being the case primarily, but I primarily signify the understanding that is the natural sign of 'a stone is not in the soul' being the case. Therefore, although 'a stone is not in the soul' being the case is outside the soul, and the utterance signifies primarily the understanding of this being a sign, it will not on this account be false because I am not denying being by something that is in the soul, nor am I affirming the being or non-being of the species.

[29] To the other [argument], 'a name signifies what is primarily understood,'[37] I say that utterances are made into signs by imposition; but the imposition of an utterance, since it is conventional, can be upon the very likeness existing in the soul in that a likeness is the sign of a thing, just as it can be imposed upon a thing as it is understood. That is why the argument concludes that a name can signify a thing as it is understood.

[IV. The Opinion of Scotus]

[30] Neither way is very necessary,[38] but the second seems more consonant with the words of Aristotle and Boethius. But it is completely absurd to say that a thing is signified absolutely.[39]

[*An interpolated comment follows:*[40]] Again, concerning composition and division, note that real composition of the extremes is not always required, but only the composition of reason, because the understanding can use one and the same thing as two things, and thus compose the same thing with itself.

Against this: then a composition in reality would not correspond to a true composition in the understanding, and the composition is of diverse things; however, the concept of the subject and the concept of the predicate do not here fall into the union made by 'is [*est*].'

Or it can be said that a composition is not signified but is what holds on the

---

37. See n. 8 above.
38. See n. 14 of q. 2 below.
39. Simon of Faversham, *Periherm.*, q. 5 (155): "Therefore, by names we signify things and not the species of things. But it should be noticed that utterances do not signify things according to the concept according to which it would have being outside the soul, nor according to the concept by which they have being in the soul; rather, they signify things absolutely, as that which exists absolutely, by leaving out any accident, as is apparent in connection with the name 'man.'"
40. See comment in ms. codex Z: "This is lacking in the Vatican codex" (i.e., ms. [N]).

part of the sign; accordingly, one thing is not composed with another, but the predicate is composed with the subject, because what is intentional pertains to composition, and so the predicate and subject are two. Nevertheless, it must not be so in the ground of those intentions.

[Question 2. Does a Name Signify a Thing Univocally When the Thing Is Existing and When It Is Not?]

It is asked whether a name signifies a thing univocally when the thing is existing and when it is not.

[1] It seems not, because the thing itself in its proper aspect is signified by the name, although it is not signified primarily since the affection of the understanding is the sign of the thing under a proper aspect. Therefore, once a thing has been altered in its proper nature, the signification of the name is altered as well. But the proper nature of the thing is altered 'between a thing's existing and not existing'; therefore, the significate of the name is altered as well.

[2] Again, in *De substantia orbis*,[41] Averroes says that in substantial change a thing loses its name and definition; therefore, the name of the thing will not remain the same when it is and when it is not, because it will not be named by the same name after its corruption as before.

[3] Likewise, Aristotle says that a dead animal only has a foot or a hand equivocally,[42] just as a hand that has been cut off is a hand only equivocally.

[4] Again, there is nothing univocally common to what is and what is not; therefore, the nature of the name is not the same in beings and non-beings.

[5] On the opposite side: the nature of a thing in the soul is the same when the thing is existing and when it is not; but through this the significate of the utterance is the same because the nature of the thing is the same in the soul. This is obvious in the case of accidents frequently generated and corrupted, for if 'an animal runs [*animal currit*]' is said, even though there is nothing running, what is understood by the name is the same as it would be with running existing.

---

41. Averroes, *De substantia orbis*, c. 1 (IX, f. 3rb); AA 229: "In individual substances, there are two kinds of change. One change is substantial, which changes the thing in name and definition. This is called generation or corruption."

42. Aristotle, *De partibus animalium* I.1.640b33–641a55.

Also, it would not otherwise be possible to produce a demonstration from non-existing things,[43] because in saying 'Socrates is [*Socrates est*]' in this way, if by 'Socrates' the same thing is not understood that is understood when he is existing, but rather, the name now signifies a dead man, then this proposition will be true because it signifies that this man is dead.

Also, if an expression signified nothing except what is, no proposition where the verb 'is [*est*]' was asserted would be false, for the subject would always signify something under the aspect by which 'being [*esse*]' belonged to it. And likewise, 'Socrates was [*Socrates fuit*]' would not be true, because it would signify what now exists was, and is not [now]—which is impossible.

[6] Also, Aristotle says[44] that the same proposition is true and false, but it is not the same proposition unless the extremes remain the same per se. But the extremes do not remain the same unless the significates remain the same per se.

[I. Reply to the Question]

[7] It must be said that a name signifies a thing univocally whether the thing is existing or not. In this connection, it should be known that the name 'Socrates' signifies Socrates as he actually is but it does not signify that Socrates exists. Yet Socrates is an actual being by his form, for the name, as has been stated,[45] primarily signifies a likeness of the thing in the soul; but that [likeness] is his form as he actually is; therefore, the name signifies Socrates as he actually is.

[8] Another thing: it must be understood that, whether things are or not, likenesses are signs of them univocally. From these [assumptions], it follows that a name equally signifies a thing whether it is or is not, because it represents the thing in the way that its likeness is in the soul, and is its sign.

[II. Reply to the Main Arguments]

[9] To the first argument,[46] I say that the thing is a per se significate through the utterance, as it is related to the utterance by a mediating immutable likeness.

---

43. Aristotle, *Anal. post.* I.30 (AL IV^1 61; I.30.87b22–26); cf. Robert Grosseteste, *Anal. post.* I.18 (265): "But every demonstration is of a thing that is always or of a thing that is for the most part."
44. Aristotle, *Praedic.*, c. 5 (AL I^2 53; 5.4a36–b2): "For the statement remains the same insofar as someone is sitting; but once the person has moved, the statement becomes true at one time and false at another."
45. See n. 16 of q. 1 above.
46. See n. 1 above.

For a thing signified under its proper aspect by the utterance, insofar as [it is] a likeness of the thing in the soul, is immutably its sign. Thus, because the name is the mediated sign of a thing, as the likeness in the soul is the immediate sign of the thing (the likeness, however, is the sign of a thing whether it is or not), it follows that the name is unchangeably the sign of a thing whether the thing is or not.

[10] To the other,[47] I say that in substantial change, the substance of a the thing that is corrupted does not remain, just as when Socrates dies,[48] the substance of Socrates does not remain but the cadaver is left behind, which does not have the definition Socrates had before, or the name, except equivocally. But even so, the name 'Socrates' still signifies the same when he does not exist as it signified when he is existing; all the authorities proceed on this understanding.

[11] To the other:[49] [it must be said that] there is not some per se common concept univocal to the concept of that which is the being of Socrates and to the concept of that which is the non-being of Socrates, but there can be a common concept of Socrates, who is not (though not as he is not), and of John, who now is. This, however, suffices as regards the fact that a name is common to being and non-being.

[III. Noteworthy Remarks on the Signification of a Name]

[12] Based on what has been said before, it should be known that a name signifies a thing according as its sign is a likeness existing in the soul. But that likeness is a likeness of what is and of what is not, for it is shared in, [both] equally and in itself, by what is and what is not, though not by what is not as it is not. For this reason, Caesar does not share in the name 'man' according to the being that Caesar has now.

Nor is the name 'man' shared in by the Antichrist under potential being, because the Antichrist, understood under the being he has now, is not a particular concept sharing in the per se concept of that which is a man; but it is another concept entirely, as he is a particular, sharing per se in what is understood of what is a man in potentiality. If the Antichrist is understood under the aspect beneath which, in what is understood of him, is included the particularized actuality of a

---

47. See n. 2 above.
48. Cf. Duns Scotus, *Quaestiones super Librum Elenchorum Aristotelis*, q. 37, n. 15 (*OPh* II, 441) and q. 50, n. 7. (*OPh* II, 499).
49. See n. 3 above.

man [*actum hominis particulatum*], then there is a *suppositum* univocal with the man now actually sharing in the form of man; and it shares in both common [natures] completely under an undivided aspect. The reason for this is that a name is per se the sign of a thing. But signifying a thing that is, or was, or will be, is beyond the signification of the name.

[13] And so logically speaking, viz., as regards the formal nature of what is common, and regarding the *suppositum* particularizing the understanding of what is common, any relation of what common to the *supposita* under any time will be beyond the understanding of what is common and the *suppositum*; but things that are[50] beyond [both] the per se understanding of what is common and the *suppositum* in [its] participation in what is common cause no priority or posteriority, and no equivocation in [their] participation in what is common according to the *suppositum* per se. Nevertheless, it does not follow from this that 'Caesar is a man [*Caesar est homo*]' is true or false; but I say that the univocal *suppositum* of man is the Antichrist, Caesar, and John, and the understanding of the names.

[IV. Reply to the Preceding Question]

[14] Therefore, we can briefly say to the [preceding] question:[51] what is strictly speaking signified by the utterance is a thing, not as it exists or does not exist, but as it abstracts from them [that is, existing or non-existing] absolutely and is extraneous to any one of them. Even so, taking into consideration the arguments made and the authorities, it should be noticed that signs—viz., the letter, utterance, and concept or affection of the soul—of the same significate, viz., of the thing, are ordered just as many effects of the same cause are ordered, none of which is the cause of another, as is clear from the sun illuminating many parts of a medium, each of which is illuminated by the sun immediately, but in a certain order, because the more remote parts [are illuminated] by mediation of parts that are more proximate [to the source].

And where there is an order in things that are caused, without one being the cause of the other, in that place there is [also] an immediacy of one in respect of the same, by excluding one under the aspect of cause, but not under the aspect of

---

50. Reading '*sunt*' with mss. OR.
51. This paragraph has many similarities to the *Ordinatio* of Scotus (I, d. 27, qq. 1–3, n. 83; VI.97) and to the *Perihermenias* of Antonius Andreas (f. 66va); it is inserted here in mss. ELOR and S, and omitted from mss. NW, but we do not know the sources from which it derives.

a more immediate effect. And then it could be said that the more proximate effect is in some way the cause of the more remote effect, not strictly, but on account of the proximity that exists between such effects in relation to their cause. So in the case at hand it can be granted as regards many ordered signs of the same significate that one is in some way the sign of another, because it provides an understanding of the very first point (viz., that a letter is the sign of an utterance and an utterance is the sign of an affection), because the more remote would not signify unless before that, in some way, the more immediate were to signify;[52] and the one is not on that account the sign of the other, as was stated in another part as regards a cause and things caused, among which things caused there is an order of posterior effect to prior effect but not of the cause to the effect or the effect to the cause.

[Question 3. Do Truth and Falsity Only Concern Composition and Division?]

It is asked whether truth and falsity only concern composition and division of the sort I have now described.[53]

[1] It seems that they do not only concern composition and division: division, which is the separation of composites, is terminated in simples; but truth or falsity is not designated by simples not united in composition; therefore, there is no truth or falsity concerning division.

[2] Again, we say that there is true gold, and brass is false gold.

[3] Again, being and truth convert, for "as each thing is related to being, so it is related to truth."[54]

[4] Again, a power of sense [*sensus*] is said to be true of its proper object.[55]

[5] Again, in Book III of *De anima*, it is said that understanding,[56] when grasp-

---

52. Here following Antonius Andreas (*Perihermenias*; Venice: 1508, f. 66rb), who has the active *significaret* where the edition has the passive *significaretur* after 'because,' and the comparative adjective *immediatius* instead of *immediatum*.

53. Cf. Thomas Aquinas, *De interpr.* I.3 (I^1 15b–17a).

54. Aristotle, *Metaph.* II.4 (AL XXV^2 37; I.1.993b30–31); AA 118: "As each thing is related to being, so it is related to truth."

55. Cf. Aristotle, *De an.* II.161 (II.30.428b18–20).

56. Averroes, *De an.* III, com. 36 (490–93).

ing the what-it-is of a thing, is true understanding and never deceived; therefore, truth and falsity do not only concern composition and division.

[6] On the opposite side is Aristotle, in Book VI of the *Metaphysics*,[57] when he says that 'the true and the false are not in things as if the good [were true] and the bad [were false],' but [they are] in thought; and not in every thought, but in [those that involve] composing and dividing.

[II. Reply to the Question]

[7] It must be said that the true and the false only concern the composition and division of the understanding, as in someone who is cognizing.[58]

It should be noted in this connection that each and every thing is said to be true because it is equal to its measure; but the measure of each thing is the understanding; thus, each thing is said to be true in some manner by comparison to the understanding.

[8] But it should be known that understanding is twofold: one is measured by things; the other is the measure of things. Our understanding is measured by comparison to natural things and is said to be true because it conforms to the thing that is its measure. But artifacts are related to our intellect just as things that are measured are related to what measures them, and so artifacts are said to be true because by their forms they attain the perfection of the form of the craftsman. For a house is said to be true because it is assimilated, in its form in matter, to the form of a house in the mind of the craftsman.

And natural things are said to be true in relation to the divine understanding, for each natural thing in its form imitates in a certain way its species in the divine mind; for this reason, it is said to be true because it attains the nature of that species. And in this way, each and every being is said to be a true being, like brass: even though it is said to be false gold, it is nevertheless true brass. Likewise, a sense is said to be true because it conforms to its measure, which is its proper sensible. Our simple understanding is said to be true because it conforms to its measure.

[9] For this reason, it is obvious that each and every thing is said to be true because it is in conformity to its measure. But the measure of each thing is a concept

---

57. Aristotle, *Metaph.* VI.8 (AL XXV[2] 37, 122; VI.5.1027b26–27): "For the true and false are not in things, as if the good were true and the bad false, but [they are] in thought [*in mente*]."
58. Duns Scotus, *Metaph.* VI, q. 3, nn. 23–71 (*OPh* IV, 65–83).

formed by some understanding. Therefore, each thing is said to be true by comparison to such an understanding, but primarily by comparison to its measure. However, even though a sense is said to be true—and an understanding is likewise, because of its conformity to its measure—sense by itself does not recognize its own conformity to what it cognizes, nor does it recognize itself conforming to what it is able to cognize. It is likewise as regards simple understanding.

[10] But an understanding that is composing recognizes its conformity to a thing. That is why the composing and dividing of the understanding is nothing but the understanding judging that it is so in reality [*ita esse in re*] or that it is not so, just as the thing conforms to the understanding. For the understanding does not compose because it says that one intelligible species is [the same as] another, but because it judges that it is so in reality, just as the understanding is in conformity with the thing. For whatever judges being composes [it] as it is in reality, and so no understanding other than the composing understanding recognizes what is true. But a simple understanding is true, although it does not recognize what is true, because to recognize what is true is to recognize the conformity of the understanding to the thing. But the understanding does this only because it judges that it is so in reality and for this reason it composes or divides, which is why no understanding other than a composing and dividing understanding can recognize what is true.

[11] And thus Aristotle says in Book VI of the *Metaphysics* that the true and false are in thought.[59] On this basis, I say that the true and the false are in the composing and dividing understanding just as [they are] in the person cognizing. Even so, they are not in the composing and dividing understanding as in what is true, since a simple understanding is true because it conforms to its intelligible; and so is sense, because it conforms to its sensible. But neither understands what is true, and Aristotle understands this.

[Reply to the Main Arguments]

[12] The arguments prove that the true is in something other than composition and division, viz., in what is true. For this reason, it must be said to the first argument[60] that likenesses in the soul can be considered in two ways: [i] inso-

---

59. See n. 6 above.
60. See n. 1 above. See Antonius Andreas, *Periherm.*, f. 64va: "From this [the reply] is clear to all

far as the soul compares one likeness to another, and there is always a comparison or composition of likenesses in this way, whether it wishes to affirm or deny something—whether in this way or that, the soul always relates the likeness of one thing to another. But [ii] if likenesses are considered as they are related to things, likenesses are distinguished just as things are, as when I say, 'a man is not an donkey,' I put forward likenesses as they are related to things, distinguishing one from another.

[Question 4. Does an Indefinite Name Posit Something, Such That the Predication of the Being of That Thing Is Required?]

It is asked whether an indefinite name posits something, such that for it to be predicated of something, the being of that thing must also be predicated.

[1] That it is so is apparent from Aristotle at the end of Book I of the *Prior Analytics*,[61] where he says that there is something underlying what is not equal [*non-aequale*], namely, the unequal [*inaequale*]; but 'unequal' posits something; therefore, so does 'not equal.'

[2] Again, 'the negation of something is the removal of something from something';[62] therefore, negation added to 'man' removes something from him, and if so, it takes something away and leaves something behind, for the removal of the whole thing is not [the same as] the removal of something from something.

[3] Again, if it posits nothing, this follows, viz., 'if a man is not just, therefore a man is non-just [*si homo non est iustus, ergo homo est non-iustus*].' Yet Aristotle denies that consequence.[63]

---

arguments, other than the first, to which I reply that affections or likenesses which are in the soul can be considered in two ways."

61. Aristotle, *Anal. priora* I.46 (AL III^1 87; I.46.51b25–28): "Nor is 'being not equal [*esse non aequale*]' and 'not being equal [*non esse aequale*]' [the same], for something underlies the one, i.e., what is not equal [*non aequale*], and this is the unequal [*inaequale*]; but there is nothing [underlying] the other."

62. Cf. Aristotle, *Metaph*. IV.4 (AL XXV^2 62; IV.2.1004a14–16); AA 122: "Negation and privation differ, because negation is the removal of something *simpliciter*, but privation is the removal of something in a subject naturally suited to it."

63. Aristotle, *De interpr*. II.10 (AL II^1 19–20; II.19.19b20–20a3).

[4] It is said that this is a good consequence, nor does Aristotle deny it except in the case of composite predicates, because 'a is not a white log; therefore, a is a non-white log [*a non est album lignum; igitur a est non-album lignum*]' does not follow.[64]

[5] Against this: when Aristotle denies that consequence, he says that the verb 'is' will be added to 'just' or to 'non-just.'[65]

Again, if the consequence were good, then when the minor is negative in the first figure, a good syllogism would follow. For the syllogism 'every non-animal is a non-man; a stone is a non-animal; therefore, a stone is a non-man [*omne non-animal est non-homo; lapis est non-animal; igitur lapis est non-homo*]' is valid. But what follows from a consequent with something added follows from the antecedent with the same thing added. Therefore, in the place of the minor, assuming that 'a stone is not an animal [*lapis non est animal*],' the same conclusion follows: 'therefore, a stone is a non-man.' And it will be a negative minor in the first figure.

[6] Again, returning to the main argument, Boethius says that an indefinite name is a privation of the species that is present, but it leaves behind other indefinite names.[66]

[7] On the opposite side: what is equally truly predicated of what exists and what does not exist, posits nothing. But an indefinite term is like this, because an ox is a non-man, and equally, a chimera is a non-man.

[8] Again, in contradictories, a consequence holds from the contrary proposition. Therefore, just as 'a is a man; therefore, a is something [*a est homo; igitur a est aliquid*]' follows, so also, 'a is a non-something; therefore, a is a non-man [*a est non-aliquid; igitur a est non-homo*]' should follow. But the consequent never determinately posits the opposite of the antecedent, because if it did, whenever anything is posited by another, it follows from that other thing. But from the antecedent the consequent follows; therefore, from the opposite of the consequent the opposite of the antecedent follows. Therefore, from the consequent and the

---

64. Cf. Aristotle, *Anal. priora* I.46 (AL III[1] 87; I.46.51b29–31).

65. Aristotle, *De interpr.* II.10 (AL II[1] 19; II.19.19b25–26): "I say, however, that 'is' will be added either to 'just' or to 'not-just.'" The edition has "to 'just' and to 'non-just,'" which we have corrected to 'or,' following AL.

66. Boethius, *De interpr.* IV.10 (259; PL 64:522CD): "For 'non-man' takes away the signification of what we call 'man'; there is one thing and one per se signification is being removed."

opposite of the consequent the opposite of the antecedent follows—which is impossible, for then the same thing would follow from the same thing affirmed and denied, which is contrary to Aristotle in *Prior Analytics* II.[67]

[9] It is said that this is in error,[68] because 'something' cannot be infinitized [*non potest infinitari*].

Against this: 'being [*ens*]' can be infinitized, and 'being' is no less a commonality than 'something [*aliquid*].' For Aristotle says that being is produced from non-being.[69]

[10] Again, to the main argument: if so, 'every man is an animal; therefore, a stone is something [*omnis homo est animal; igitur lapis est aliquid*]' follows. The consequent is false; therefore, so is the antecedent. Proof of the consequence: 'every man is an animal, therefore, every non-animal is a non-man [*omnis homo est animal; igitur omne non-animal est non-homo*]' follows, and furthermore, since 'a stone is a non-animal, therefore a stone is a non-man [*lapis est non-animal, igitur lapis est non-homo*],' therefore a stone is something, since an indefinite name posits something; therefore, by transitivity, etc.

[11] Again, an indefinite term is imposed by the negation of form, but with the privation of the form of something, nothing remains of it having being through that form; therefore, etc.

[I. Reply to the Question]
[A. The Opinion of Others]

[12] It is said in reply to the question that indefinite terms are of two kinds: one substantial, one accidental.[70] A substantial indefinite term posits nothing because the negative particle adjoined to the term per se deprives it of quality. But in things signified substantially with privation of quality, what has being through that quality is deprived; therefore, etc.

[13] However, I call a 'substantial term [*terminus substantialis*]' every term

---

67. Aristotle, *Anal. priora* II.15 (AL III[1] 124; II.15.64b9–13).
68. Albert the Great, *Periherm.* I.2 (1:393a–393b): "Nevertheless, it should be noticed that transcendental names such as 'thing [*res*],' 'being [*ens*],' and 'something [*aliquid*]' cannot be infinitized, because once the qualities of those names have been removed when they are indefinite, an indefinite substance cannot remain, not even in apprehension; furthermore, they cannot be infinitized."
69. Aristotle, *Physics* V.7 (AL VII[1] 195; V.1.225a16–17): "But what comes from non-being *simpliciter* in a substance is generation *simpliciter*."
70. Albert the Great, *Periherm.* I.2 (1:393a).

signifying in the manner of a substance, such as 'whiteness [*albedo*]' and 'man [*homo*].' But an indefinite accidental term posits something, because with the privation of an accidental quality, what persists through that quality does not have [to suffer] privation because that quality is not the principle of [its] being *simpliciter*. Furthermore, in saying 'Socrates is non-white [*Socrates est non-albus*]' in this way, something is posited.

[14] Using this distinction, we say to the argument taken from Aristotle at the end of Book I of the *Prior Analytics* that he understands of an indefinite accidental term that something is subject to it.[71] Similarly, to Aristotle's remark in Book II of that work,[72] [we say] that Aristotle denies the consequence for accidental terms because the indefinite term posits something in them. But for substantial terms, '*a* is not a man; therefore, *a* is a non-man [*a non est homo; ergo a est non-homo*]' holds.

[B. Against the Opinion of Others]

[15] Against: just as in an accidental term there is a sort of composition of the accident with a subject, so in a substantial term there is a composition of form with matter. Accordingly, just as with the privation of an accidental quality, a subject can remain under an indefinite quality—and for that reason an indefinite accidental term posits something—so with the privation of substantial form from matter, the matter could remain under the negation of a determinate form. Therefore, since the matter would be something, it seems that a substantial indefinite term would posit something.

[16] Again, an accidental term does not signify a subject, but only a quality; therefore, negation added to an accidental term negates only its per se significate, because there are not two things there of which there could be a privation of one and not of the other that remains. Therefore, much less can an indefinite accidental term [signify a subject]. For there is a difference between a privative and an indefinite term, just there is a difference between 'blind [*caecum*]' and 'not-seeing [*non-videns*].' For 'blind' determines a subject by itself and posits the removal of a determinate form, and in this it agrees with an indefinite term. But it also signifies the removal of a form in a determinate subject, and in this it is different from an indefinite term because it[73] does not determine a subject by itself of which it is

---

71. See n. 1 above.
73. That is, an indefinite term.

72. See n. 3 above.

predicated. In that case I argue as follows: if an indefinite accidental term were to posit something, then an indefinite term and a privative term [would] in no way differ—because negation removes that quality and designates the removal of a quality from a determinate subject.

[III. The Reply of Scotus]

[17] To the question it must be said that to ask whether an indefinite term posits something is to ask whether the essential nature of an indefinite term is such that it requires some nature to be subjected to it for the proposition to be true in which it is the subject. For that which is 'an indefinite term positing something [*terminum infinitum aliquid ponere*]' can have a twofold sense: either there is something subjected to it as regards its essential understanding, or it requires a thing or nature as regards its own nature. I say that 'something [*aliquid*]' is taken in several [senses], viz., for a thing and a nature that exists, or for everything that can be signified by an utterance.

[18] I say, therefore, that an indefinite name does not posit something such that in its essential understanding it includes some being according to a nature, yet it does include something indeterminate as regards the being of a nature and intelligible being. For in saying 'non-man [*non-homo*]' in this way, whatever can be understood under the negation of 'man' can be called a 'non-man.'

For this reason, Boethius says[74] that [the predication of an indefinite term] is indifferent in anything that exists or does not exist absolutely. But a being that exists only in belief, such as a chimera, is a non-man. For the negation added to a finite term is the privation of the determinate form signified by the term, and it leaves behind a being indeterminate in relation to any intelligible and capable of being apprehended under the aspect of a determinate quality. And for this reason, 'non-man' agrees with anything with which the being of a nature or an intelligible

---

74. Boethius, *De interpr.* I.2 (62; PL 64:424D): "But when I say 'non-man,' I signify a certain something—that which is not a man. But this is indeterminate [*infinitum*]. For a dog and a horse and a stone can be signified, and anything that was not a man. And it is said equally, either of that which exists or that which does not." Cf. Thomas Aquinas, *De interpr.* I.4 (I^1 23ab): "Therefore 'non-man' can be also said indifferently, both of that which does not exist in the nature of reality, such as if we say 'a chimera is a non-man,' and of that which exists in the nature of reality, such as when we say 'a horse is a non-man.' But if it is imposed from privation, it would require a subject that is at least existing; but because it is imposed from negation, it can be said of a being and a non-being, as Boethius and Aristotle say."

being in any way agrees, as it is understood under the privation of the finite quality conveyed by the name 'man.'

That is why it is customarily, and rightly, said that 'being [*ens*]' and 'something [*aliquid*]' cannot be made indefinite, because an indefinite name posits something, and does not suffer privation through the name which is posited. For the name 'non-man' signifies a signifiable being, because if 'non-man' signified nothing, when 'non-man' was uttered, no more would the mind of the hearer pause [in order to hear it] than if the utterance '*bers bars*' were uttered.[75] From this it is clear that an indefinite name posits something as 'signifiable being.'

[III. Reply to the Main Arguments]

[19] To the first,[76] I say that there is something underlying what is not equal, as unequal, in the sense of 'that of which it is predicated,' but not that 'unequal' is posited on the strength of the signifying utterance by reason of its signification through 'not equal.'

[20] To the second,[77] I say that negation added to a term leaves something behind that has not suffered privation, which is an intelligible and signifiable being, but it leaves nothing behind of the nature that was there before.

[21] To the third,[78] I say that the verb 'is [*est*]' is not only a union or mode of unifying the extremes, but that there is also a certain unified content to which the predicate is applied. For there are two things in the verb, namely the composition and the content, which is why 'this is not just; therefore, this is non-just' does not follow; because in 'this is non-just,' the content of the verb is affirmed, but in 'this is not just,' the content of the verb is denied—and in both cases justice is denied. For this reason, just as from the negation of the content of the verb, the affirmation of the same content does not follow, so 'this is not just; therefore, this is non-just' does not follow.

[22] Or it can be said that it is doubtful whether the verb is only a copula, or whether it yields to its content on the side of the extreme. For 'just [*iustum*]' gives us to understand a subject, since it is an accident signified concretely, for in saying 'a man is just,' it is signified that a man is something in whom justice inheres.

---

75. Aristotle, *De interpr.* I, 'On Verbs' (AL II[1] 7; I.3.16b20–21): "For the one who speaks establishes an understanding and the one who hears pauses [in order to hear it]."
76. See n. 1 above.   77. See n. 2 above.
78. See n. 3 above.

Therefore, the predicate has the power of the two extremes or terms. Thus, just as 'it is not a white log; therefore, it is a non-white log [*non est album lignum; igitur est non-album lignum*]' does not follow, so 'it is not just; therefore, it is non-just [*non est iustum; igitur est non-iustum*]' does not follow.

[23] To the first argument against this,[79] I say that Aristotle's remark in *De interpretatione* II is to be understood as applying to composite predicates.[80]

[24] To the passage of Boethius,[81] I say that this passage is to be understood as follows: negation added to a finite term removes the form of the term, not by removing some form belonging to another thing. So it is [in the case of] 'non-man [*non-homo*]': for 'non' applied to 'man' removes the species of man, not by removing the species of donkey or horse, though it does leave behind those species which are not removed. But Boethius does not understand that an indefinite name posits those species of its understanding that are not removed through negation applied to the term.

[Question 5. Is the Verb 'Is' Only a Copula of the Predicate with the Subject?]

It is asked concerning the chapter 'On Verbs' and primarily whether [the verb 'is'] is only a copula of the predicate with the subject, or whether it is a predicate, or something belonging to the predicate, when we say, 'a man is white [*homo est albus*].'

[1] That it is not only a copula I prove [as follows]: the verb 'is' predicates the same thing when it predicates second and when it predicates third because it does not change its significate on account of what is adjoined to it. But when it predicates second, its content is the predicate; therefore, when something is adjoined to it, it seems that the specified content of the verb is predicated through another.

[2] Again, when 'a man is [*homo est*]' is said in this way, the content of the verb 'is' is understood to be united with the subject or with the *suppositum* through a verbal mode of signifying, which is composition. Therefore, when 'a man is white' is said in this way, the content of the verb is still understood to be united by the same mode, because what is joined to it does not change per se modes of signifying.

79. See n. 4 above.
80. See n. 3 above.
81. See n. 6 above.

[3] Again, Boethius says that 'a categorical proposition is divided into two parts only,' viz., into subject and predicate.[82] Therefore, it follows that 'is' will not be a per se part when I say 'a man is white,' but something belonging to a single part, that is, to the predicate and not to the subject, because composition holds more reasonably on the part of the predicate, since Aristotle says in *De interpretatione* II, "the noun or verb 'is' [*est*]' is a third element in a sentence."[83]

[4] Again, to be is the actuality of every being. Therefore, when I say 'a man is an animal [*homo est animal*],' I designate that a man is actually an animal, and [what is designated is] not only the expression, 'animal,' but the animal in actuality.

[5] Again, Aristotle says, "'is' is predicated as a third element";[84] therefore, it is not only a copula.

[6] On the opposite side: if it were part of the predicate, no proposition would be converted *simpliciter* in the same terms because in saying 'a man is white,' the content of the verb is according to you part of the predicate. Therefore, if it should be converted into terms, the content of the verb in the converted proposition must be part of the subject, which is false; for then every syllogism in the first figure would be from four terms, because the middle term in the major premise would be taken absolutely, such that 'being [*esse*]' is not part of it. But when 'being' is predicated in the minor premise, it is part of it.

[7] Again, 'a man is an animal' would be nugatory, for if 'being [*ens*]' is predicated, then so is 'animal,' and in 'animal' being is understood. Then from the same part of speech, the same thing would be said twice, i.e., 'being.'

[8] Again, Boethius says in Book II of this work that 'is [*est*]' is posited as a third element, 'not as if it were some part of a proposition, but as the demonstration of a quality in a proposition; for it demonstrates how the proposition is—that it is affirmative.'[85] And it does not establish the proposition as its part; therefore, it is only a copula.

---

82. Boethius, *De interpr.* IV.10 (251; PL 64:519D): "But predicative and categorical propositions are those that consist of two simple terms only."

83. Aristotle, *De interpr.* II.1 (AL II[1] 19; II.10.19b21–22): "But [when] I say 'he is a just man [*est iustus homo*],' I say that the noun or verb 'is' [is] a third element in the affirmation."

84. Ibid., 19b20.

85. Boethius, *De interpr.* IV.10 (265–66; PL 64:525D–526A): "But the third [element] is predicated with respect to the entire proposition, not as if it were a sort of part of the entire proposition, but rather as the demonstration of quality. For we do not say that 'is [*est*]' constitutes the entire proposition, but that it demonstrates how it is [*qualis sit*], i.e., that it is affirmative."

[9] Again, it is commonly said that when 'is [*est*]' predicates as a third element, it predicates what is in another such that it does not predicate its content by itself, but by another.[86] And Boethius says that it is not predicated, but that it adjoins the predicate.[87]

[Question 6. Is a Present-Tense Verb a Copula for the Present 'Now' or Indifferently for Anything Present?]

In this connection, it is asked whether a present-tense verb is a copula for the 'now' that is current [*nunc quod instat*] or indifferently for anything present.

[10] And that it is not [a copula for] the current 'now' I prove [as follows]: 'I run, if I run [*curro, si curro*]' is true, even though I am sitting. If 'running [*currere*]' only[88] supposited for the time that is current, the proposition would be false.

[11] Again, if it were a copula for the current 'now,' 'Socrates always is [*Socrates semper est*]' would be a conflict of understandings.

[12] It is said that it is a copula for the present time that is current: as 'now' for that [moment] which exists now and otherwise for another [moment] when it will be present.[89]

Let the example be given that there was a gate so narrow only one man could pass through, and let whatever being [*ens*] was in the gate, when it was in the gate, be called *a*. Then *a* will stand always for a being in the gate, viz., now for John, now for Robert. Thus, in 'a man is [*homo est*],' 'is' is a copula for this 'now,'

---

86. Cf., e.g., William Arnauld, *Lectura super Peryermenias*; in Aegidius Romanus *Expositio in Artem Veterem* f. 59ra: "Sometimes it is predicated as a third element, and in that case it predicates what is in another."

87. Boethius, *De interpr.* IV.10 (265; PL 64:525D): "I call the predicate in that proposition which posits a just man, 'just [*iustus*],' for this predicate belongs to the man. But 'is [*est*]' is not predicated [as such], though it is predicated as a third element, i.e., in the second position and adjoining the 'just.'"

88. It seems that this exclusive 'only' should be read after 'supposited.'

89. Cf. Simon of Faversham, *Periherm.*, q. 11 (170): "But a present-tense verb signifies the present time by, as it were, excluding what is past and future; but this applies to each designated part of time: future, present, and past. If this is so, then no designated part of time can be consignified by the verb; but then one will assume that it would signify in this way what it would consignify without confusion, and so it would not consignify any present significate. And this is more manifestly obvious if the present that is now present is called *a*: if someone were to say that a present-tense verb consignifies *a*, then it follows that, since the verb would always consignify that same *a*, what is true at present will be past later; and then it will be necessary to say that a present-tense verb will consignify a time already past."

and when I say 'a man is' tomorrow, it will be a copula for the 'now' that is then under the aspect of the present, and not for this singular now. For this reason, a present-tense verb acts as a copula for anything present—so long as it has the aspect of the present—and not for the instant designated. This is shown as follows: if it were to act as a copula only for the 'now' that is current (let it be designated and called *a*), then in saying 'a man exists,' the sense is 'a man exists at *a*.' But it is false should *a* pass away and 'a man exists' be uttered, because the man is not at *a* since *a* does not exist.

Therefore, if that proposition is true now as before, it must be necessary that at a designated instant it be a copula now as before—or one must say that the verb 'is' was imposed as often as it designates under a new time.[90]

[13] Against this: no determination under which a determinable is understood restricts the determinable beyond the form of the determination, because in saying 'a white man [*homo albus*],' 'white' does not restrict 'man' except insofar as it stands for what is white, and it is not restricted to stand for something more contracted than being white in virtue of *white* at least not with regard to anything except what is white. But the significate of a verb is primarily understood absolutely according as it is something in itself [*quid in se*]. Next, the mode of 'signifying with time' is added to it via the mode of 'predicating of another,' beneath which is understood the mode of signifying with the present time, beneath which the primary significate is understood. But now the aspect of this, i.e., the present time, no more respects the 'now' than the 'then,' but rather it is said of the present insofar as it possesses the aspect of the present. Accordingly, the significate of the verb, understood under that presentness as it is a mode, is no more understood as existing than as non-existing [*exsistente quam non-exsistente*] under that presentness.

[14] Again, unless the present-tense verb were a copula for this determinate present, 'a man runs' could be true for a man running tomorrow, because the power of speech [*virtus sermonis*] would not restrict it to this present more than that.

---

90. Cf. Simon of Faversham, *Periherm.*, q. 1 (168): "But this cannot be the case, for then a word would change its significate many times in one day. For if the word 'runs' were imposed to signify the present which is now current, either it will now not co-signify the present which will be current, or, if it does, it must be said that it will change its consignificate, and so there is a new imposition for the whole day."

[15] Again, to the main argument: if this is so, then any present-tense proposition would be necessary *simpliciter*, for what is or is not at this instant necessarily is or is not at this instant.

[16] On the opposing side: if it were not so, then 'everything that is, is at this instant [*omne quod est, est in hoc instanti*]' would be false. And thus something would be and not be at this instant.

[17] It is said that 'everything that is, is at this instant' is true,[91] and the current present is governed by the copula, but *per accidens*, viz., because there is not another present.

[18] Against this: this solution shows that many things are present at the same time, and then it need not act as a copula for this, because no other exists, since "the present is [that] of which part is past, and part is future";[92] and the present is not indivisible, because then time would not exist. Therefore, there are many partial presents [existing] at the same time, just as there are many pasts.

[19] Again, if it does not literally act as a copula for this instant, but *per accidens*, the proposition, 'everything that is, is in this "now" [*omne quod est, est in hoc nunc*],' need not be true.

[I. To the Fifth Question]
[A. First Opinion]
[1. Exposition of the Opinion]

[20] To the question: those who say[93] that the copula is part of the extreme term make the following assumption: 'to be' is the actuality of being [*esse est actualitas entis*]. Therefore, when 'this is white [*hoc est album*]' is said, the predicate is signified as being in the subject under the aspect of the act of the subject itself,

---

91. Cf. Simon of Faversham, *Periherm.*, q. 11 (169): "And so when there is only one thing that is always disposed in this way, distinct from the past in reality and the future in reality [*distinctum a praeteritione in re et futuritione in re*], it must be that that one thing consignifies a present-tense verb and consequently without any confusion."

92. Priscian, *Institutiones grammaticae* VIII.10 (1:414): "The present tense is properly said of that of which part is past, and part is future."

93. Cf. William of Sherwood, *Introductiones in logicam*, n. 1.3.2 (Kretzmann, 268): "Some say that the word 'is' is a third part, the copula. But that is not the case; for since it is a verb it signifies that which is said of something other than itself, and thus it is a predicate"; Thomas Aquinas, *De interpr.* II.2 (I¹ 88a): "To make this clear, it should be recognized that the verb 'is' is itself sometimes predicated in an assertion in itself; ... but sometimes it is not predicated per se as the main predicate, but as conjoined to the main predicate, to connect it to the subject."

and by the mediation of a verb of being. For, just as in saying 'Socrates is [*Socrates est*]' in this way, the actuality of being in Socrates is signified, so when 'Socrates is white' is said, Socrates being under the predicate is signified, as being under the act [of that subject]. For this reason, 'being [*esse*]' is assumed to be a part of what is predicated, because 'white' does not signify per se the act of the subject, and by way of that act.

[2. Reply to the Main Arguments of the Fifth Question according to This Opinion]

[21] To the arguments: in this way it can be said to the first argument[94] that it is possible to consider two things in the predicate, viz., the thing that is predicated and the aspect under which it is predicated. 'Being [*esse*]' can be understood to be a part of the predicate in two ways: either as part of the thing that is predicated, as in 'a rational animal runs [*animal rationale currit*],' where 'rational' is part of what makes up the subject; or as the aspect under which the thing itself is predicated. In the first way, 'being [*esse*]' is not part of the predicate because it does not form a composite with the thing. For 'being' and 'white' do not form a composite as 'man' and 'white' do, because the actuality of a thing does not form a composite with that of which it is the actuality. But in the second way, 'being' is part of the predicate because it is the aspect of the thing insofar as it is predicable.

[22] To the other,[95] it must be said that 'animal,' juxtaposed to that which is 'being [*esse*],' is not juxtaposed to it as the content of the thing, but as a potentiality is understood to be juxtaposed to actuality. For 'animal' is taken as a potentiality whose actuality is conveyed by [the verb] 'to be [*esse*].' But if one were to say, 'a man is an existing animal [*homo est ens animal*],' it would be nugatory because in the essential understanding of that which is an animal, being [*ens*] is understood, in the way it is signified by 'being [*ens*].' That is why, in saying 'a man is an existing animal,' the whole [expression] 'existing animal' is taken to be the thing predicated, whose actuality is what is conveyed by [the verb] 'to be [*esse*].'

[23] To what is said by Boethius,[96] I grant that 'is [*est*]' is not in any way the main part in a proposition when it is predicated as a third element, because it is neither the subject nor predicate; even so, it can in some way be part of a part in the proposition. And when he says that it is the demonstration of a quality in

---

94. See n. 1 above.
95. See n. 4 above.
96. See n. 3 above.

the proposition,[97] I say that he says this about it because of the composition it conveys. For every verb conveys two things: [i] the content of the verb, which belongs to the essential understanding of the verb insofar as it signifies the content conceived by the mind; and [ii] the composition, which belongs to it insofar as it is a verb. Therefore, because of the content conveyed by the verb 'is,' since that is an actuality, there is an aspect beneath which anything that is predicated of another is predicated.

[24] To the other,[98] it is said that when the verb 'is' predicates as a third element and adjoins another, it primarily predicates being of what it adjoins, [that is,] of a third. For example, in saying 'Homer is a poet [*Homerus est poeta*],' one predicates being a poet [*esse poetae*] of Homer, not the being of Homer [*esse Homeri*] of Homer. Accordingly, Boethius says that in 'Homer is a poet,' two things are predicated, viz., poet [*poeta*] primarily, and being [*esse*] secondarily.[99] Therefore, [the verb 'is'] predicates the being [*esse*] that is in another because it predicates the being [*esse*] the subject has, not of itself, but relative to something else, e.g., the being [*esse*] that belongs to Homer as a poet. But when it is predicated per se, it predicates a being [*esse*] [that is] actual and *simpliciter*, and this is as it is in itself. Therefore, 'being a third [*esse tertium*]' is the aspect according to which something is predicated, and not part of it insofar as the concept 'predicable' is applicable to it.

[25] But the aspects of things are distinguished by actuality and potentiality. For just as in a natural composite there is one thing having the aspect of potentiality as matter, and another having the aspect of actuality as form, so it is in the artificial composite that is the proposition—for the subject is like the matter, and the predicate like the form. Accordingly, because the predicate is made from that which is the subject, something other than the subject is required, which makes it known that what was previously the subject is to be taken under the aspect of actuality and form; and this is the verb 'is [*est*].' Therefore, there are three things, viz., [i] the thing of which it happens to be predicated, [ii] the intention of predicating, and [iii] the thing as informed by such an intention. And it is not part of the predicate in the first two modes, but in the third mode.

---

97. See n. 8 above.   98. See n. 5 above.

99. Boethius, *De interpr.* IV.11 (374; PL 64:578D): "For of Homer, we predicate poet primarily, since we say that Homer is a poet; but the verb we predicate of poet primarily, and of Homer secondarily."

[B. Second Opinion]
[1. Exposition of the Opinion]

[26] Otherwise,[100] it is said that the content of the verb and that which follows the content of the verb, together with the composition, make the one extreme of the proposition, which is the predicate, into a whole. And we must not understand that the composition is like a sort of middle term and not one or the other of the extremes, because the nature of the predicate is the nature of being predicable of another, and the nature of being predicable of another is the nature of being dependent on another. But the content of the verb is not [so] inclined in itself. Rather, there are two things in the verb: the content of the verb and the composition. That by reason of which the content of the verb is inclined in another establishes the nature of the predicate, because the composition formally establishes the predicate.

[2. Against the Second Opinion]

[27] Against this: the composition that the question is concerned with is a composition uniting the extremes, in keeping with the fact that what is true or false is signified by composition. But this composition is not a verbal mode of signifying, which is the principle of construing a *suppositum* with what is juxtaposed [to it], because this composition is the same in an affirmative and a negative proposition, just as the nominative case is the same. But it is manifest that the composition by which something is signified to be or not to be [*esse vel non esse*] is not the same in the affirmative and the negative—therefore, the reply is not relevant to what is assumed here, because it only replies about the composition that is a verbal mode of signifying.

[28] Again, what is said[101]—[viz., that] the composition, the content of the verb, and the predicate make a single predicate into a whole—is not true, because the mode in the proposition is never the extreme term, nor part of the extreme.

---

100. Precisely where this is said has not been found.
101. See n. 26 above.

[Scotus's Reply to the Fifth Question]
[1. Exposition]

[29] And so [in reply] to the question it should be known that when the verb 'is [*est*]' is predicated as a third [element], it is strictly speaking neither the subject nor part of the subject, nor the predicate nor part of the predicate. But it denotes the predicate being the same as the subject in act.

[30] In this connection, it should be known that every understanding is understood through the mode of actuality, because each thing is understandable based on the fact that it possesses actuality. But the actuality of each thing is that according to which its proper nature is predicated. But in this way, a potentiality is said to be in actuality, for something is the proper nature of a potentiality in that it is distinguished from a non-potentiality. Thus, privation is also in actuality.

[31] The other thing to be understood is that 'to be [*esse*]' signifies the actuality of being [*ens*]. Therefore, when we want this to signify an actual being [*esse actu*], we say 'this is [*hoc est*].' And because the actuality does not form a composite with that of which it is the actuality, 'being [*esse*]' does not form any composite with what is juxtaposed to it. For it designates that what is juxtaposed to it is the same as another thing in act. For that reason, in saying 'Homer is a poet,' it is signified that a poet in his act is the same as Homer, because the aspect of the being of things and the thing do not form a composite. Therefore, the predicate is not understood to be a composite of two things, viz., of the thing juxtaposed and the verb of being [*verbum essendi*].

[32] For this reason, it must be understood that composition is twofold: one [type] is the mode of signifying in the verb, in which act is inclined to substance; this is the composition generally in every personal verb, which is why it is called by some 'personation [*personatio*].'[102] Another is the composition designated by the verb 'is [*est*]'; it is not a mode of signifying but a thing verbally signified. The second composition differs from the first because the first does not make a proposition affirmative or negative, but is in the personal verb. But the second, because it designates something being the case or not being the case of something [*aliquid esse vel non-esse de aliquo*], makes a proposition affirmative or negative. For from this composition, a proposition is called affirmative or negative, and is

---

102. To whom Scotus is referring here is not known.

different in the affirmative and negative. The first is not. And this is understood of every verb in that it is part of an assertion.

[2. Reply to the Main Arguments in the Mind of Scotus]

[33] To the first argument,[103] I say that if something were juxtaposed with the verb 'is' in the way that something is juxtaposed with 'man,' then when I say 'Socrates is a white man,' the consequence would hold because the verb 'is [*est*]' would be part of the predicate. But it is not so, because when it is predicated per se, the act of being [*actus essendi*] is predicated absolutely. But when it is predicated as a third [element], the other is predicated primarily, and it [is predicated] secondarily insofar as it designates the other (viz., the predicate) in an act of the same thing as regards a third [element]; or it would be the same, i.e., as regards the subject.

[34] To the other,[104] I say that when 'is [*est*]' is predicated per se, the composition (which is a verbal mode of signifying) is the mode of uniting the predicate with the subject, but it is not a principle of signifying what is true or false—nothing pertains to the logician in that composition, but rather to the grammarian. But the composition, which the verb conveys on this basis of its verbal signification, is a composition that signifies what is true or false, so that the grammarian's verbal content is the logician's composition in the verb 'is,' when it is predicated as a third element. Therefore, the grammarian also says that it requires the nominative case after it due to the force of the copula or the signification.[105] But that composition is not a verbal mode of signifying in the way the argument supposes. Therefore, the argument only shows that composition, which is a mode of signifying, is something other than the thing designated in being, and this is true.

[35] The argument of the final position[106] proceeds from the mode of signifying.

---

103. See n. 1 above.
104. See n. 2 above.
105. Cf. Priscian, *Institutiones grammaticae* XVII.27 (2:206); cf. Peter Helias, *Summa super Priscianum maiorem*, in *Petrus Helias, Summa super Priscianum*, ed. Leo A. Reilly, 2 vols. (Toronto: Pontifical Institute of Mediaeval Studies, 1993), 186–87: "Again, it is never joined to a substantive verb except in the nominative case."
106. See n. 26 above.

[II. Reply to the Sixth Question]
[A. Scotus's Reply]

[36] To the second question,[107] it must be said that the verb acts as a copula under the time of the discrete present.

[37] In this connection, it must be known that a present-tense verb, taken per se, signifies the present. But a present-tense verb signifies its content not as something that exists having being in the past or the future, but rather, it denotes its content under the mode of present being [*sub modo essendi praesentis*]. For no part of the past or future is current; but the present is current, and a present-tense verb signifies its content through the mode of what exists at this instant. There is also in a certain way a similarity between a name with respect to its *supposita* and a present-tense verb. For 'man' signifies the form of man or an actual man—not a man in potentiality or a man who was under those aspects or names, but a man according to his actuality. And when anything is understood as the having actuality of a man, it is understood to be a man.

Thus, a present-tense verb denotes its content according as it has the actuality of what is present, and any time, whenever it is understood as having present actuality, is consignified by a present-tense verb. Nevertheless, there is a difference in the fact that, because a common term signifies without time, nothing prevents it from being understood to apply to several things at the same time, any of which is understood to have its actuality. But as regards present times, which are many in order and succession, it cannot be understood that they are many at the same times to which the present actually belongs, because there is a dissimilarity between a name as regards its *supposita* and a present-tense verb.

[38] Second, it must be known that a present-tense verb serves as a copula between one extreme term and another as regards the same time, which it consignifies. Therefore, just as it consignifies the present discrete time as distinct from the past and the future, so it serves as a copula under such a time. That is why it cannot be understood that it serves as a copula for the signified 'now,' because then, when this 'now' has passed, it would not signify a present-tense verb, as was argued before.[108] Nor does it join a common present to a present that was or a

---

107. See nn. 10–19 above.
108. See n. 12 above.

present that will be in the way that a common name signifies, for then 'you will be white [*tu eris albus*]' could verify 'you are white [*tu es albus*].' Therefore, it serves as a copula for any present time, when it was actually present.

[B. Reply to the Main Arguments of the Sixth Question]

[39] To the first argument,[109] I say that in conditionals, the present time is not predicated absolutely or of anything present absolutely, but the present of the one is posited under the relation of the one to the other, so that it is signified that, when the one has present being [*esse praesentiale*], the other will have it too. That is why a confused present serves as the copula there, because it is related to the other. But here we speak of the verb serving as the copula for something absolutely.

[40] To the second,[110] I say that although the verb 'is [*est*]' serves as a copula for the time that is current under the aspect by which it is current, yet there is no inconsistency in understanding when we say 'Socrates always is [*Socrates semper est*],' for here extreme is joined to extreme under the present time as distinct from the aspect of the present and the aspect of the future. For what is past does not exist [*non est*] and similarly, the future does not exist. But because 'always [*semper*]' is determinative of the verb 'is [*est*]' and[111] is not repugnant to it, as it is understood to be distinct from the past and future, for that reason there is no conceptual inconsistency in saying, 'Socrates always is,' because it serves as a copula for any time, as it is distinguished from the past and the future.

[41] To the other,[112] I say that based on its signification, 'present' signifies the present that is current, because otherwise it would not be present. For the present that will be or was is not present, and for that reason, it restricts the content of the verb by its form, as it is understood under the present that is current. But even though, due to the fact that a name could be understood to have many *supposita* at the same time, like the name 'man,' nevertheless, 'the present time,' because of the form of the content it signifies under its proper aspect, cannot have many things at the same time under the aspect of the present. For that reason, the con-

---

109. See n. 10 above.
110. See n. 11 above.
111. Cf. the notation in earlier editions (Wadding, *Opera Omnia* I, 220b; Vivès, *Opera Omnia* I, 596ab): "Another reading: and it is repugnant to it, as it is understood not to be distinct from the past and future, and so there is no repugnancy of understandings [omitted from the Vivès edition]."
112. See n. 14 above.

tent of a verb understood under the aspect of the present is not understood under indifference to many things present at the same time. That is why 'a man runs' is not verified because a man will run tomorrow.

[42] To the other,[113] I say that if the present served as a copula for this present necessarily, 'the Antichrist exists [*Antichristus est*]' would be impossible, just as 'the Antichrist exists at *a* [*Antichristus est in a*]' would be impossible. But because it does not serve as a copula in this way, but for any 'now' when it was present, and the proposition 'the Antichrist exists' uttered today is no different from the one uttered tomorrow; for these reasons it is not an impossible proposition, although it could not be verified now. But it only follows that it is impossible now, not that it is impossible.

[43] To the other,[114] I say that the whole time, which is understood as distinct from the past (viz., by reason of the past), and distinct from the future by reason of the future, is called the present time. Therefore, the quantity of the present time is taken in comparison to action, just as we say that someone builds a house in a week, understanding that he performs such an action over the whole time, and not that he acts immediately or that the action occurs immediately. And by comparing part of a time to part of an action, we distinguish the same time via the present and future, because the present is understood with respect to the whole of what has happened. Thus, Priscian says, "the present time is that of which part is past, and part is future."[115] Yet the whole is taken as one time in comparison to a completed work. So, although there are several parts in a single present, yet none has the aspect of the present, as could be said of many present things together. But that [single whole] is said to be present in comparison to one complete work, and the past to another. For there is an accommodation of time to the verb, as measured by its actuality.

[Question 7. Is a Proposition about the Future Determinately True or False?]

It is asked whether a proposition about the future is determinately true or false.

---

113. See n. 15 above.
115. See n. 18 above.

114. See nn. 17–19 above.

[1] It seems that it is false, because it signifies being otherwise than is in reality; therefore, etc. The consequence is clear, because sentences are true based on the fact that a thing is present. And in the text he says, 'sentences are true as things [actually are].'[116] The antecedent is clear, because a proposition about the future signifies now that a thing will have determinate being [*esse determinatum*], and this being is indeterminate.

[2] Again, Boethius[117] comments on the second argument of Aristotle:[118] "Someone who says, 'there will be a sea-battle tomorrow,' as if it were necessary to happen, pronounces what is to be. But if it did happen, someone who says that it happens contingently is not now correct, [but only someone who][119] says that it happens by necessity; for this reason, there is no falsity in the occurrence of the thing, but in the mode of predication."

[3] Again, every proposition signifies itself to be true. Therefore, in saying, 'you will run at *a* [*tu curres in a*],'" it is signified that 'you are going to run at *a* [*tu esse cursurum in a*]' is true. But this is determinately false because it is signified that a truth is inherent at a time that exists now. Therefore, 'you will be white [*tu eris albus*]' also signifies determinately what is true or false.[120]

[4] On the opposing side is Aristotle,[121] who says that where there are real alternatives [*in his quae sunt ad utrumlibet*], a sentence is no more true than false; therefore, etc.

[Question 8. Is '*a* will be' Now Determinately True?]

Assuming that '*a*' will happen later, it is asked whether '*a* will be [*a erit*]' is now determinately true.

---

116. Aristotle, *De interpr.* I.9 (AL II¹ 17; I.9.19a33): "So, sentences [*orationes*] are similarly true, in the way that the things [actually are]."

117. Boethius, *De interpr.* III.9 (212; PL 64:500C): "But someone who begins to say, 'tomorrow there will be a sea-battle,' pronounces it as if it were necessary—which, if it were to happen, he will not have already spoken the truth because he predicted it, since what was going to happen contingently he predicted as a future necessity. Therefore, there is no falsity in the occurrence, but in the mode of prediction ['predication' is an alternative reading in the apparatus of Meiser's edition]."

118. Aristotle, *De interpr.* I.9 (AL II¹ 14; I.9.18b9–16).

119. Adding *sed ille qui* to the Latin text.

120. Perhaps the conclusion, 'therefore ... it signifies what is true or false,' should be read, 'therefore ... it signifies what is false.'

121. Aristotle, *De interpr.* I.9 (AL II¹ 17; I.9.19a37–39).

[5] It seems so: no proposition is judged to be true or false except for the time at which the predicate can inhere in the subject, as is clear from past propositions, which are not judged according to the disposition of the reality they have now, but according to what they had. Therefore, it will be likewise in propositions about the future, for in saying 'you will be white at *a* [*tu eris albus in a*],' it is not that something is signified to be or not to be [*esse vel non esse*] as regards reality now, but rather it is signified that at *a* it will be true to say, 'you are white [*tu es albus*].' Accordingly, if reality will stand at *a* just as the proposition now asserts reality to stand at *a*, it is now determinately true.

[6] Again, a singular proposition about the future asserts that reality is going to be the way that it will happen, for it asserts that reality will be at a determinate time such that it would be able not to be [*posset non esse*]. But the reality stands now to being, such that tomorrow it would be able not to be; therefore, etc.

[7] It is said that a proposition about the future signifies now that it is determinately so in the reality that will be then. For that reason, its being determinately true now is not consistent with the reality being able not to be tomorrow.

[8] Against this: 'this will be; therefore, this will necessarily be [*hoc erit, ergo hoc necessario erit*]' does not follow; therefore, the opposite, 'this is able not to be tomorrow [*hoc potest non fore cras*]' stands.

[9] On the opposing side is Aristotle.[122]

[Question 9. Is It Possible That Neither Part of a Contradiction Is True?]

It is asked whether it is possible that neither part of a contradiction is true.

[10] It seems so: any proposition signifies itself to be true; therefore, 'you will be white' signifies itself to be true. The antecedent is clear because from every true proposition it follows that its *dictum* is going to be true. Similarly, the contradictory of an affirmative such as 'you will not be white' implies that '"you are not going to be white [*te non fore album*]" is true.' Therefore, each member of a pair of contradictories about the future signifies itself to be determinately true. Therefore, since neither is [determinately] true, it follows that both are false—

122. Ibid.

this is granted[123] because each part of the contradiction is false at the same time in future propositions, due to the mode of being, which is not denied in either of the contradictory propositions.

[11] Against this are the arguments of Aristotle: if each part of a contradiction is false at the same time, it is not the case that "either the affirmation or the negation is said to be true of any [subject]."[124] This is impossible because the opposing negation is the removal of the same thing from itself in the same way; for example, the contradictory of 'every man runs [*omnis homo currit*]' is 'not every man runs [*non omnis homo currit*].' In 'every man runs,' then, negation not only removes the affirmation, but also what is affirmed. And so in the way that 'you will be white at *a* [*tu eris albus in a*]' affirms, in the same way, 'you will not be white at *a*' denies, and [as it says] in the text,[125] "both will not be false together in such circumstances."

[12] Again, if 'you will be white at *a*' is determinately false, it is now true to say that when *a* occurs, you will not be white. Similarly, if 'you will not be white at *a*' is determinately false,[126] it will be true to say that you will be white. Therefore, contradictories will be true at *a*.

[13] Aristotle is on the opposing side.[127]

[I. Reply to the Seventh Question]

[14] To the first question,[128] it must be said that a singular proposition about a future contingent is neither true nor false *simpliciter*, nor determinately true nor false.

In this regard you should know that 'true [*verum*]' signifies a being that is [*esse quod est*], and 'false [*falsum*]' a being that is not. It follows from this that 'just as a

---

123. Where this is granted has not been found.
124. Cf. Aristotle, *De interpr.* I.9 (AL II[1] 13; I.9.18a29–30): "And so with regard those things that are and that have happened [*facta*], it is necessary for the affirmation or the negation to be true or false." Cf. also *Anal. post.* I.11 (AL IV[1] 26; I.11.77a30); *Topica* VI.6 (AL V[1] 125; VI.6.143b16); *Metaph.* IV.9 (AL XXV[2] 66; IV.3.1005b19–24); AA 123: "The first principle [*dignitas*] is [that] the affirmation of any [proposition], or the negation [is true]; otherwise, everything is either the case or not the case, and of none [is the affirmation and negation true] at the same time."
125. Aristotle, *De interpr.* I.9 (AL II[1] 14; I.9.18a38–39): "For both will not be false together in such circumstances."
126. Omitting the 'not' from the critical edition, which seems required to make sense of the argument.
127. Aristotle, *De interpr.* I.9 (AL II[1] 13; I.9.18a29–30).
128. See nn. 1–4 above.

thing is related to being, so it is related to truth.'[129] But what actually exists in the present has what is true in itself, just as it has being [*esse*] per se. However, what is going to be does not exist in itself, but in [its] cause, which happens in three ways: in the first way, there is something that exists 'in a cause' when it necessarily follows from it [the cause]; in another way, when it has a tendency to be produced by the cause, but can nevertheless be prevented; [and] in the third way, when it is related indifferently to being or non-being. In these three ways, things are related to being in the future [*se habent res in futuro ad esse*].

[15] Second, it must be understood that 'sentences are true just as things are related to being [*orationes sunt verae sicut res se habent ad esse*].'[130] For a sentence asserting being of a thing is true in keeping with the way it is related to being; otherwise, the sentence asserting it is false.

[16] Third, it must be understood that a proposition about the future, based on its significate or mode of signifying, equally designates the being [*esse*] of each thing determinately, because the being of things does not change the meaning of a piece of discourse [*non mutat significationem sermonis*], since an expression and a sentence signify the same when the thing is existing and when it is not existing.

[17] Fourth, it must be understood that a proposition about the future can be understood to signify something in the future in two ways: [i] either in such a way that the proposition about the future signifies that it is true now that something in the future will have to be true[131] (e.g., 'you will be white at *a*' signifies it now to be in reality such that at time *a* you will be white); or [ii] it can be understood that it signifies now that you will be white then—not that it signifies it now to be such that then you should be white, but that it signifies now that then you will be white. For to signify it to be the case now that you will be white at *a* signifies more than to signify that you will be white at *a*.

[18] Accordingly, I say that the proposition, 'you will be white at *a*,' asserted *simpliciter*, is determinately false if it signifies a thing to be related to being [*esse*] in such a way that you ought to be white at *a*, because "sentences are true [*orationes sunt verae*],"[132] etc., by the second of the premises [above].[133] But when a thing of

---

129. Aristotle, *Metaph.* II.3 (AL XXV² 37; I.1.993b30–31); cf. AA 118: "As each thing is related to being, so it is related to truth."
130. See n. 1 above.
131. Reading *habere* as an auxiliary verb. This is unusual (although Ockham uses it) but it seems to be required for agreement with the earlier *significet nunc verum esse*.
132. See n. 1 above.   133. See n. 15 above.

this sort is asserted, it is not now related to its cause in such a way that it must have being [*esse*] then, because if the thing were now related to its cause in such a way that it must have being then, this will of necessity be [the case] now, and it would be determinately true now. And so go the first two arguments Aristotle makes.[134] For on this interpretation, a proposition about the future signifies something that is not determinate to be now determinately related to being at a future time.

[19] But if a proposition about the future signifies any future for which it signifies only if [that future] were present, which it is true to say then—since that is what is now asserted as future—a proposition about the future is indeterminately true or false. The reason for this is that when a proposition about the future makes an assertion in this way, it does not assert the existence [*esse*] or non-existence of what is now as something determinate, since on that interpretation, the existence a thing has in its cause is not asserted because the proposition is about the future. Because of this, although a thing now has determinate existence in its cause and although existence is asserted of the thing at some future time, the proposition would not now be called true or false. For it is not asserted to be determinate now as it would be at some future time, but it is asserted now that it will be so disposed, and it is not asserted that the thing is disposed [now] as it must be then.

[20] Accordingly, Aristotle says that in things that involve real alternatives, the affirmation is no truer than the negation.[135] That is why it is not possible for someone reading the proposition dividedly to say that this definitely will be, or that this definitely will not be. But definitely one says this will be when one asserts it to be now, as something will have being in the future.

[*Here there is an interpolated note:*] Therefore, it is concluded from what was said that a singular proposition about a future contingent taken in this second way, as Aristotle also takes it, is not true or false *simpliciter*, nor determinately true or determinately false.

[II. Reply to the Main Arguments of the Seventh Question]

[21] To the first argument,[136] I say that if a proposition about the future signifies it now to be such that a thing in the future will have existence [*esse*] then, it signifies it to be other than it is, and—even if the thing happens that is asserted

---

134. Aristotle, *De interpr.* I.9 (AL II¹ 13–14; I.9.18a39–b9, 18b9–16).
135. See n. 4 above.
136. See n. 1 above.

to happen—it is false, not because of the occurrence of the thing, but because of the mode of assertion. For it is asserted to happen otherwise than it happens. If it is understood in the second way (which determinately asserts the existence of the thing at a determinate future time),[137] the proposition is now neither true nor false, because it is now indeterminate which of the contradictories will have being for that time.

[22] To the other,[138] I say that the argument proceeds on one reading of a proposition about the future.

[23] To the third,[139] it is said '"that you will be white" is true [*"te fore album" est verum*]' must be distinguished according to composition or division. In the sense of composition, the proposition is false, and it signifies that truth [*verum*] inheres in the *dictum* 'that you will be white' for the present; nor does it follow in this way from the first proposition. In the other way, it is taken in the sense of division, and signifies only 'that you will be white' is true, and this indeterminately, just like the first proposition.

[24] Yet in another sense, it must be said that the proposition, '"that you will be white" is true,' signifies in the sense of composition not that the thing is now disposed as 'you will be white at *a*' asserts—for then it would determinately signify a falsehood—but a truth asserted about the *dictum* is understood as a sort of true assertion about the thing conveyed by the *dictum* for the time for which the extremes of the *dictum* are denoted to be united. And thus the proposition in the sense of composition is indeterminately true, because the truth asserted of it should be understood as a sort of assertion of composition conveyed by the *dictum* for the time for which the predicate is asserted to be said of the subject.

[III. Reply to the Eighth Question]

[25] To the second query,[140] it must be said that a proposition about the future is not determinately true, as is clear from what was said.

[Reply to the Main Arguments of the Eighth Question]

[26] To the first argument,[141] I say that a proposition about a future contingent does not assert its being now to be just as the thing is related to being, nor

137. See n. 17 above.
139. See n. 3 above.
141. See n. 5 above.

138. See n. 2 above.
140. See nn. 5–9 above.

does it assert now its not being otherwise than the thing is related to being. But I say that for this time, it asserts determinate being of a thing for a future time. That is why, since it is not determinate for that time (as is clear), a proposition now asserting it to be determinate for that time will be said to be neither determinately true nor determinately false now.

[27] To the other,[142] I say that it is not consistent that it is now determinately true that 'this will be [*hoc erit*]' and that 'this is able not to be in the future [*hoc potest non fore*],' because if 'you will be white tomorrow [*tu eris albus cras*]' is determinately true now—just as 'you are white now [*tu es albus nunc*]' and 'you are now able not to be white [*tu potes nunc non esse albus*]' are not consistent—so that it is now true that 'you will be white tomorrow' and that 'you could possibly not be white tomorrow [*tu possis non esse albus cras*]' are not consistent.

Nevertheless, it is consistent that it is determinately true that 'you will be white tomorrow' and that 'tomorrow you could possibly not be white [*cras possis non esse albus*],' because it is not necessary when you were white that you could not possibly be non-white in the future. But because 'you will be white tomorrow' does not prevent your possibly being non-white tomorrow, therefore, 'you will be white tomorrow' and 'you could possibly be non-white tomorrow [*possis esse non-albus cras*]' are consistent.

[V. Reply to the Ninth Question]

[28] To the third question,[143] I say that if a proposition about the future asserts it to be determinate now that an asserted thing has being [*esse*] in the future, both parts of a contradiction with respect to those propositions about the future are false, because one part asserts it to be definite that it will be, and the other to be definite that it will not be, and (as is clear) it is false, since neither is determinate, but both are indeterminate. And if a proposition about the future only asserts a thing to exist for a future time, and not determinately something about the being that a thing now has in its cause, then both parts are indeterminately true or false.

[VI. Reply to the Main Arguments of the Ninth Question]

[29] To the first argument to the contrary,[144] I say that the proposition, '"that you will be white" is true [*"te fore album" est verum*],' is not now determinately

142. See n. 6 above.
143. See nn. 10–13 above.
144. See n. 10 above.

true or false, because by that proposition, 'being white in the future [*fore album*]' is understood to be affirmed of you for some future time, not for the time that is now current. That is why, although 'that you will be white' is not indeterminate in the future—because for you to be white involves real alternatives [*est ad utrumlibet*] in its cause—nevertheless, because it is not signified that you are now white or not, nor is it signified that there is some respect, determinate in its cause, such that it has this being in the future, the proposition 'you will be white' is not determinately true or false now.

Yet if the proposition were to signify that what is now asserted about the future, and would have being in the future, is now determinate, the proposition would be determinately false because it would signify now that what is contingent is determinate on one side; given this, both parts of the contradiction are false, because one part would signify that this is determinate with respect to being [*ad esse*], whereas the other would signify that this is determinate with respect to non-being [*ad non-esse*]—and that is contingent.

[VII. Some Counterexamples and Replies]

[30] Still, it can be argued that a proposition about the future is determinately true, because 'the future is future, therefore the future is [*futurum est futurum, igitur futurum est*]' follows. The antecedent is determinately true; therefore, so is the consequent.

[31] Again, as it is said now, a proposition about the future does not assert something to be now determinately, but asserts future being as regards a thing—not by determining something to be or not to be. Accordingly, just as a proposition about contingency is now determinately true—because it asserts the occurrence of the thing determinately; even so, it does not determine something to be or not to be now—in this way a proposition about the future will be true.

[32] To the first,[145] it must be said that the consequence is deficient according to "figure of speech," because a 'what [*quid*]' is changed into a 'how [*quale*]'; for in saying 'everything future is future [*omne futurum est futurum*],' what is future is predicated, but in 'the future will be [*futurum erit*]' being is predicated under a future mode; therefore, etc. That is why 'the future is future' concerns the present, just like 'a man is a man [*homo est homo*],' but 'the future will be [*futurum erit*]'

---

145. See n. 30 above.

does not concern the present. Yet if it is supposed that 'the future will be' is determinately true, it does not on account of this follow that a proposition about a future singular contingent is determinately true.

For,[146] if it is argued, 'every future thing will be; "you will be a bishop" is future; therefore, this will be [*omne futurum erit; haec "tu eris episcopus" est futurum; igitur hoc erit*],' this is a figure of speech, because in the major premise there a distribution is made for the *supposita*, whose quiddity it predicates as having been distributed;[147] but in the minor premise, the future is predicated of a certain thing, as predicating a quality of it, on account of which 'what' is changed into 'how'[148]—just as in 'what is written, someone has written; what is written is false; therefore, someone has written a falsehood [*quod scriptum est, scripsit aliquis; falsum scriptum est; igitur falsum scripsit aliquis*].'[149]

But if one descends thus: 'everything future will be; the proposition "'you will be' is future" is future'; therefore, this future will be [*omne futurum erit; hoc est futurum "'tu eris' est futurum"; igitur hoc futurum erit*],' the conclusion may follow, but the minor premise implies a falsehood.

[33] To the other,[150] I say that a proposition about the future does not assert now that something is or is not as regards what exists, but for a future time. For that reason, it is not now determinately true or false. But a proposition about contingency now asserts something determinately, because when it is said 'this will happen contingently [*hoc contingenter eveniet*],' it is signified that its occurrence is contingent, and so it determinately is or is not; accordingly, that proposition about contingency is determinately true or false.

[34] It is argued in a different way as regards the main argument: if 'this will be [*hoc erit*]' is said, it is the same as saying, 'and this is future [*et hoc est futurum*].' But the second proposition is determinately true or false; therefore, so is the first.

---

146. Here there is an interpolated note: "It suggests here that in the major premise, the 'is [*est*]' predicates what is in another, because it is in the future [*esse futuri*]. But when it is posited per se, it predicates what is in itself [*in se*], i.e., as existing through a future mode [*per modum futuri*]—this is not part of the literal sense of the text."

147. 'Distributed' appears to refer to quiddity, though *distributum* is neuter. There seems to be no other way to make sense of the Latin.

148. Cf. Aristotle, *De soph. elench.* II.7 (AL VI¹ 45–46; II.22.178b36–179a1).

149. Cf. Duns Scotus, *De soph. elench.*, q. 40, n. 12: "Here there is a figure of speech: 'what is written, someone has written; a false sentence is written; therefore, someone has written a false sentence [*quod scriptum est, scripsit quis; falsa oratio scripta est; ergo falsam orationem scripsit quis*]'; and here there is a change in cause."

150. See n. 31 above.

On Book I   141

[35] I say that in saying, 'this will be,' the actuality joined to the subject [*actus copulatus subiecto*] is understood to be joined for a future time, whose initial boundary is the present; and so when 'this will be' is analyzed into 'this is future,' the actuality measured under a future time is understood to be joined to a subject for the present time, which is the initial boundary of the same future, on account of which 'a man will be [*homo erit*]' and 'a man is going to be [*homo est futurus*]' are equally valid. But because it is now indeterminate whether a future actuality will have being [*esse*]—since the time measuring it is present—for this reason 'this is future' is indeterminately true, just like 'this will be.' And when it is said that this is of the present,[151] I say that this is not of the present because it is necessary for what is present that the designated actuality be measured of the present time, and not only consignificatively. But it does not happen in the case at hand; therefore, it is not of the present.

151. See n. 34 above.

OPUS II 🙰 QUESTIONS ON THE TWO BOOKS OF *PERIHERMENIAS:* ON BOOK II

[Question 1. Does an Indefinite Verb Remain Indefinite in a Sentence?]

Concerning the second book, it is asked whether an indefinite verb remains indefinite in a sentence [*oratio*].

[1] It seems so: for Aristotle says, "an indefinite verb is predicated in the same way of what is and of what is not,"[1] and it is only predicated of something in a sentence.

[2] Again, he says that it is "a sign of what must be predicated of another,"[2] and this is not the case except in a sentence.

[3] Again,[3] an indefinite verb is a substantive word [*dictio*] to which belong modes of signifying, which are the principles of construing it with another substantive word. Therefore, since it possesses per se modes of signification through which it can be construed with another, it can remain indefinite in a sentence.

[4] Again, it seems absurd that a substantive word should lose its definition

---

1. Aristotle, *De interpr.* I.3 (AL II[1] 7; I.3.16b15–16).
2. Ibid., 16b10–11.
3. Cf. Simon of Faversham, *Periherm.*, q. 10 (165–66): "Again, what has modes of signification through which it is capable of being ordered with another in an assertion [*enuntiatio*], is part of the assertion; ... but an indefinite verb that remains indefinite has modes through which it is capable of being ordered with another; therefore, when an indefinite verb is a substantive word ... it will be capable of being ordered with another in a sentence."

solely on account of its order in a sentence [and] that its significate should not remain, but two substantive words are produced—words that on account of the beginning or ceasing of a sentence do not change their proper significate.

[5] Again, Boethius argues as follows:[4] "if this were not the case, it would follow that one syllogism posited by Plato is made from negatives." For Plato argues syllogistically when he places an indefinite verb in the minor premise of a first figure syllogism. If this were purely negative, his syllogism would possess a negative minor in the first figure.

[6] On the opposing side is Boethius,[5] who says that an indefinite verb placed in a sentence does not retain its force, but is purely negative. The reason for this is that someone who says 'a man is not running [*homo non currit*]' does not affirm anything of a man but rather removes something from a man.

[7] Again, if this were so, it would be the same to say 'a man is not running' and 'a man is non-running [*homo est non-currens*].' But 'therefore, what is non-running is a man [*igitur non-currens est homo*]' follows from the latter; therefore, it follows from the former—which is false, because the antecedent can be true without the consequent or with the consequent being false [*consequente exsistente falso*], e.g., assuming that no man exists, because then 'what is non-running is a man' would be false and 'a man is not running' true.

[8] Again, in Book II of *De interpretatione*,[6] it is said that 'there is no affirmation or negation by an indefinite verb,' because if there were affirmation or nega-

---

4. Boethius, *De interpr.* IV.10 (316; PL 64:551A): "But there were those who gathered this both from many others and at the same time from some syllogism of Plato, and they defined on the basis of that thing what they recognized on the authority of those most learned men. For a syllogism cannot be produced from two negatives. For in a certain dialogue [*Theaetetus* 186d–e], Plato investigates a syllogism of this kind: 'the senses (he says) do not reach the nature of a substance [*ratio substantiae*]; that is not attained, nor does the truth of the thing reach the apprehension; therefore, sense does not extend to the apprehension of truth.' For he appears to have produced a syllogism entirely from negatives, which cannot be done."

5. Boethius, *De interpr.* II.10 (258; PL 64:522B): "But since he [Aristotle] knew that an indefinite name preserves [the quality of] the proposition that receives it (so that if it is predicated in the affirmative, it would keep the proposition affirmative, as in 'a non-man is walking [*non homo ambulat*]'; if it is predicated in the negative, it would keep the proposition negative, as in 'it is not the case that a non-man is walking [*non homo non ambulat*]'), but indefinite verbs that are joined to a proposition do not preserve affirmation, but perfect negation; on that account he remained silent about these matters—[i.e.,] that those features which arise more from the infinite verb, pertain to a single quality of a proposition, i.e., to the negative quality. For negation is always produced from an indefinite verb."

6. Aristotle, *De interpr.* II.1 (AL II[1] 18; II.10.19b11–12): "Apart from the verb, there is no affirmation or negation." The edition erroneously gives the reference here as *De interpr.* I.10.

tion by an indefinite verb, it would follow that when 'is [*est*]' is predicated as a second element, different opposing propositions could be generated in as many ways as when it is predicated as a third element.

[Reply to the Question]

[9] It must be said that when an indefinite verb is placed in a sentence, it does not differ from a purely negative verb. For just as Boethius says, "verbs are indefinite when they are by themselves [*sola*]; when they are joined to some noun, however, they are definite, though they are understood with negation in the entire proposition,"[7] because in an affirmative sentence, something is affirmed of something;[8] but nothing is affirmed of a man when it is said, 'a man is not running [*homo non currit*].'

[10] The reasoning behind what is said here is this: a verb is composed of two [elements],[9] viz., the content and the composition by which something is signified to be or not to be. But an indefinite verb is produced by the addition of a negative particle,[10] which removes the verb in itself. Therefore, when it is added to a noun, it removes what is signified of another by the verb 'to be [*esse*].' But it is not a negative proposition for any other reason than that something is removed from being to non-being. Therefore, an indefinite verb is a verb understood with negation, which does not occur on the part of the noun.[11] For when 'a non-man is running [*non-homo currit*]' is said, something is not removed from something being. But an indefinite verb is understood outside a sentence as a single substantive word, and it is not [so understood] inside a sentence, because indefinite verbs are understood as nouns when they are by themselves; nor is something removed from something.

---

7. Boethius, *De interpr.* II.10 (261; PL 64:523D): "For indefinite verbs are indefinite when they are by themselves. But if they are joined with a noun or an indefinite noun, they are no longer indefinite, but definite, since they are understood with negation over the entire proposition."

8. Cf. Aristotle, *De interpr.* II.1 (AL II^1 18; II.10.19b5): "But because affirmation is signifying something about something."

9. Cf. Simon of Faversham, *Periherm.*, q. 9 (163): "It must be understood here that there are two [elements] in a verb, viz., the content of the verb and also the composition."

10. Cf. Boethius, *De interpr.* II.10 (261; PL 64:523C): "As the negative particle 'not [*non*]' joined with 'was walking [*ambulat*]' makes the indefinite verb 'was not walking [*non ambulat*]'"; cf. Thomas Aquinas, *De interpr.* II.1 (I^1 85a): "An indefinite verb is established by the addition of a negative particle, which, when added to a verb said per se ... removes it absolutely."

11. Cf. Thomas Aquinas, *De interpr.* II.1 (I^1 85a): "When negation is added to a verb placed in an assertion, the negation removes the verb from something, and so makes the sentence negative, which does not happen on the part of the noun."

[11] Nevertheless, if infinitizing negation [*negatio infinitans*] is understood to refer to the content of the verb, it would be appropriate to say that an indefinite verb remains indefinite in a sentence just as a privative verb remains privative in a sentence, as in this case: 'he is blinded [*ille excaecatur*].' That is because in privative verbs, the composition is affirmed and the privation of a thing is merely understood.[12]

[Reply to the Main Arguments]

[12] To Aristotle's first pronouncement,[13] I say that an indefinite verb is thus called 'indefinite' because the content designated by the verb is equally suited to what is and to what is not. It follows from this that an indefinite verb does not signify any determinate concept, just as an indefinite name does not. But it does not follow from this that an indefinite verb, insofar as it is indefinite, is said of something, but only that the concept of an indefinite verb is not distinct or determinate.

[13] To Aristotle's other pronouncement,[14] I say that an indefinite verb is 'a sign of what should be predicated of another' since it is taken per se. But when it is placed with another, something is denoted to be removed from something, because in predicating 'non-being [*non esse*]' of a man, I am predicating the true removal [of being] from a man, since the composition by which something is signified to be or not to be belongs to the definition of the verb and is not merely a mode of signifying. Therefore, negation is not related to the content of the verb, but to the composition, and so when an indefinite verb is placed in a sentence, that sentence is a negative proposition *simpliciter*. That is why, although it has in itself a sign of what must be predicated of another, it does not remain a sign of predicating in itself in a sentence.

[14] To the other argument:[15] indefinite verbs are not modes of signifying by which there can be ordering with another substantive word in a sentence such that the definition of the indefinite verb remains. The reason is that if this were so, it would not now be signified that the being of something is removed from

---

12. Here there is an interlinear note: "But it is not so as regards an indefinite verb, for as Boethius says, the one who says, 'a man is not running [*homo non currit*],' affirms nothing of a man, but rather, removes something from a man. This is the addition of Antonius Andreas; for further details, see that work."

13. See n. 1 above. 14. See n. 2 above.
15. See n. 3 above.

something, but it is only signified that the negation of something is in something.

[15] To the other argument,[16] I say that it is necessary as regards an indefinite verb outside a sentence that two substantive words occur in the sentence, because when a verb signifies something to be of something, a negative particle added to the verb insofar as it is a verb will remove the being [*esse*] of something from something. And this is to make a negative proposition *simpliciter*, so that a negative proposition differs in nothing real or of reason from a proposition where an indefinite verb is posited.

[16] To the other argument,[17] Boethius[18] says that if an indefinite verb is understood as a single substantive word only in the minor premise of such a syllogism, it is understood to be referred to the act, as if the sense were: 'Socrates does not run [*Socrates non currit*],' i.e., 'he is not running [*est non currens*].' Boethius shows this,[19] because it is the same to say 'Socrates runs [*Socrates currit*]' and 'Socrates is running [*Socrates est currens*].' But in 'Socrates is not running [*Socrates non est currens*],' the negative particle added to the verb 'is [*est*]' immediately makes the proposition negative.[20] Therefore, since the verb 'is' was primarily contained in the verb 'runs,'[21] in 'Socrates does not run [*Socrates non currit*],' the 'is running [*est currens*]' is removed because [it is] the entire verb, so that the negation of running is understood in the entire verb. Boethius[22] also says a little earlier that when I say 'Socrates does not walk [*Socrates non ambulat*],' I affirm nothing of Socrates, but rather I remove something, because if there were an affirmation, i.e., if there were an indefinite verb, something would be affirmed of some being. Therefore, he wants it to be that the composition is affirmative if the indefinite verb remains, and so there would not be an indefinite verb, but only the content of the verb.

---

16. See n. 4 above.
17. See n. 5 above.
18. Boethius, *De interpr.* IV.10 (316–17; PL 64:551AB): "And so they affirm that an indefinite verb, e.g., 'it does not happen [*non contingit*]' has been replaced by an indefinite participle, i.e., 'it is not happening [*non contingens est*].'"
19. Ibid., IV.10 (315; PL 64:550C): "Therefore, the verb 'runs [*currit*]' signifies the same as 'is running [*currens est*].'"
20. Ibid., IV.10 (317; PL 64:551C): "A negative particle joined to the verb 'is [*est*]' does not make an affirmation, but rather, a negation."
21. Ibid., "'Runs [*currit*]' contains the verb 'is [*est*]' within it."
22. See n. 6 above.

[Question 2. Does 'This is not just; therefore, this is non-just' Follow?

It is asked whether 'this is not just; therefore, this is non-just' follows.

[1] It seems not: for Aristotle says that of four propositions,[23] viz., two with an indefinite predicate and two with a definite predicate, the two affirmatives are related to the two negatives such that from the affirmation of one there follows the negation of the other; but the two negatives are not likewise related to the two affirmatives.

[2] It is said that Aristotle means that the consequence is not valid for composite terms.

[3] Against this: he says in the text, "but I say that in this case, one adds 'is [*est*]' to 'just [*iustum*]' and 'non-just [*non-iustum*]'."[24] 'Just' and 'non-just' are simple terms.

[4] Again, in *Prior Analytics* I,[25] he says, "it makes a difference in affirming and denying [whether we take an expression to be saying] 'to be non-this [*esse non hoc*]' and 'not to be this [*non esse hoc*]'." He also says there[26] that an affirmative proposition with an indefinite predicate does not follow from a negative proposition with a definite predicate, because 'to be non-white [*esse non-album*]' and 'not to be white [*non esse album*]' are related in the same way as 'to be able to not-walk [*posse non ambulare*]' and 'not to be able to walk [*non posse ambulare*]'. Just as the first does not follow from the second of these, so neither does it follow, 'it is not white; therefore, it is non-white [*non est album; igitur est non-album*]'."

[5] Again, the verb 'is [*est*]' is affirmed in the proposition, 'this is non-white,' on account of which it is signified that this is a being [*ens*] which is non-white, just as in the case of 'this is able to not-walk,' it is signified that it has the capacity such that it might not walk. But in the case of 'this is not white,' being a white

---

23. Aristotle, *De interpr.* II.1 (AL II[1] 19; II.10.19b22–25): "For this reason, then, there will be these four cases, two of which will be sequentially related to affirmation and negation as privations, but two of which will not."

24. Ibid., 19b30: "For in this case, one is adding 'is' and 'is not' to 'just' and 'non-just.'"

25. Aristotle, *Anal. priora* I.46 (AL III[1] 86; I.46.51b5–6): "But it makes a difference in affirming or denying [*construendo vel destruendo*] whether we assume 'not to be this' and 'to be non-this' mean the same or something different."

26. Ibid., 51b7–10.

thing is completely negated. Therefore, the first does not follow from the second because something is posited in the first that is not posited in the second.

[6] Again, a negative proposition can have two causes of truth, but not an affirmative proposition.[27] Therefore, moving from the negative to the affirmative is the fallacy of [affirming] the consequent, just like moving from a disjunctive proposition to one of its parts.

[7] Again, Aristotle says that 'there is something underlying what is not equal [*non aequale*], and this is the unequal [*inaequale*]';[28] but 'it is not equal; therefore, it is unequal [*non est aequale; igitur est inaequale*]' does not follow; therefore, 'this is non-equal [*hoc est non-aequale*]' does not follow.

[8] On the opposite side: 'just' and 'non-just' are 'said of anything.'[29] Therefore, if 'just' is not said of a thing, 'non-just' will be true of it or contradictories would be true at the same time.

[9] Again, Aristotle says,[30] if it is true to deny what was asked about, it is true to affirm the indefinite predicate, e.g., for someone who is asked, "Is Socrates wise [*Socrates estne sapiens*]?" if it is said, 'no,' there follows 'therefore, he is non-wise [*igitur est non-sapiens*]'; therefore, etc.

[10] Again, it is said in the text[31] that this follows: 'not every man is non-just; therefore, some man is just [*non omnis homo est non-iustus; igitur aliquis homo est iustus*]'; and likewise, 'no man is just; therefore, every man is non-just [*nullus homo est iustus; igitur omnis homo est non-iustus*].' Therefore, 'this is not just; therefore, this is non-just [*hoc non est iustum; ergo hoc est non-iustum*]' follows in the same way, for each negative proposition is similarly related to each part.

---

27. John Styckborn, *Periherm.* (ms. Cambridge, Gonville and Caius College, 344–54: f. 213rb): "Thus, it was usually said that any negative proposition has two causes [of its truth], but an affirmative only one."

28. Aristotle, *Anal. priora* I.46 (AL III^1 87; I.46.51b25–28): "Nor is 'to be non-equal [*esse non-aequale*]' [the same] as 'not to be equal [*non esse aequale*]'; for there is something underlying the one, and this is the unequal, but there is nothing underlying the other."

29. That is, of any subject.

30. Aristotle, *De interpr.* II.1 (AL II^1 21; II.10.20a24–26): "If it is true to deny what was asked about, it is also true to affirm it, e.g., 'do you think Socrates is wise [*putasne Socrates sapiens est*]?'; 'he is not [*non est*]'; [it follows] that 'Socrates is non-wise [*non sapiens est*]'."

31. Aristotle, *De interpr.* II.1 (AL II^1 21; II.10.20a21–23).

[Question 3. Does a Consequence of This Sort Hold for Relational Terms?]

It is asked whether a consequence of this sort holds for relational terms.

[11] It seems not; because in *De sophisticis elenchis*[32] it is said that it is not inconsistent to admit that the same thing is both double and non-double.

[12] Again, 'it is unequal; therefore, it is non-equal [*est inaequale, igitur est non-aequale*]' does not follow; nor, further, does 'therefore, it is not equal [*igitur non est aequale*]' follow.

[Question 4. [Does a Consequence of This Sort] Hold with Past-Tense Verbs: First, Would 'It was non-white; therefore, it was not white' Follow?]

It is asked whether a consequence of this sort holds with past-tense verbs: first, whether 'it was non-white; therefore, it was not white [*fuit non-album; igitur non fuit album*]' follows.

[13] It seems so, because a proposition of the past and a proposition of the future differ only with respect to [their] times, but time does not change the disposition [*habitudo*] [of a proposition] because the consequence is *simpliciter* and not as-of-now [*ut nunc*]; therefore, it follows with a past-tense verb just as with a present-tense verb.

[14] On the opposite side: if you were at one time black, this is true: 'you have been non-white [*tu fuisti non-albus*]'; and if you were at one time white, this is false: 'you have not been white [*non fuisti albus*].' And from this truth, a falsehood does not follow.

---

32. Aristotle, *De soph. elench.* II.11 (AL VI[1] 51; II.26.181a5–8): "But if one were to ask at the outset, one must not admit that it is impossible for the same thing to be both double and non-double; but it must be said in such as way as not to refute what was granted"; cf. Duns Scotus, *De soph. elench.*, q. 56 (*OPh* II, 525–27).

[Question 5. Conversely, [Does a Consequence of This Sort] Follow, Assuming the Constant Existence of the Subject?]

Conversely, [does a consequence of this sort] follow, assuming the constant existence of the subject [*constantia subiecti*]?

[15] It seems so, because 'you have not been white, and you have been; therefore, you have been non-white [*non fuisti albus, et fuisti; igitur fuisti non-albus*]' follows, since at every time you existed, you were white or non-white.

[16] On the opposite side: it is the same to say 'you have been white [*fuisti albus*]' and 'you are previously white [*es praeteritus albus*].' But 'you are not previously white, and you are; therefore, you are previously non-white [*tu non es praeteritus albus, et es; igitur es praeteritus non-albus*]' does not follow, just as 'you are not a white log, and you are; therefore, you are a non-white log [*non es album lignum, et es; igitur es non-album lignum*]' is not valid.[33]

[Reply to the <Previous> Questions]

[17] It must be said that with respect to the four existing propositions regarding the same subject—with the predicates varied as definite and indefinite, [understood] affirmatively and negatively, taken with simple or complex terms in an existing composition concerning the present, past, or future—if the two predicates of the affirmative propositions are 'said of anything,'[34] the affirmative propositions follow from the negative propositions; and if not, not.

[18] The reason for this is given by Aristotle in *Prior Analytics* I:[35] for take the simple terms [in] 'Socrates is good [*Socrates est bonus*],' 'Socrates is non-good [*Socrates est non-bonus*],' 'Socrates is not good [*Socrates non est bonus*],' 'Socrates is not non-good [*Socrates non est non-bonus*].' If 'being good [*esse bonum*]' and 'being non-good [*esse non-bonum*]' are 'said of anything,' "and of none of them both,"[36] the negative propositions follow from the affirmative propositions, and

---

33. Aristotle, *Anal. priora* I.46 (AL III^1 87; I.46.51b29–31): "Further, 'it is a non-white log' and 'it is not a white log' are not the same. For if it is a not-white log, it will be a log, but it is not necessary for what is not a white log to be a log."
34. That is, of any subject.
35. Aristotle, *Anal. priora* I.46 (AL III^1 87–88; I.46.51b31–41).
36. Cf. Aristotle, *De interpr.* I.9 (AL II^1 13; I.9.18a29–30): "And so with regard those things that

conversely by conversion. That is because if they did not follow, contradictories would be true at the same time. For if Socrates is not good, if it does not follow that he is non-good, and 'non-good' and 'good' are 'said of anything' according to the hypothesis, then Socrates will be good; therefore, he is good and not good at the same time; and the converse holds in the same way.

[19] Again,[37] the same argument works with composite terms, because if 'being a white log [*esse album lignum*]' and 'being a non-white log [*esse non-album lignum*]' were said of anything, 'it is not a white log; therefore, it is a non-white log' would follow, or else a contradiction would occur and then contradictories would be true at the same time. But because in some cases, both of the composite predicates are denied of the same thing and are not 'said of anything,' as in 'this is a white log, and this is a non-white log,' and both are false of Socrates; therefore, the consequence does not hold.

[20] But beyond this there is a doubt whether in 'this is non-good [*hoc est non-bonum*],' 'being [*ens*]' would be predicated, and 'non-good [*non-bonum*],'[38] on the grounds that this inference is excluded from the negative [proposition], 'this is not good [*hoc est non bonum*],' just as in other composite predicates.

[21] To this I say that it is certain that the consequence is not prevented if 'is [*est*]' is only a copula when predicated third, for then only 'non-good' is predicated, and 'good' and 'non-good' are said of anything. But if 'is' is part of the pred-

---

are and that have happened [*facta*], it is necessary for the affirmation or the negation to be true or false." Cf. also *Anal. post.* I.11 (AL IV[1] 26; I.11.77a30); *Topica* VI.5 (AL V[1] 125; VI.6.143b16); *Metaph.* IV.9 (AL XXV[2] 66; IV.3.1005b19–24); AA 123: "The first principle [*dignitas*] is [that] the affirmation of any [proposition], or the negation [is true]; otherwise, everything is either the case or not the case, and of none [is the affirmation and negation true] at the same time."

37. Cf. Duns Scotus, *Reportatio* I, d. 4, q. 1, n.[7] (Vivès XXII, 124a): "If it is argued that the affirmative of an indefinite predicate follows from the negative of a definite predicate, just as 'a man is not just; therefore, he is non-just' follows, then 'God did not create another God; therefore, God created another non-God [*Deus non genuit alium Deum, ergo Deus genuit alium non-Deum*]' follows. I reply that even though that rule is true, as can be demonstrated from the nature of contradiction, it never holds for composite predicates. For 'a stone is not a white log; therefore, a stone is a non-white log' does not follow, because in the second, something is affirmed that was not affirmed in the first"; cf. Duns Scotus, *Reportatio* III, d. 3, q. 1, n.[10] (Vivès XXIII, 266a): "And it does not follow from this that he is in himself non-just, just as 'a surface is not in itself white; therefore, it is in itself non-white [*superficies non est ex se alba, igitur ex se est non-alba*]' is not valid."

38. The point of 'non-good' is to make a distinction in English between the negative 'Socrates is not good' and the affirmative 'Socrates is non-good,' i.e., between denying goodness of Socrates and affirming the non-goodness of Socrates. The sentence makes less sense in English than in Latin, but smoothing out the English might obscure the logico-philosophical issue under discussion here.

icate in keeping with its own understanding, is not [the consequence in which] 'being non-white [*esse non-album*]' and 'being white [*esse album*]' are not said of anything prevented by this? In that case, the consequence does not hold: when the antecedent and consequent are put in different ways, one says the same of the consequence.

[II. Reply to the Main Arguments of the Second Question]
[A. Reply to the Arguments on the Opposing Side]

[22] Reply to the main arguments of the second question: to the first argument,[39] it is obvious that 'man [*homo*]' and 'being a non-man [*ens non-homo*]' are not 'said of anything.'

[23] To the other argument:[40] I say that the questions have an order, as composites presuppose simples. That is why someone looking for something adjoining the verb 'is [*est*]' presupposes its existence [*esse*]. For this reason, in asking whether Socrates is wise, the existence of Socrates is presupposed. And if Socrates exists, and he is not wise, he is an unwise being [*ens*].

[24] To the third argument:[41] Aristotle assumes that the man exists in that inference.

In this way, it is obvious [what must be said] to the arguments showing that the consequence holds.

[25] But if it is said that the consequence does [not] hold, it must be said that 'is [*est*]' is only the copula and 'non-man [*non-homo*]' or 'man [*homo*]' only the predicate; and then one of the predicates 'is said of one or the other and neither of both [*dicitur de altero et de nullo eodem modo*],'[42] and in that case, 'a being that is a non-man [*ens non-homo*]' is not predicated.

[B. Reply to the Main Arguments on the Negative Side]

[26] To the first argument,[43] when he speaks of 'the two,' etc., I say that Aristotle means that affirmatives are not inferred from negatives because they are not universally inferred, like the converse—except when what is predicated of the affirmatives 'is said of anything [*dicuntur de quolibet*],'[44] which does not occur in composite predicates.

---

39. See n. 8 above.
40. See n. 9 above.
41. See n. 10 above.
42. See n. 18 above.
43. See n. 1 above.
44. We omit *eodem ambo*, with mss. EOR.

[27] And when it is argued 'against this':⁴⁵ "I say that 'is [*est*]' will be added to just and non-just," Aristotle says this only in order to distinguish definite and indefinite predicates. But as it happens, the predicate is simple or composite.

[28] And when it is said in the *Prior Analytics*,⁴⁶ etc., I say that the difference is with regard to the mode of assertion [*ad modum enuntiandi*]; however, in certain assertions there is no real difference, just as with regard to the mode of assertion, 'Socrates's non-running is true [*Socratem non currere est verum*]' differs from 'Socrates's running is not true [*Socratem currere non est verum*],' because the second contradicts something, though not the first. But even so, they do not differ as regards truth.

[29] To the other argument,⁴⁷ I say that the affirmative proposition can be verified in as many ways of an indefinite predicate as the negative proposition can of a definite predicate. For 'being non-human [*esse non hominis*]' posits no more than 'not being human [*non esse hominis*],' although being [*esse*] in an unqualified sense posits more, as is obvious.

[Question 6. Is 'A white man runs' One?]

It is asked concerning this chapter on the unity of the proposition whether 'a white man runs [*homo albus currit*]' is one.

[1] It seems not, for Boethius says,⁴⁸ "if something one is not made from what you make into the subject or predicate, the proposition is not one." But from 'man' and 'white' one thing is not made; therefore, etc.

[2] Again, Boethius says,⁴⁹ "if something one is not made from what you make into the subject, e.g., from animate sensible substance, the proposition is not one." But from 'man' and 'white' one thing is not made in that way; therefore, etc.

[3] It is said that where that under which the term is taken does not make one thing, e.g., one species, Boethius understands that the proposition will not be

---

45. See n. 3 above.
46. See n. 4 above.
47. See n. 6 above.
48. Boethius, *De interpr.* V.11 (353; PL 64:568CD): "If something one is not made from the several things you make into the predicate or the subject, in the way that something one (that which is an animal) is made from what we predicate (animate sensible substance), a single affirmation or negation is not made."
49. Ibid.

one. But that under which the term is taken, e.g., a white thing, is one in this way; therefore, etc.

[4] Against this: when we say, 'a white man runs,' running is attributed principally to a white man, or to a white man *per accidens*; therefore, man is not taken with respect to running under the aspect of white.

[5] Again, by the same argument, the entire proposition, 'a walking white man runs [*homo albus ambulans currit*],' would be one, because what precedes it could be taken under the aspect of walking, which Aristotle and Boethius deny.[50]

[6] Again, Aristotle says in the text that of two things predicated of a third *per accidens*, or of two things, one of which is predicated of the other *per accidens*, one thing is not made from them in relation to which something could be affirmed or denied [of it] as one thing. But 'white [*album*]' is said of a man *per accidens*. Therefore, the proposition will not be one.

[7] Again, there is one negation of any one affirmation. But there is not one negation of 'every white man runs [*omnis homo albus currit*]' because if there were, it would be 'a white man does not run [*homo albus non currit*],' which is not consistent because both are false at the same time on the assumption that no man is white. For it is implied in both that there is an intermediary between man and white, just as there is between something needing completion [*exigens*] and something needed for completion [*exactum*]. For both imply that a man is white; therefore, both are false on account of the implication of what is false.

[8] Against this: when something taken universally is affirmed of some subject in a proposition contradicting it, it is sufficient to deny the whole that was previously affirmed of the same [subject], and to deny it of the same subject taken particularly. But in 'every white man runs' the predicate is universally affirmed of the subject 'white man.' Therefore, to deny the same predicate by the same subject taken particularly is the contradiction of the first.

[9] Again, 'every rational animal runs [*omne animal rationale currit*]' is one, which 'some rational animal does not run [*aliquod animal rationale non currit*]' contradicts, notwithstanding the intervening implication between animal and rational. Therefore, notwithstanding the intervening implication between man and white, 'every white man runs [*omnis homo albus currit*]' and 'some white man does not run [*aliquis homo albus non currit*]' are contradictories.

50. Not found in these sources.

[10] It is said that the implication is not the same, on account of the accident not relating to the subject and the *differentia* not relating to the genus in the same way; for this reason, although the one prevents the contradiction, the other does not.

[11] Against [this]: it is not held why it is said that the implication falls under an intermediary unless because there is one thing needing completion and another needed for the completion. Likewise, then, since 'animal' needs 'rational' or conversely, as 'man' needs 'white' or conversely, the reason for the implication will not be changed.

[12] On the opposing side: in that proposition there is one truth; therefore, it is one. For it is not the same to say 'every white man runs [*omnis homo albus currit*]' and 'every man is white and every man runs [*omnis homo est albus et omnis homo currit*].' For if it were, there would be composite propositions: 'man' would be the subject in both absolutely, and 'every white man runs; therefore, every man runs [*omnis homo albus currit, ergo omnis homo currit*]' would follow, because 'white [*album*]' is the predicate in one, and 'running [*currere*]' in the other.

[13] Again, when Aristotle is asking which things predicated dividedly as two could be predicated as one, he says that Socrates is a man and white, and [that we can unite these predicates] as one.[51]

[14] Again, Ammonius says that 'Socrates is a white man [*Socrates est homo albus*]' is one.[52]

[Question 7. Is 'A white thing is musical' One?]

In this connection, it is asked whether 'a white thing is musical [*album est musicum*]' is one.

[15] It seems not: for 'musical' is predicated of 'white' by reason of some third thing, such as Socrates or Plato. Therefore, it is the same as if one said, 'Socrates, who is white, is musical [*Socrates, qui est albus, est musicus*].' But Aristotle would

---

51. Aristotle, *De interpr.* I.11 (AL II^1 23–24; I.11.20b31–37).
52. Ammonius, *Periherm.* 11 (II, 373): "Therefore, Aristotle shows that some things are naturally suited to be compounded in the generation of a single predicate, taking 'animal' and 'two-footed,' which are predicated of man not dividedly, [of each] alone, but together, when we assert man to be a two-footed animal; and again, [the same is true of] 'man' and 'white,' which are predicated of this man both dividedly and together, when we say, 'Socrates is a white man.'"

have it that 'Socrates, who is white, is musical' is composite, because he says in the text, 'when two things are taken, one of which is predicated of the other *per accidens*, or both of a third *per accidens*, one thing is not made from them.'[53]

[16] Again, there are as many compositions implicit in 'a white thing is musical' as there are in 'there is a white musical thing [*est albus musicus*]'; but on account of the implicit compositions, 'Socrates is a white musical thing' is composite; therefore, 'a white thing is musical' is also composite. For when 'a white thing is musical' is said, there are two propositions involved, as in 'Socrates is white, who is musical [*Socrates est albus, qui est musicus*],' and the same compositions are implicit in 'Socrates is a white musical thing.' What is assumed is clear. For when I say 'a white thing is musical,' I call that in which whiteness inheres musical, properly speaking.

[17] On the opposing side: a proposition is one in which one thing is predicated of one thing. However, the same unity of extreme suffices for the subject as for the predicate. But 'Socrates is a musical thing' is one, and similarly, 'Socrates is white'; therefore, 'a white thing is musical' is also one.

[Question 8. Is 'A white man is a musical man' One?]

In connection with this, [it is asked if] 'a white man is a musical man' is one.

[18] It seems so: 'a white man runs' is one, as was shown.[54] Therefore, the unity of the white man suffices for the unity of the extreme, and for the same reason, 'a musical man' is one. Therefore, [in] propositions of this sort, 'a white man is a musical man,' each extreme is one.

[19] Again, from man and white one thing is made, just as [one thing is made] from actuality and potentiality.

[20] Similarly, by the same reasoning, [one thing is made] from man and musical. Therefore, each extreme is one thing; therefore, etc.

[21] On the opposing side: Aristotle says, 'of things that are made the subject or predicate, [where] any two or more are said of a third *per accidens*, and one is said of another *per accidens*: one extreme is not made from these.'[55] Nor is the af-

---

53. Aristotle, *De interpr.* I.11 (AL II[1] 24; I.11.21a7–10).
54. See nn. 12–14 above.
55. See n. 15 above.

firmation or negation one. But it is so in the case at hand, because 'man' and 'musical' are said of a white man *per accidens*, and one is said of the other *per accidens*. Therefore, this will not be one, just as 'Socrates is a white man' is not.

[Question 9. Is 'A man, who is white, runs' One?]

It is asked whether 'a man, who is white, runs' is one.

[22] It seems so: for the word 'who [*qui*]' has the nature, implicitly understood [*subintellectus*], of an article, on account of the fact that it makes what follows restrict what goes before. For this reason, what goes before is taken under the aspect of what follows, as compared to a third thing; therefore, etc.

[23] Again, the unity of the subject of distribution suffices for the unity of the subject of the act. But the entire expression, 'a man, who is white [*homo, qui est albus*],' is one subject of distribution, because from 'every man, who is white, runs [*omnis homo, qui est albus, currit*],' it is possible to construct a syllogism as follows: 'this is a man, who is white; therefore, this runs [*iste est homo, qui est albus; ergo iste currit*].' In a syllogism, however, the middle is the whole [of] what is taken in both propositions, and in the major the sign falls over the whole as one thing that is distributable.

[24] Again, the unity of the proposition 'a man, who is white' suffices for the unity of the syllogistic middle; therefore, it suffices as well for the unity of the extreme in a proposition, because no syllogism is made from a proposition that is composite.

[25] Again, the unity of a name and of its quality is the same. But the plurality resulting from composition of the act and its quality does not impede the unity of the proposition. For 'this runs fast [*iste currit velociter*]' is one [proposition].

[26] Again, when a proposition is composite, it is necessary for the extremes to be composite, because [there are] at least four, because there are two extremes in every proposition. For suppose I take another that does not restrict the subject. Then, if in 'a man, who is white, runs,' 'running [*currere*]' is predicated of 'man' as its subject and 'white' is predicated of man as its subject, 'man' is not restricted by the [word] 'white.' Therefore, 'every man, who is white, runs; therefore, every man runs [*omnis homo, qui est albus, currit; ergo omnis homo currit*]' would follow.

[27] On the opposing side: a 'relative of substance [*relativum substantiae*]' re-

fers to what is the same in number as its antecedent; 'who [*qui*]' is a relative of substance; therefore, in saying 'a man, who is white, runs,' man is meant to be replicated such that 'man' taken once appears as the subject of the act of running, and taken again appears as the subject of what is being white [*esse album*]. But there cannot be one subject of a proposition from 'man' taken again with respect to diverse things.

[28] Again, there are several compositions here; therefore, there is not one proposition.

[29] It is said that one composition is material with respect to another, and therefore it does not impede the unity of the proposition.

[30] Against this: even though a man is referred to by the word 'who,' this *dictum* always formally unites 'white' with 'man' as if 'a man is white' were said. Therefore, the composition in which 'white' is united to 'a man' related to it is in some respect formal and not material.

[31] Again, a composition is called material because it is per se like matter with respect to another. But the composition conveyed by the verb 'is [*est*]' is thereby formal *simpliciter*, like the composition conveyed by the verb 'runs [*currit*].'

[32] Again, to the main [question]: a proposition that is one has a contradiction that is one. But 'every man, who is white, runs' does not have one contradiction because if it did, it would be 'a man, who is white, does not run.'

[33] It is said [by certain persons] that [the contradictory] is 'a man, who is not white, does not run.'

[34] Against this: according to those persons, a proposition whose subject is 'a man, who is white' is one, but if the particular negative of the same subject and predicate contradicts the universal affirmative, then 'a man, who is white, does not run' contradicts the former if it is one.

[35] Again, the understanding of any categorematic composition is resolved into two simple understandings without truth or falsity. But this proposition is not resolved in this way, for in saying 'a man, who is white,' without the addition of the other [part], truth or falsity follows, because it is meant that a man is white. But because 'man' is being referred to, and the relation is to another actuality, the mind of the person hearing it is thereby suspended until something else is added to 'man,' e.g., if 'a man, who runs' is said, what is true is signified by that proposition, but even so, the mind of the person hearing depends on what must be said beyond this.

[36] Again, negation added to one proposition only negates the composition by which the unity and truth of the proposition is accepted. Therefore, if 'a man, who,' etc., is one in 'not every man,' etc., the negation is related to one composition only, which is not possible. For no matter which composition the negation is related to, 'not every man,' etc., is false because, given that there are many white men and that some are running and some are not running, 'every man, who is white, runs' is false, and similarly 'not every man, who is white, runs'—but on the understanding that the negation is related to the material composition.

Similarly, given that no man is white, 'every man, who is white, runs' is false, and similarly, 'not every man,' etc., on the understanding that negation is referred to the principal composition in that it is implied that some man is white. Therefore, the negation cannot be referred to any one composition. But if it were one, in its contradictory the negation could be referred to one composition.

[I. Reply to the Sixth Question]
[A. Reply]
[1. The Opinion of Others and an Objection]

[37] To the first question, it is said that 'a white man runs' is composite on account of the authoritative passages of Boethius cited above,[56] because there are two compositions, one implicit and the other explicit. For 'man' and 'white' are related as something requiring completion and something that is required for completion, between which 'who is' falls as a middle.

[38] Against this: then 'a rational animal runs [*animal rationale currit*]' would be composite, because between 'animal,' which requires completion, and 'rational,' for which completion is required, 'who is' falls as a middle.

[2. Reply of Scotus to the Question]

[39] It can be said that the proposition is one, which is why one extreme is made from 'man' and 'white' with respect to composition, though not something one *simpliciter*. It should be known in this connection that the unity in a proposition is analogous to the unity in things. But in reality, certain things have unity absolutely, such as those that are beings *simpliciter*. Certain things are called one in a qualified sense [*secundum quid*], e.g., those composed out of such-and-such

---

56. See nn. 1–2 above.

things, e.g., a house. There is an example of this in propositions: this is why 'a man is an animal' is one *simpliciter* where a simple predicate is asserted of a simple subject. But 'a white man runs' is not one *simpliciter*, unlike the former, because the proposition is said to be one based on the unity of extremes. But 'to run [*currere*]' is not thereby affirmed of one thing in keeping with the [unqualified] concept when it is said, 'a white man runs,' as [opposed to] saying 'a man is an animal.' Yet the first is one, because there belong to it the conditions of one proposition, which are: opposition, contradictories, contraries, being divided by affirmation and negation, and syllogism-making [*syllogizatio*]. And according to the meaning of these conditions, it is clear that in *De interpretatione* I[57] Aristotle does not divide any proposition into affirmative and negative unless it is one.

[B. Reply to the Main Arguments of the Sixth Question]

[40] To the first argument,[58] I say that Boethius understands that a proposition is not one *simpliciter* unless one thing is made from the predicates and subjects in the way that one species is also one thing.

[41] Yet a proposition can in some way be one even though an extreme is not one. For one thing is made from actuality and potentiality. And a white thing is in some sense the actuality of a man, although not *simpliciter*; yet it is, as he says,[59] a superficial actuality, because from man and white, a thing is in a certain way made one.

[42] [The reply] to the other argument[60] is clear by the same reasoning.

[43] To the third argument,[61] I say that its contradictory is 'some white man does not run [*aliquis homo albus non currit*].' And when it is said, 'both are false, given that no man is white,' I say that [they are] not, for 'a white man does not run [*homo albus non currit*]' does not posit that a man is white.

[44] When it is said that 'who is [*qui est*]' is a middle,[62] I say that an adjective

---

57. Aristotle, *De interpr.* I.5 (AL II[1] 8; I.5.17a9–10): "The first single sentence [*oratio*] is the affirmative assertion; negation is next. The others are one by virtue of a connective [*coniunctio*]."

58. See n. 1 above.

59. Ammonius, *Periherm.*, c. 11 (II, 379): "Of the things that are predicated according to this single mode, Aristotle rejects the idea that they cannot be joined to each other, since the white of a man is naturally suited to be joined and signifies a non-substantial quality of a man, though a quality that is superficial relative to the aforementioned quality *simpliciter*."

60. See n. 2 above.   61. See n. 7 above.

62. See n. 7 above.

conforms to its substantive [noun] and is united to it as the actuality of a potentiality. But a potentiality with respect to its actuality has the nature of a sort of actuality according to which the actuality is the nature of something or other. It is likewise when we say that 'the Antichrist is actually now in potentiality [*Antichristus est actualiter nunc in potentia*],' and also when I say 'a white man [*homo albus*],' in taking 'man' as having the nature of potentiality with respect to white—a potentiality that is naturally suited to be actualized by a white thing. Therefore, in order to indicate the actuality of a potentiality in comparison to its quality or its act, I interpose 'being [*ens*]' or 'who is [*qui est*].' But of course, 'being' or 'who is' does not signify that something is or is not [*esse vel non esse*], but designates the nature of the conformity of the adjective to the substantive [noun], as if it were a certain mode of understanding or signifying. For this reason, I say that the 'being' or the 'who is' implicitly understood in 'a white man runs' does not assert that white is or is not with respect to the man, but is still a simple concept, without truth or falsity. For it remains that 'a white man runs' does not posit that a man is white, just as 'rational animal' does not posit that an animal is rational.

[45] To the other argument,[63] I say that it is not the same argument, because walking and white are two things, each of which is an accident of the other, and neither is an act or a potentiality with respect to the other, on account of which 'a white man' is taken as one subject with respect to the predicate. Therefore, from 'man' and 'white' and 'walking,' one thing is not made, although one thing is made from man and from each of the others dividedly. But perhaps 'a white-coated substance runs [*substantia superficiata alba currit*]' is one because a coated substance is a potentiality with respect to white, and therefore one thing is made from those, just as from man and white, for accidents come to a substance in an order, such that one accident is like a disposition to another.

[46] To the other argument,[64] I say that when two accidents, each of which is an accident of a third thing, are predicated of it or are made subject to it, then the proposition is not one. It is not so in the case at hand, for 'man' and 'white' are not accidents of a third thing, e.g., of Socrates, although white is an accident of man.

---

63. See n. 5 above.
64. See n. 6 above.

[II. Reply to the Seventh Question]
[A. Reply]

[47] To the second query,⁶⁵ it must be said that 'a white thing is musical' is one, since the white thing makes itself the subject *per accidens*. For that reason, it is not one *simpliciter*, just as 'a white man is musical' is not one, for one thing is made the subject and one thing is predicated. For if the unity of a concrete term did not suffice for the unity of the extreme, one proposition would be converted into a composite, because 'Socrates is white' is one, which is converted into 'a white thing is Socrates [*album est Socrates*].'

[B. Reply to the Main Arguments of Question 7]

[48] Reply to the main arguments: to the first argument,⁶⁶ I say that the sentence shows that the extreme of the proposition is not one *simpliciter*, and yet it is one to a degree sufficient for the unity of truth and falsity and affirmation and negation, and sufficient for a syllogistic sentence.

[49] To the second argument,⁶⁷ I say that when 'a white thing is musical' is said, the composition implied in the subject is the composition of act and potentiality; likewise, the composition implied in the predicate is the composition of act and potentiality, on account of which one thing is made from the things taken in the subject, and likewise from the things taken in the predicate. But when 'a man is a musical white thing' is said, white and musical are two things, neither of which is in potentiality with respect to the other, but both are actualities. For that reason, they cannot be predicated of the same thing in the manner of something one. But when both are taken as predicates, it is necessary for both to be predicated per se. Therefore, the proposition is composite where two accidents are predicated or made into the subject.

[III. Reply to the Eighth Question]
[A. Reply]

[50] To the third question,⁶⁸ it must be said that 'a white man is a musical man' is one for the reason stated:⁶⁹ because white is related to man as act to poten-

---

65. See nn. 15–17 above.
66. See n. 15 above.
67. See n. 16 above.
68. See nn. 18–21 above.
69. See n. 47 above.

tiality, and musical similarly. Hence, one extreme is made from man and white, and another extreme is made from man and musical. Accordingly, one thing is predicated of one thing. But the 'being [*ens*]' implicitly understood between the adjective and the substantive noun does not designate that something is or is not [*aliquid esse vel non esse*], like the composition of an affirmative or negative proposition, but a certain conformity between the adjective and substantive noun,[70] in the sense that one has the nature of something disposed and the other the nature of something able to be disposed. Thus, it is more a mode of understanding than a verbal copula designating that something is.

[Reply to the Contrary Argument in Question 8]

[51] To the argument on the contrary,[71] I say that the proposition is not composite even though several things are predicated, both of which are accidents of the third and one an accident of the other. But if two things are predicated, one of which is an accident of the other via some third thing in which they inhere and of which they are actualities, then the proposition will be composite. For if two accidents that are actualities of some third thing are predicated of each other, one thing will not be made from these as from act and potentiality, though it can be made from others. From this it is clear that the argument proceeds from an insufficiency, because it leaves out the ultimate particle.

[IV. Reply to the Ninth Question]
[A. Reply]

[52] To the fourth question,[72] it is said that 'a man, who is white, runs' is one, because it is able to enter into a syllogism, and because it has contradictories, and the like. But in keeping with this, contradiction in such things cannot be adequately preserved because the particular negative of the same subject and the same predicate should contradict the universal affirmative. Accordingly, if this [proposition] is one, it follows that 'some man, who is white, does not run' is its contradictory. For this reason, 'a man, who is white' will be the subject taken particularly—[the same subject] that was taken universally in the universal [proposition].

[53] Therefore, it can be said that 'a man, who is white, runs' is composite *sim-*

---

70. See n. 44 above.
72. See nn. 22–36 above.

71. See n. 21 above.

pliciter because two acts are attributed to 'man' by two formal compositions. For 'white' is attributed to the man by the verb 'is,' implying a formal composition. For this is how 'white' is formally attributed to the man, although the man is referred to by 'who,' as if 'a man is white' were said, because the formal attribution takes [its] species from the verbal composition. But the 'who is' in respect of the related man denotes that 'white' is also attributed to what 'running' is attributed to. Nor is running attributed to the man who is white, such that the whole is taken as one subject. For what formally signifies the being or non-being [*esse vel non-esse*] of another is never taken as one subject with respect to a third thing. But something is signified to be [so] of another by the 'who is white,' even though the mind of the hearer is suspended by reason of the relation conveyed by the 'who,' as 'man' meanwhile refers to another. Otherwise, when no white man exists [*exsistens*], 'some man, who is white, does not run' would not be false, just as if I were to say that you run, the true or the false is signified. Yet the mind is suspended to the extent that something is added, for the antecedent signifies the true or false hypothetically, as it is part of the proposition. Nevertheless, if the 'who is' is understood as a certain mode of understanding between the adjective and substantive noun, then the proposition is one, just as 'a white man runs'—and its contradictory is 'a man, who is white, does not run.'

[B. Reply to the Main Arguments of Question 9]

[54] [Reply] to the arguments of the fourth question: to the first argument,[73] when it is said, "'who' has the nature of an article implicitly understood," I say that in 'a man, who is white, runs,' 'man' is restricted by what follows because it is denoted that the same man is the subject of running and whiteness. Thus, 'man' is restricted such that it does not stand universally for each one of them. Nevertheless, it does not follow from this that the entire expression, 'a man, who is white, runs,' is one subject with respect to the running, because in saying 'a man, who is a white walker, runs [*homo, qui est albus ambulans, currit*],' 'man' is more restricted by this whole than if I were to say, 'who is white, runs.' The reason is that three things are denoted to inhere in the same man, and these three accompany one another in each case; thus, 'man' is not restricted such that one subject is made with respect to any of them.

---

73. See n. 22 above.

[55] To the second argument,[74] I say that the whole [expression], 'a man, who is white,' is not distributed in the first instance and absolutely, but 'man' per se is nevertheless [distributed] in relation to the 'who is white,' because 'man' is taken to be restricted in a certain way by the fact that it is taken together with it, insofar as white and running inhere in him.

[56] To the third argument,[75] I say that that which is the 'who is white' is not per se part of the syllogistic middle, nor should such determinations be added to subjects, just as other determinations should not, e.g., if one were to make it into a syllogism as follows: 'every man and two men are three; this is a man; therefore, this man and two men are three [*omnis homo et duo homines sunt tres; iste est homo; ergo iste et duo homines sunt tres*].' In the case at hand, one should construct the syllogism as follows: 'every man, who is white, runs; this is a man; therefore, this man, who is white, runs [*omnis homo, qui est albus, currit; iste est homo; ergo iste, qui est albus, currit*].'

[57] Or it can be said that 'every man, who is white, runs' lacks the capacity to be made into a syllogism *simpliciter* because it is composite *simpliciter*. And when it is said that "'white man' is one distributable ['*homo albus' est unum distribuibile*],"[76] it is to be denied.

[58] The fourth argument[77] shows that 'a white man runs' is one, but there is no similarity to 'a man, who is white, runs.' [And] that which is adduced, 'what is one extreme [*quod est unum extremum*],' signifies what is true or false in a single proposition.

[59] To the fifth argument,[78] I say that there are four extremes: 'man' and 'running,' 'man related [*homo relatus*],' and 'white' are denoted to inhere in the same place; therefore, the proposition is composite.

74. See n. 23 above.
76. See n. 23 above.
78. See n. 26 above.
75. See n. 24 above.
77. See n. 25 above.

COMMENTARY

OPUS I

[Question 1. What Is the Subject of *On Interpretation*?]

First we must settle what a name is and what a verb is [I.1.16a1]

Summary

According to Scotus, the proper subject of interpretation is the assertion (*enuntiatio*) or proposition, a composite entity whose primary parts are nouns and verbs (nn. 1–2). Thus, the subject matter of "this book," *De interpretatione* or *On Interpretation*, falls midway between the *Categories*, which considers nouns and verbs by themselves, and the *Prior Analytics*, which is about arguments, that is, higher-level composites whose parts are propositions. The three-fold division of the subject matter of logic corresponds to three kinds of intellectual activity: simple apprehension; composition and division; and speculative reasoning.

Likewise, there are three kinds of existence enjoyed by the subject matter of each book: spoken, written, and mental. Of these, thought, which has mental existence, is assumed to be the basis for significant speech and writing, although this will require clarifying what Boethius means when he defines interpretation as "articulate *sound*," since a noun or verb (or proposition, or argument) can be expressed without being spoken (n. 8).

Discussion

There is a parallel treatment in the prologue to *Opus II* of Scotus's commentary, which appears to be based on the prologue to the *De interpretatione* commentary of Thomas Aquinas. There again, the focus is also on why interpretation is primarily about propositions rather than nouns and verbs, which can also be interpreted.

Commentary

[n. 1] Scotus begins by ordering the subject matter of *De interpretatione* in relation to the subject matter of the texts that precede and follow it in the logical canon of Aristotle: the *Categories*, which concerns nouns and verbs (that is, syncategorematic or significant words), and the *Prior Analytics*, which is about the syllogism, or the form of argumentation that forms the basis of Aristotle's propositional logic.

However, a puzzle is introduced by the concept (*ratio*) or definition of interpretation offered by Boethius, the main authority on this text throughout the medieval period: "Articulate sound, uttered with the aim of signifying." How can interpretation be primarily about articulate sound if it can occur in the mind, without any words being spoken? The Boethian definition appears to make spoken sounds the proper subject of logic, but as Scotus has already argued in his commentary on the *Categories*, "no part of logic concerns the utterance, because all the properties of a syllogism and all its parts can be in it according to the mode of being they have in the mind, even if they are not uttered."[1]

[n. 2] The solution to the puzzle is to make assertion (*enuntiatio*) the proper subject matter of interpretation, by which is meant mental rather than spoken assertion. Interpretation involves the composition and division of apprehended simple terms, through which we determine their integral and specific parts and other significant properties. Spoken assertions have these properties too, but derivatively, that is, only insofar as they are signs of mental assertions.

Objections to Scotus's Solution

[n. 3] Here we get an objection: if a science (*scientia*) is common to all of the things treated in it—think of the way medicine treats of both hearts (cardiology) and kidneys (nephrology)—then assertion does not really treat of nouns and verbs, since it is not predicated of them, that is, only the composite of a noun and verb is an assertion, rather than a noun or verb by itself. This means that on Boethius's definition there will be no 'science' of interpretation—the Latin *scientia* here means something like 'body of knowledge'—because on the Aristotelian account, a science is unified by being about a single subject, for example, the human

---

1. Duns Scotus, *Praedic.*, q. 1, n. 11 (*OPh* II, 251).

body in the case of medicine, the soul in the case of psychology, and so on. But if nouns and verbs, and arguments, can be interpreted along with propositions, then there will be no true science of interpretation, or only a quasi-science with a subject that equivocates among these three kinds of being.

[n. 4] The second objection is similar in that it tries to use the multiplicity of things we can inquire about when we inquire about propositions to undermine the claim that there is any single proper subject of interpretation. Thus, the authority of Boethius is invoked as saying that 'interpretation' applies "to words as well as to names and significant speech."

[n. 5] Finally, Scotus mentions the literalist objection that even if assertions or propositions are taken to be the proper subject of interpretation, they cannot be 'in the mind' because they must be uttered, and articulations of vocal sounds cannot be in the mind.

Replies to Objections

[n. 6] To the first objection (n. 3), Scotus replies that the first or 'major' premise of the objector's argument is false if it assumes that the subject of this science must be predicated as a whole of its parts, since the assertion is not predicable of its noun or verb components—no noun or verb by itself can be said to be a proposition or assertion (setting aside cases in which a single word is really being used to stand for an entire proposition). Interpretation, Scotus implies, has a complex subject. But where complex subjects are concerned, the fact that all inquiry in the science is related to that subject, which 'determines' or orders everything else that is included in it, is sufficient for the unity of a science. In this sense, nouns and verbs on the one hand, and arguments on the other, both seem essential to any inquiry into the nature of propositions.

[n. 7] The reply to the second objection (n. 4) is to distinguish between the subject of a science in the sense of something a science happens to be about (in the way that body is a subject of psychology because it studies living bodies), and the principal or primary subject of a science, which is the goal of our inquiry, the pursuit of which drives and organizes whatever else we study in relation to it. Scotus here quotes from his earlier commentary on Porphyry's *Isagoge* or *Introduction* to the *Categories*.

[n. 8] Scotus replies to the literalist objection (n. 5) by pointing to the tripartite mode of existence enjoyed by assertions—spoken, written, and mental—

where we can find parallel parts and structure. But does not Boethius's use of the term 'utterance' [*vox*] in his definition rule out thoughts (and inscriptions) from being proper subjects of interpretation? Scotus parries this objection in two ways. First, it may be that utterances are seen by us as primary because they become more known to us than thoughts or inscriptions as we achieve linguistic competence even though their corresponding descriptions in the mind are clearer. Second, perhaps there is a difference between a noun existing as an 'utterance' [*vox*] or 'as spoken' [*in voce*], which would be that utterances need not be verbally spoken, for example, when they are merely considered in the mind.

[Question 2. Do Names Signify Things, or Species in the Mind?]

And so there are [spoken sounds], etc. [I.1.16a3–4]

Summary

The subject of this question is Aristotle's statement that utterances are signs of affections in the soul. Do names signify things outside the mind, or species or affections or likenesses of things in the mind?

The initial discussion consists of seven arguments (nn. 2–8) that names signify species, followed by four arguments for the opposing thesis that a thing is signified (nn. 9–12), which are supported by a further six arguments showing that a species is *not* signified.

Scotus provides two different determinations of the question, neither of which he fully endorses. According to both determinations, names signify species as well as things. According to the first (beginning at n. 20), a name is the sign of a sign of a thing and so is both the sign of a thing outside the mind and a sign of its sign, the species. On this view, he concedes the arguments that a thing is signified (n. 25). This is followed by replies to the arguments that a species is not signified (nn. 26–38).

According to the second determination (n. 39), a name primarily signifies a thing not as it exists but as it is conceived by the understanding, according to its essence; nn. 40–44 are replies to the main arguments according to this view. Finally, in nn. 45–51 we find a discussion of doubts about both views, in particular the problem of explaining how individuals are signified or understood. The question is similar in structure to q. 1 of *Opus II*, which has two similar determinations, as well as the same doubts.

Discussion

The problems raised by this question are fundamental to the whole work. If a name (which for Scotus and all traditional logicians means both a common and a proper name) signifies a thing, how can it preserve its meaning when that thing is destroyed (q. 3)? How do we explain what names signify when they are used for things which no longer exist (for example, 'Caesar' in qq. 7–8), or whose scope covers non-existent (qq. 5–6), or future, or possible objects (qq. 9–11)?

Although modern philosophical logic no longer regards such questions as problematic for *common* names, they are still pertinent to *proper* names. Since Brentano and Frege,[2] logicians treat the universal statement 'every man is an animal' as the conditional statement 'if any x is a man, x is an animal,' which is in turn equivalent to the negative statement 'no x is both an animal and not a man.' This is both meaningful and true when no men exist. However, the question remains of how a *proper* name can be meaningful without a referent. How can 'Socrates' signify Socrates when Socrates no longer exists and there is nothing for 'Socrates' to signify? Russell and others tried to resolve the problem by arguing that proper names in ordinary language are really disguised descriptions, so that the sentence really expresses the universal judgment, 'if any x is a Socrates, x was a man.' However, following Kripke's persuasive objections in the 1970s,[3] the disguised descriptions view has largely been abandoned, and many philosophers of language now hold that sentences with empty proper names are meaningless, since they cannot have a truth-value.

Commentary

Names Signify Species

[n. 1] Scotus considers seven arguments that names signify species (nn. 2–8). He excludes names already imposed for signifying species, presumably expressions such as 'species,' 'idea,' 'concept,' and so forth. Some logicians who were

---

2. Franz Brentano, *Psychologie vom empirischen Standpunkt* (Leipzig: Duncker & Humblot, 1874 and 1911), II.7; Gottlob Frege, "On Concept and Object," in *Translations from the Philosophical Writings of Gottlob Frege*, eds. and trans. Peter Geach and Max Black (Oxford: Blackwell, 1952), 48.

3. See especially Saul Kripke, *Naming and Necessity* (Cambridge, Mass.: Harvard University Press, 1980).

contemporaries of Scotus, such as Radulphus Brito, Simon of Faversham, and Durand of St. Pourçain, appeal to the distinction between first and second impositions as a way of resolving the question.[4] Primarily, their arguments are from the authority of Aristotle, Priscian, and Boethius.

[n. 2] Aristotle famously writes, "and so there are spoken sounds that are signs of affections in the soul, and written marks that are signs of spoken sounds" (*De interpretatione* I.1.16a3–4). 'Affections' is a translation of *passio* in the medieval Latin translation of Aristotle. The modern English 'passion' usually means strong affection or sexual love, or sometimes the suffering and death of a martyr, neither of which is intended here. *Passio* is not classical Latin, although it is derived from *patior*, to undergo, suffer, or endure. It first appears in 730 CE to signify the martyrdom of saints. By the 1260s, it had acquired the philosophical meaning of a state of mind affected by something external, a state or power of being acted upon, or attribute or affection.[5] The Greek word that *passio* translates is *pathema*, an affection, enduring, or suffering.

[n. 3] The next argument on behalf of the view that names signify species in the mind is the authority of *De interpretatione* I.1.16a5–8, where Aristotle says that species are likenesses of things outside the soul, and that these species are "primarily" signified by utterances, which are also likenesses of extra-mental things. Therefore signification appears to work via likeness.

[n. 4] The proposition signifies what is true or false. Aristotle says that truth and falsity involve composition and division (*De interpretatione* I.1.16a13–14), but the simples from which a composite is made up are concepts or species, and thus species or concepts are signified.

This raises a problem to which Scotus returns a number of times. The initial assumption, that propositions have a truth-value, equally supports the opposite conclusion because the truth or falsity of a proposition depends on how things are combined in reality, rather than in the mind (see nn. 15–17 below).

[n. 5] The view that names signify species has the additional authority of Boethius, who appears to second what Aristotle says in *De interpretatione*.

---

4. See, e.g., Robert Andrews, "The Modistae and John Duns Scotus's *Quaestiones super Perihermenias*," in *Aristotle's* Peri Hermeneias *in the Latin Middle Ages: Essays on the Commentary Tradition*, eds. H. A. G. Braakhuis and C. H. Kneepkens (Groningen-Haren: Ingenium, 2003), 69.

5. See entry for '*passus*' in R. E. Latham, *Revised Medieval Latin Word-List from British and Irish Sources* (London: British Academy, 1965), 334.

[n. 6] Next we have the authority of the great sixth-century Roman grammarian, Priscian, who in Book XI, chapter 2 of his *Institutiones grammaticae*, asks rhetorically, "for what is a part of speech other than an utterance indicating a 'concept of the mind,' i.e., a cognition?"[6]

[n. 7] The argument that things do not exist in the understanding consists of two syllogisms:

P1—Understanding and understandable are more truly joined than matter and form;

P2—Nothing outside the understanding is more truly joined than matter and form;

C1—Therefore, nothing outside the understanding is understandable.

P1—Nothing outside the understanding is understandable (from C1);

P2—Things do not exist in the understanding (Aristotle, *De anima* III.8.431b29–432a1);

C2—Therefore, things are not understandable.

Accordingly, names must signify species rather than things because things are not understandable.[7]

---

6. In *De Signis*, Roger Bacon argues that we should read the word *conceptum* in this passage as a substantiated adjective (*adiectivus substantivatus*), i.e., as the thing conceived; see Karin Fredborg (ed.), "The Commentary on *Priscian Maior* ascribed to Robert Kilwardby," *Cahiers de l'Institut du Moyen-Age grec et latin* 15 (1975): 137; Karin Fredborg, Lauge Nielsen, and Jan Pinborg (eds.), "An Unedited Part of Roger Bacon's *Opus maius*: 'De signis,'" *Traditio* 34 (1978): 134; and Karin Fredborg, "Roger Bacon on *Impositio vocis ad significandum*," in *English Logic and Semantics from the End of the Twelfth Century to the Time of Ockham and Burleigh, Acts of the Fourth European Symposium on Mediaeval Logic and Semantics, Leiden/Nijmegen 23–27 April 1979*, eds. H. A. G. Braakhuis, C. H. Kneepkens, and L. M. de Rijk (Nijmegen: Ingenium, 1981), 171. Bacon's view has some affinity with the Modist doctrine that names signify things as conceived, rather than concepts. The Modists, or speculative grammarians, were philosophers and proto-linguists who analyzed human discourse in terms of universal modes of signifying, which they related to parallel modes of understanding and being; see Zupko, "Thomas of Erfurt."

7. Something similar is found in AA 194: "In an understanding that is capable of understanding itself, both the understanding and the thing understood are in every way the same." Cf. Averroes, *De an.* III, com. 5 (404): "Let us say, then, that it is clear that a man does not actually understand except through actual contact with what is understood. It is also clear that matter and form are joined to each other such that their combination makes something one and that this holds even more as regards the material intellect and the intention that is actually understood. For what is joined together from them is not some third thing different from them, as is the case with other composites of matter and form." See also Thomas Aquinas, *Sent. De an.* III.3.

[n. 8] "Nothing is understood except through a species." Presumably, what causes a thing to exist or is a principle of its existence is greater or more significant. But a species is the cause or principle of understanding, and hence of signification; therefore, it is the species that is signified more than the thing.

Arguments That Names Signify Things

[n. 9] Next, there are four arguments (nn. 9–12) from the authority of Aristotle to show that a thing is signified. The first is Aristotle's remark in *De interpretatione* I.3.16b19–21 that verbs signify something, such that when a speaker establishes an understanding of a thing in the mind of a hearer, or gets the hearer to figure what he means by an utterance, what is signified by that utterance is the thing, not the concept.

[n. 10] The second authority is Aristotle's famous (tongue-in-cheek?) remark, "because we cannot bring things with us into the discussion, we use names as symbols of things" (*De sophisticis elenchis* 1.175a6–8).[8]

[n. 11] The third authority is also from Aristotle's *De sophisticis elenchis* (1.165a11–12): if things are infinitely many and names are finite, then a single name or expression must signify multiple things.[9]

[n. 12] Finally, there is Aristotle in *Metaphysics* (IV.7.1012a24–25), where he says that the nature or aspect (the Latin term is '*ratio*') signified by the name is the definition of a thing, which indicates its true essence. So that essence, which belongs to the thing, is signified by the name.[10]

---

8. The same passage is quoted in "*Omnis homo est*" (NL 16135, f. 49vb–52vb), in *César et le Phénix: Distinctiones et sophismata parisiens du XIIIe siècle*, ed. Alain de Libera (Pisa: Scuola Normale Superiore, 1991), in the question regarding whether a term supposits for existing things only, or indifferently for past, present and future things, in order to justify the view that names can signify not things that fail to be present not only in space but also in time (and which are therefore non-existent): "It is not necessary that one disputing about things should have the things present; therefore, neither do things have to be present among those imposing the names: they can also not be present. Therefore, anything both present and not present to the one imposing the name can be represented unequivocally with a single name [Non est necesse ut disputans de rebus habeat res praesentes, sed "utitur nominibus notis pro rebus," ut dicit Aristoteles ... ergo nec apud imponentes oportet res esse praesentes, sed possunt esse absentes; igitur omnes—tam praesentes quam absentes—apud imponentem poterunt una voce repraesentari et univoce]" (ibid., f. 49vb [147]).

9. See also another anonymous text published in *César et le Phénix* entitled "*Omnis homo de necessitate est animal*" (NL 16135, f. 52vb–62vb) where the same authority is used to defend the proposition that when things are destroyed, the terms lose their signification. Scotus addresses himself to the same proposition in the following question.

10. Cf. Thomas Aquinas, *Summa Theologiae* Iª, q. 85, a. 2, ad 3.

Arguments That Names Do Not Signify Species

[n. 13] The question moves on to consider six arguments (nn. 14–19) that species are *not* signified by names.

[n. 14] If a species were signified, then the name would signify an accidental property, since an intelligible species is an accidental property of the soul: it is present when we are actually understanding it, but not when we are not.

[n. 15] The next three arguments (nn. 15–17) work from the assumption that truth and falsity depend on how things are combined in reality, not in the mind. The first (n. 15) is that the proposition 'a man is an animal' would be false since it would state that the species of a man is the same as the species of an animal, which it is not.

[n. 16] Furthermore, Aristotle would have said something self-contradictory in stating, "a stone is not in the soul, but the species of a stone," since it would mean that something in the soul (viz., the signification of 'stone') is not in the soul.

[n. 17] Furthermore, any predication of the verb 'is' by itself would produce a true proposition, since the species of that subject exists, even if the thing does not; thus, 'Socrates is' and 'Antichrist is' would both be true, despite the fact that the former no longer exists and the latter does not yet exist.

[n. 18] The argument here is not clear. By 'perfect syllogism,' Scotus probably means what he elsewhere calls a 'regular' syllogism, that is, one regulated by *dici de omni*, or the rule that what is affirmed (or denied) of any subject is affirmed (or denied) of everything belonging to that subject. Perhaps, then, the point is that we would have an undistributed middle if the middle term signified a species of the soul, although this would make the syllogism invalid rather than imperfect.

[n. 19] Next are three brief arguments that an intelligible species is not understood. First, there is an argument from analogy: just as the visible species is not seen, so the intelligible species is not understood (note that the same argument occurs in *Opus II.I*, q. 1, n. 11 below). Second, the intelligible species is that by which what can be understood is understood, but according to Boethius in chapter 2 of *De hebdomadibus*, what exists and that by which it exists are different. Third, because otherwise, there would be an infinite regress: if understanding any a requires understanding some b by means of which we understand a, there must be a further c by whose means we understand b, and so on.

First Determination of Question 2
Reply to the Question

[n. 20] In nn. 20–24, Scotus presents the first of two determinations of q. 2.

According to the first determination, a species is immediately signified by a name, and a thing is signified indirectly. Scotus uses the impersonal verb *dicitur* ('it is said') to indicate that this is the view of others. Boethius, Ammonius, Albert the Great, and Thomas Aquinas are mentioned in the edition as possible sources here.

Modists such as Siger of Courtrai, Martin of Dacia, and others also held this view.[11] It was commonly used to explain how propositions such as 'every man is an animal' [*omnis homo est animal*] can be true even when no men exist. Robert Kilwardby held that existence in reality is not necessary for the truth of such propositions; rather, existence in the conceptual order is sufficient because regardless of whether any man exists or not, 'animal' is understood in what 'man' signifies.[12] The same idea underlies Kilwardby's analysis of inferences involving indefinite terms, a problem discussed by Scotus in *Opus II.II*, q. 2 below. In Kilwardby's commentary on the *Prior Analytics*, he concludes that indefinite substantial terms such as 'non-man' do not involve actual being, because in 'a being that is not-a-man' [*ens quod non est homo*] the word 'being' refers not to actual being, but to being that is common to being in the mind.[13]

In the sections below, Scotus gives three arguments to justify this view:

---

11. Siger of Courtrai, *Expositio in librum Aristotelis Perihermeneias*, in *Zeger van Kortrijk, Commentator van 'Perihermeneias,'* ed. C. Verhaak (Brussels: Paleis der Academiën, 1964), 9; Martin of Dacia, *QQ. Periherm.*, in *Martini de Dacia Opera*, ed. Heinrich Roos (Copenhagen: G. E. C. Gad, 1961), q. 7 (242.13–4); Peter of Saint-Amour, Vat. Bibl. Apost. Pal. lat. 1007, 21rb, cited in Robert Andrews, "The Modistae and John Duns Scotus's *Quaestiones super Perihermenias*," in *Aristotle's* Peri Hermeneias *in the Latin Middle Ages: Essays on the Commentary Tradition*, eds. H. A. G. Braakhuis and C. H. Kneepkens (Groningen-Haren: Ingenium, 2003), 77.

12. P. Osmund Lewry, "Oxford Condemnations," 246. See also the sophism 'Every man of necessity is an animal' in Kilwardby, Erfurt ms. Amplon Q328, 9vb; cited in Lewry, "Oxford Condemnations," 267.

13. P. Osmund Lewry, "Robert Kilwardby on Meaning: A Parisian Course on the *Logica Vetus*," in *Sprache und Erkenntnis im Mittelalter*, eds. J. P. Beckmann et al. (Berlin: De Gruyter, 1981), 382, quoted in A. Tabarroni, "The Tenth Thesis in Logic Condemned at Oxford in 1277," in *Aristotle's* Peri Hermeneias *in the Latin Middle Ages: Essays on the Commentary Tradition*, eds. H. A. G. Braakhuis and C. H. Kneepkens (Groningen-Haren: Ingenium, 2003), 350.

Commentary: *Opus I*   179

1. *The representation argument.* A likeness can be considered in two ways: (i) as it is in itself, in which case it has all the properties and features of the matter of which it is composed; or (ii) as it is a likeness representing something else, in which case it is said to have the properties of the thing it represents.[14]

2. *The transitivity argument.* The sign of a sign of *a* is itself the sign of *a*, and so a name directly signifies a species. But the species naturally represents something outside the soul, which makes it a sign of it. Thus, the name is indirectly a sign of the thing outside the soul.[15]

3. *The argument from analogy.* Scotus frequently uses this to support the transitivity argument. Letters signify utterances, but the written sentence 'a man is an animal' does not say that the utterance 'man' is the same as the utterance 'animal.' Likewise, utterances signify species, but the uttered sentence 'a man is an animal' does not assert that the species *man* is the species *animal*.[16]

[n. 21] Scotus considers an objection to this view, which is that every name would be equivocal if a name signified the species immediately and the thing only indirectly (nn. 21–22). That is because the thing and its species—understood here as the likeness that is in our understanding—belong to different categories.

[n. 22] This objection has the authority of Aristotle on its side, viz., the argument in chapter 1 of the *Categories* (1.1a1–2) that things having different definitions are equivocals, in the way we say that a man and the picture of a man are animals.

---

14. Thomas Aquinas gives a similar argument in his *De interpr.* commentary (I.1.3, n. 4), where he writes that as a statue of Hercules exists in itself, it is said to be made of bronze; as a likeness of Hercules, it is called a man.

15. Neither Thomas nor Albert uses this argument in the places mentioned. But the argument must have been current, as Lambert of Lagny mentions it in his *Logic*, claiming that just as the cause of a cause is the cause of the thing ultimately caused, so the sign of a sign is the sign of the thing [ultimately] signified. Thus, an utterance is the directly the sign of an understanding, but this is a sign of thing, and so an utterance is indirectly the sign of a thing; see Lambert's *Logica (Summa Lamberti)*, ed. Franco Alessio (Firenze: La Nuova Italia Editrice, 1971), 205. According to Paul Vincent Spade, in using the language of immediate and ulimate significates, Scotus is here defending the transitivity of signification ("The Semantics of Terms," in *The Cambridge History of Later Medieval Philosophy: From the Rediscovery of Aristotle to the Disintegration of Scholasticism, 1100–1600*, eds. Norman Kretzmann, Anthony Kenny, and Jan Pinborg [Cambridge: Cambridge University Press, 1982], 189n5). Spade notes further that Scotus seems to have changed his mind about this being a signification relation between *Opus I* of his *Perihermenias* commentary and his more mature *Ordinatio* (189n7).

16. This analogy is also used by William Arnauld, writing earlier in the mid-thirteenth century: "Written letters are marks of utterances, and utterances are signified by written letters, and are signs of affections; affections are signified by utterances, and are signs of things" (*Lectura super Peryermenias*; in *Aegidius Romanus Expositio in Artem Veterem* 47vb).

[n. 23] Scotus replies to the objection that a term is only equivocal when it signifies many things in different acts of signification. But (in the case of indirect signification considered here) a thing and its representation are signified in the same act because the utterance is the sign of a sign insofar as it is a sign and also a sign of what is signified by it.

[n. 24] Furthermore, with regard to the example of the man and the painted man in n. 22, Aristotle was clearly talking there about different acts of signifying, and so the objection is invalid.

Reply to the Arguments on the Opposing Side

[n. 25] Next, Scotus concedes the arguments that the name signifies the thing (nn. 9–12), including, presumably, the arguments against the view that the name signifies the species (nn. 13–19).

Reply to the Arguments Proving That Names Do Not Signify Species

[n. 26] To the argument that a species is an accidental feature of the mind (n. 14), Scotus replies that a name can signify absolutely, but not directly. This is the first appearance of his argument from analogy: letters signify utterances, but the written sentence 'a man is an animal' does not say that the utterance 'man' is the same as the utterance 'animal.' Likewise, utterances signify species, but the uttered sentence 'a man is an animal' does not assert that the species *man* is the species *animal*.

[n. 27] Next are seven sections (nn. 27–38) replying to nn. 15–17 above, which argued that truth and falsity depend on composition outside the mind.

The first argument (n. 15) asserted that the proposition signifies the identity of what are signified by its terms, and the terms cannot signify species—otherwise, propositions such as 'a man is an animal' and 'a stone is not in the mind' would be false and 'Socrates exists' would be true even when Socrates does not exist.

Scotus replies that a proposition asserts the identity not of the primary significates (the species) but of the ultimate significates (the things). He now uses the argument by analogy with written letters and spoken sounds: the written sentence, 'man is an animal,' is not false even though the utterance 'man' is not the utterance 'animal.' That is because the written letters do not signify the utterances as they are in themselves but as they are signs of other things.

[n. 28] Scotus says that this answers all of the arguments about truth and falsity (nn. 15–17), because truth is proper to the "ultimate significates" of written letters and spoken sounds, that is, to things.

[n. 29] To this it is objected that the primary significates, that is, the species, are denoted to be the same in the proposition, 'man is an animal.' But since they are obviously not the same, the proposition is false.[17]

[n. 30] Scotus replies to this objection (n. 29) that truth and falsity are not concerned with the signs qua signs, but with their ultimate significates, that is, the things.

[n. 31] Next is an objection to the representation argument: the species *man* insofar as it represents man is not the same as the species *animal* insofar as it represents animal. Thus, things that are not the same are represented in the proposition as being the same, which is false.

[n. 32] Scotus admits that this is difficult to resolve, but repeats his argument from analogy: the written sentence, 'man is an animal,' is not false even though the utterance 'man' is not the utterance 'animal.' The utterances are joined first because they are signified first, but that is not what the proposition asserts.

[n. 33] Thus, the spoken assertion, 'man is an animal,' signifies the composition not of species or utterances, but of things.

[n. 34] Next, Scotus replies to the argument about the syllogism in n. 18 above, arguing that the *suppositum* of a term in a perfect syllogism must be understood with respect to its ultimate significate, which is "the thing as it is considered by reason." This is the first mention of the view in the second determination that names signify things as they are considered or understood by the mind, although it occurs here where the first view, viz., that a name is the sign of a sign of a thing, is still being considered.

[n. 35] The next four sections reply to the three arguments of n. 19 showing that names do not signify species, that is, the argument from analogy (n. 36), the argument from the distinction between what exists and that by which it exists (n. 37), and the argument from infinite regress (n. 38). Each reply is based on the idea mentioned here, in n. 35, that the species is understood not primarily or in the first instance, but "by reflection [*per reflectionem*]."

---

17. 'Denote' is not quite right for the Latin *denotare*, which has psychological and epistemic connotations missing from the modern sense of 'denote.' The psychological side of the Latin meaning would be closer to the English word 'notify.'

[n. 36] In reply to the first argument, Scotus denies the analogy. Sense is not reflexive because it is a material or corporeal power and a material power cannot reflect on its own act. Understanding, however, is immaterial, and so there is no obstacle to its reflecting on itself and "going beyond" what it immediately cognizes.

[n. 37] In reply to the second argument, Scotus agrees that the species is different from what is cognized indirectly by it (that is, the ultimate object of understanding), yet the species is still something intelligible.

[n. 38] In reply to the third argument, Scotus argues that there is no infinite regress because the species of what is understood is not cognized through another species. Only what is primarily cognized by the understanding, namely the quiddity or 'what-it-is [*quod quid est*]' of a thing, produces a species in the understanding. According to the edition, he adds, somewhat puzzlingly, "All other things cognized by reflection and discursive thought are cognized by a proper species." Mss. L and R have *sine propria specie* ["without a proper species"], which makes more sense.

Second Determination of Question 2
Reply to the Arguments Proving That Names Signify Things

[n. 39] Scotus now begins the second determination of the question, viz., the view that a name signifies a thing as it is conceived by the understanding, that is, it signifies the essence of the thing signified by the definition, the primary object of our understanding. In other words, a thing is not signified as existing because it is not understood in this way; rather, it is signified as it is conceived by the understanding. This is the view of the Parisian Modists, who held that existence in reality and existence in the understanding share an unchanging common nature that simultaneously underlies the essence of reality, our understanding of it, and the signification of the language expressing that reality. According to the Modists, the grammar of a sentence reveals not just the structure of human language, but also the structure of thought and the external reality underlying it.

Although this was a Parisian view, it seems to have been known in England in the latter part of the thirteenth century. Peter of Cornwall, who was teaching in England at about the same time as Scotus, says that a name primarily signifies a thing, not absolutely but as it is apprehended, and that it is different to say 'a thing

Commentary: *Opus I*   183

as it is apprehended' and 'species of a thing.'¹⁸ An anonymous writer, probably English and writing in the 1280s, mentions the argument that when a man has been corrupted, the species corresponding to the man remains in the understanding, so the thing in reality is not the cause of truth, but the thing as understood. He also says that 'every man is an animal' is necessarily true, because even when no man exists, the intellectual species corresponding to the term 'man' remains in the understanding.¹⁹

    18. Peter of Cornwall, "*Omnis homo est*," in "Talking about What Is No More: Texts by Peter of Cornwall (?), Richard of Clive, Simon of Faversham, and Radulphus Brito," ed. Sten Ebbesen, *Cahiers de l'Institut du Moyen-Age grec et latin* 55 (1987): 150 (quoting ms. Worcester Q.13, 49va): "I say that if we call a concept (*intellectum*) the species or likeness of a thing, an utterance is not primarily a sign of that concept, and if it does signify this in any way, it is equivocal. Rather, primarily and principally it signifies a thing, yet it does not signify a thing absolutely, but as it is apprehended. And it is different to say, "thing as it is apprehended," and "species of a thing," because a species is in the soul through itself, and a thing is in the soul through a species, and not as though in a subject, but in external reality [Dico quod si vocamus intellectum speciem vel similitudem rei, quod vox non est primo modo signum illius intellectus, et si hoc significet aliquo modo hoc est aequivoce; sed primo et principaliter significat rem, non tamen significat rem simpliciter sed secundum quod apprehenditur. Et differt dicere "rem secundum quod apprehenditur" et "speciem rei," quia species est in anima per se ipsam, et res est in anima per speciem et non est in anima ut in subiecto, sed in re extra]."
    19. Anonymous sophisma in Caius 611/341, quoted in Lewry, "Oxford Condemnations," 268: "Again, it was argued as follows. He [the Master] supposed first that, according to Aristotle in *De anima*, species remain in the senses from sensible things; otherwise it would not be possible to recollect or remember. From this supposition he held that with a man corrupted, the species still remains in the intellect. He supposed further that a thing is not in any way the cause of truth except as it is understood. Then argue from these suppositions as follows: with the cause remaining, the effect remains, since the thing as it is understood always remains. Therefore, since a proposition is a sort of effect of reason, the same truth will always remain in speech [Item, arguebatur sic: Supponebat primo per Aristotelem in libro de Anima quod ab entibus sensibilibus manent species in sensu, aliter non contingit reminisci nec memorari. Ex ista suppositione habebat quod corrupto homine adhuc manet species hominis penes intellectum. Supponebat aliud, res non quocumque modo est causa veritatis, sed res [ut/unde] intellecta. Tunc ex istis suppositionibus argue sic: manente causa manet effectus; cum res secundum quod intellecta est semper manet, ergo cum propositio sit quidam effectus rationis, semper manebit eadem veritas in oratione]" (59ra; cf. Kilwardby, Erfurt ms. Amplon. Q.328: 8va). The author later rejects this reasoning, however, arguing that the sophism "Every man of necessity is an animal" is false because the truth of a proposition requires that its terms be measured by realities—they must really exist and agree with one another (ibid., 59ra): "The last point was replied to, and the supposition was denied. The truth of a proposition is caused by the fact that an understood thing is caused by a truly existing thing. For it does not suffice for the truth of a proposition that the extremes are commensurate, but that the extremes are really and truly beings, and that there is a consistency of the extremes with one another. And therefore just as before, since these conditions are by hypothesis lacking, the proposition 'a man is an animal' is false, given that no man exists [Ad ultimum respondebatur, et negatur ista suppositio, veritas in propositione causatur ex hoc quod res intellecta causatur ex vera entitate rei: non enim sufficit ad veritatem in propositione quod extrema mensurentur, sed quod realiter et vere extrema sint entia, et quod fuerit convenientia extremorum ad invicem. Et ideo sicut

184   *Opus I*

The extent to which Scotus agrees with the Modist view is not clear, but the positions he takes in many of the questions that follow seem to depend on it, especially his defence of the notion that a name can have the same signification even when the thing it signifies ceases to exist. For example in *Opus I*, q. 3, n. 13 below, he says that when the thing signified is destroyed, so is the sign. But, even though the thing as it exists is destroyed, it is not destroyed as it is understood; thus, the significate of the utterance is not destroyed.

Reply to the Main Arguments

[n. 40] Scotus claims, not quite convincingly, that when the authorities quoted above (nn. 2–8) talk about 'affection,' 'species,' or 'concept,' they mean 'thing as understood,' to contrast with 'thing as existing.'[20]

[n. 41] Scotus replies to the argument (n. 4) about composition and division. The composition in question is not of the species but of the things, and not as they exist but as they are understood. In the same way, the parts of a composition exist in the understanding as simples, that is, "as what is cognized in the one cognizing it [*ut cognitum in cognoscente*]"—which could be rendered more prosaically, 'as the thought exists in the thinker.' Thus, there are things in the intellect, not just species.

[n. 42] In reply to the argument that what is primarily signified is also primarily understood (n. 7), Scotus says that the thing is understood primarily, that is, the 'thing as existing,' whereas the species, or 'thing as understood,' is understood only reflexively, or by a further act in which this primary act is understood.

Scotus also replies to the argument that understanding and the understandable form a single composite that is "more truly [*verius*]" one than other composites. The argument comes from Averroes, in Book III of his commentary on Aristotle's *De anima*, where he says that the material intellect and understood intention form a tighter metaphysical unity than other composites of matter and form, presumably because the act of cognition involves receiving form without matter, unlike material changes where a substance is physically moved, augmented, or diminished.

In reply, Scotus directs his audience to his commentary on Porphyry's *Isagoge*

---

prius: cum istae conditiones per positionem deficiunt, ista propositio est falsa, 'Homo est animal,' posito quod nullus homo sit.]"

20. Cf. *Opus II.I* below (q. 1, n. 16).

or *Introduction* to Aristotle's *Categories*, where Scotus says that Averroes cannot be read as saying that the understanding and the understandable form a single composite, because then the essences of all sensible things (rather than their intelligible species or concept) would enter into its composition, and the intellect would become actually colored, warm, etc. Rather, the composite of understanding and the understandable is deemed more truly one because it can be understood reflexively, that is, the understanding can grasp that what it is doing is thinking about some sensible thing. The assumption seems to be that it could not do this if the latter act formed anything less (or more) than a unity.

[n. 43] Replying to the argument (n. 8) that the species is signified more than the thing, Scotus argues that the inference, 'nothing is understood except by a species; therefore, nothing is signified except by a species,' can be denied if we read the word 'by' causally. The point seems to be that Aristotelian causation has multiple senses, and the species figures differently in the acts of signifying and understanding, causing the one and being caused by the other. Thus, if a name signifies the thing as it is conceived by the understanding (the thesis of the second determination above), then the species is the efficient cause of the thing being signified, but not the formal or essential cause. Because the thing is signified as it is understood, an act of understanding must be presupposed, which provides the content or 'sine qua non' cause of the act of signification in Scotus's terminology.

[n. 44] Continuing his reply, Scotus adds that even if we grant that nothing is signified except by the species, then regardless of how we read the preposition 'by [*per*],' it does not follow that the species is signified in a way that would make Aristotle's maxim true (that is, "that on account of which each and every thing [exists] is greater"). That is because the latter references what Scotus calls "the efficient and univocal, per se and total, cause," which the species, understood merely as the efficient cause of signification, is not. Presumably, the "per se and total" cause of something would invoke all of the various agencies that bring it into existence, not just its immediate predecessor in a chain of efficient causes.

Returning to the Question

[n. 45] Of the two views that names signify species or things, Scotus says that he will choose "what seems more probable." In this context, the Latin *probabilis* has the sense of 'plausible' or 'readily believable.' Next are a series of doubts (nn. 46–51) about the two determinations.

[n. 46] Scotus says that on behalf of the first view (that a species is immediately signified), we have the authorities, and in particular the argument about the truth and falsity of propositions (the edition refers us to nn. 4 and 26–27). This is confusing. In n. 4 we have the argument that the proposition is a composition in the understanding, and not in reality. But nn. 27–28 are not consistent with this view, since it is argued there that "every truth of any proposition must be related to things because it is things rather than signs that are the ultimate significates" and that "truth is only to be judged as belonging to the ultimate significates, which are things." Moreover, in his comment on the second view (n. 41), Scotus argues that there is composition not of the species themselves but of the things, although not as existing but as understood. So it appears that neither the first nor the second view is consistent with n. 4, and both apparently agree with each other that the composition signified by a proposition is of things, not species.

[n. 47] Arguing for the second view (that a thing is signified as understood) there is the reasoning "that a thing is understood in time and nature prior to its species being understood reflexively." If this is correct, then every understanding of a species will depend on some prior understanding of a thing.

[n. 48] Against both views, Scotus mentions the problem of singulars (for example, Socrates or Plato). This is more of a problem for the view that the species is immediately signified by a name, as opposed to the thing, because singulars do not immediately produce species in the intellect, as there are no intelligible species of singulars per se. This goes back to the Aristotelian principle that sensation is of singulars, whereas understanding is of universals.

[n. 49] Scotus notes that the same argument from singulars (n. 48) can be made regarding imaginary entities as well, since they are singular in the relevant sense, being metaphysically particular or not common to many. In Aristotelian psychology, the faculty of imagination belongs to the sensory part of the soul, which means that its objects are generated by a power that trades in singulars: the chimera or golden mountain that I imagine is always a particular chimera or a particular golden mountain.

[n. 50] Finally, a further argument against 'the second way,' that is, the view that the species is immediately signified by the name, is that if a name only signifies something as it is understood, no proposition in which we say that some attribute or property really inheres in a subject would be true. That is because it is, for example, the quality 'white,' not our understanding of the quality 'white,' that really inheres in Socrates if 'Socrates is white' is true. Thus, the second way cannot easily avoid the fallacy of accident (treating something accidental as essential and vice versa) in syllogistic arguments involving both real and intentional predicates.

[n. 51] Coming down squarely on the fence, Scotus tells us that the first way is more plausible according to the authorities, although the second is more plausible according to reason.

[Question 3. Does a Change Occur in the Signification of an Utterance Given That a Change Has Occurred in the Thing Signified?]

Summary

The question begins with four arguments (nn. 1–4) in support of the thesis that substantial change in the thing signified causes a change in the signification of the utterance, and five arguments (nn. 5–9) against.

Scotus's determination, expressed by the neutral *dicitur* ["it is said"], is that no change will occur in the signification of the utterance. This follows from the position introduced in q. 2 above: a thing is not signified as it exists, but as it is understood. Thus, we have the same understanding of it whether it exists or not.

Unhelpfully, Scotus uses the same term (*transmutatio*) to refer to both change in the thing and change in the utterance. But where the thing is concerned, it is clear that he must mean substantial change because merely accidental change (movement, growth, decay, etc.) would not raise the question of whether the same substance is signified by the name. Socrates is a man both before and after changing his cloak, walking to the Piraeus, getting a haircut, and so on. In addition, Averroes specifies that he is talking about substantial change in the authoritative passage quoted in n. 2. Scotus accepts this without comment in his reply at n. 12.

Scotus replies to the four arguments for the thesis (nn. 11–17), and adds a further objection (n. 18) and its solution (n. 19).

Discussion

The question corresponds to *Opus II.I*, q. 2: "Does a name signify a thing univocally when the thing is existing and when it is not?" Beginning and ceasing to be, of course, is what is meant by substantial change in the sublunary realm.

Scotus's treatment of the question has some affinity with the treatment by an anonymous author writing in Paris, probably in the 1270s, who asks whether the signification of a term "falls away" if the thing it signifies is corrupted.[21] Closer to Oxford in the 1290s, an anonymous sophisma in Caius 611, probably written in the early part of that decade, discusses the question of whether, if a man is destroyed, the species of man remains in the understanding, saying that some argue that it does because a thing or reality remains as it is understood.[22]

The question is also discussed by Radulphus Brito in the early fourteenth century in his *Questions on the Perihermenias*[23] and somewhat later by William of Ockham.[24]

Commentary
Arguments That a Change in Signification Does Occur

In nn. 1–4, Scotus presents arguments for the thesis that a change in signification accompanies a substantial change in the thing signified.

The first argument is from the authority of Boethius, who says that if no thing *is* the subject of an utterance, it is not significative. Scotus's reply to this depends on the interpretation of the emphasized '*is*.'

[n. 2] The second argument is from the authority of Averroes: in a substantial change, the definition of something is changed; hence, the name with the original definition that signified it before no longer does so.

There is a corresponding argument in *Opus II.I*, q. 2, n. 2.

[n. 3] The third argument is from the authority of Aristotle. A correlative is an object that, when so designated, must be related to another object in some way; thus, we only call a person a slave when someone is their master. But the sign and thing signified are correlatives: when the latter ceases to exist, so does the former insofar as it is called a sign. In the same way, a slave is no longer a slave once freed,

---

21. See *Utrum rebus corruptis termini cadant a suis significationibus* [Whether once the things (falling under terms) destroyed, the terms fall away from their signification], NL 16135, 54va–55ra (*César et le Phénix*, 187–91).
22. See Anonymous sophisma in Caius 611/341, f. 59ra, quoted at note 19 above.
23. Radulphus Brito, *Quaestiones in Perihermenias*, in *Questiones subtilissimae Magistri Rodulphi Britonis super arte veteri* (ed. Vercellensis & Vercellensis; Venice: 1499).
24. William of Ockham, *'Quodlibetal Questions' Vols. 1–2, Quodlibets 1–7*, trans. Alfred Freddoso and Francis Kelly (New Haven, Conn.: Yale University Press, 1991), V.16 (454): "Utrum cadente re cadat vox a suo significato."

and the master is no longer his master. As Aristotle puts it in the *Categories*, "relatives are related in such a way that when one is posited, so is the other, and when one perishes, so does the other."

A similar point is made by the anonymous Parisian author mentioned above,[25] who says that sign and signified are called correlative at least *qua* sign and signified. But an utterance is a sign of an understanding in the soul, and an understanding is a sign of an external reality, so that with the external reality destroyed, the understanding and the utterance are destroyed *qua* signs.[26]

[n. 4] The fourth argument consists of two syllogisms:

P$_1$—What is not understood is not signified (*maior principalis*);
P$_2$—Non-being is not understood;
C$_1$—Non-being is not signified.

The proof of the minor premise involves a second syllogism:

P$_1$—Everything capable of being understood produces a species in the intellect;
P$_2$—A non-being does not produce a species in the intellect;
C$_2$—A non-being is not capable of being understood.

There is a further argument to prove the second minor: when a cause is destroyed, so is the effect; but the thing signified causes the species; therefore, when the thing is destroyed, so is the species. Also (repeating the earlier argument about correlatives), when the thing signified is destroyed, so is the sign.

Arguments on the Opposing Side

The five arguments in nn. 5–9 are marshaled against the thesis that substantial change causes a change in signification.

[n. 5] The first argument invokes the authority of Aristotle. The same sentence (*oratio*) can be true or false; therefore, what is signified by the sentence is the same in either case. Note that this argument is not valid without further prem-

---

25. NL 16135, f. 54.
26. See also Roger Bacon, *De signis*, in "An Unedited Part of Roger Bacon's *Opus maius*: '*De signis*,'" eds. Karin Fredborg, Lauge Nielsen, and Jan Pinborg, *Traditio* 34 (1978): n. 146 (128); Bacon, *Compendium studii theologii*, in *Roger Bacon, Compendium of the Study of Theology*, ed. and trans. Thomas Maloney (Leiden: Brill, 1988), c. 5, n. 114 (100).

ises—presumably when the sentence is false it has to signify the same thing that was the case when it was true—otherwise it could not be false. But the state of affairs signified when the sentence is true is changed when it is false, for it has ceased to be the case.

[n. 6] The second argument is similar. Aristotle says that a statement about sitting remains the same as far as someone is sitting, but becomes false (though still significative) when the person moves. The statements themselves remain unaltered in all respects; it is by alteration in the facts that they become false. Otherwise, sentences that signify states of affairs that sometimes exist and sometimes do not (for example, 'Socrates is sitting') would stop being significative when their states of affairs cease to exist. Then, when the state of affairs comes into existence again, the utterance would have meaning again. Perhaps this could happen many times.

Radulphus Brito makes a similar argument:[27] if an utterance did not signify the same when its significate is destroyed, we would have to impose a new meaning on utterances every time that which they signified was destroyed.

[n. 7] Another similar argument: unless a sentence signified the same thing as when it was true, it could not be false.

[n. 8] The fourth argument is that since we can meaningfully assert that 'Socrates exists' is false when Socrates does not exist, it is clear that the assertion has the same meaning when Socrates does exist. To signify a thing is to "establish an understanding" of it.

[n. 9] The fifth argument is that Aristotle says it is possible to signify and understand non-existent things, such as goat-stags, so we can know what the account or name signifies without knowing whether what it signifies actually exists.

Determination

[n. 10] Scotus's determination, neutrally expressed via *dicitur* ['it is said'] rather than *dico* ['I say'],[28] invokes a passage of Aristotle often cited by scholastic logicians, viz., his claim in the *Posterior Analytics* that it is possible to give proofs and demonstrations of things that do not always exist, or exist only from time to time,

---

27. Radulphus Brito, "*Utrum vox significet idem re existente et non existente, quod sic*," in *Quaestiones super arte veteri* (ed. Vercellensis & Vercellensis; Venice: 1499).

28. This might indicate that Scotus is simply agreeing with the consensus view in his determination.

such as eclipses. Scotus argues that this is the case because a thing is not signified as it exists, but as it is understood. This clearly seems to be a consequence of the essentialist view introduced in q. 2 above.

Radulphus Brito makes the same argument in his questions on the *Perihermenias*, viz., that the significate of an utterance does not exist absolutely, but as it is signified. Thus, the significate as signified remains the same even if the object signified is destroyed. The significate has 'understood being.'[29] Writing a few decades earlier, Siger of Brabant says that when a thing ceases to exist, the understanding of it does not cease to exist.[30] It follows that signification relates to a thing as it is related to the understanding. When the thing ceases to exist, the understanding of it remains.

Replies to the Main Arguments

In nn. 11–14, Scotus replies to the main arguments for the thesis.

[n. 11] "To the first authority" refers to n. 1 above, the argument of Boethius that if no thing *is* signified by the utterance, the utterance is not said to be significative. Scotus replies that if the emphasized copula '*is*' is read as a 'third element,' that is, if it merely denies that the predicate 'is signified by *a*' applies to any thing, then of course it is true that *a* is not significative, that is, it signifies nothing or has no significance.

By implication, if the copula is read as a 'second element,' that is, if it means that when the thing signified does not exist, then the utterance is not significative, then it is false. Boethius of Dacia, who also mentions [Severinus] Boethius in this context, says exactly this: "If [the copula] is predicated as a second element then [Severinus] Boethius's statement is false, as though its meaning were: 'if the thing is not a thing, the utterance stops being significative,' as is commonly said."[31]

---

29. Radulphus Brito, "*Utrum vox significet idem re existente et non existente, quod sic,*" in *Quaestiones super arte veteri* (ed. Vercellensis & Vercellensis; Venice: 1499).

30. Siger of Brabant, "*Utrum nomen idem significet et univoce re existente et non existente,*" from Questions on Aristotle's Metaphysics, in *Siger de Brabant, Questions sur la Métaphysique*, ed. Cornelio Graiff (Louvain: Éditions de l'Institut Supérieur de Philosophie, 1948), 224–48.

31. Boethius of Dacia, sophisma: "*Utrum rebus corruptis necesse sit terminos cadere a suis significatis* [Whether, with the things [falling under a term] destroyed, it is necessary that the terms fall from their significates]," in the sophisma, "Every Man Is of Necessity an Animal," in Martin Grabmann, "Des 12 und 13 Jahrhunderts mit Textausgabe eines Sophisma des Boethius von Dacien," *Beiträge zur Geschichte der Philosophie und Theologie des Mittelalters* 36, no. 1 (1940): 90.

[n. 12] Scotus's reply to the second main argument of n. 2 above is to distinguish between the significate of a common name and a *suppositum* or individual falling under it. Thus, when some individual of a species is transformed or corrupted so that it no longer belongs to that species, it does not follow that the name of the species thereby loses its significate, because the common name does not signify any particular individual.

[n. 13] His reply to the third argument (see n. 3 above) is that if the significate is destroyed, so is the sign. But when a thing as it exists is destroyed, it is not destroyed as it is understood. Therefore, the significate is not destroyed.

Our anonymous Parisian author replies in a similar way: when the thing signified is destroyed *qua* thing signified, so is the sign *qua* sign. But the existing thing is not signified because it exists, but rather because the thing had impressed a species in the soul, and under this aspect the sign is not destroyed.[32]

[n. 14] Scotus's reply to the fourth argument (n. 4 above) is to deny the first major premise, that is, the assumption that "signifying presupposes understanding," from which it follows that what is not understood is not signified. Signifying presupposes understanding in the sense that in order to impose a name, we have to understand what it would mean. But once it has been imposed, it can continue to signify in the same way, even when the thing it signifies has been destroyed.

To this, our anonymous Parisian author replies that there are two sorts of cause: extrinsic and intrinsic. An extrinsic cause is only the cause of something coming into existence, and not the cause of continuing to exist. An intrinsic cause maintains something in existence. The argument is true only of an intrinsic cause, not an extrinsic one. But species in the soul have an extrinsic cause only, since Aristotle says[33] that when the sensible object has gone away, the species remains in the soul.[34] See also Scotus's argument at n. 16 below.

---

32. "*Omnis homo de necessitate est animal,*" NL 16135, f. 52vb–62vb, 61ra (206): "To the second it must be said that it is certainly true that 'when the significate is corrupted qua significate the sign is also corrupted qua sign,' but an existing thing was not signified because it is existing, but because the thing had impressed a species on the soul through the medium of the senses joined to it, and under this aspect its sign is not corrupted [Ad secundum dicendum quod bene verum est quod 'corrupto significato inquantum significatum et corrumpitur signum in quantum signum est,' sed res existens non erat significata quia existens, sed quia res impresserat apud animam speciem mediante adiuncto sensuum et sub hac ratione non corrumpitur eius signum]." Note that the collection of texts in NL 16135 covers at least two periods, and probably several authors were in fact involved.

33. See Aristotle, *De an.* III.2.425b25.

34. "*Omnis homo de necessitate est animal,*" NL 16135, f. 52vb–62vb, 61ra (206): "To the first we say: when you say that 'when the cause is corrupted what is caused, by it is corrupted,' it must be said that

[n. 15] Scotus next argues against the minor premise of the same argument (that non-being is not understood), appealing to Aristotle in *Posterior Analytics* (see n. 9 above), who says it is possible to understand non-beings. Furthermore, the proof of the minor premise is defective. Its major premise (that everything capable of being understood produces a species in the intellect) is false, in that it is true only of the primary object of understanding. So also the minor (that a non-being does not produce a species in the intellect) is false, because a non-being can be understood through a species that it previously produced in the understanding, and which can remain the same after the thing has been destroyed.[35]

[n. 16] Furthermore, replying to the argument (of n. 4) that the species cannot exist when the cause is destroyed, Scotus argues this is only regarding the 'cause in being,' and not the 'cause in becoming.' In other words, the initial cause of something does not have to continue to exist in order for the effect to continue to exist, and this applies to an intelligible species, as he argued above. To impose a name upon a kind of thing (for example, an extinct animal such as a dodo), we must understand what that kind of thing is, which requires the existence of that kind of thing. But the species can perish without the meaning of the name perishing.

[n. 17] Continuing his reply to the fourth argument that "when the significate is destroyed, so is the sign," he repeats the argument made in n. 13 that the thing as it exists is not what is signified by an intelligible species in the soul, but rather, the thing insofar as it is understood. In that sense, it is not destroyed.

A Further Objection and Its Solution

[n. 18] An objection to this solution to the question is that if an utterance signifies the same with the thing existing and non-existing, then what is signified is

---

the cause has two aspects: one extrinsic, and this is a cause of becoming only and not of conserving <the effect in being>; and another intrinsic, and this is a cause of being and of conserving <what is caused in being>. The major is true regarding the latter. It is not true regarding the former because Aristotle says that 'after sensible things have gone away, <their> species still remain in the soul' [Ad primum dicimus: cum dicas quod 'corrupta causa corrumpitur quod ab ea causatur,' dicendum quod duplex est causa, quaedam extrinseca, et est causa fiendi tantum et non conservandi, quaedam intrinseca, et est causa essendi et conservandi; et de ista ultima vera est maior. De prima non est verum, quia dicit [61rb] Aristoteles quod 'abeuntibus sensibilibus adhuc remanet species in anima']."

35. The further question of how this applies to non-beings that never existed is not addressed here; perhaps Scotus's point is simply to question the validity of the general assumption that it is not possible to understand non-beings.

the same. The argument appeals to the logical equivalence of active and passive expressions of the same action, for example, 'Tom hits John' and 'John is hit by Tom.' What is signified is the same in both cases.

[n. 19] Scotus replies to this objection by simply pointing out that because what is signified is the thing as it is understood, the thing's real existence or non-existence is irrelevant to the meaning of the utterance.

[Question 4. Does Aristotle Designate a Proper Difference between Inscriptions and Utterances, and Affections and Things?]

Summary

The question begins with four arguments (nn. 1–4) against the proposition that there is a proper difference, followed by one argument (n. 5) on the opposing side. The determination (n. 6) is that the difference is proper. The reply to the first argument is in n. 7, which gives rise to an objection (n. 8) and its reply (n. 9). The three replies to the main arguments (nn. 2–4) are given in nn. 10–12.

Commentary

Arguments against the Question

[n. 1] The first argument is that the distinction is not a good one. If affections are the same for all, and if the process by which affections lead to cognitions of things is also the same, then all things would be equally known to everyone.

[n. 2] Scotus's second argument, "some things are for some that are not for others, nor are they the same in number or species," refers to the fact that the things that correspond to certain affections may not be the same for all. For example, the particular dog(s) on which my concept of dog is based may vary greatly from those underlying your concept of dog; and likewise for the species underlying each person's generic concept of 'animal.'

[n. 3] The third argument is that inscriptions and utterances are naturally the same for all, which is an odd thing to say unless Scotus is thinking of Adamitic language, that is, human language before it became divided after the Tower of Babel. Thus, God ordained that human spoken and written language be naturally significative, but human pride intervened and conventionalized all except mental discourse.

[n. 4] The fourth argument looks to be a development of n. 3 rather than a separate argument. In any case, it contends that what is natural is the same for everyone, but a significant utterance is a natural sign. Proof of the latter: the power of expressing ourselves is natural. But there must also be a natural instrument of this power, namely language. Therefore, language signifies naturally. In the context of the Babel story, the natural instrument of expression was damaged during the construction of the Tower, leaving humankind to fashion its own conventional instruments.

Argument on the Opposing Side

[n. 5] On the opposing side is Aristotle, who is of course responsible for the distinction.

Determination

[n. 6] Scotus replies that Aristotle's distinction is appropriate because ideas or affections are the same in everyone insofar as they represent the same thing.

Scotus does not address the difficulty of explaining what a representation is. His later discussion of representation (see *Opus II.I*, q. 1, n. 23 below) is about statues, where a comparison can be made between a statue of someone and the person represented, since both are visible to many observers. The philosophical problem of how an essentially private object in the mind of one observer can be compared with the real object by another observer is not addressed here.

However, inscriptions and utterances do not represent the same thing. As Scotus says, "inscriptions and utterances in themselves are not the same for all insofar as they are signs because the same inscription does not represent the same utterance for all, but either another or none at all." He means that (i) an inscription in a foreign language can represent a different utterance for a speaker of that language than it does for us—think of how the written word 'also' represents a different utterance in German than in English, or the same *kanji* symbol represents different sounds for Chinese than for Japanese. Or (ii) the same inscription may not represent any utterance for all. For example, some *kanji* have no equivalents in the different spoken languages.

Replies to the Main Arguments

[n. 7] In connection with the first argument (n. 1), Scotus interjects another argument: it could be said that simple ideas are the same for everyone, but the compositions of simple ideas are different, citing Aristotle.[36] People may be deceived about the quiddity or essence of a thing in the way they combine it with something else.

[n. 8] Scotus replies that this is false, since many people apprehend simple ideas not apprehended by others at all. The passage cited from Aristotle is not relevant, for he says in *Metaphysics* IX that we either understand quiddity completely, or not at all. If the latter, there is no deception, since deception implies that something has been cognized.

[n. 9] Continuing, Scotus says that the correct reply is that ideas, or "affections," are not the same in everyone per se, but only insofar as they are signs of things.

Note Scotus's remark: "Affections are not the same for all in themselves, but insofar as they are signs of things. For every affection that is the same in itself always represents the same thing in whomever's mind it was." This seems inconsistent, for he says in the first sentence that all affections are not the same in themselves, but then logically implies in the second that they are in fact the same. Perhaps there is a distinction being assumed here between representing (inside the mind, to the person conceiving it) and signifying (outside the mind, via utterances).

[n. 10] To the second argument (n. 2), which was that people regard different things in different ways, he replies, "a thing insofar as it is signified by an affection is the same for all." But here we have what looks to be another inconsistency, as the criterion of sameness Scotus used in the determination (n. 6) is that ideas x and y are the same, or alike, when they represent the same thing. But here, the criterion of sameness for a thing is that it is signified by the same idea or affection.

[n. 11] To the third argument (n. 3), he replies that different tokens of the same inscription (when used for different utterances) are not the same, in the sense that they are not signs of the same utterance. Signs are made by imposition, which is different for different people.

[n. 12] To the fourth argument (n. 4), Scotus replies that the natural instrument of the power of interpretation is not the significant utterance, which is the product of interpretation, but the throat and lungs, or that by which it is produced. In the same way, clothing and weapons are only instruments in a secondary sense, as products of man's natural ingenuity.

---

36. The edition mistakenly gives the Aristotle reference here as 430a26–28 and 431b16–18.

Questions 5–8. Summary Outline

These four questions involve an extended discussion of the signification of common terms and proper terms that have no existing significate or supposit: q. 5 concerns whether a term can signify in the same sense ('univocally') both existing and non-existing things, q. 6 asks whether a term can stand for any things apart from ones that exist, q. 7 asks whether terms correctly predicated only of existing things ('man') can also truly be predicated of non-existing things ('Caesar is a man'), and q. 8 concerns whether propositions with an identical predicate and subject ('Caesar is Caesar') are true when the subject does not exist.

[Question 5. Is a Common Term Said Univocally of Existing Things and Non-Existing Things?]

Summary

This question begins with three arguments (nn. 1–3) against the thesis that a common term can be predicated in the same sense ('univocally') of both existing and non-existing things, followed by three arguments (nn. 4–6) for the thesis. Scotus's determination (nn. 6–8) is in favor of the thesis, that is, a common term is predicated in the same sense of both existing and non-existing things.

There are two replies to the arguments against. The first is at nn. 81–86, after the replies to the arguments of the eighth question; the second is at nn. 89–91.

Discussion

The general history of the problem is obscure. According to Roger Bacon, the controversies over whether the proposition 'a man is animal' is true when no man exists and whether 'Caesar is a man' is true given that Caesar is dead, arose around the same time.[37] Bacon says that Richard Rufus of Cornwall was the first to claim, during his lectures on the *Sentences* at Oxford in 1250, that 'man' could be predicated univocally of Christ during the *Triduum*, that is, the three days his body was in the tomb prior to his resurrection.[38] However, Landgraf has shown

---

37. Roger Bacon, *Compendium studii theologii*, 87.
38. Ibid., 88.

this is not so.[39] In any case, the question became especially controversial at both Oxford and Paris during the second half of the thirteenth century. Bacon also says that the majority still held Richard's views in the 1290s, and that there was much discussion of the question at Oxford at this time, which happens to be when Scotus would have been a student there. For further discussion of the signification of empty proper names such as 'Caesar,' see the commentary on q. 7 below.

Roger Bacon discusses a question similar to this, giving nine arguments (nn. 88–96) on behalf of the thesis that a name cannot signify anything 'univocal' that is common to a being and a non-being.[40]

However, it is noteworthy that Scotus does not mention Bacon's view here, and none of the arguments that he discusses are found in Bacon; nor, conversely, are any of the arguments found in Bacon mentioned directly by Scotus.[41]

Commentary

"Therefore, a name is a spoken sound." The lemma is from the opening line of *De interpretatione* II.16a19-20: "A name is a spoken sound significant by convention, without time, none of whose parts is significant separately."

Arguments against

[n. 1] The first three sections (nn. 1–3) argue against the position that a name is predicated univocally, or said in the same sense, of a being and a non-being. The first argument (n. 1) is that anything said in one sense of an inferior is said in the

---

39. A. M. Landgraf, "Das Problem *Utrum Christus fuerit homo in triduo mortis* in der Frühscholastik," in *Mélanges Auguste Pelzer. Études d'histoire littéraire et doctrinale de la scolastique médiévale offertes à Mgr Auguste Pelzer, scriptor de la bibliothèque Vaticane, à l'occasion de son soixante-dixième anniversaire* (Louvain: éditions de l'Institut supérieur de philosophie, 1947).

40. Roger Bacon, *Compendium studii theologii*, 88. This work is usually dated to the 1290s. Bacon also discusses the question in his *Sumulae dialectices* (c. 1252) and *De signis*. For an analysis of Bacon's semantics, see H. A. G. Braakhuis, "The Views of William of Sherwood on Some Semantical Topics and Their Relation to Those of Roger Bacon," *Vivarium* 15 (1977): 111–42, which compares theories presented in William of Sherwood's *Introductiones in logicam* and *Syncategoremata* with Bacon's *Sumulae dialectices* and *Compendium studii theologii*.

41. But see the third argument in n. 3 below. See also "*Omnis homo de necessitate est animal*" (NL 16135, ff. 52vb–62vb), especially the question, "*Utrum terminus sit aequivoce nomen praesentium et non praesentium*" (55vb; 193); Porphyry, *Isagoge* 2; and Robert Kilwardby, *Omnis Phoenix est* (Erfurt Q 328: f. 20a), cited in H. A. G. Braakhuis, "Kilwardby versus Bacon? The Contribution to the Discussion on Univocal Signification of Beings and Non-Beings Found in a *Sophisma* attributed to Rober Kilwardby," in *Medieval Semantics and Metaphysics. Studies dedicated to L. M. De Rijk*, ed. E. P. Bos (Nijmegen: Ingenium, 1985), 127.

same sense of a superior: for example, if 'animal' is predicated in the same sense of Socrates and Aristotle, then it is predicated in the same sense of those two men. Conversely, if a term is not predicated in a certain sense of a superior, it is not predicated in that sense of an inferior. But 'being' belongs to a superior category than 'animal,' and 'being' is predicated in a different sense of existing and non-existing things because the latter are non-beings, or beings in potentiality.

[n. 2] The second argument is that univocal predication is essential predication and the truest form of essential predication made with the verb 'is.' But this kind of predication cannot be applied to non-existing individuals. No support for the argument is given, but it is one of two arguments (the other being the first main argument against q. 6 at n. 12 below) where Scotus says that he will "show later" how nothing common can be predicated of non-existing supposits. The edition refers in both cases to n. 88, which is an alternative reply to the argument: viz., predication cannot be made with the verb 'is' in the present tense, though it can be made with the verb in the past tense (for past individuals who no longer exist) or with the verb in the future tense (for future individuals who do not yet exist). But we are not convinced that Scotus is referring to n. 88 here.

[n. 3] The third argument is that no univocal expression is common to being and non-being, which is clear from the topic of 'greater to less.' A 'topic' (called a *locus* in scholastic Latin) is a principle of reasoning to which the dialectician can appeal. Boethius calls it "the seat of an argument, or that from which one draws an argument appropriate to the question under consideration."[42] The topic 'from greater to less' applies when one thing exceeds another in power or scope. It is said to hold destructively (*destructive*): that is, if there is nothing in common to all beings that is univocal, then there is nothing in common to all expressions that is univocal, because beings exceed expressions in scope. The logician John Buridan (c. 1300–1361) provides another example, based on power: "The king cannot take this castle; therefore, neither can the count."[43]

---

42. Boethius, *De topiciis differentiis*, ed. Eleonore Stump (Ithaca, N.Y.: Cornell University Press, 1978), I:1174D (30).

43. John Buridan, *Summulae de dialectica*, trans. Gyula Klima (New Haven, Conn.: Yale University Press, 2001), 6.5.6 (472); for the topic *a maiori*, see Boethius, *De topiciis differentiis* II:1191A (55). Cf. Aristotle, *Physics* IV.8.215b19–20; Roger Bacon, *Compendium studii theologii* 4, n. 89 (88); "*Omnis homo de necessitate est animal*" (NL 16135, f. 11rb–12vb [26]); "*Caesar est homo, ipso mortuo*," q. 4 in "*Album fuit disputaturum*" (NL 16135, 12rb, in *César et le Phénix*). Scotus does not mention the passages in Aristotle's *Metaphysics* (II.987b6 or III.999a6–8) cited by some authors, including Bacon. See also q. 21 of

Arguments for

[n. 4] Next are three arguments (nn. 4–6) for the proposition. First, the same term is predicated univocally when it has the same definition: as Aristotle says, "things having a name in common and the same definition of substance corresponding to that name are called univocals" (*Categories* 1.1a6–7). But it is predicated of non-existing things according to the same definition; therefore, it is predicated univocally.⁴⁴

[n. 5] The second argument is that what signifies beyond any *differentia* of time "is not determined with respect to the *supposita* of any time," meaning that its past, present, and future significations are not relevant or not determinately of any specific time. But a common term belongs to a specific time. This argument was used by other writers to justify natural supposition—the view that the signification of a noun does not include tense or time—in view of Aristotle's belief that a noun "signifies without time" that time or tense is signified by the verb alone (*De interpretatione* I.1.16a20, 16b5–6).⁴⁵ For example, Nicholas of Paris, probably writing in the middle of the thirteenth century, says in his *Syncategoremata* that although the subject term cannot be restricted, it is a noun and it is a property of nouns to signify neutrally (*in quiete*) and without time.⁴⁶

But perhaps Scotus intends to contrast a common term with a 'discrete' term

---

Siger of Brabant's *Commentary on the Metaphysics* (224–28): "Whether a name signifies the same with the thing [signified] existing or not existing"; and Radulphus Brito, *Perihermenias*, "Whether an utterance signifies the same with the thing [it denotes] existing or [vel//et] not existing," third argument, in *Quaestiones super arte veteri* (ed. Vercellensis & Vercellensis; Venice: 1499).

44. There seems a simple objection to this, however, since the definition of the existing thing would *not* be the same as the non-existing thing, as though the non-existing thing could even have a definition. See "*Omnis homo est*" (NL 16135, f. 49vb [147]): "What can be understood can be signified. But one term—according to the reason and species of a name—can be understood to be ampliated indifferently for present, past, and future entities. Therefore it can also be understood to signify this [Quod contingit intelligere contingit significare'; sed contingit unum terminum secundum rationem et speciem nominis intelligere indifferenter ampliari pro praesentibus, praeteritis et futuris entibus, ergo et hoc contingit significare]."

45. See ibid.: "Does a term from its natural supposition supposit for existing things alone, or indifferently for things present, past and future?"

46. See H. A. G. Braakhuis, *De 13de eeuwse Tractaten over syncategorematische Termen: Uitgave van Nicolaas van Parijs' sincategoreumata*, 2 vols. (Meppel: Krips Repro, 1979), 2:31–35 [hereafter "*Syncategoremata*"]: "If in the subject, this cannot be, for the subject is a name, but it is a property of a name to signify at rest and without time [Si in subiecto: hoc non potest esse, quia subiectum nomen est, sed est proprium nominis significare in quiete et sine tempore]."

suppositing for something absolutely discrete (for example, Socrates or *that man there*)?[47] Geoffrey of Aspall says that common and discrete terms are imposed to represent their significates in different ways.[48] A common term is imposed 'beyond any *differentia*' of time, but a discrete term is imposed with respect to a particular time as long as the supposit and the significate are the same Geoffrey argues further that if the supposit and the significate are identical, the signification of a discrete term is destroyed when its referent is destroyed.[49]

[n. 6] The third argument is that accidental differences in the objects signified by a term do not make it equivocal, and temporal differences are accidental. In the logical terminology of the late thirteenth century, an 'aggregate [*aggregatum*]' is formed when one entity is joined with another that is less fundamental, such as when the fundamental significate Caesar is joined with existing-in-the-past. The argument is then that if 'Caesar' signified such an aggregate, it would signify it accidentally and not so as to place Caesar-existing-in-the-past in a different genus. Therefore, there is no equivocation when 'Caesar' is said of existing and non-existing things.

Determination

[n. 7] Scotus gives his determination of the question in nn. 7–8. The replies to the arguments are given later, after the replies to qq. 7–8 (nn. 81–91). He says that a term imposed to signify a single nature is predicated univocally.

[n. 8] This is for two reasons. First, the term has a single definition. This repeats the argument of n. 4 above: according to Aristotle, a name signifies the definition of the thing to which it applies. As he writes, "the formula [*ratio*] which the name signifies is the definition" (*Metaphysics* IV.7.1012a23–25).[50] Thus, if everything with the same nature has the same definition, the term signifying that nature must have the same definition, and hence the same signification.

---

47. See Ps.-Lambert of Auxerre on the properties of terms, in *Logica (Summa Lamberti)*, 209–10, translated in Kretzmann and Stump, *Cambridge Translations of Medieval Philosophical Texts*, 111.

48. Geoffrey's logical works are lost, but his views are mentioned in "*Dubitationes et notabilia circa guilelmi de shyreswode introductionum logicalium, tractatum V*" (Worcester Q.13, 59vb–62va, f. 62va).

49. See also the third condemned proposition of Kilwardby, and Scotus's distinction between supposit and significate at n. 8 of q. 9, below, saying that a common term primarily supposits for its *significatum* in every proposition, and does not supposit for a *suppositum* unless it is because the *suppositum* is the same as the *significatum*; otherwise, no universal [proposition] would be true.

50. See also Thomas Aquinas, *Summa Theologiae* I^a, q. 13, a. 1, co.: "Ratio enim quam significat nomen, est definitio."

Second, equivocation does not involve merely the diversity of supposits: the term 'man' is not equivocal merely because it applies to John, Tony, Gordon, and other men. To be equivocal is to apply to something in a different sense.[51]

[Question 6. Are There Any *Supposita* Belonging *Simpliciter* to a Common Term Signifying a True Nature, apart from Things That Exist?]

Summary

This question asks whether there are any *supposita* that belong absolutely to a common term signifying a 'true nature' other than existing ones. First there are three arguments (nn. 9–11) for the affirmative. The arguments against are found at nn. 12–14. Scotus gives his determination in nn. 43–44, following the main arguments of q. 8. The replies are at nn. 45–48.

Note that in Scotus's opening remark, "we ask, then, on account of its truth and in order to resolve the arguments," the pronoun 'its [*istius*]' probably refers to the proposition expressed in final sentence of the previous question, that is, "if [a common term] is said of all supposits absolutely, it follows that it is said of all supposits univocally."

Discussion

A common term is taken absolutely when it is not ampliated or restricted. Scotus says later (at n. 88 below) that *supposita* belong absolutely to a common term whenever they involve the same definition (*ratio*) of the term for any *differentia* of time. According to another view, common in the mid-thirteenth century,[52] a common term taken absolutely with a present-tense verb supposits only

---

51. See also "*Omnis homo de necessitate est animal*" (NL 16135, 55vb), discussing this same question: "Equivocation does not exist because of a small or a large number of supposita, but because of the significates alone [Nulla aequivocatio est per paucitatem vel pluralitatem suppositorum, sed significatorum solum]"; ibid., 58vb: "equivocation does not require diverse *supposita*, but rather diverse significates [aequivocatio non requirat diversa supposita sed diversa significata]." See also Thomas Aquinas, *Quaestio Disputata de Unione Verbi Incarnati* a. 2, ad 4, in *Thomas von Aquin, Quaestio disputata 'De unione Verbi incarnate' (Über die Union des fleischgewordenen Wortes)*, eds. Obenauer, Senner, and Bartocci (Stuttgart-Bad Cannstatt: Frommann-Holzboog, 2011), 58: "equivocation and univocation are considered according to signification and not *supposita* [aequivocatio et univocatio secundum significationem attenditur, et non secundum supposita]."

52. See "*Omnis homo de necessitate est animal*," NL 16135, 58vb (201).

for things existing in the present; thus, 'Caesar is a man' is false, but 'Caesar was a man' is true. See also q. 7 below.

Commentary

Arguments for

[n. 9] The first three arguments (nn. 9–11) support the view that there are non-existing *supposita*. The first argument (n. 9) depends on the definition of suppositing absolutely, or without qualification: "everything for which a term can supposit absolutely and verify a proposition is its *suppositum simpliciter*." '*Suppositum simpliciter*' in this context probably refers to natural supposition (see q. 5 above). The definition Scotus later gives of absolute supposition in n. 88 is consistent with the definition of natural supposition: the supposition that a term has when it is not restricted or ampliated when it applies to any thing(s) sharing the same *ratio*, definition, or aspect. The question of whether a term taken absolutely supposits indifferently for past and future (and hence non-existing) things as well as for presently existing ones, or only for presently existing ones, was frequently discussed in the *sophisma* literature of the mid-thirteenth century, which is the broader context of many of the questions here.[53]

Given this definition, Scotus argues that it is obvious that propositions such as 'a man was' or 'a man will be,' and especially 'a man can run,' are not true of existing things.

[n. 10] The second argument invokes Aristotle, who says that a universal term is that which is "naturally suited to be predicated of many." The claim is that nothing more is required for the common nature to be predicated of many (passively, as what is attributed to a subject) than for the supposit to participate in it (actively, as its subject).

[n. 11] The third argument anticipates Scotus's determination of the question at n. 43 below, where he says that the nature of the common or the *suppositum* is not attributed to a thing as it actually exists, but as it is conceived in the understanding. In the latter sense, it is indifferent to whether the thing actually exists or not. In this section, he is saying that the conception of the *suppositum* and the

---

53. See, e.g., "*Omnis homo est*," NL 16135, f. 49vb–52vb (145–85). De Libera also cites John le Page in "Les *Appellationes* de Jean le Page," *Archives d'histoire doctrinale et littéraire du Moyen Age* 51 (1984), II, n. 9 (228); Ps.-Lambert of Auxerre, *Summa* VIII, "De appellation" (*César et le Phénix*, 52–56). See also "*Album fuit disputaturum*," NL 16135, f. 13ra (52) and "*Omnis Phoenix est*," NL 16135, f. 14vb (52).

common term does not depend on the being of the thing, but on the consideration of the understanding. This is consistent with the position taken throughout the commentary that the signification of language does concern reality, albeit reality as conceived, which is independent of its actually existing or not. A further point is that the distinction between what is common to many things and the individual supposit is also a function of our understanding. Later (in n. 43), he argues that we conceive a nature in the understanding in the same way: both as predicable of many and as not predicable of many.

A passage in Scotus's *Ordinatio* helps to explain this: "Every inferior includes in itself something that is not included in the understanding of the superior; otherwise, the concept of the inferior would be just as common [that is, universal] as the concept of the superior."[54] Likewise, in the present passage, he says that there is an order according to superior and inferior as they are compared in the understanding.

Arguments against

[n. 12] In nn. 12–14, Scotus argues against the view that there are non-existing *supposita*. The first argument concedes that what is common belongs to the per se understanding of any supposit without qualification, and is thus predicated of it per se "in the first mode." However, it is not predicated of non-existing *supposita*, "as will be shown later." The edition mentions n. 88 below as a possible reference for 'later.' However, the view put forward in n. 88 is that there can be non-existing *supposita* belonging absolutely to a common term, although the common term cannot be predicated of them with the verb 'is.' For example, Caesar is an absolute *suppositum* of the name 'Caesar,' and it is true that Caesar was a man. But 'Caesar is a man' is not true. This is not the same as the present argument, which argues against the proposition that there can be non-existent *supposita* belonging absolutely to a common term.

When Scotus speaks of predication "per se in the first mode," he is tacitly referring to Aristotle's *Metaphysics* V.1022a25, which talks about the different modes

---

54. Duns Scotus, *Ordinatio* II, d. 3, q. 6: "Every inferior includes within itself something that is not included in the superior; otherwise, an inferior concept [would be] equally common as the superior concept [Omne inferius includit in se aliquid quod non includitur in intellectu superioris, alioquin conceptus inferioris esse aeque communis sicut conceptus superioris]."

of per se belonging.[55] What belongs to a thing per se in the first mode is the essence of that thing.

[n. 13] The second argument is obscure. The point is perhaps that if there is nothing—literally, no thing—particular for which the utterance can stand (for example, 'Caesar' cannot stand for Caesar the man because he is dead), then the utterance must stand for itself ("the utterance would be the *suppositum* of the utterance"). But this, says Scotus, "is obviously false," presumably because the utterance 'Caesar' is not a man, but an articulate spoken sound. The only other alternative would be for the utterance to stand for something "essentially the same as its common nature," call it 'humanity.' But that cannot be true either, because then a true nature ('humanity' or 'man') would be predicated of a non-being (Caesar), and non-beings are not essentially the same as their true natures.

Put this way, the argument looks mildly question-begging, since the issue is whether beings and non-beings can exist in some absolute sense by virtue of their true common nature. But Scotus may simply be reporting the argument of an opponent here.

[n. 14] The third argument is that if there were non-existing *supposita*, the rule of *dici de omni* ('being said of all') would require that all universal affirmative assertoric propositions be false whenever the predicate did not apply to non-existing *supposita*. This is also the first mention of the *dici de omni*, a logical principle used to demonstrate that a syllogism is conclusive.

John Buridan, writing a generation after Scotus, says that according to the principle of *dici de omni*], the predicate should "be true about the subject with respect to each of its *supposita*; thus it is necessary that of whatever term the subject is truly affirmed, of that also the predicate is truly affirmed."[56] Since 'man' in the proposition 'every man is rational' is a "common distributed term," this proposition would be false according to the third argument if just one of the individuals for which it stands, such as Caesar, does not exist. Since there is no shortage of men who no longer exist, this would falsify all universal assertoric propositions about man, or rather, human beings.

As for Scotus's claim that no *de inesse* (assertoric) proposition would be true, compare our anonymous thirteenth-century author, who says that no assertoric

---

55. See also Aristotle, *Anal. post.* I.4.
56. John Buridan, *Summulae* 5.1.2 (307).

'as of now' proposition would be true if the word 'man' in the proposition 'every man is white' were to supposit for existing and non-existing things, past and future.[57] Why not? Because in that case, the proposition would be 'every man who is, was, and will be, is white,' which is impossible. The same is true for 'every sheep is white.' An anonymous author mentions al-Ghazali saying that "being is the actuality of being."[58]

Scotus's argument here concerns the exposition of contingent propositions and in particular two ways of reading '*contingit esse P*' discussed in the *Prior Analytics*.[59] Thus, '*a contingit esse b*' could not be expounded as (i) '*a non est b*' and (ii) '*Possibile est a esse b*' because (i) is *de nunc* or 'as of now'; but such a proposition is not possible. The idea is that neither of the *exponentes* is possibly true, and so the proposition is not possible either.

[Question 7. Are the Propositions 'Caesar is a man' and 'Caesar is an animal' True When Caesar Does Not Exist?]

Summary

This question concerns whether terms truly predicated only of existing things ('man') can also be truly predicated of non-existing things ('Caesar'). Thus, is 'Caesar is a man' true?

There are six main arguments (nn. 15–20) that 'Caesar is a man' is false, followed by five arguments that it is true (nn. 21–29). The determination is given in nn. 49–50 and the replies in nn. 51–73 and 92–94.

Discussion

For a discussion of the history of the problem of empty common names, see the commentary on q. 5 above. The problem of empty proper names, such as

---

57. "*Omnis homo est*," NL 16135, ff. 49vb–52vb, 50va (156): "If a predicate could not restrict the subject to existing supposita, then no proposition would be true or necessary, and no universal assertoric affirmative as-now proposition [would be true], which is against Aristotle [Si praedicatum non possit subiectum restringere ad supposita entia, tunc nulla esset propositio vera et etiam necessaria [et] nulla propositio universalis affirmativa esset de inesse ut nunc quod est contra Aristotelem]."

58. Al-Ghazali, *Metaphysica*, in *Algazels's Metaphysics: A Medieval Translation*, trans. J. T. Muckle (Toronto: St. Michael's College, 1933), 1 (26) and 2 (52); "Logica" (Venetiis 1506, f. 2vb; cited in *César et le Phénix*).

59. Aristotle, *Anal. priora* I.13.32b23–37.

'Caesar,' probably occupied a similar place in the 1250s. However, Lambert of Lagny[60] mentions the 'Caesar' arguments, and the origin of the discussion may date from well before this. The examples 'Caesar is praised' and 'Caesar was a man' are given in *Summa Metenses* (1220–40),[61] and 'Caesar is a non-man' occurs as an example in the *Dialectica Monacensis*, probably dating from the late twelfth century.[62] 'Caesar' seems to have been the stock example in the Middle Ages for a deceased and therefore non-existent man, and 'Socrates' the example of a living, existent man (though both are, and were then, in fact, dead).

There were three main positions on the question in the thirteenth century:

1. 'Caesar is a man' has no truth value. 'Caesar' signifies nothing because Caesar is dead (or rather, 'Caesar' is now used in a different sense than when he was alive). If the name is used in the same sense as when Caesar was alive, it signifies nothing. The expression in which it occurs is not really a sentence or a proposition, nor does it signify what is true or false.[63] This implies that neither 'Caesar exists' nor 'Caesar does not exist' is true; likewise, neither 'Caesar was the Roman emperor' nor 'Caesar was a man' is true.[64]

2. 'Caesar is a man' is false, but 'Caesar was a man' is true. This was the most common position according to the anonymous author of NL 16135: "And

---

60. Previously identified with Lambert of Auxerre, the Dominican friar under whose name Lambert's work appeared. See Alain de Libera, "Le traité *De appellatione* de Lambert de Lagny (Lambert d'Auxerre)," *Archives d'histoire doctrinale et littéraire du Moyen Age* 48 (1982): 229–32.

61. L. M. de Rijk, *Logica Modernorum: A Contribution to the History of Early Terminist Logic*, 2 vols. (Assen: Van Gorcum, 1962 and 1967), II.i:460.

62. Ibid., II.ii:621–22.

63. Roger Bacon, *Compendium studii theologii*, c. 5, n. 123 (104, 112–15): "And because of this, the utterance 'Caesar is Caesar' will signify nothing: neither is it an expression nor [is it] a proposition nor does it signify either what is true or false, for the whole "statement" does not signify because of one or two [of its] parts that do not signify [Et propter hoc haec vox 'Caesar est Caesar' nihil significabit: nec est oratio nec propositio, nec verum vel falsum significat, quia ab una vel duabus partibus non significativis est totius sermo non significativus]."

64. Cf. "*Omnis homo de necessitate est animal*," NL 16135, f. 55ra: "Then 'Caesar exists' would not be true, nor 'Caesar does not exist,' nor 'Caesar was the Roman emperor'—and so would perish all knowledge of history—which is absurd [Tunc haec non esset vera 'Caesar est' nec ista 'Caesar non est' vel 'Caesar fuit imperator romanus' et si sic perisset omnis historiae scientia, quod est inconveniens]." Cf. also ibid., 52va (182–83): "Some say that ... with Caesar destroyed and with no man existing who is called by the name 'Caesar,' the term 'Caesar' is a non-significant term, and therefore it is neither true nor false if 'Caesar is a man' is uttered. But whether that is true, we shall not say now [Dicunt tamen quidam ... Caesare destructo et nullo homine existente qui vocetur hoc homine 'Caesar,' iste terminus 'Caesar' est terminus non significativus, et ideo non est vera nec falsa si dicatur 'Caesar est homo.' Utrum autem hoc sit verum non modo dicamus]."

almost all adhere to this position, which they derive from the rule of appellation: 'a common term suppositing with a verb of the present tense, taken *simpliciter*, not having a force of ampliation either from itself or another, nor restricted nor otherwise ampliated, supposits for things which actually exist, or for things existing in the present.'"[65] The rule is much older than this, however, dating back at least to the late twelfth century.[66]

3. 'Caesar is a man' is true. This is the position defended by Scotus. Some argue that it is true because it does not posit actual existence, or the existence of a composite of soul and body.[67] Others, such as Scotus here, invoke the distinction between 'being' used as a participle (that is, when 'being' is related to 'is' rather like 'running' is to 'runs'), and 'being' used as a noun. In the former sense, it implies real existence, and in this sense 'Caesar is a man' does not imply that Caesar exists. In the second sense, it merely signifies having a certain 'essence,' which does not imply real existence.[68]

Others argue that it is true because the 'is' in 'Caesar is a man' signifies tenselessly, meaning 'Caesar is or was or will be a man.'[69]

According to Roger Bacon,[70] the second and third positions arose from two serious errors, viz., (i) the assumption that an utterance can signify something common to being and non-being, and (ii) the idea that an utterance cannot lose its signification. Practically everyone is trapped "most obstinately" by these errors, he says, "so that they make up not only numberless errors but also heresies that are to be detested." He continues: "from ignorance of these two problems, the multitude holds that Caesar [when] dead is a man, that a dead man is an animal, and that Christ was a man during the *Triduum*, and infinitely many additional most false and foolish things." Writing in the 1290s, Bacon claims that the errors were first promoted in Oxford by Richard of Cornwall in the 1250s, and later spread to Paris when Richard read the *Sentences* of Peter Lombard there. He

---

65. NL 16135, f. 55ra, 52vb–62vb. On this view, see Peter of Cornwall, "*Omnis homo est*," (Worcester Q.13, q. 2). Peter says that the proposition is false, because presentness is signified by the verb. Thus 'Caesar was a man' is true, but not 'Caesar is a man.'

66. For example, it is mentioned in the "*Logica 'Cum sit nostra'*" (Rijk, *Logica Modernorum* II.ii:451).

67. "*Caesar est homo, ipso mortuo*," q. 4 (NL 16135, f. 11rb–12vb; 41).

68. See Scotus, n. 70 (below), for a similar objection, and similar reply.

69. Richard Clive, "*Quaestiones in libros metaphysicorum*" (in Ebbesen, "Talking about What Is No More," Worcester Q.13, 121ra).

70. Roger Bacon, *Compendium studii theologii*, c. 4 (85).

is incredulous that the multitudes have persisted in these errors for some forty years, and that this "infinite madness" has become powerful especially in Oxford, where it began.[71]

Interestingly, although Bacon was teaching in Oxford in the 1290s, when Scotus is thought to have been there, qq. 5–8 do not mention Bacon's view that the sentence has no truth value (position 1, above). Scotus inclines to the third view here, although in q. 12 below he appears to hold the opposite view.

Commentary

Arguments against

[n. 15] There are six main arguments given in nn. 15–20 against the view that 'Caesar is a man' is true.

The first is that being cannot be predicated of (a) being, but a man is a true being; therefore, it cannot be predicated of Caesar, since he does not exist.

[n. 16] The second argument invokes Aristotle, who says that we can infer '*a* is a man' from '*a* is a white man,' although not from '*a* is a dead man,' for that would involve 'opposition in the adjunct [*oppositio in adiecto*]' (*De interpretatione* I.11.21a19–24). Thus, if the 'is' in 'Caesar is a man' predicates being or existence, we can infer 'Caesar is,' that is, Caesar exists, because 'existing' and 'man' are not opposed in the way that 'dead' and 'man' are. But Caesar does not exist. Therefore 'Caesar is a man' is false.

When Scotus remarks, "the consequence holds from what is conjoined to what is divided," he means that there is no fallacy of division here. The fallacy of division is one of the six fallacies of words (*in dictione*) given by Aristotle in *De sophisticis elenchis* 4.165b23–166b27. It obtains when things taken together in the premises of an argument are taken separately in the conclusion.[72]

[n. 17] The third argument is that if 'Caesar is a dead man' is true, then 'Caesar is a man' is false. The consequence is valid because 'dead' conflicts with 'man,' that is, 'Caesar is a man' implies 'Caesar is a living man.' But if Caesar is a dead man, he is not a living man. Therefore Caesar is not a man.

In support of the antecedent ('Caesar is a dead man'), Scotus gives two proofs,

---

71. Roger says: "But among the wise he was 'insane' and reproved at Paris for the errors which he devised [and] promoted, when he solemnly read the *Sentences* there, after he had read the *Sentences* at Oxford in the year of our Lord 1250" (ibid., n. 86 [87]).

72. See also Scotus, *Praedic.*, q. 9.

which he later refers to in nn. 67–68 below. In 'Caesar was a man,' the word 'was' means an actuality that is now finished. Second, 'dead' and 'living' are opposed to one another. Therefore, since Caesar is not living, it follows that he is dead.

[n. 18] The fourth argument cites Averroes: in substantial change, a thing loses both its name and its definition. The same argument was used in q. 3 above, and will crop up again below, in *Opus II.I*, q. 2, to show that there must be a transformation in the signification of an utterance if there is a transformation in the thing signified.

[n. 19] The fifth argument begins with the assumption, "if the proposition 'the Antichrist is a man' were true, by parity of reasoning it would be necessary." What Scotus seems to mean is that if the proposition 'the Antichrist is a man' were tenselessly true, it would have to be necessary, and so every syllogistic mode that is *de contingenti* would be impossible, "since it would denote a middle term being said contingently of such a *suppositum*," which, going back to the starting assumption, it is not. Scotus replies to this argument at n. 72 below.

[n. 20] The sixth argument invokes Aristotle's remark that if all primary substances (that is, particular things) were destroyed, nothing else (that is, universals) would remain (*Categories* 2.2b6–7).[73] Therefore, if Caesar does not exist, the secondary substance signified by 'man' could not be said of Caesar, and so 'Caesar is a man' would be false.

Arguments for

In nn. 21–29, we have the six main arguments for 'Caesar is a man' being true.

[n. 21] The first is that 'Caesar is running; therefore, a man is running' is necessary, because it was true at one time, that is, when Caesar was alive, and the understanding of the consequence is the same now as it was then. Therefore, the implied middle of the consequence, 'Caesar is a man,' is also necessary. 'Necessary' here means that the conclusion follows from the premises; we might also say, 'valid.'

An objection to this would be either that the understanding of the consequence is not the same in both cases, or that the understanding is the same, but the tense of the verb restricts the terms 'Caesar' and 'man' to presently existing *supposita* such that 'Caesar is running' is false, although 'Caesar was running' is true.

---

73. The same argument is used in "*Omnis homo de necessitate est animal*," q. 4, "Whether Caesar is a man, when he is dead" (NL 16135, 12va [41]).

A similar argument is to be found in the sophism 'every man exists' by our anonymous Parisian author. Some writers thought that the consequence 'Caesar exists; therefore, a man exists' is necessary, and similarly 'the Antichrist exists; therefore, a man exists.'[74]

[n. 22] The second main argument is not exactly clear, though it alludes to an argument given by Aristotle: "What I mean by 'signifying one thing' is this: if that thing is a man, then if anything is a man, that thing will be to be a man [i.e. 'being a man']" (*Metaphysics* IV.4.1006a33–34).[75]

Aristotle's argument is part of his attempt to justify the principle of non-contradiction, viz., that something cannot at the same time both be the case and not be the case. His reasoning seems to be as follows: if 'non-man' meant for some people the same thing as we mean by 'man,' it would be trivial and true for such people to say of a man that he is a 'non-man.' They would simply mean that a man is a man. But that is not the intention of those who deny the principle of non-contradiction; they need the 'non-man' in the 'a man is a non-man' to mean something different from 'man.' The question is not whether a man can be a non-man in name, but whether this can be so in reality, and therefore in definition.

However, the definition of 'man' and 'non-man' cannot be the same. Aristotle's argument for this is what Scotus has in mind. As Aristotle goes on to explain, "what I mean by 'signifying one thing' is this: if that thing [that is, the thing signified] is a man, then if anything is a man, that thing will be *to be a man.*"

Thus if, as critics of the principle of non-contradiction assert, a man is both a man and a non-man, then they must mean that a man is different from a non-man in definition, not just in name. But then 'man' would have two different definitions, and hence the word 'man' would have different meanings, which is not possible for, as Aristotle explains, "not to signify one thing is to signify nothing ... it is not possible even to conceive if one is not conceiving of one thing" (*Metaphysics* IV.4.1006b8). Scotus's point is presumably that 'Caesar is a man' must be unconditionally true because it asserts that 'man' is included in the definition of 'Caesar,' which is true whether or not Caesar exists.[76]

---

74. See also "*Album fuit disputaturum,*" ad 4 (NL 16135, 14va [73]).
75. As translated by Christopher Kirwan in *Aristotle's 'Metaphysics,' Books G, D, E* (Oxford: Clarendon Press, 1971), 9.
76. See q. 8, n. 34 and q. 12, n. 1 below. Scotus agrees with the argument here, and so does not reply to it. However, in q. 12, he disagrees with the argument, to which he replies in n. 8. See the commentary below.

In short, Aristotle's proof of the principle of non-contradiction is based on the assumption that where the proposition '*a* is *b*' predicates a definition *b* of the thing defined *a*, the proposition is true by virtue of its meaning alone and does not require the existence of an object satisfying the definition. The proposition 'Caesar is a man' predicates a definition of the thing defined; therefore, it is true whether or not Caesar exists. We might also say that 'man' is part of the significate of 'Caesar' such that the meaning of the proper name 'Caesar' includes the meaning of 'man.' Therefore, 'Caesar is a man' is true.

[n. 23] Scotus records the objection that Aristotle is talking here only about the predication of a definition such as 'two-footed animal' of 'man,' not about cases where only part of the definition is predicated. But 'man' is only part of the definition of 'Caesar.'

[n. 24] The reply to this objection is that the whole of what is signified implies the part. Thus, 'two-footed animal' implies 'animal,' and if it does not imply it when no man exists, it cannot imply it when some man exists, for as Scotus says, "the same diminution will occur on both sides [*eadem deminutio fiet utrobique*]." The 'diminution' being referred to here is in meaning rather than in extension, that is, from 'two-footed animal' to 'animal.' Thus, if no man exists, then no two-footed animal (that is, man) exists. Note that the diminution is the same in both cases, with no man existing and with some man existing, because the meaning of 'animal' is contained in the meaning of 'two-footed animal,' whether or not such a thing exists. The concept of diminution is also used in n. 66 below.

[n. 25] The third argument is similar to the second: 'man' belongs to the per se understanding of 'Caesar.'[77] According to Scotus, "all these consequences are clear from Book I of the *Posterior Analytics*." The edition refers to chapter 4 of Book I, where Aristotle discusses attributes that are always true of a subject, that is, the so-called 'essential attributes' that belong to a subject (i) as part of its very nature, or (ii) as part of its defining formula or *ratio*. It is the second type of belonging that Scotus presumably has in mind here: a thing as it is understood is the essence of a thing; what always belongs to the thing-as-understood always

---

77. Peter of Cornwall mentions a similar argument, that "the predicate is in the understanding [*de intellectu*] of the subject," but rejects it, saying that not only is 'man' predicated, but also 'presentness.' See "*Omnis homo est,*" Worcester Q.13, 49vb: "To the first argument, [that] 'the predicate is in the understanding of the subject,' I say that not only is 'man' predicated here, but at the same time, along with this, I consignify presentness [Ad primum argumentum 'praedicatum est de intellectu subiecti,' dico quod non solum praedicatur hic homo sed simul cum hoc consignifico praesentialitatem]."

belongs to the essence; hence, it is always true of the thing (whether it exists in reality, or whether it is simply understood). Accordingly, since 'man' belongs to the understanding of 'Caesar,' it follows that it is always true of Caesar.

[n. 26] Objection to the third argument: according to Aristotle, there is no definition of singulars such as Caesar. Therefore, 'man' cannot form part of the definition of 'Caesar.' Nor can there be a definition of something that does not exist, presumably because there would be no subject for the definition to be predicated of.

[n. 27] Scotus replies to this objection that, also according to Aristotle, there can be demonstrative arguments about things that do not exist. In fact, there must be definitions of such things because we must already grasp of the subject of a demonstration 'that it is [*quia est*]' and 'what it is [*quid est*],' which is how we can know that thunder is a terrifying sound even when no thunder is present.

[n. 28] The fourth argument is similar: there can be definitions of non-existent things, or at least a definition explaining what the name means. Presumably, Scotus has in mind the example from *Posterior Analytics* II.7.92b5–7, where Aristotle says that we can know the meaning of 'goat stag,' although he denies we could ever know its essential nature.

[n. 29] The fifth argument is that 'Caesar is Caesar; therefore, Caesar is a man' is a valid consequence. Thus, since 'Caesar is Caesar' is true, so is 'Caesar is a man.' In nn. 9–10 of q. 12 below, Scotus discusses two views on this: some deny the identity statement, 'Caesar is Caesar,' whereas others deny the consequence itself.[78]

[Question 8. Are the Propositions 'A man is a man' and 'Caesar is Caesar' True When Neither of Them Exists?]

Summary

This question asks whether propositions with an identical predicate and subject, such as 'Caesar is Caesar,' are true when the subject does not exist. There are three arguments (nn. 30–32) for the thesis that such propositions are false, followed by eight arguments against (nn. 33–42). The determination is in nn. 74–77, and the replies in nn. 78–80.

78. See also "*Omnis homo est*," NL 16135, ff. 49vb–52vb.

Commentary

Arguments against

[n. 30] First is the argument given in n. 16 of q. 7 that 'Caesar is Caesar' is false because it implies 'Caesar exists,' which is false.

[n. 31] According to the second argument, 'Caesar is a man' follows from 'Caesar is Caesar,' and 'a man is an animal' follows from 'a man is a man' because they are included in the concepts of their antecedents. But in the case where no man exists, 'Caesar is a man' is false, and so is 'a man is an animal.' Therefore, so are their antecedents: 'Caesar is Caesar' and 'a man is a man.'

[n. 32] The third argument is that for a proposition to be true, it is not enough that the predicate concept agrees with the subject concept; there must also be agreement or composition or union in reality. But since there is nothing in reality that corresponds to the name 'Caesar,' it follows that there is no agreement or composition in reality corresponding to the agreement expressed in 'Caesar is Caesar.' Therefore, the proposition is false.[79]

Arguments for

[n. 33] The first is that no proposition is truer than one in which the same thing is predicated of itself. Here Scotus is citing a well-known remark from the second Commentary on Boethius's *De interpretatione*, where it is stated that the proposition 'what is good is good' is closer to the nature of goodness than 'what is good is useful.' For this reason, a proposition in which the same thing is predicated of itself is truer than one in which something else is predicated of it accidentally.[80]

---

79. In the third quarter of the thirteenth century, Boethius of Dacia argued in a similar way: "Composition in speech cannot be true unless the corresponding composition in the understanding is true; but composition in the understanding cannot be true unless there is a corresponding composition in reality; therefore, the proposition is false [Sicut se habet compositio sermonis ad compositionem intellectus, sic se habet compositio intellectus ad compositionem rerum. Sed compositio sermonis non potest esse vera, nisi sit vera compositio intellectus, ex qua ipsa est. Ergo nec potest esse vera compositio intellectus nisi sit talis compositio in re]," in "*Omnis homo de necessitate est animal,*" taken from Martin Grabmann, "Des 12 und 13 Jahrhunderts mit Textausgabe eines Sophisma des Boethius von Dacien," *Beiträge zur Geschichte der Philosophie und Theologie des Mittelalters* 36, no. 1 (1940), q. 1, *quod contra* (78).

80. See also n. 3 of q. 12 below, and Thomas Aquinas, *Scriptum super Sententiis* I, d. 4–7. Ockham (*Summa logicae* II.14) denies the Boethian principle and contends that "the chimera is a chimera" is false, arguing, as Russell did six hundred years later, that it is not true because it covertly makes the false assertion that the chimera is something.

The edition mentions Albert the Great, whose statement of the principle is similar to that of Scotus. However, the principle was cited by many medieval authors, such as Ockham, and Scotus may not have had Albert explicitly in mind.

[n. 34] The second argument is the same as in n. 22 above.[81]

[n. 35] The third argument cites Aristotle's remark that what is per se is something of which nothing else is a cause (*Metaphysics* V.1022a33–34). Thus, for example, man has a plurality of causes such as 'animal' and 'two-footed,' and yet a man is still per se a man. Perhaps, then, the argument is that something true by itself in this way requires no external reality to cause it to be true. If so, it does not matter how reality is: 'a man is a man' is true regardless of how things stand in the world, even if no men exist.

[n. 36] The fourth argument cites another passage from Aristotle (*Metaphysics* VII.1041a20–24). Presumably, the idea is that if nothing else needs to be assumed about whether propositions such as 'a man is a man' are true, we need not ask how things are in reality, e.g., whether Caesar, or a man, exists.

[n. 37] The fifth argument cites Aristotle again (*De interpretatione* I.5.23b16–18): every negative proposition can be reduced to some affirmative proposition that is more basic or fundamental. For example, 'good is not evil' can be reduced to the more basic 'good is good.' Similarly, 'Caesar is not a donkey' and other similar propositions that remove something from Caesar can be reduced to the more basic 'Caesar is Caesar.'

[n. 38] The sixth argument involves what is known as a 'syllogism from opposites.' According to Aristotle, we have such a syllogism when the premises are related as contradictory opposites and when the terms are either identical or related as whole and part. Aristotle says that the conclusion of such premises is always 'contrary to reality.' Thus: every a is b; some a is not b; some non-b is b. But 'Non-Caesar is Caesar; Caesar is non-Caesar; therefore, Caesar is Caesar' is a syllogism of this form. Thus, "the premises are true based on what makes the conclusion false" because denying the conclusion (asserting not-p) implies the conclusion (p); therefore, the conclusion is true.

The same argument is used n. 4 of q. 12. Boethius of Dacia also mentions the argument: "every animal is a substance; some man is not a substance; therefore, some man is not an animal," although he objects that Aristotle says only that a syl-

---

81. See also n. 1 of q. 12 below.

logism from opposites is contrary to reality.[82] Scotus makes a similar point in his reply to q. 12, saying that the argument is only valid for terms that are not empty.

[n. 39] A syllogism from opposites also shows that 'every man is a man' is necessary. The syllogism, 'no man is white; some man is white; therefore, some man is not a man,' has opposed premises, and so according to Aristotle (*Prior Analytics* II.16.64b7–10, 15–16), the conclusion is impossible. Therefore, the opposite conclusion, 'every man is a man,' is true.

"In the third [mode] of the second [figure]"; the figure of a syllogism is determined by the position of the middle term, in this case 'white.' When the middle term is in the predicate position in both premises, the syllogism belongs to the second figure. The 'third syllogism' is in the *Festino* form, where the first premise is the E-proposition (no p is m), the second the I-proposition (some s is m), and the conclusion the O-proposition (some s is not p). In this case, the subject s and the predicate p are the same ('man'); thus, the premises contradict one another or 'are opposites' with regard to one another; hence the term, 'syllogism from opposites.'

[n. 40] The eighth argument, which is stretched over nn. 40–42, is that the subject of a proposition and of its negation is the same. Thus, the subjects of 'Caesar is Caesar' and 'Caesar is not Caesar' are the same. But if the subject (Caesar) is the same, it follows that 'Caesar is Caesar' is true.

[n. 41] Scotus next considers two objections to this argument. The first, which he attributes to Boethius, is that the proposition 'Caesar is Caesar' asserts the existence of Caesar (as well as the identity of subject and predicate). This is because the content of the verb 'is' includes existence, which is predicated together with what 'specifies' the verb, that is, the predicate 'Caesar.' Thus, 'is Caesar' really means 'is-an-existing Caesar.' Thererfore, the same thing (existing Caesar) is not asserted of itself (Caesar *simpliciter*).

[n. 42] Scotus replies to the objection that in such propositions, the copula 'is' simply predicates 'what is in another,' that is, the being of Caesar is predicated of Caesar, but Caesar is the being of Caesar, so the proposition is true. Similarly, we can concede that 'a non-being is a non-being' and 'a chimera is a chimera' are both true simply because the being of the predicate is the same as the subject. See also n. 2 of q. 12 below.

---

82. Boethius of Dacia, "*Omnis homo de necessitate est animal.*"

Scotus mentions that this reply involves a difficulty about the content of the verb 'is' when it is used as a copula, which he will discuss later. The edition mentions nn. 32–33 of qq. 9–11 below. These sections in turn look ahead to *Opus II.I*, qq. 5–6, nn. 21–25 and 29–34. This suggests not only that qq. 5–11 were written so as to form an organic whole, but also that Book I of *Opus II*, which is supposedly just a different version of *Opus I*, is part of the same work, rather than a revision.[83]

Replies to Questions 6–8
Determination of Question 6

In nn. 43–44, Scotus replies to the sixth question, which is referred to as the first question of the group: "To the first of these questions."[84] This reference suggests that qq. 6–8 belong together and did not originally include q. 5. It is possible that the present grouping is the work of an anonymous editor. Further evidence is the fact that the replies to the main arguments of q. 5 (nn. 81–86) occur after the replies to qq. 6–8.

[n. 43] Scotus's argument here follows the principle established in qq. 2–3 above, viz., that a thing is not signified as it exists, but as it is understood. And so the aspect [*ratio*] of what is common is not attributed as it exists, but as it is conceived in the understanding. The distinction between the common and the individual *suppositum* is also a matter of conception: we conceive the common nature as what is predicable of many individuals;[85] likewise, we conceive the individual supposit through the same nature conceived as predicable of no more than one. Since our conception of the suppositum already includes the concept of the common, it follows that there are other individuals of a common term besides things that exist.

---

83. See Peter of Cornwall: "Likewise, Boethius would have it the same way—the verb 'is' sometimes is a copula, such that it is an extreme, as when it is given per se, and then it predicates what is in itself; and sometimes a copula such that it is not an extreme, and then it predicates what is in another. But it predicates inherence more truly when it predicates what is in itself than when it predicates what is in another, for inherence is more true when it predicates what is in itself, therefore more truly should being actually, or [being] relationally be distinguished in saying 'a man is' than in saying 'a man is an animal' [Item, hoc idem vult Boethius [*Boethii Int. ed. 2a, 1.3 et V.11*]: hoc verbum 'est' aliquando est copula ita quod extremum, ut quando per se ponitur, et tunc praedicat quod in se est; aliquando est copula ita quod non extremum, et tunc praedicat quod in alio est. Sed verius praedicat inesse quando praedicat quod in se est quam quando praedicat quod in alio est, quia verior est inhaerentia quando praedicat quod in se est, ergo verius debet distingui penes esse actu vel habitu sic dicendo 'homo est' quam sic dicendo 'homo est animal']" ("*Omnis homo est*," Worcester Q.13, f. 48va [142]).

84. Cf. the main arguments of q. 6 in nn. 9–14 above.

85. Cf. n. 10 of q. 6 above.

This is one of the few places in these *Questions* which seem to anticipate Scotus's later thought, particularly in the *Lectura, Ordinatio*, and the *Questions on the Metaphysics*, where he argues that the principle of individuation is a positive feature distinguishing one individual (such as Socrates) of the same nature (man) from another individual (such as Plato).[86]

A characteristic mode of expression here is the use of the demonstrative pronoun 'this [*haec*]' as though it were an adjective or noun. Scotus speaks of a nature conceived as 'this,' almost as though it were 'a this,' or 'something that is this.'[87]

[n. 44] Scotus adds an argument of Aristotle's that there can be demonstrative reasoning about things that do not currently exist, such as eclipses (*Posterior Analytics* I.87b22–26; cf. also n. 27 above). And so, as was argued above, a nature conceived as a 'this' is related in the same way to human nature conceived as 'predicable of many' whether or not it is conceived as existing.

"As was stated in the resolution of the third question"; see n. 10 of q. 3 above. Unless this was itself an addition of a later editor (the word 'third' is missing in

---

86. For example, compare n. 43 above: "To the first of these questions, it can be said that the nature of what is common or of the *suppositum* is not attributed to a thing as it exists, but as it is conceived in the understanding, because to posit something existing as the nature of what is common is attributed to it just is to posit ideas, as Plato thought [Ad primam quaestionem illarum dici potest quod ratio communis vel suppositi non attribuitur rei ut existit, sed ut concipitur apud intellectum. Quia ponere aliquid exsistere secundum quod sibi attribuitur ratio communis est ponere ideas, sicut Plato posuit]," with *Ordinatio* II, d. 3, n. 160, solution to q. 6: "There follow absurdities in metaphysics. First, because the idea of Plato would be supposed, or [even] more than the idea of Plato would be supposed. For Plato supposed that the idea is a nature existing per se, separated and without accidents, just as is attributed to him by the Philosopher, in which the entire nature of the species would consist... [In Metaphysica sequuntur inconvenientia. Primum quia poneretur idea Platonis vel plusquam idea quam posuit Plato, Plato enim posuit ideam esse naturam per se exsistentem, separatam, sine accidentibus, sicut sibi imponitur a Philosopho, in qua esset tota natura specie ...]."

87. Cf. *Ordinatio* II, d. 3 (*Opera Omnia* [Vatican edition] VII, n. 172 (476): "A nature is naturally prior to this nature, and proper unity following from a nature as nature is naturally prior to its unity as this nature [Natura prius est naturaliter quam haec natura, et unitas propria consequens naturam ut natura prior est naturaliter unitate eius ut haec natura]." See also n. 165 (473): "Therefore, to say that a nature is of itself 'this,' according to the aforementioned understanding of 'a nature which is of itself "this,"' and for that still to be able to be this thing or that thing, whatever other thing is at hand, is to utter a contradiction [Dicere ergo naturam esse de se hanc, secundum intellectum praeexpositum de natura quae de se est haec, et tamen ipsam posse esse hanc et illam, quocumque alio adveniente, est dicere contradictoria]." For discussion, see Richard Cross, "Divisibility, Communicability, and Predicability in Duns Scotus's Theories of the Common Nature," *Medieval Philosophy and Theology* 11, no. 1 (2003): 43–63. See also the question, "Utrum intellectus animae Christi novit omnia in genere proprio a principio" in *Lectura* III, d. 14, q. 3.

mss. L and N), this is further evidence that these *Questions* were intended as a single work by their author, and are not a redaction.

Reply to the Arguments of Question 6

[n. 45] The first reply is to the argument in n. 12 above (although the edition erroneously says n. 9). The argument was that although a common nature belongs per se to the understanding of any supposit, it is not predicated of non-existing things.

In connection with Scotus's remark that the reply "will be obvious from the solution to the following question," see nn. 49–50 below, where he argues that the union of the terms is sufficient for the truth of an affirmative proposition, and so it is sufficient that the understanding of the subject is included the understanding of the predicate. Thus, 'man' can be predicated of 'Caesar' because the understanding of Caesar involves the understanding of man.

[n. 46] To the second argument (the edition refers to n. 10, although this should be n. 13), a nature conceived in the understanding as a 'this' is essentially the same as the nature, but not in such a way that the aspect [*ratio*] of conceiving it falls into a union made with the verb 'is,' and so (presumably) we are not forced to conclude that the supposit is essentially the same as its common nature. Thus, when we entertain the proposition 'Caesar is a man,' we are not thinking that the nature 'man' conceived as this man (Caesar) is identical with the common nature of man. Rather, we are conceiving the common nature under the aspect 'this man.'

[n. 47] To the argument that non-being cannot be the same as a true nature, Scotus replies that that non-being as conceived in the understanding can be the same as true being.

[n. 48] To the third argument (n. 14 above), which was that every universal affirmative assertoric proposition would be false because of the predicate not being true of non-existing supposits, Scotus says the reply "will be clear later." This appears to look ahead to qq. 9–11, especially (according to the edition) nn. 23–24. This is further evidence that these questions, or questions very similar to them, were part of the original work.

Determination of Question 7

[n. 49] Scotus replies to q. 7 (nn. 15–29 above) that propositions such as 'Caesar is a man' are true because the union of the extremes—by which is meant the outer terms of the proposition, that is, 'Caesar' and 'man'—is sufficient for the proposition being true, and in this case the understanding of the predicate 'man' is included in the understanding of the subject 'Caesar.'[88]

[n. 50] Scotus's second argument for the truth of 'Caesar is a man' is that if it were false, then any proposition predicating a common term of its supposit can sometimes be true (such as when 'man' was predicated of Caesar while he was alive) and sometimes false. But then the rule of *dici de omni* (see n. 14 above) would not apply to a first figure affirmative syllogism whose major is necessary but minor is assertoric. This is contrary to Aristotle in *Prior Analytics* I. The edition gives I.15.34a35–b6, as a reference, but Scotus is almost certainly talking about I.9.30a15–b6, where Aristotle discusses mixed necessary and assertoric propositions.

Medieval logicians distinguished between modal propositions understood in the 'sense of division [*sensu divisionis*],' where 'necessarily' attaches to the predicate, and propositions understood in the 'sense of composition [*sensu compositionis*],' where 'necessarily' attaches to the whole proposition.[89] In syllogisms where the major proposition is necessary in the sense of division, a necessary conclusion follows when the minor is assertoric: every *b* is necessarily-*c*; every *a* is *b*; every *a* is necessarily-*c*.

This is because according to the rule of *dici de omni*, whatever the subject (*b* is predicated of, so is the predicate (necessarily-*c*). This is true whether the minor premise is 'simply assertoric [*de inesse simpliciter*],' that is, one in which the predicate cannot belong to the subject at one time without belonging to it at any other

---

88. Peter of Cornwall, "*Omnis homo est*" (Worcester Q.13, q. 13; 48va, 49vb), mentions a similar reason, but rejects it, arguing that present existence is signified by the verb 'is,' but 'man' is not in the understanding with the present existence co-signified by 'Caesar.' A similar reason is also mentioned, and rejected, by Boethius of Dacia around 1270 in "*Omnis homo de necessitate est animal.*" Replying to the argument that composition in the understanding (in this case 'animal' with 'man') alone is sufficient for the truth of a proposition, Boethius replies that if that is so, a composition of the understanding could be true that compounds things that are in reality divided, e.g., 'man' and 'donkey'—which is impossible.

89. William of Ockham, *Summa Logicae* III.31 (440). There are similar arguments in Scotus at the beginning of q. 11 (n. 17), and in q. 13 (n. 15).

time, or 'as of now assertoric [*de inesse ut nunc*],' that is, where the predicate may sometimes be true of the subject, and sometimes not. If 'every *a* is *b*' is only true now, and every *b* is now necessarily-*c*, it still follows that (now) every *a* is necessarily*c*. It is in the sense of division, says Ockham, that we must understand Aristotle's observation. In the sense of composition, it is clearly not true when the minor is an 'as of now' proposition. Thus, the following syllogism is not valid: necessarily every *b* is *c*; every *a* is (now) *b*; necessarily every *a* is *c*.

Reply to the Main Arguments of Question 7
Reply to the First Main Argument

In nn. 51–57 we have replies, objections, and counter-objections to the first main argument (n. 15 above) that being cannot be predicated of non-being.

[n. 51] The first reply is that something existing is not predicated of something non-existing, but human nature conceived as predicable of many is predicated of the same nature conceived as a 'this.' This is essentially the same answer Scotus gave in the determination of q. 6 above: the nature of the common or the supposit is not attributed to a thing as it exists, but as it is conceived in the understanding.

[n. 52] It is objected that if 'Caesar is non-existing' is true and 'a man is existing' is true, then in 'Caesar is a man,' what is existing is predicated of what is non-existing.

[n. 53] Scotus replies that this is Aristotle's 'fallacy of accident,' which happens when an attribute is said to belong to a thing and its accident in the same way. Thus, if 'man' is the thing and 'Caesar' is its accident, to say that we are predicating what is existing of what is non-existing when we say 'Caesar is a man' would be to commit the fallacy of accident.[90]

[n. 54] A further objection: but the subject 'Caesar' and the predicate 'man' are not actually united, since Caesar does not exist.

[n. 55] Scotus replies that the predication is incidental (*per accidens*). See the more detailed comments in n. 58 below. He does not mention this reason in his determination of q. 7 in n. 49 above.

[n. 56] Scotus mentions another objection that we have met before, in q. 5 above: nothing is univocal to being and non-being. Note that the reply to q. 5

---

90. Cf. Peter of Spain, *Tractatus, called afterwards Summule logicales*, ed. L. M. de Rijk (Assen: Van Gorcum, 1972), VII.102 (146–47); cf. also Thomas Aquinas, *De fallaciis* 12.

is not made until n. 81 below. The fact that the same question is also raised here further suggests that q. 5 was not part of the text to which qq. 6–8 originally belonged.

[n. 57] Scotus replies that existing and non-existing are extraneous to the nature as it is signified by the term. For related arguments, see n. 19 of q. 3 and n. 11 of q. 6; see also n. 58 below, n. 64 (reply to q. 7), and n. 84 (reply to q. 5).

Reply to the Second Main Argument

In nn. 58–65, Scotus gives his replies to the second main argument (n. 16) and to counter-objections.

[n. 58] His first reply invokes the same passage from Aristotle used in the argument itself. Aristotle says that even when opposite elements (such as 'dead' and 'man') are predicated, the inference from the compounded to the divided sense does not always hold. This is the case, for example, when being is predicated 'incidentally' (*secundum accidens* in Boethius's translation). He says that in the sentence 'Homer is a poet,' being is predicated only incidentally, and so we cannot infer 'Homer exists.'

[n. 59] In nn. 59–62 we get four objections to the reply. The first is that 'Caesar is white; therefore, Caesar is' is valid, and so 'Caesar is man; therefore, Caesar is' is also valid. Therefore, since the being of an accident such as 'white' implies true being, a substantial being such as 'man' implies being, which is in fact a truer being than an accident. But 'Caesar exists' is false; as is, therefore, 'Caesar is a man.'

[n. 60] The second objection is that being in an unqualified sense (*simpliciter*) follows from the being of an essence like 'man.'

[n. 61] The third objection is that according to Aristotle (*Posterior Analytics* II.2.89b36–90a12) the question of whether something exists can be the subject of inquiry, and so is truly knowable. Therefore 'being' must be predicated of anything that can be a subject of inquiry and per se, and so it follows from anything.

[n. 62] The fourth objection is that it is not possible to know what something is if we do not know whether it exists or not.

[n. 63] Scotus replies to the first objection (n. 59 above) that the being posited in 'Caesar is white' is not incidental being (*esse secundum accidens*). For a real accident such as 'white' belongs only to existing subjects. But as Caesar does not exist, 'Caesar is white' is false, and so the inference fails (that is, no being is posited in an unqualified sense).

[n. 64] Scotus replies to the second objection (n. 60 above) that the assumption of the argument (viz., that being either belongs to the essence of something, or else necessarily follows from it) is only true of the essence as it exists. So we do not have to assume it is predicated of Caesar except as he is understood.

[n. 65] Scotus replies to the third and fourth objections (nn. 61–62 above) that the question of whether something exists, as Aristotle understands it, is to be taken in the sense of 'whether something has an essence.' We cannot know what essence we are talking about without knowing that what we are talking about has an essence in the first place.

Reply to the Third Main Argument

In nn. 66–70 we find replies to the third main argument (n. 17) and two objections. The main argument was that the consequence 'Caesar is a dead man; therefore, he is not a man' is valid, because what is predicated of something ('man') with a conflicting determination ('dead') is truly denied of it.

[n. 66] Here Scotus argues that the consequence is not valid if 'dead' and 'alive' signify actuality rather than aptitude, for if so, it is true that Caesar is dead, but 'is a dead man' taken in that sense does not imply 'is not a man.' In that sense, the meaning of 'man' does not include the opposite of 'dead.' If, on the other hand, they are aptitudes, then they are *differentiae* of 'substance,' and in that sense 'Caesar is dead' is true (see also n. 24 above).

[n. 67] Next, Scotus addresses the two proofs supporting the antecedent, 'Caesar is a dead man.' The first was that the 'was' of 'Caesar was a man' means an actuality that is complete and terminated. Scotus objects that this is only true if 'was' is predicated as a second element, that is, so as to imply 'Caesar used to exist.' If it is predicated as a third element, it is still true that Caesar is a man.

[n. 68] Recall that the second proof was that 'dead' and 'living' are opposed to one another. Since Caesar is not living, it follows that he is dead. Scotus replies to the second proof as in n. 66 above, that is, this is only true when 'living' and 'dead' are aptitudes.

[n. 69] But then it is objected that if living is existing, as Aristotle says (*De anima* II.4.415b13), then Caesar does not live, and so does not exist.

[n. 70] In reply to the objection, Scotus concedes that Caesar is not alive, but he appeals to the ancient distinction between 'being as a participle [*ens participium*]' and 'being as a name [*ens nomen*],' which implies a distinction between existential being (*esse exsistere*) and essential being (*esse essentiae*, or, as Scotus puts it, having an essence; *habens essentiam*). 'Being as a participle' signifies actual being, which is not the case here, but rather 'being as a name,' or 'essential being.' Caesar, being dead, is not alive, and so does not have the being of existence, but only of essence.[91]

91. Peter John Olivi (d. 1298), *Quaestiones in secundum librum Sententiarum*, ed. B. Jansen (Quaracchi: Collegium S. Bonaventurae, 1922–26), q. 13: "*An universalia sint in individuis suis secundum suam universalitatem an tantum in intellectu* [Whether universals are in the individuals [instantiating them] in their universality or in the understanding]": "But others say that universals have a sort of conditional or potential being which these persons call essential being, and in this being they remain even when the individuals [which instantiate them] perish. But they have another sort of being in the individuals, which they call actual being, and in this being the universals do not remain when their instantiators perish. Nor, in this being, do they have universality, but rather they are made particular and multiplied in the individuals. But according to the first kind of being [i.e. potential being], they have true universality, without any individuation [Alii vero dicunt quod universalia habent quoddam esse habitudinale seu potentiale in se ipsis quod vocant esse essentiae et secundum hoc esse manent ipsis individuis destructis, aliud vero habent in suis individuis, quod vocant esse actuale; et secundum hoc esse non manent individuis destructis nec secundum hoc esse habent universalitatem, immo sunt particulata et multiplicata in suis individuis; secundum vero primum esse habent veram universalitatem sine aliqua individuatione]." An anonymous commentator on the *Perihermenias* writes that "when we say that when a thing perishes, the signifying utterance corresponding to it does not perish, this is only in a qualified sense, viz., insofar as it represents the thing under existential being. For, when the thing has perished, that utterance does not represent it as existing; but the utterance is not destroyed as it represents a thing under the aspect of understood being [cum dicitur quod destructa re, non destruatur vox significativa, dico quod immo secundum quid; videlicet inquantum repraesentat tale sub esse existere, quia destructa re, amplius ipsa vox non repraesentat ipsam exsistere; sed non destruitur in quantum repraesentat aliquod tale sub esse intellectum]" (*Quaestiones super logicam veterem*; Paris Bib. Nat. Mazarine 3523, ff. 57ra–70ra; QQ. *Periherm.* q. 3, f. 68rb). Cf. also "*Omnis homo de necessitate est animal*" (NL 16135, ff. 11rb–12vb), whose anonymous Parisian author writes: "Being has two senses. One is essential being, and this is the actuality of being as it is a noun. The other is existential being, and this is the actuality of being as it is a participle. And so one being does not imply the other, nor one entity the other. But when the verb 'is' is added, it joins essential being, or not, depending on the requirements of the subject. Therefore 'it is a being, therefore it exists' does not follow, for the copula is always modified by what is added [Duplex est esse. Uno modo est esse essentiae, et tale est actus entis ut est nomen; alio modo est esse existentiae, et tale est actus entis ut est participium. Et ita nec unum esse infert aliud, nec unum ens aliud. Cum autem superadditur huic verbo 'est' secundum exigentiam subiecti, copulat tunc esse essentiae, tunc autem non, (sed) copulat esse actuale. Ideo non sequitur 'est ens, ergo est'; semper enim copula contrahitur per adiunctum]"; Siger of Brabant, "*Quaestio Utrum haec sit vera: Homo est animal, nullo homine existente*," in *Siger de Brabant, Écrits de logique, de morale et de physique*, ed. B. C. Bazán (Louvain-Paris: Publications Universitaires-Éditions Béatrice-Nauwelaerts, 1974), 52–56, 54; Henry of Ghent, *Syncategoremata*, 2:368; Richard Clive, "*Quaestiones in libros metaphysicorum*" (Worcester Q.13, f. 125 [157]): "It should be said that there are two senses of 'a being' or 'to be,' viz., quidditative and the being of actual existence. Quidditative being is what is common to past, future, and present; Avicenna calls this being 'non-prohibited being' [Dicendum quod duplex est ens vel esse, sc. quidditativum et esse actualis existentiae. Esse quidditativum est quod communiter se habet ad praeteritum et futurum et praesens et vocat Avicenna illud esse 'esse non prohibitum' in 5 Metaphysicae suae" [Avicenna, *Liber de philosophia prima sive scientia divina, V–X*, ed. Simone van Riet (Leiden: Brill, 1980), V.1 (227)]]"; and "*Utrum haec possit esse vera 'caesar est homo,'*" in "*Omnis homo est*" (NL 16135, f. 49vb–52vb).

[n. 71] The fourth argument in n. 17 above was that in substantial change, a thing loses [its] name and definition. Scotus argues that change really happens to a thing existing in reality, and so Averroes is correct concerning a thing as it exists. But as it is conceived in the understanding, in the mode of singularity (that is, as 'not predicable of many,' in Scotus's terminology), it does not undergo a substantial transformation, and so does not lose its name or its definition.

[n. 72] Here Scotus replies to the argument of n. 19, which was that if the proposition 'the Antichrist is a man' were tenselessly true, it would have to be necessary, and so every syllogistic mode involving contingency would be impossible "since it would denote a middle term being said contingently of such a *suppositum*." Scotus replies that this is no objection to Aristotle, because it is still a valid syllogistic form. See also our commentary on qq. 9–11 in n. 18 below.

[n. 73] The sixth argument (n. 20 above) was about the destruction of the 'primary substances.' Scotus replies by mentioning his book on the *Categories* (q. 13, nn. 18–21, 24–25).[92]

Replies to Question 8

[n. 74] Scotus says that propositions such as 'Caesar is Caesar' and 'Caesar is a man' are true because of "the arguments made earlier." He probably means nn. 33–42 above, although the edition refers the reader to nn. 38–40.

With regard to the proposition 'Caesar is a man,' some editions have '*homo est homo*' because: (i) q. 8 is clearly about propositions of the form '*a* is *a*,' where the predicate is identical to the subject; (ii) the title (n. 30) has '*homo est homo*'; and (iii) the argument in n. 33 cites Boethius's claim that no proposition is truer than one in which the same thing is predicated of itself. Possibly the author is referring to both q. 7 and q. 8 here.

[n. 75] "One of the arguments is this"; our translation of *quarum una est ista* here follows the division of the edition. Scotus appears to be referring to the argument about the syllogism from opposites in nn. 38–39 of the main arguments, particularly in n. 39, where it was argued that 'every man is a man' is true because its contradictory opposite 'some man is not a man' is the conclusion of a syllogism from opposites. In this section, for reasons that are not clear, he argues that 'every man is an animal' is true because its opposite is the impossible conclusion of the

---

92. *OPh* I, 369-70; 371-72.

syllogism 'every animal is white; not every man is white.' It is unclear what this argument is doing here, other than repeating the argument made in n. 39 above.

Scotus says that the argument in n. 39 "can be reduced to the solution of the preceding question." The edition refers to nn. 49–50 here, which is indeed the solution to the preceding q. 7. In n. 49, it was argued that the understanding of the subject per se is included in the understanding of the predicate. More confusingly, n. 50 apparently refers back to n. 49.

[n. 76] Scotus next addresses an objection: what if non-existence removes the nature (*ratio*) of an inferior from man by reason of 'animal'? Perhaps he means: to have the nature of inferior (in the case of man) requires having the nature of animal (because the species 'man' belongs to the genus 'animal'). But if no man exists, no man has the nature of animal, and thus no man has the nature of what is inferior to animal.

Scotus objects that the nature belongs to 'man' insofar as man exists (and so it is not a nature of animal *simpliciter*) by the work of the understanding, for the work of the understanding does not depend on existence in reality. This is proved because (appealing to the *Posterior Analytics* again, as in nn. 27–28 above) there can be proofs involving non-existing things, as well as definitions of them. Scotus here seems to be rejecting the 'diminution' approach to solving the dead man sophism, which was the solution advocated by Peter of Spain.[93]

[n. 77] Scotus then mentions an argument about 'per se' made in "the first question," but this clearly refers to n. 25 and nn. 27–28, which are part of the main argument of q. 7. Elsewhere, he refers to q. 6 as the first question.

Scotus repeats the arguments of those earlier sections: since there are definitions of non-existing things, and since 'animal' is part of the definition of 'man' even when no men exist, it is true to predicate 'animal' per se of 'man' (n. 28). And in the definition, 'animal' would be predicated necessarily, since it is part of the meaning of 'man' and because names signify the same even when they denote nothing.

These arguments all prove that 'a man is an animal' is true, even though no man exists; they do not prove that 'Caesar is Caesar' or 'a man is a man' is true.

[n. 78] The first argument was that 'Caesar exists' follows from 'Caesar is Caesar.' Scotus replies that it was stated in a previous question how being [*esse*] is predicated as a second element. But in 'Caesar is Caesar,' being is predicated as a

---

93. See Sten Ebbesen, "The Dead Man is Alive," *Synthese* 40 (1979): 44–45.

third element, and so it does not imply 'Caesar exists,' where it is predicated as a second.

[n. 79] The second argument (n. 31 above) was that 'Caesar is a man' follows because the consequent belongs to the understanding of the antecedent, and 'Caesar is a man' is false. Scotus replies that 'Caesar is a man' is not false, as he contended in n. 74 above and in other similar propositions earlier.

[n. 80] The third argument (n. 32 above) was that for an affirmative proposition to be true, there must be a composition (*unio*) in reality in the way the proposition signifies. But in the case of 'Caesar is Caesar,' there cannot be such a union if Caesar does not exist. In keeping with what he has already said, Scotus replies that the nature (*natura*) signified by the name 'Caesar' is a being in the understanding; otherwise, the understanding could not compose anything from it. Thus 'Caesar is Caesar' signifies the composition of the same thing with itself in the understanding, and this composition is sufficient for it to be true, just as 'a chimera is a chimera' and 'a non-being is non-being' are true, even though chimeras and non-beings do not exist in reality.

Reply to the Arguments of Question 5

These next sections (nn. 81–94) present some difficulty. They begin with the replies to q. 5 (nn. 81–86) that should have preceded the replies to q. 6 if qq. 5–8 really belong together, or after the determination of q. 5 (nn. 7–8) if q. 5 stands on its own. There follow two sections (nn. 87–88) that the edition considers to be "another reply to the sixth question," but which could also be another reply to the second argument of q. 5 (n. 2). The next sections (nn. 89–91) offer alternative replies to the three arguments of nn. 1–3, and nn. 92–94 are replies to the opposing arguments of q. 7.

[n. 81] "To the first argument of that question"; this refers to the first argument of q. 5 (n. 1 above). Scotus gave his determination of this question in nn. 7–8, but offered no replies to the three arguments of nn. 1–3; qq. 6–8 and their replies are sandwiched in between despite the fact that there is nothing in the material covered in qq. 6–8 and their replies that would justify placing the replies to q. 5 here.

The first reply invokes the distinction, first introduced in n. 70 above, between being as a name and being as a participle. Being as a name is not equivocal. Being as a participle is perhaps equivocal, but in that case the first argument is not valid, for as a participle it is not a superior genus to man.

[n. 82] The reply to the second argument (n. 2 above) is that it has already been conceded (in n. 43 above, according to the edition) that the common is predicated of its supposit using the verb 'is.' But it is not clear that n. 43, which is the determination of q. 6, is the passage being referred to here. The phrase "predicated of its supposit with the verb 'is'" occurs nowhere in n. 43. Rather, the central ideas of that section are (i) that the nature of the common is attributed to something as it is conceived, not as it exists; and (ii) that a nature can be conceived either as predicable of many, or as not-predicable of many, that is, as an individual.

[n. 83] This section and the three sections that follow (nn. 83–86) reply to the third argument of n. 3 above, viz., Roger Bacon's argument that no univocal expression is common to being and non-being. Scotus replies that insofar as they have the nature of contradictories, this is perhaps true.

[n. 84] However, Robert (who exists) and Caesar (who does not exist) can still have something in common (presumably, being a man) even though it happens that the one is existing and the other non-existing. As those accidents inhere in them, they do not have such a common nature, that is, one that involves contradictories.

[n. 85] Scotus compares this argument to one that is clearly invalid: one might equally argue that there is nothing univocally common to white and non-white, since they are contradictories; this man is white and that man is not white; therefore, there is nothing univocally common to this man and that one. The claim (in n. 3) that there is nothing univocal to all beings is false because (according to Scotus) there can be something the same, conceived in the intellect, as regards the understanding of what happens to exist and what happens not to exist.

[n. 87] This section presents considerable difficulty. Scotus refers to the second of three questions and then mentions "what was said in connection with the preceding two questions." But what are the three questions, and where are the preceding two questions?

According to the edition, the three questions are qq. 5–7, the second of which must be the sixth; thus, nn. 87–88 receive the title, "Another Reply to the Sixth Question." The edition identifies the "preceding two questions" as qq. 7–8.

But if this is so, it is hard to explain why n. 43 (the reply to q. 6) refers to q. 6 as the first question of the group and not the second.[94] And if "the preceding two

---

94. Some of the older editions have "the third," on the assumption that "the preceding two questions" must refer to the first and second of the "three questions."

questions" refers to qq. 7–8, why does he say that what was said to them was that "both existing and non-existing supposits are supposits of a common term without qualification," which is the reply to q. 6, and which uses terminology (*"simpliciter supposita termini communis"*) found only in q. 6 (just before n. 9)?

[n. 88] What is said here suggests that nn. 87–88 are actually an alternative reply to the one given in n. 82 to the second argument of q. 5, and that we must read "to the second question of those three" in n. 87 as "to the second argument [*ratio*] of those three." This can only be conjecture, but it is strongly suggested by the repeated terminology of "predicated with the verb *is*," which occurs only in the second argument (n. 2), in the reply to the argument in n. 43, and here. Note also the recurring use of the terms "the former ... the latter [*de his et de illis*]" in n. 2 and the present section.

The alternative reply involves the notion of "diverse appellation." The understanding of a common term involves neither the idea of the present (*praesentialitas*), nor the past, nor the future, and does not specify any *differentia* of time. Therefore, a term such as 'man' can be univocal when used more than once with the same signification, but different or 'diverse' appellation. Thus "univocation is when the appellation of a name varies and the signification remains the same." This kind of explanation is given in the anonymous *Treatise on Univocation*: "Univocation therefore is when the appellation of a name varies and the signification remains the same."[95]

Alternative Replies to Question 5

[n. 89] The point of the first reply (to n. 1 above) seems to be that 'Socrates is' and 'Robert is' are both true, but 'Socrates is a being' is false because Socrates, unlike Robert, is dead.

[n. 90] The second reply is consistent with the idea of diverse appellation mentioned above.

[n. 91] The third reply is as before (n. 83).

---

95. *Tractatus de Univocatione Monacensis*, in Rijk, *Logica Modernorum* II.ii:333–51. For discussion of the historical origin of univocation, see ibid., II.i:492; see also Lambert of Lagny, *Summa Lamberti* (ed. Alessio), 205–45 (translated in Kretzmann and Stump, *Cambridge Translations of Medieval Philosophical Texts*, 102–62) and Jeremiah Hackett, "Roger Bacon," in Jorge J. E. Gracia and Timothy Noone (eds.), *A Companion to Philosophy in the Middle Ages* (Oxford: Blackwell, 2003), 620.

Reply to the Opposing Arguments of Question 7

[n. 92] The first argument (n. 21) was that 'Caesar is running; therefore, a man is running' is necessary[96] because it was true at one time (when Caesar was alive), and that our understanding of the consequence is the same now as it was then, so the implied middle of the consequence, 'Caesar is a man,' is also necessary.

It is replied that the consequence is not valid, for Caesar is not now the appellate of 'man' with a verb in the present tense. But the consequence is clearly true when the tense is changed appropriately, that is, 'Caesar is running in the time during which he was appellated by man with a verb in the present tense; therefore, a man ran' is valid.

[n. 93] The second main argument probably alluded to Aristotle's argument in *Metaphysics* IV.4.1006a33-34: "I say, however, that this signifies one thing; if this exists, [and] if this [is] a man, this will be the being of a man." Scotus replies, "Aristotle's remark must be understood as regards the composite signified by a verb of any *differentia* of time."

[n. 94] The final reply is to the fifth main argument of n. 29, that 'Caesar is Caesar; therefore, Caesar is a man' is a valid consequence. It is objected that the consequence is not valid, although it did follow at the time that Caesar was appellated by 'man' with a verb in the present tense. See n. 13 of q. 12 below: "For the thing that 'Caesar' signifies does not exist now, nor does it have its being [*suum esse*] at every time."

Questions 9–11. Summary Outline

These three questions address some of the problems that arise when terms stand for non-existent things: q. 9 concerns whether a common term with a verb in the present tense supposits only for things existing in the present; q. 10 asks whether the subjects of past- and future-tense propositions stand for only things have existed and will exist, respectively; and q. 11 considers whether a common term distributes for all of its *supposita* without qualification, including past and future things.

---

96. 'Necessary' here means that the conclusion follows from the premises; we might also say, 'valid.'

[Question 9. Does a Common Term Suppositing with a Present-Tense Verb Supposit Only for Presently Existing Things?]

Summary

The question begins with four arguments (nn. 1–4) that a term is restricted, followed by five arguments (nn. 5–10) against. The reply to the first affirmative argument (n. 1) is at nn. 26–30; to the second, at nn. 31–33; and to the third and fourth, at nn. 34–35. Two objections to the first negative argument are considered at nn. 36–37, followed by two replies to these (nn. 38–39).

Discussion

The topic is revisited in q. 13 of *Opus I*, which consists of many of the same questions, though the opposite conclusion is drawn. In reply to q. 9, Scotus determines that a term is not restricted by the present tense of the verb; in reply to q. 13, however, he determines that it is.

This was a common topic in *sophismata* literature of the mid-thirteenth century, and almost certainly traces its origins to the twelfth century or earlier. It is connected with q. 7, whether 'Caesar is a man' is true, and with the sophism 'every man exists': if every man exists and Caesar is a man, it follows that Caesar exists, which is false. Therefore, Caesar is not a man, and the present tense restricts the term 'man' to present men. Alternatively, we can hold that some men do not exist, in which case 'Caesar is a man' is true, and the term is not restricted by the tense of the verb.

Those who disagree with restriction (as Scotus does in q. 9) also hold that 'Caesar is a man' is true (as he does in q. 7), and that 'every man exists' is false. On the other hand, those who agree with restriction (as Scotus does in q. 13) also hold that 'Caesar is a man' is false (as he does in q. 12), and that 'every man exists' is true. Thus q. 7 and q. 9 are consistent, as are q. 12 and q. 13, though for opposite reasons. This suggests that qq. 12–13 were written at a different time from the rest of *Opus I*.[97]

---

[97]. For the connection between this and the question of whether Caesar is a man, see "*Omnis homo est*" (NL 16135, ff. 49vb–52vb) and "*Omnis homo de necessitate est animal*" (NL 16135, f. 58vb).

Our anonymous Parisian commentator tells us that the position that the term is restricted was the most common and that almost everyone adhered to it, taking it from the rule of appellation:[98] "A common term suppositing with a verb of the present tense, taken *simpliciter*, not having a force of ampliation either from itself or another, nor restricted nor otherwise ampliated, supposits for things that actually exist, or for things existing in the present."[99]

Scotus's position here (but not in the corresponding q. 13) would have fallen under the censure of the ninth of the ten propositions condemned by Robert Kilwardby in 1277: "That a term with the verb in the present is distributed for all *differentia* of time."[100] The reasons for the condemnation are not exactly understood, but may be connected with Kilwardby's defence of Augustine's view that past-tense propositions can be translated without loss of meaning into present-tense propositions. Kilwardby says, in his commentary on the *Perihermenias*,[101] that the content (*res*) of the proposition 'Caesar existed' truly exists now, and cites Augustine in the *Confessions*, saying that every verb of the past or future tense can be analyzed into a verb of the present tense. For example, when I say 'Caesar existed,' this is to be analyzed into 'Caesar is a thing of the past,' that is, the pastness of Caesar, or the record (*memoria*), exists.[102]

---

98. The rule is also mentioned by *Ps.*-Lambert of Auxerre (*Summa* VIII, "De appellatione," in *César et le Phénix*); see also John le Page (*Appellationes* II, n. 9; 228). It is mentioned as early as the late twelfth century in the logical works *Dialectica Monacensis* (Rijk, *Logica Modernorum* II:623) and *Logica 'Cum sit nostra'* (ibid., 449).

99. *César et le Phénix*, NL 16135, 58vb (201): "And this position is the most common. Hence almost all adhere to this position, and they wish to extract it from the rule of appellation, which says, 'a common term suppositing with a verb of the present tense taken *simpliciter*, [and] not having the force of ampliation either from itself or from another, neither restricted nor otherwise ampliated, supposits for those things that are actual, or for things existing in the present [Et ista positio communissima est. Unde omnes fere adhaerent huic positioni et istud volunt extrahere ex illa regula appellationum: 'terminus communis supponens verbo praesentis temporis simpliciter sumpto, non habenti vim ampliandi nec ex se nec ex alio non restrictus nec ampliatus aliunde, supponit pro eis quae sunt actu sive pro praesentibus].'" The position that a common term is restricted by the verb should be distinguished from the position held by William of Sherwood (*Introductiones* 5.16; Kretzmann, 123) and by Roger Bacon (*Summulae* II, n. 560; 280): that a common term naturally stands only for things existing in the present, and so requires no restriction.

100. Robert Kilwardby, *Perihermenias*, lib. 1, lect. 9, in Lewry, "Oxford Condemnations," 275n140: "Quod terminus cum verbo de praesenti distribuitur pro omnibus differentiis temporum."

101. Ibid., 250.

102. See Augustine, *Confessions* XI.18.23, 20.26, 27.35, *et passim*. See also Kilwardby, *De tempore*, in *Robert Kilwardby O.P.: On Time and Imagination*, ed. P. Osmund Lewry (Oxford: Oxford University Press for the British Academy, 1987), §§4, 10, 75–77. Kilwardby attempts to balance the Augustine

Commentary

Arguments for

The first four sections (nn. 1–4) give four arguments in defence of the proposition that a common term is restricted by the tense of the verb.

[n. 1] The first argument is that if a common term is not restricted by the tense of the verb, 'a white thing is black' would be true (for example, of a person who was previously pale, but is now dark having spent months in the Mediterranean sun). Also 'a sitting thing can walk' would be true in the sense of composition, because the proposition 'a sitting thing is walking' could possibly be true. But in *De sophisticis elenchis* I.4, Aristotle says that in the sense of composition, such a proposition is false.

The two senses of composition and division correspond roughly to the modern distinction between the wide and narrow scope of an operator. 'It is possible that someone sitting can walk' can be understood such that 'it is possible' applies to the entire proposition, 'a sitting thing walks' (which is obviously false, since nothing can both sit and walk at the same time), or such that 'possible' applies to the predicate only (which is true, since someone who is now sitting can possibly walk). This can be expressed as follows:

Sense of composition: Possibly $(\exists x)[\text{sitting}(x) \text{ and walking}(x)]$
Sense of division: $(\exists x)(\text{sitting}(x) \text{ and Possibly } [\text{walking}(x)])$

According to William of Ockham, "when the *dictum* of a proposition is given with a mode, the [sense of the] proposition must be distinguished in terms of composition, division, and amphiboly."[103] He continues: "In the sense of composition, it is denoted that the mode is predicated of the whole proposition; in the sense of division, it is denoted that the predicate is predicated of the subject by an intermediate verb determined by such a mode, or by an intermediate modal verb."[104] For example, in 'for a pale thing to be dark is possible,' it is denoted in

---

'internalist' account of time with the Aristotelian 'externalist' account by arguing that time as unlimited and undetermined does not require mind, and is therefore external to us. However, as limited and determined (e.g., divided into contingent units) it does require mind, and is therefore 'internal.' Also, q. 14 (ibid., §73) raises the interesting question of whether time could exist without a mind.

103. Amphiboly is ambiguity in the sense of a whole sentence that results from a cause other than the ambiguity of a single word. See Ockham, *Summa logicae* III-I.5-7 (377–82).

104. Ockham, *Summa logicae* III-I.20 (411–12): "When the *dictum* of a proposition is supplied

the sense of composition that the mode 'possible' is verified by the whole proposition 'a pale thing is dark.' In the sense of division, however, it is denoted that the predicate 'dark' is verified of the subject 'pale' by the intermediary verb 'is,' determinately with one adverb or by some other equivalent determination corresponding to such a mode, or by an intermediary corresponding verb adjoined with the infinitive 'to be,' as in, for example, 'a pale thing is able to be dark.'

[n. 2] The second argument for restriction is that "the predicate in such a proposition is restricted to standing only for things that exist; therefore, so is the subject." It consists of a proof of the consequence: if we could not infer that the subject stood for the same things as the predicate, we could not convert propositions such as 'some *a* is *b*' to 'some *b* is *a*' without committing the fallacy of 'figure of speech.' This is the last of the fallacies in the *Topics* that Aristotle says depend on language (*in dictione*). The Latin *figura dictionis* literally means 'figure of speech,' but the fallacy does not involve a non-literal use of language. Rather, it occurs when the conclusion relies on the ambiguity of some verbal inflection, which is wrongly implied to hold in one case where it correctly holds in others. It may also (wrongly) suggest that one form of words has the same kind of semantic analysis as another.[105]

The argument is unclear, but perhaps Scotus means that the predicate forms something that is 'one' with the subject, such that conversion follows, and so 'Caesar is a man' is false because you cannot form 'one' out of an existing predicate and a non-existing subject, or at least not without tweaking the meaning of 'is.'

Then Scotus gives two proofs of the antecedent, that is, that the predicate is restricted. The first is that if we add *a* to '*b* is' to make '*b* is *a*,' this is equivalent to '*a* is a being-that-is-*a*,' and so *a* is a presently existing thing. The second is that otherwise, 'a man is pale; therefore, a man is' would not be valid. He gives a further proof of the second argument: if the predicate 'pale' stood indifferently for what exists and what does not exist, the consequence from the conjoined to the

---

with a mode, that proposition must have distinct senses of composition and division, or according to amphiboly. In the sense of composition, it is denoted that the mode is predicated of the entire proposition. In the sense of division, it is denoted that the predicate is predicated of the subject with an intermediate verb determined by such a mode, or with an intermediate verb of such a mode [Quando dictum propositionis ponitur cum modo, illa propositio est distinguenda penes compositionem et divisionem vel secundum amphiboliam. In sensu compositionis denotatur quod ille modus praedicetur de illa propositione tota; in sensu divisionis denotatur quod praedicatum praedicetur de subiecto mediante verbo determinato per talem modum vel mediante verbo tali modali]."

105. See, e.g., H. W. B. Joseph, *An Introduction to Logic* (Oxford: Clarendon Press, 1906), 543.

divided would be faulty in every case because 'being' would be predicated only incidentally. Yet Aristotle teaches (*De interpretatione* II.2) that this inference is sometimes valid. See the discussion of 'incidental being' in n. 16 of qq. 5–8.

[n. 3] The third argument is that the composition of the proposition is 'measured' by a time. Since we do not understand the proposition without understanding its 'extremes' or terms, we must understand the terms as existing at the same time as the composition. Lambert of Lagny mentions a similar argument in his *Logic*: "The consignification that is its time [or tense] is first the measure of the verb's signification, or action, and last the measure of the *suppositum*, or the subject of the action. But a measure restricts the thing measured (since if [a thing] is measured with respect to quantity, there is [a restriction] of the quantity of the thing measured). And so even though the restriction is not brought about by reason of the verb's signification, it can be brought about by reason of the verb's consignification."[106] Scotus's rejection of this argument is consistent with his later resolution of Aristotle's sea-battle problem.[107]

[n. 4] The fourth argument is similar to the third. The composition of the proposition is the form of the terms. But form is the principle of understanding something according to its logical aspect (*ratio*), and so the terms are understood under the logical aspect of the composition, that is, in the present.

Arguments against

In nn. 5–10, Scotus presents arguments that the subject term is not restricted by the verb.

[n. 5] The first argument is that if no men existed, the contradictories 'every man exists' and 'some man does not exist' would both be false, which is impossible. Proof: 'every man exists' is clearly false, since no men exists; but 'some man does not exist' is false, because by hypothesis the subject 'some man' stands only for existing things; thus, it signifies 'some man who exists does not exist.'

---

106. In Kretzmann and Stump, *Cambridge Translations of Medieval Philosophical Texts*, 123; see also *Logica (Summa Lamberti)*, 128. For further discussion of the time of composition, see Peter of Auvergne on justifying the idea of restriction from a 'Modistic' point of view: a term with a present-tense verb supposits for present things because the composition signified by the verb is present in a present tense verb, past in a past tense, etc.; quoted in Costantino Marmo, "The Semantics of the *Modistae*," in *Medieval Analyses in Language and Cognition*, eds. Sten Ebbesen and Russell L. Friedman (Copenhagen: Royal Danish Academy of Sciences and Letters, 1996), 95.

107. See *Opus II.I*, qq. 7–9, below.

Note that Scotus, like other medieval writers, is not committed to the existential sense of 'some,' or to Quine's principle 'to be is to be the value of a variable.' The falsity of 'some man does not exist' arises only from the assumption that 'some man' must stand for existing men. Lambert of Lagny gives an almost identical argument, saying "when no man is in existence, 'Every man exists' is false, and so its contradictory 'Some man does not exist' will be true. But if the common term in the negative proposition supposits for existing things, the proposition will be false—which is impossible."[108]

A commonly accepted resolution of this difficulty was that a term supposits for existing things when there are existing *supposita*. When there are not, the term reverts to suppositing for non-existent things. This is captured by the rule mentioned by Lambert: "A substantial or accidental common term that is not restricted by any other means and that serves as the subject or the predicate of a present-tense verb that has no ampliating force of its own or from anything else is restricted to suppositing for present things if it has *appellata*; but if it does not have *appellata*, it reverts to nonexistents."[109] Scotus does not accept this principle, however (see his comment at n. 39 below), because he accepts the argument given here.

[n. 6] The second argument is that if the subject ranged only over existing things, propositions such as 'a house is [being] made' would be false. Something that is being made does not exist in the full sense. A house under construction is not yet a house, so a house that exists now cannot be made. Hence Aristotle: "nature in the sense of generation is a path to nature" (*Physics* II.1.193b12–13).

[n. 7] The third argument is that 'the Antichrist runs, therefore a man runs' is valid; therefore the implicit minor premise, 'the Antichrist is a man,' must relate to a not-yet-existent thing (the Antichrist). Compare n. 22 of q. 13 below, where

---

108. Lambert of Lagny, *De suppositionis et de significationis*, in *Logica (Summa Lamberti)* VIII, 219 (translated in Kretzmann and Stump, *Cambridge Translations of Medieval Philosophical Texts*, 123). See also John le Page, *Appellationes* II, nn. 12–13 (228–29); "*Omnis Phoenix est*" (NL 16135, f. 64ra); "*Album fuit disputaturum*" (NL 16135, 13vb).

109. Lambert of Lagny, *De suppositionis et de significationis*, 213 (translated in Kretzmann and Stump, *Cambridge Translations of Medieval Texts*, 116). See also Roger Bacon, *Summa de sophismatibus et distinctionibus* in *Opera hactenus inedita Rogeri Bacon*, ed. Robert Steele, 16 vols. (Oxford: Clarendon Press, 1937), 144; "Introductiones parisienses" (Rijk, *Logica Modernorum* II.ii:372, 8–9); William of Sherwood, *Introductiones* 5.16.2 (124), in Norman Kretzmann (trans.), *William of Sherwood's Introduction to Logic* (Minneapolis: University of Minnesota Press, 1966), 16.2; "*Omnis Phoenix est*" (NL 16135, f. 14vb.); and "*Album fuit disputaturum*" (NL 16135, f. 13ra).

the same argument is mentioned but without endorsement, unlike here. In q. 13, it is rejected because the premise is false: 'the Antichrist runs; therefore, a man runs' is not valid unless 'the Antichrist is a man' is true, which it is not because the Antichrist is a not-yet-existent thing.

[n. 8] The fourth argument is obscure: "A common term primarily supposits for its significate and not for a *suppositum* unless because the *suppositum* is the same as the significate." This is a comment about the 'primary' signification of a common term, "otherwise, no universal [proposition] would be true." Why would this follow? If a term primarily supposited for the individuals falling under it (the *supposita*), why could not the predicate of the proposition apply to all these individuals, and so at least one universal proposition be true? Why would it follow that no universal proposition is true?

Perhaps we can make sense of this in terms of the distinction between personal and simple supposition. The significate of a common term is the corresponding concept or nature, for which the term supposits primarily (or simply). So when we are talking about man being an animal or mortal, we are primarily referring to relations between concepts or natures. But secondarily, or personally, we are saying that there are no individuals for which 'man' stands that are not also individuals for which 'animal' stands. Therefore, the common term supposits equally for all individuals, although not in the same way as it supposits for the concept or nature. Scotus seems to be operating with the notion of something being true or false "in the understanding [*secundum intellectum*]," where what is signified is the "mental concept," as in n. 10 below. See also Walter Burley,[110] who says that everything which is a *suppositum* of a present man is a present *suppositum* of a present man, and every past *suppositum* of a past man is a past *suppositum* of a present man.

[n. 9] The fifth argument (nn. 9–10) is that the subject is not constrained by the verb. Two reasons are given. The first (n. 9) seems to be that a term in one part of a sentence cannot affect the semantics of a term in another part. Otherwise 'a

---

110. Walter Burley, *Quaestiones in Perihermenias*, in "Walter Burley, Questions on the Perhermenias," ed. Stephen Brown, *Franciscan Studies* 34 (1974): 280: "All that is a supposit of a present man is a present supposit of a present man, and all that is a past supposit of a man is a past supposit of a present man [Omne quod est suppositum praesentis hominis est suppositum praesens hominis praesentis, et omne praeteritum suppositum hominis est suppositum praeteritum hominis praesentis]." This text was probably produced in 1301, after Scotus's *Questions*, but not long after. It demonstrates a common understanding of the same problem, at around the same time and in the same place (Oxford).

man is dead' could be true; that is, if 'is dead' qualified 'man,' so that 'man' only meant dead men, the sentence would be true. Then there would be no difference between a 'contracting' determination (*determinatio contrahens*) and a 'diminishing' determination (*determinatio diminuens, determinatio specificans*). A diminishing determination occurs when an adjectival modifier negates the scope of what it determines, as in 'dead man.' A contracting determination does not, as in 'wise man.' In the first case, we cannot reason from the valid predication of the qualified expression ('dead man') to the predication of the unqualified one ('man'). Thus, we cannot infer from 'there is a dead man' to 'there is a man.' In the second case, we can validly infer this, from 'there is a wise man' to 'there is a man.' Hence Aristotle: "But when in what is added some opposite is contained that gives rise to a contradiction, it is not true but false (e.g., to call a dead man a 'man')" (*De interpretatione* II.11.21a21–23).[111]

[n. 10] The second reason for the subject not being constrained by the verb is that we can understand 'the actuality measured by the present time' to exist in the subject for any *suppositum* falling under the subject term. Therefore (assuming the Modist principle that signifying follows understanding) it should be possible to signify this. But this would destroy the point of discourse, which is to signify every possible mental construct. See q. 13, n. 6, which uses the same premise in support of the opposite conclusion.

[Question 10. In a Past-Tense Proposition, Does the Subject Stand Only for Things That Were, and in a Future-Tense Proposition, Only for Things That Will Be?]

Summary

The main arguments consist of three arguments (nn. 11–14) that in past- and future-tense propositions, the subject stands only for things that used to exist or will exist, followed by two arguments (nn. 15–16) against. The reply to the question is at n. 24.

---

111. See Stephen Dumont, "Duns Scotus's Parisian Question on the Formal Distinction," *Vivarium* 43, no. 1 (2005): 7–62, for a discussion of Scotus's use of the distinction in a later work. Dumont suggests that Simon of Faversham is a source for much of Scotus's terminology; see *Simon of Faversham, Quaestiones super libro Elenchorum*, eds. Sten Ebbesen et al. (Toronto: Pontifical Institute of Mediaeval Studies, 1984), q. 22 (156–58).

Arguments for

[n. 11] The first argument cites the arguments of the previous question, concerning composition. This apparently means nn. 1–4 of q. 9 above, i.e., that if the subjects in past- and future-tense propositions did not stand for things that used to exist or will exist, respectively: (i) 'a white (or pale) thing is dark' would be true; (ii) the subject and predicate of the proposition could stand for different things; (iii) the composition expressed by the proposition would not be measured by the time of the verb; and (iv) there would be no logical composition of its terms in the present, which is how the proposition is understood.

[n. 12] The second argument is that 'a man was' follows from 'a man who was, was,' and similarly for 'a man will be' from 'a man who will be, will be.' But if the subject could stand for presently existing men, neither consequence would follow, since it is not true to say of any presently existing man that he was among the men who used to exist (and whose act of existence terminated in the past), or those who will exist (and whose act of existence has not yet begun).

[n. 13] The third argument is that if all men who exist now had just begun to exist, and other men besides these had existed in the past (that is, if the whole of humanity were suddenly wiped out and replaced by a new set of humans), then 'a man was' would be false if the subject term did not stand for the men who existed previously. And then 'no man was' would be true.

[n. 14] Here Scotus notes that the two previous arguments prove that the subject may stand for past and future things, although not only for past and future things. So also for the second argument of q. 9 (n. 2 above) that "the predicate in such a proposition is restricted to standing only for things that exist; therefore, so is the subject."

His point is not altogether clear, given that n. 2 explicitly says that the predicate only stands for things that exist now. Perhaps Scotus is saying that although n. 2 attempts to show that the subject of present-tense propositions stands only for presently-existing things (restriction-to-the-present), the proof shows only that it may stand for presently-existing things. Likewise for the second and third arguments (nn. 12–13). He does not say why, though it is possible that n. 14 is not one of the arguments for the thesis, but rather a transitional observation.

There is an ambiguity in the referent of "the two final arguments [*duae ultimate rationes*]" which occurs here and again at n. 15. Here, at n. 14, context and logic indicate that it must refer to the final two of the three affirmative main arguments of q. 10, that is, to nn. 12–13 above. But the same phrase in n. 15 below either has the same referent as before (nn. 12–13), or else refers to nn. 9–10 of the preceding question. This affects the translation: if it refers to nn. 12–13, we take "against the opposite of the preceding question [*ad oppositum praecedentis quaestionis*]" as the object of "works—or proves [*probant*]"; if to nn. 9–10, we take "against the opposite of the preceding question [*ad oppositum praecedentis quaestionis*]" as qualifying "the two final arguments [*duae ultimate rationes*]." The latter is the more natural reading outside the context of the discussion, but makes little sense. The second reading would be something like: "the two final arguments [of q. 10] prove 'not only' in respect of the opposite of the preceding question [q. 9]." Therefore, to someone defending the "not only" of q. 10, that is, that the arguments do not rule out reference to present things, it is objected that by the same reasoning, we must accept the objections (that is, the opposites) to q. 9, which are that a common term with a verb in the present tense does not just supposit 'only' for things existing in the present.

Arguments against

[n. 15] The first argument (that the predicate is restricted) is that the 'not only' of the two final arguments (nn. 12–13) works against the opposite of the preceding question (q. 9). When Scotus speaks of "the 'not only' of the two final arguments," he means the claim that the subject of a future-tense proposition stands 'not only' for things that were.

[n. 16] The second argument in opposition is that otherwise 'a white object was dark' would be true: for example, being 'a white object' is now true of Socrates who has lost his tan, and it was true that he was dark in the past. So 'a white object (Socrates) was dark' is true.

[Question 11. Is a Common Term Distributed for Any of Its *Supposita* without Qualification in Every Proposition in Which Some Immediate Contracting Term Is Not Added to It?]

Summary

Four arguments against the proposition (nn. 17–20) are followed by three arguments against (nn. 21–23).

Discussion

The term *simpliciter* seems to be a reference to natural supposition: the doctrine that the range of a common term can include absolutely everything that falls under the meaning of a term, whether present, past, future, or non-existing. "Some immediate contracting term" would then be any adjectival qualification of the original term which restricts its scope, such as when we say 'presently existing men' rather than 'men.'

Commentary

Arguments against

[n. 17] The first argument considers the case where the major premise is an assertoric as-of-now proposition ('every moving thing is [now] a man') and the minor is contingent ('every horse is contingently moving'). But Aristotle says (*Prior Analytics* I.15.34a24–b19) that we must read the universal assertoric proposition without limitation of time (*simpliciter*). Otherwise, the syllogism will not be valid: it may possibly be true that everything moving is a man, that is, that only men are moving, and it may be true that every horse is moving (even though none are moving right now); but the conclusion that 'possibly every horse is a man' is false. The major must be taken *simpliciter*.

The same point is made later in the determination of q. 13 at n. 15, arguing for the same conclusion (Scotus rejects the conclusion in the determination of the present question).

[n. 18] The second argument alludes to *Prior Analytics* I.13.32b26–38, where Aristotle says that 'every b can be a' has two senses: either everything that is b can possibly be *a*, or that everything that can be *b* can possibly be *a*.[112] Thus, 'every man can fly' could mean that every man who exists now can fly, or it could mean that, at some time in the future, every man who exists then will have the ability to fly.

The argument contrasts two possible cases of the first sense ('everything that is *b*'). The first case is that the subject could stand for all of its per se *suppositа*. A per se *suppositum* is one that falls under a term because of its form, as this man falls under the term 'man.' This is contrasted with an 'accidental' *suppositum*, which falls under a term because of some accident of a per se *suppositum*, as Socrates falls under the term 'white' because he happens to be white. However, 'this white man' is a per se *suppositum* of 'white.'[113] Scotus discusses this distinction later in his reply to this argument (nn. 46–52 below). In this case, any *de inesse* and any *de contingenti* proposition would be impossible. Scotus says puzzlingly that this is because 'the same actuality could not inhere contingently in supposits belonging to any *differentia* of time.' The anonymous Parisian author of "*Album fuit disputaturum*" is more helpful, saying that a proposition such as 'every man runs' would assert that Caesar runs, or the Antichrist runs, and in neither case can both be true at the same time.[114] The anonymous author of the sophism 'every man exists' says that if a term had natural supposition, this would destroy the rules of appellation and restriction, since all universal affirmatives in the present tense would be impossible or necessary, and none would be *de contingenti*.[115] Ockham deals with this problem in the *Summa Logicae*.[116]

The second sense of 'every *b* can be *a*,' namely 'everything which can be *b*, can be *a*,' is discussed in Scotus's reply to the argument in n. 48 below.

The second case is where the subject stands only for existing things. In that case, if the assertoric (*de inesse*) proposition—meaning, presumably, the major proposition of the syllogism which has a minor premise about contingency or *de*

---

112. This is not noted in the edition. The same *Prior Analytics* passage is also alluded to (again, without being noted in the edition) in q. 13 at n. 15.
113. See Aristotle, *Anal. priora* I.22.83a1–20.
114. "*Album fuit disputaturum*," NL 16135, 14rb (73). See also John le Page, *Appellationes* I, nn. 33–36 (222–24).
115. "*Omnis homo est*," NL 16135, 51ra (162): "Tales videntur destruere regulas appellationum et restrictionum; et omnes universales affirmativas de praesenti videntur ponere impossibiles vel necessarias et nullam de contingenti, quod absurdum est dicere." See also "*Omnis Phoenix est*," NL 16135, 63vb (212).
116. Ockham, *Summa logicae* III-I.23, 26 (420).

contingenti—has natural supposition, standing for all of its per se *supposita*, the *de contingenti* proposition would be true, but the *de inesse* would be impossible. But the argument is not clear. It is possible Scotus means that the *de contingenti* proposition would be false, not true, but no alternative reading is given. See our remarks on the reply to the argument in n. 46 below.

[n. 19] The third argument seems to repeat the logic of the first. With an assertoric major and a contingent minor, the syllogism would be 'regular,' that is, regulated by the principle of *dici de omni*, such that whatever the subject is predicated of, so is the predicate.

[n. 20] The fourth argument refers to the arguments in nn. 1–4 above, which purport to show that a common term with a present-tense verb supposits only for things in the present, and nn. 11–13 above, where Scotus purports to show that in a past-tense proposition, the subject supposits only for past things, and in a future-tense proposition, only for future things.

Arguments for

[n. 21] The first argument on the opposing side is that 'every man runs; therefore, Caesar runs' is valid, and likewise, 'every man will run; therefore, Caesar will run.' They are valid because the implicit minor premise that is supplied to make a proper syllogism is necessary, that is, 'Caesar is a man.' Scotus says this is clear from "what was previously said," that is, in n. 7, where he argues that 'the Antichrist runs; therefore, a man runs' is valid, from which it follows that the implicit minor premise, 'the Antichrist is a man,' must relate to a not-yet-existent thing (the Antichrist).

[n. 22] The second argument evokes nn. 7–8 of qq. 5–8, where Scotus says that a term imposed to signify a single nature is predicated univocally because a term has a single definition, and because equivocation is not diversity of *supposita*, but diversity of sense. Any term used in the same sense is common to all of its *supposita*.

[n. 23] The third argument appeals to the principle of *dici de omni*. In a universal proposition, the distribution is for everything that can be taken under it, including all of the *supposita*. For the principle of *dici de omni* see Aristotle (*Posterior Analytics* I.4.73a28–31) and n. 14 of q. 6 above. See also Scotus's *Quaestiones super libros Elenchorum Aristotelis*, q. 52, n. 8.

Determination

[n. 24] Scotus replies to qq. 9–10 that a common term supposits for all of its *supposita*, whether existing or non-existing, and whether the *supposita* exist in the past, present, or future.

[n. 25] In reply to q. 11, Scotus repeats his remarks from n. 21 that the implicit minor of the consequence, 'every man runs; therefore, Caesar runs' is 'Caesar is a man,' and that this proposition is necessary. He notes that when the common term "is not specified by something directly added to it," that is, when it is not qualified in such a way as to restrict its scope, the common term stands for its significate "absolutely." Note that in n. 9 above, he argued that the subject is not constrained by the verb.

Reply to the Main Arguments of Both Parts of Question 9

[n. 26] To the first argument of q. 9 (see n. 1 above), Scotus replies by distinguishing between subject and *suppositum*: a common term is always predicated of a *suppositum* (though not a subject) in the present tense. Thus we cannot say of a *suppositum* of white that it 'once was black,' although we can truly say of a subject that it once was white and may now be black. This suggests that Scotus's notion of a *suppositum* is analogous to the modern concept of an object in a possible world (or a past or future world), or to what is intended when we say 'the past Socrates,' meaning Socrates as he existed in the past.[117]

Scotus says that the reply to the other example (a sitting thing can walk) will also be clear. Those who make a distinction between the sense of composition and the sense of division do not mean that a contrary predicate (walking) could be predicated of a *suppositum* of sitting. The contrary predicate applies only to the subject. Thus 'a sitting thing can walk' is false in the sense of composition, that is, 'a sitting thing is walking' is necessarily false. But as long as 'sitting' does not apply (in some possible or future situation) to the subject, the predicate 'walking' can apply to it.

[n. 27] Scotus then considers an objection to this: we can predicate both 'black' and 'was a white thing' of the present Socrates.

---

117. Walter Burley makes similar remarks about the nature of the *suppositum*: see q. 5 of Burley, *Quaestiones in Perihermenias* (200–295).

[n. 28] Replying to this objection, Scotus says that 'was a white thing' is not predicated of the present Socrates (that is, the present *suppositum*) but of the past Socrates. And we cannot arrive at a present-tense proposition from a past-tense proposition and a present-tense proposition. Thus, it does not follow that the 'previously white thing,' that is, the *suppositum* that existed in the past, is black. The reason is that 'this is a white thing that was,' which asserts the identity of 'this' (the present *suppositum*) and 'a white thing that was' (the past *suppositum*), does not follow from 'this was white,' for the past *suppositum* no longer exists. Scotus notes, preempting the objection that 'a white thing is black' follows from 'what was white is black,' that '*what* was white is black' has two senses: either (i) 'what' relates to the subject, in which case the inference is not valid because it commits the fallacy of *quid in quale*; or (ii) it relates to the *suppositum*, in which case the inference is valid but the antecedent ('what was white is black') is false, since the suppositum was white. Rather, 'a is white' was true at some time, and so 'a is black' could be true.

The fallacy of *quid in quale* is one of a number of fallacies of equivocation mentioned in Aristotle's *Topics*, and also explained by Thomas Aquinas in chapter 10 of his treatise *On Fallacies*, 'On the fallacy of figure of speech.' The fallacy occurs when there is an apparent likeness between two expressions having diverse modes of signifying. This can happen in several ways; in the present case, an expression signifying in the mode of one category is used in the same argument to signify in the mode of another. Thomas gives the following example: 'whatever you have seen yesterday, you see today; you saw a white thing yesterday; therefore, you see a white thing today.' This is not valid because something in the category of substance has been changed into something in the category of quality (*mutatur quid in quale*). Thus, even though you could have seen one person yesterday and the same person today in such a way that you have seen the same substance (person), the person may have been pale yesterday and become tanned in the sun today. Thus, the category of substance (person) has been changed into the category of quality (white), making the argument invalid.

When Scotus says "the consequence is valid and the antecedent false," recall n. 26 above, where we were told that "the common term is the same essentially as its *suppositum*" and distinct from its subject, so that "although a subject that once was white may now be black, yet it is not true of the *suppositum* of white, that the *suppositum* once was black." So, if what was white (talking about the *suppositum*) is never black, the antecedent is false, and the consequence valid.

[n. 29] Scotus here raises the further objection that we are not predicating a contrary of a contrary when we say what was white is (now) black.

[n. 30] Replying to this objection, Scotus says that if 'the white thing that was' means the past *suppositum*, then being black is contrary to this object. In keeping with his earlier point that predication only applies to a *suppositum* in the present tense, he says that there is as much contrariety in that case as in the case of a white thing that presently exists and a black thing. The same is true in the case of 'a sitting thing is walking,' which cannot be true because "a past or future *suppositum* of sitting is never walking." When such propositions are taken in the sense of composition, they are false because "the *suppositum* of any time from one part cannot be united to any *suppositum* from the other part."[118]

[n. 31] To the second argument (n. 2 above), namely that if we could not infer that the subject stood for the same things as the predicate, we could not convert (for example, from 'some *a* is *b*' to 'some *b* is *a*') without the fallacy of 'figure of speech,' Scotus replies that the predicate stands equally indifferently in a proposition as the subject because similar reasoning proves both. We can understand the predicate, as applied to any of its *supposita*, to be predicated of the subject, as applying to any of the subject's *supposita*.

[n. 32] Scotus replies here and in n. 33 to the two proofs given for the second argument. The first was that if to '*b* is' we add *a* to make '*b* is *a*,' this is equivalent to '*a* is a being-that-is-*a*,' and so *a* is a presently existing thing. He replies that if the content of the verb 'is' is part of the predicate when predicated as a third element, it does not specify what follows it, but rather the opposite. Thus, in 'every man is an animal,' the content of 'is' is part of the predicate but does not specify 'animal.' Rather 'animal' specifies 'is,' and the being specified by 'animal' is indifferent to the *supposita* it supposits for (that is, it can supposit for animals that existed in the past, not just present ones).

He adds that perhaps "as will be seen later" the content of the verb does not form part of the predicate. The editors' reference here to *Opus II.I*, qq. 5–6,

---

118. It may be helpful to think of a *suppositum* for Scotus as a sort of 'time slice' of an individual that only has existence at a particular time or possible situation, though it must be remembered that the concept of a time slice is a modern one suggesting a view of individuals as *continua* existing through time, whereas Scotus seems to view individuals as wholly constituted at any instant you choose. Thus, if 'sitting Caesar is walking' is to display the requisite contrareity, then 'is walking' would have to be contrary to the past *suppositum*, 'sitting Caesar,' and the proposition is false, just as if sitting Caesar actually existed now.

nn. 21–25 and 29–34 suggests that either (i) *Opus II.I* is not a revision of *Opus I*, but a continuation of it;[119] or (ii) *Opus I* was originally larger and included counterparts to *Opus II.I*, qq. 5–6. In the latter case, however, it is difficult to explain why *Opus II* omits the parts corresponding to qq. 5–11, which contain material crucial to understanding the later questions in *Opus II.I*, particularly the 'sea battle' questions (qq. 6–9).

[n. 33] To the second proof of q. 9, which is that otherwise 'a man is white; therefore, a man is' would not be valid, he replies that a proposition where 'being' is predicated as a second element never follows from one where 'being' is predicated as a third element. He has already argued for this in n. 42 and n. 63 of qq. 5–8 above.

[n. 34] To the third argument (n. 3 above, where it is argued that since the composition of a proposition is 'measured' by a time, we do not understand the proposition without understanding the extremes as existing at the same time as the composition), Scotus replies that the extremes, or subject and predicate terms in a proposition, "are understood for the same time for which the composition is understood, but from this it does not follow that they are understood only for the *supposita* of a single time." In other words, although the time of the verb "measures" or temporally restricts the subject and predicate terms in a proposition, it is still possible, as mentioned in n. 31 above (replying to n. 2), to understand the predicate as attributed to the subject for any of their respective *supposita*, and by any mediating composition. For example, 'a white thing was black' is false if we understand its terms to refer only to white things and black things existing at the same time in the past, since then it would say that some completely white thing was also black at the same time. But if we understand the predicate to be attributed to the subject for any of their *supposita*, that is, for anything white or black existing at any time, then the proposition is true, since a thing could be white now that was previously black.

[n. 35] To the fourth argument—n. 4 above, which, like n. 3, seems to assume that propositions are understood holistically as the 'formal' composition of 'material' parts, that is, subject, predicate, and tensed verb—Scotus again replies that we can understand a term for any of its *supposita* under the aspect (*ratio*) of pres-

---

119. However, this does not explain why the two questions in *Opus I* (qq. 2–3) have doublets in *Opus II.I* (qq. 1–2).

entness or pastness. Thus, our actual understanding of a common term such as 'white' ranges over all of its *supposita*: past, present, and future, even though we can restrict or limit this understanding in the way specified by the mode of composition, for example, in a proposition with a temporal verb.

Reply to the Arguments in Opposition of Question 9

[n. 36] Scotus also mentions other replies to the arguments on the opposing side. To the first argument (n. 5 above), he notes that some people say that it is impossible that no man exists, otherwise the contradictories 'every man exists' and 'some man does not exist' would both be false, which is impossible.

[n. 37] Scotus notes further that others say that if a term has no existing *supposita*, then it stands for non-existing things. But then 'some man does not exist' will be true, although not in the sense that 'some man who exists, does not exist,' that is, not reading 'some men' existentially, but rather in the sense 'some man who does not exist, does not exist.'

This view is mentioned by Lambert of Lagny,[120] who says that a common term which is the subject of a present-tense verb is not restricted to suppositing for existing things, because when no men exist, 'every man exists' is false, and so 'some man does not exist' is true, in the sense that 'some man who does not exist does not exist.' Generally, this seems to have been the view of all who held that 'every man exists' is false. These thinkers also seem to have held that 'man' has natural supposition and supposits for things existing in the present, past, and future, and that the predicate does not restrict the subject of a proposition.[121]

[n. 38] To the first reply (n. 36 above) Scotus says that even if the assumption is impossible, it is nonetheless possible to conceive it without inconsistency.

[n. 39] To the second reply (n. 37 above), he says that if this is the case, then the inference 'a man who does not exist, does not exist; therefore, a man does not exist' is valid, and by parity of reasoning it will be valid when a man exists. But then "the same sentence will not change from truth to falsity and conversely, which is contrary to Aristotle" (see *Categories* 5.4a36–b2).

---

120. Lambert of Lagny, *De suppositionibus et de significationibus*, in *Logica (Summa Lamberti)*; ed. Alessio, 219.

121. See "*Utrum haec possit esse vera 'Caesar est homo,'*" in "*Omnis homo est*" (NL 16135, ff. 49vb–52vb, 51ra [161]). Another view held that the subject naturally supposits only for present things, but can 'revert to [*recurrit ad*]' non-existing *supposita* under certain conditions.

The argument in n. 37 is against n. 5 above, which argued that contradictories would be false at the same time if the subject stands for presently-existing things only. For in a case where no man exists, 'every man exists' is false, but so is 'something that is a man does not exist,' because 'some man who exists does not exist' is signified. What n. 37 says is that we should not read 'some man' in 'some man does not exist' as a sort of existential quantifier.

However, n. 39 contends that the inference is valid both when no men exist and when men exist because the understanding, that is, the semantics, of the inference is the same. But then there is a problem, because according to n. 37, when there are existing *supposita*, the subject stands only for them, and therefore not for any non-existing ones. Thus, the consequent ('a man does not exist') is false, and so the argument is not valid, assuming that the antecedent 'a man who does not exist, does not exist' remains true when men do exist.

[n. 40] Scotus here gives the view of others to the fifth argument on the opposing side. According to the edition, this argument is in n. 10. However, it is clear from the context that the view is about the first proof in n. 9, viz., that the subject is not constrained by the verb because a term in one part of a sentence cannot affect the semantics of a term in another part.

The view of some is that this proves only that the subject is not restricted by composition, because predication involves terms that "stand apart from [*distant*]"; thus, only the predicate is restricted by a "real contracting thing [*contrahens reale*]"—'dead' in the case of 'a man is dead' —because it "gives way [*cedit*]" when it is with the subject. Again, if the subject 'man' were diminished by 'dead,' 'a man is dead' would be true even though Aristotle says in *De interpretatione* II that 'dead' includes the opposite of man.

[n. 41] The second proof of n. 9 above (which the edition gives at n. 10) was that the subject is not constrained by the verb because the purpose of speech is to signify any possible mental concept, and so it is possible to signify "the actuality measured by the present time" existing in the subject for any *suppositum* of the subject. It is said, according to Scotus, that it is possible to signify a predicate to be in a subject for all *supposita* of any time by means of a disjunction such as 'every man who is, or was, or will be, is white,' where the entire disjunction is the subject.

[n. 42] Scotus rejects the second proof. It is possible to understand (and hence to signify) a predicate to be in a subject as it participates in a common form, abstracted from past, present, or future. But this understanding is not signified by a disjunction, for the disjunction signifies more than is actually understood. He means presumably that the disjunction includes the concepts of past, present, and future, whereas the common concept does not: past, present, and future are 'beyond' our understanding of it.

[n. 43] Continuing the argument, Scotus says that the second proof leads to an infinite regress. The sense of the present-tense proposition 'a man who is white' will be 'every man who is, or was, or will be, is white.' This disjunction itself is equivalent to the present-tense 'man who is,' and there will be an infinite regress, according to Scotus, but it is not clear why. Perhaps he means that it is because the verb 'is' appears in both the *definiens* and the *definiendum*.

Scotus's Reply to Question 11
The Position of Scotus

[n. 44] Scotus finally replies to q. 11: when there is no contracting term added, the common term is distributed for any of its per se *supposita* because of the rule of *dici de omni*. He refers to the arguments made on the opposing side of q. 11 (nn. 21–23 above) and also to the determination of q. 9 and q. 10 (n. 24 above).

Reply to the Main Arguments of Question 11

[n. 45] Scotus replies to the first argument on the contrary side in n. 17 above. It was argued there that the common term is not distributed, because in cases where the major premise is assertoric as-of-now (for example, 'every moving thing is [now] a man') and the minor is contingent ('possibly every horse is moving'), absurd conclusions result, and this is against Aristotle, who says (*Prior Analytics* I.15.34a24–b19) that we must read the universal assertoric proposition *simpliciter*.

Scotus replies, apparently conceding the point. A syllogism is invalid (*inutilis*) when the major premise is assertoric and as-of-now (the edition notes to add the qualification that the minor is *de contingenti*, following n. 17) and it is valid when the major premise is assertoric *simpliciter*.[122]

---

122. Cf. Ockham, *Summa logicae* III-1.3 (363–65): "If both are affirmative, then it is in the first mood and valid; if both are negative, then there is a different conjugation and it is invalid because it has a negative minor. If one premise is affirmative and the other negative, either the major is negative and the minor affirmative, or vice versa; if the former, we have the third conjugation, and it is valid; if

Commentary: *Opus I* 251

[nn. 46–47] Scotus next replies to the second argument of n. 18 above, viz., either (i) the subject of 'that which is *b*' stands for all per se *supposita*, in which case any proposition about contingency in which it is posited would be impossible, or (ii) it stands only for existing things, in which case a universal contingent proposition would be true even though its assertoric equivalent is impossible. Scotus replies that no per se *suppositum* is contingently joined to that of which it is the per se *suppositum*, but necessarily; that is, 'white thing' necessarily stands for white things. Therefore (ii) above is true, and the subject of 'that which is *b*' means all things that are *b*, and so the universal proposition about contingency is true (reading *vera* for *falsa*), and the assertoric proposition corresponding to it is impossible. This is not a problem, he says, because the validity of a syllogism does not depend on the truth or falsity of its premises, but on the relation of premises to conclusion.

Note that the punctuation in n. 46 is wrong, and n. 47 really belongs to n. 46. It should read:

When it is said 'therefore, every universal proposition about contingency, in that sense it is false, and every assertoric proposition corresponding to it will be impossible'—this can be conceded [*cum dicitur 'ergo omnis universalis de contingenti in illa acceptione est falsa, et omnis de inesse ei correspondens erit impossibilis,' hoc potest concedi*].

A problem with this reading (actually for any reading) is that n. 18 actually reads: "a universal *de contingenti* proposition would be true [correcting 'false'], and yet its assertoric equivalent would be impossible." The 'yet [*tamen*]' of n. 18 suggests that 'true,' not 'false,' is the correct reading. However, no alternative reading for n. 46 is given.

[n. 48] In nn. 48–52 we have a digression on the reply to the second argument, which discusses case (i) of the argument in n. 18, while nn. 46–47 above discuss case (ii). In case (i), the subject 'which is *b*' stands for all of its per se *supposita*, with the absurd implication that it is impossible for a proposition about contingency to be true. (According to the standard 'synchronic' view that past and

---

the latter, it is the fourth and it is invalid because it has a negative minor [Si utraque sit affirmativa, sic est primus modus et utilis, si utraque sit negativa, sic est alia coniugatio et est inutilis, quia habet minorem negativam. Si una sit affirmativa et alia negativa, aut maior est negativa et minor affirmativa, vel e converso; si primo modo, habetur tertia coniugatio, et est utilis; si e converso, est quarta et inutilis, quia habet minorem negativam]." Cf. E. J. Ashworth, "Some Notes on Syllogistic in the Sixteenth and Seventeenth Centuries," *Notre Dame Journal of Formal Logic* 11, no. 1 (1970): 17–33.

present states of affairs are necessary, any proposition asserting that they are not necessary, such as a proposition about contingency, cannot be true).

Scotus now considers the objection that though it is impossible for something to be contingently in past things insofar as they are past, because there is no potentiality in respect of the past, nevertheless it is not impossible for something to be contingently in them insofar as they share a common form. He repeats the earlier remark (n. 42) about pastness being extraneous to anything insofar as it is a per se *suppositum* of a common form. In that case, at least in the second sense of 'every *b* is contingently *a*' mentioned by Aristotle, viz., where *b* means 'that which is contingently *b*' rather than 'that which is *b*,' the subject stands for the same things 'under another aspect.'

[n. 49] Scotus clarifies this point. Something which is taken absolutely and per se as a *suppositum* of a certain term can be taken under another aspect contingently. For example, man is necessarily a per se *suppositum* of the term 'man,' but this white man is a contingent *suppositum*, that is, under the aspect 'white thing,' it is accidentally a *suppositum* of 'man.' Thus, the proposition has another sense, viz., 'which is contingently [*b*],' where we take the same things under another logical aspect acquired from the contingent mode.[123]

[n. 50] The logic is not clear, but nn. 50–51 seem to be Scotus's reply to the points made in nn. 48–49. The first seems to be a *reductio*: if taking the proposition in the sense of 'what is *b*' requires contingent composition, then this mode

---

123. This view has similarities to the one expressed by the anonymous Parisian author of "*Album fuit disputaturum*." Against the argument that a term restricted to things existing in the present has accidental rather than natural supposition, he says that a term can have both natural and accidental supposition at the same time, but in diverse ways. If a predicate relates to its subject for some fixed *differentia* of time, but indifferently for any time, then the subject has natural supposition. But if the predication is *per accidens*, then it relates to the subject for some *differentia* of time, and so has accidental supposition (NL 16135, 14rb [73]); cf. "*Omnis Phoenix est*" (NL 16135, 67rb [216]). De Libera also cites Nicholas of Paris (in H. A. G. Braakhuis, *De 13de eeuwse Tractaten over syncategorematische Termen: Uitgave van Nicolaas van Parijs'* sincategoreumata, 2 vols. [Meppel: Krips Repro, 1979], 2:316). See also Peter of Cornwall, "*Omnis homo est*" (Worcester Q.13, 48vb [147]), who mentions the argument that unless the predicate could restrict the subject, Aristotle would never have said that the proposition 'every *b* is contingently *a*' has two senses, and similarly a *de inesse ut nunc* proposition would never be true. Against this view is the argument mentioned by the anonymous author of "Every Man of Necessity Is an Animal": if a term were to supposit indifferently for present, past, and future *supposita*, then the distinction made by Aristotle between 'every thing that is *b* is contingently *a*' and 'every thing that is contingently *b* is contingently *a*' would be pointless; for if *b* is applied to present, past, and future *supposita*, then nothing would be contingently *b* except what was *b* ("*Omnis homo de necessitate est animal*," NL 16135, ff. 99rb–103vb, 101vb [238]).

of understanding is transferred to the extreme terms. But in that case there is no difference between this sense and the sense 'what is contingently *b*.' Taking something under a contingent mode does not give the proposition a different sense because a mode of understanding makes no difference to the way the term is taken for its per se *supposita*. In other words, there is nothing about the mode of contingency that changes the way a term is related to the things falling under it.

[n. 51] Again, Scotus argues that the *supposita* must be understood in terms of "some real superadded determination" if the *supposita* per se are to be taken *per accidens*; merely understanding the composition of the terms in a proposition as necessary or contingent "does not convey anything real," as was said at n. 9 above.

[n. 52] Scotus concludes the digression. The first sense or acceptance (*acceptatio*), namely 'what is *b*,' is a literal sense, and holds in virtue of the meaning of the words. However, the second sense, namely 'what is contingently *b*,' does not hold by signification, nor even *per accidens*, but rather "from our pre-determination [*ex praefixione nostra*]." What Scotus means is not entirely clear. Perhaps he means that the sense or acceptance is pragmatically conveyed. He adds that this is why sense is called 'acceptance,' as we can take or 'accept' the proposition under such a determination.

[n. 53] Scotus replies here to the third main argument of n. 19, which was that with an assertoric major and contingent minor, the syllogism would be 'regular,' that is, regulated by *dici de omni*, such that whatever the subject is predicated of, so also is the predicate. He says that for a syllogism to be perfect, "it is not sufficient that what is taken under the minor premise is that for which distribution is made in the major premise," but rather the subject of the minor must itself be taken under the aspect or nature for which the distribution is made in the major premise. Thus, the syllogism in the example—'every man necessarily is an animal; that white man is a man; therefore, etc.'—is not perfect because 'that white man' is not taken as such, that is, as participating in the form of man, in the minor premise, but rather, under the "extraneous aspect" of white.

[n. 54] Alternatively, Scotus says it can be replied that there is a distinction between a contingent *suppositum*, like the white man referred to by the subject term of the minor, and a per se *suppositum*, like any man picked out by the subject term of the major, because the latter, though not the former, are "necessarily joined to a common term." Any man is necessarily an animal, but a white man is only contingently white.

[Question 12. Is 'Caesar is a man' True When Caesar Does Not Exist?]

Summary

The question consists of two arguments (nn. 1 and 2–4) that 'Caesar is a man' is true, followed by two arguments (nn. 5–6) that it is not. The impersonally-expressed determination (n. 7) is that the proposition is false, for "no one is a man unless he is a man now." This is followed by a reply to the first argument (n. 8), two views about the second argument (nn. 9–11), and replies to the second argument (nn. 13–15). Finally, there is an apparently unrelated discussion (nn. 16–19) about quantifying the predicate.

Discussion

This question and the following q. 13 present difficulties for the view that the questions in *Opus I* express a unity intended by its author, rather than being a later redaction. They repeat much of the material in q. 7 and qq. 9–11, respectively, but seem to arrive at different conclusions. The determination of q. 7 is that 'Caesar is a man' is true, whereas the determination of the present question is that it is false. As qq. 12–13 are not found in some of the early manuscripts, it may be that they stem from a different (and possibly later) version of the same work, and that they were subsequently appended to *Opus I* by Scotus's early editors.

On the other hand, while there are significant overlaps between qq. 12–13 and qq. 7–8, there are also arguments in the latter which are not addressed in q. 12 (conversely, all of the arguments of q. 12 are addressed in qq. 7–8). If q. 12 represents a later view of the same author, why did he not resolve some of the arguments that he was apparently persuaded by earlier?

A further problem is that qq. 12–13 are missing from some of the sources which contain only *Opus I*. These versions end: "Concerning the following questions on *De interpretatione*, there is a discussion elsewhere [*De quaestionibus sequentibus super librum Perihermenias dictum est alibi*]." This could perhaps be explained by the hypothesis of the editors of the critical edition (see page 28) that a *bifolium* was dropped. If so, presumably the scribe was aware of this in saying "*dictum est alibi*."

Finally, it has to be explained why the versions containing only *Opus I* as well as qq. 12–13 end: "[Here] end Scotus's questions on *De interpretatione* [*Finiunt quaestiones Scoti super libro Perihermenias*]," as though qq. 12–13 were missing from the other versions. Why would *Opus I* have been regarded as complete when it omits questions from Aristotle's second book?

Commentary

Arguments for

[n. 1] For a discussion of this argument, based on a somewhat cryptic passage from Aristotle's *Metaphysics*, see n. 22 of q. 7 above. Almost exactly the same argument is given there, with the additional explanation that "'man' signifies the same thing whether or not Caesar exists." See also n. 34 of qq. 5–8 above.

[n. 2] The second argument consists of two supporting reasons. The first (n. 2) is that the implication 'Caesar is Caesar; therefore, Caesar is a man' is valid. The second (nn. 2–4) is that 'Caesar is Caesar' is true.

This part of q. 12 is closer to q. 8 above than q. 7 since it is concerned with the truth of 'Caesar is Caesar.' For the argument that "man is included in Caesar and is part of what we understand by him," see n. 25 of q. 7 and n. 31 of q. 8. The first part of the argument is justified by the reason that 'man' is included in 'Caesar' and is part of what we understand by Caesar, so the implication is valid.

The second part of the argument is that 'Caesar is Caesar' is true for three reasons. The first is that the proposition 'a chimera is a chimera' is true,[124] a point mentioned in n. 42 of q. 8 above. There are prior discussions in two *sophismata* from the mid-thirteenth century,[125] and in Robert Kilwardby, who says that 'a

---

124. Cf. Thomas Aquinas, *Scriptum super Sententiis* I, d. 4, q. 2, a. 1, s.c. 2: "Item, secundum Boetium, nulla propositio est verior illa in qua idem de se praedicatur." Ockham discusses the same point in *Summa logicae* II.14, but argues for the opposite conclusion, i.e., 'a chimera is a chimera' is false because it covertly makes the false assertion that the chimera is something, i.e., something that exists: "For 'a chimera is a non-being,' and anything similar, is literally false, since every such proposition would have as its exposition, 'a chimera is something' and 'this is a non-being,' the first of which is false. And if it is said, "surely this is true: 'a chimera is a chimera'?", it seems that it is, because the same thing is predicated of itself and Boethius says that no proposition is more true than one in which the same thing is predicated of itself. It must be said [in reply] that 'a chimera is a chimera' is literally false if its terms supposit significatively, because it implies what is false [Ista enim est falsa de virtute sermonis 'chimaera est non-ens' et quaelibet consimilis, quia quaelibet talis habet istas exponentes 'chimaera est aliquid' et 'illud est non-ens' quarum prima falsa est. Et si dicatur: numquid ista est vera 'chimaera est chimaera'? Videtur quod sic, eo quod praedicatur idem de se, et Boethius dicit quod nulla propositio est verior illa in qua idem de se praedicatur. Dicendum est quod de virtute vocis ista est falsa 'chimaera est chimaera' si termini supponant significative, eo quod falsum implicatur]."

125. See "*Omnis homo de necessitate est animal*," NL 16135, f. 11vb (33).

man is an animal' is true when no men exist (proof: 'a man is a man' is true when no man exists, because 'a chimera is a chimera' is true, even though a chimera does not exist).¹²⁶

[n. 3] The second reason for the truth of 'Caesar is Caesar' was also considered in n. 33 of q. 8 above: 'nothing is truer of something than what is the same as it.' See the commentary on that section.

[n. 4] The third reason is the same as the one given in n. 39 of q. 8. See the commentary on that section.

When Scotus says, "from opposites, the impossible follows," he is referring to a syllogism from opposites (*syllogismus ex oppositis*), according to which, from opposed premises, we can draw a negative conclusion about the same subject as regards itself. John Buridan gives the following example using contrary premises: "No discipline is laborious; every discipline is laborious; therefore, no discipline is a discipline."¹²⁷

Arguments against

[n. 5] There follow two arguments (nn. 5–6) that 'Caesar is a man' is false. First, there is Aristotle's claim that "when 'is [*est*]' is posited as a copula, it is posited as of now [*ut nunc*]" (*De interpretatione* I.3.16b9–10).

[n. 6] Second, living and breathing are necessarily accompaniments of being a man. There is no mention here of the distinction between actuality and aptitude introduced at n. 66 of q. 7 above.¹²⁸

Determination of the Question

[n. 7] The determination that the proposition is false is expressed impersonally, via "*dicitur* [it is said]"; the only other question with a neutral determination is n. 20 of q. 2. The section heading of the critical edition says it is a "reply to the question, first opinion." This relies on the assumption that the 'others say' of n. 10

---

126. Robert Kilwardby, "*Omnis homo de necessitate est animal*," eds. S. Ebbesen and J. Pinborg, in "Studies in the Logical Writings attributed to Boethius of Dacia," *CIMAGL* 3 (1970): 37–40 [extracts].

127. John Buridan, *Summulae*, 5.10.7 (386).

128. Cf. Radulphus Brito, *Quaestiones super arte veteri* (ed. Vercellensis & Vercellensis; Venice: 1499): "Whether 'a dead man, therefore a man' is valid," who argues that in 'Socrates is a dead man,' 'man' here does not stand for a living or true man [Cum dicitur in illo antecedente 'Sortes est homo mortuus includuntur duo contradictoria,' falsum est, quia dicendo Sortes est homo mortuus, homo hic non stat pro homine vivo vel vero, sed secundum exigentiam mortui ut visum est]."

below refers back to the *dicitur* here, which is clearly incorrect, since it refers to the "some deny" of n. 9. Nor are there two opinions about the question. Thus, "it must be said that [*dicendum*]" was intended by Scotus, or his *dicitur* is a misreading of some earlier text, or this question is a fragment of a larger text.

The edition mentions Roger Bacon in connection with those who say 'Caesar is a man' is false. However, Bacon held that the sentence is neither true nor false.[129] The view that the sentence is false was commonly held by those who agreed with the rule that a term can be restricted by the tense of the main verb to signifying things that exist only at the present time, which is why Scotus says: "For no one is a man unless he is a man *now*."

The edition also mentions Pseudo-Boethius of Dacia,[130] who refers to a "controversy among the moderns," some of whom say that the proposition is false because 'Caesar is a man' is true per se "in the first mode." This refers to Aristotle's view (*Metaphysics* V.18.1022a25) that a proposition is true per se in the first mode when it states that the essence of a thing belongs to that thing, such as 'man' belongs to Caesar. But death takes away the substance of Caesar, so the proposition is false.

Replies to the Four Main Arguments

[n. 8] In nn. 8–15, Scotus gives a reply to the first argument (n. 8), two views about the second argument (nn. 9 and 10–12), and replies to the three reasons supporting the second premise of that argument (nn. 13–15).

According to the edition, nn. 8–9 are replies to the main arguments in keeping with the first opinion. However, as noted above, n. 8 is actually a reply to the first main argument (n. 1 above), and n. 9 is the first reply to the second main argument (nn. 2–4).

To the first argument (n. 8) Scotus replies that Aristotle is not saying that whatever a name signifies is also predicated of that name, but rather he wishes to prove the "first principle," that is, the principle of non-contradiction: if the state of affairs signified by one of a pair of contradictory statements exists, the state of affairs signified by the other does not exist.

---

129. Roger Bacon, *Compendium studii theologicae*, c. 5, nn. 122–28 (105): "'Caesar is Caesar' will signify nothing: neither is it an expression nor [is it] a proposition nor does it signify either what is true or false, for the whole "statement" does not signify because of one or two [of its] parts that do not signify ['Caesar est Caesar' nihil significabit: nec est oratio nec propositio, nec verum vel falsum significat, quia ab una vel duabus partibus non significativis est totus sermo non significativus]."

130. Ps.-Boethius of Dacia, *Quaestiones super librum Elenchorum*, q. 94 (84).

Aristotle says: "First then this at least is obviously true, that the word 'be' or 'not be' has a definite meaning, so that not everything will be 'so and not so.' Again, if 'man' has one meaning, let this be 'two-footed animal'; by having one meaning I understand this: if 'man' means '*x*,' then if *a* is a man '*x*' will be what 'being a man' means for him. (It makes no difference even if one were to say a word has several meanings, if only they are limited in number.)"[131]

[n. 9] In nn. 9–11, we have two separate views about the second argument in n. 2 above, corresponding to the two parts of the argument. The first is that "some deny the consequence," viz., that 'Caesar is a man' does not follow from 'Caesar is Caesar,' and it is therefore possible to concede that 'Caesar is Caesar' is true even though 'Caesar is a man' is false. Peter of Cornwall is referenced in the edition, but Peter does not discuss the question of whether the consequence holds, or whether 'Caesar is Caesar' is false.

Among those who do deny the consequence is Pseudo-Boethius of Dacia, who says "by this it is clear in connection with another [argument] that it is true that Caesar is Caesar, although 'Caesar is Caesar; therefore, Caesar is a man' does not follow, except for the time during which he is the suppositum of 'man.'"[132]

[n. 10] "Others say that 'Caesar is Caesar' is false." This is the view to which Scotus adheres, judging from his three replies to the second argument (nn. 13–15).[133] The edition cites Pseudo-Boethius of Dacia here as being among the 'others,' but it is clear from the passage quoted above that he does not belong to those who deny the soundness of the consequence (the 'others'), but rather its validity (the 'some'), saying that 'Caesar is Caesar' is true but that the consequence is not valid. He therefore belongs to the 'some' rather than the 'others.'

---

131. Aristotle, *Metaphysics* IV.4.1006a31.

132. Ps.-Boethius of Dacia, *Quaestiones super librum Elenchorum*, q. 94 (83): "From this the answer to the other argument is clear, namely that it is true that Caesar is Caesar, but that 'Caesar is Caesar, therefore Caesar is a man' is not valid, except at the time at which Caesar is the *suppositum* of a man [Per hoc patet ad aliud, quod verum est quod Caesar est Caesar, non tamen sequitur 'Caesar est Caesar, ergo Caesar est homo' nisi pro illo tempore pro quo est suppositum hominis]."

133. This question is also discussed extensively in "*Omnis homo est*" (NL 16135 [145–84]), particularly at q. 6, f. 50vb (question) and 52va (response). There are two arguments that 'Caesar is Caesar' is true, the first being Boethius's argument, "no proposition is truer," etc.; the second being that the proposition has the same signification whether Caesar is alive or not. The two arguments against this are (i) if the subject stands for a Caesar who exists, then the proposition is false (presumably because Caesar does not exist), but if for a dead Caesar, it is also false because the predicate stands for a living Caesar; (ii) that it is false because any proposition implying something false is itself false, but the name 'Caesar,' though imposed on a living subject, now implies the subject is dead. In reply, the Master says that the name was imposed on living person and thus still stands for a living person; therefore, the proposition is true.

According to the edition, n. 10 introduces a second opinion on the question. As already noted, this section is rather a second view of the second argument.

[n. 11] The argument also works with reference to the future, since 'this ox is an ox' is not true tomorrow, after it has been sacrificed. So the consequence follows only when the ox to be sacrificed really exists as the supposit of 'ox.'

[n. 12] Averroes's distinction between the two kinds of change (*transmutatio*), substantial and accidental, was invoked by Scotus at n. 18 of q. 6 and n. 12 of q. 3 above. See the commentary on those sections for discussion.

[n. 13] In nn. 13–15, Scotus replies to the three supporting arguments of the second part of n. 2 (first supporting argument), and nn. 3–4 (second and third supporting argument). Again, they are not, contrary to what is stated in the edition, a "reply to the main arguments according to the second opinion."

The first supporting arguments are the ones adduced "on the basis of what is similar [*a simili*]," or by analogy, just as 'a non-being is a non-being' is true, or 'a chimera is a chimera' is true, so 'Caesar is Caesar' is true. Scotus gives the odd reply that 'a chimera is a chimera' is true at any time, whereas 'Caesar is Caesar' is true only when Caesar exists (he does not explain how 'a chimera is a chimera' can be true, given that a chimera has never existed).

[n. 14] Here Scotus replies to the second supporting argument of n. 3 that 'nothing is truer of something than what is the same as it.' Scotus argues that Caesar is nothing, and we do not say of nothing that is the same as itself (because it is, presumably, nothing).

[n. 15] Scotus replies (n. 15) to the third supporting argument of n. 4. The rule about the 'conclusion from opposites' only applies when the subject of a proposition such as '*a* is not *a*' actually exists, in which case the same thing is being denied of itself, and this cannot possibly be true (that is, '*a* is not *a*' can be true when *a* does not signify any existing thing).

[nn. 16–19] These sections do not appear to belong to this question at all. In fact, nn. 17–18 are found *verbatim* in Antonius Andreas, q. 9, "whether a sign can be posited on the part of the predicate [*utrum signum possit poni ex parte praedicati*],"[134] that is, whether the predicate can be quantified by a universal or particular sign of quantity.

In that question, Antonius considers two arguments against quantification of the predicate: (i) the predicate corresponds to the mode of form and the sub-

---

134. Antonius Andreas, *Periherm.*, 71v.

ject to the mode of matter; but distribution is more appropriate to matter than to form, and so the sign (that is, the quantifier), which signifies distribution, should be added to the subject, not to the predicate; (ii) 'every man is every animal' is false, as Aristotle notes in *De interpretatione* I.7.17b15.

Antonius replies with three conclusions: (i) it is more appropriate to add the sign to the subject; (ii) even so, it can be appropriate in certain cases to quantify the predicate; (iii) in such cases, the quantifier "yields to identity with the predicate [*cedit in identitatem praedicati*]." Note the similarity in phrasing between the third conclusion and Scotus at n. 16.

In defence of the third conclusion, Antonius gives two arguments. The first is that otherwise, a falsehood would follow from a truth, for example, from 'no man is every animal' it would follow that 'man is not a man'; thus, 'every' must be part of the predicate, viz., 'man is not every animal.' The second argument is that syncategorematic terms always apply to the terms that follow them in a sentence, as in negation. Therefore, quantification before the predicate but after the subject determines the predicate alone, and hence not the subject.

Antonius mentions an objection to the third conclusion with identical wording to that found in n. 17 of Scotus. He then gives a reply which is identical to n. 18 of Scotus.

The material in n. 19 concerns the subject of conversion of the universal negative, which does not correspond to anything in q. 9 of Antonius Andreas. What it is doing here remains a mystery.

[Question 13. Can a Common Term Be Restricted?]

Summary

The structure of this question is different from the other questions of the work, which mostly follow the scholastic pattern of 'arguments for' followed by 'arguments against.' Here, each of the main arguments in support of the proposition that a common term can be restricted by the verb is followed by a series of objections. Thus, the first argument (n. 1), that the time of composition of the verbal predicate with the subject must be the same as the time at which the subject is presumed to exist, is followed by four objections (nn. 2–5). The second

Commentary: *Opus I* 261

argument (n. 6), that restriction is taken from the purpose of speech, is followed by four objections (nn. 7–10). The third argument (n. 11) that there are only presently-existing *supposita* of a term, is also met by two objections (nn. 12–13).

The determination (n. 14), that the term is restricted but for a different reason than those given by the main arguments, is followed by a lengthy discussion along with other objections.

There are no concluding replies to the three main arguments because the replies have already been made.

Discussion

Like q. 12, this question duplicates material in earlier questions (qq. 9–11), and, like q. 12, it comes to the opposite conclusion. Its structure suggests that it was written after qq. 9–11. The main arguments that were rejected in qq. 9–11 are also rejected here, perhaps to explain how Scotus comes to a different determination—almost as if to say he was wrong, but for the right reasons.

Commentary

[n. 1] The first argument is that the composition of predicate with subject "is measured by the present time" because the terms must be measured by the same measure that applies to the composition. In other words, the linguistic composition made by the spoken or written proposition, which occurs in the present, must correspond to a present composition in reality. Therefore, the *supposita* of the subject term can exist only in the present.

The argument is paralleled by n. 3 of q. 9. The "some" who propose the argument are not identified in the edition, but there are similar arguments by scholastic writers of the mid-thirteenth century, such as Lambert of Lagny, who says that the restriction is brought about by the "co-signification [*consignificatio*]" of the tense of the verb with the subject, because co-signification is the measure of the signification of the verb, which restricts the thing measured.[135]

This view is also mentioned, though not endorsed, by the anonymous author of "*Album fuit disputaturum*," who says that when the verb 'is' is predicated as a third element, it is a copula, and then its content applies to the subject, so that the term and the copula are "measured by the same *differentia* of time." For example,

135. Ps.-Lambert of Auxerre, "On the Properties of Terms," translated in Kretzmann and Stump, *Cambridge Translations of Medieval Philosophical Texts*, 123.

'Socrates was running' means 'Socrates ran.' Similarly, in the proposition 'a white person was going to dispute,' one thing is asserted of another; therefore, the time that 'measures' the composition of predicate and subject is one.[136]

Nicholas of Paris (fl. mid-thirteenth century) also argues that the verb co-signifies time because otherwise, the verb would not be "the measure of composition [*mensura compositionis*]."[137]

In *Opus II.I*, q. 9, n. 35 below, Scotus's rejection of this principle is fundamental to his solution of Aristotle's sea-battle problem.

[n. 2] The next three sections reply to this argument. The first reply rejects the Modist principle 'as in understanding, so in signifying.' To understand the composition of terms in the present, it is not necessary to understand that the

---

136. "*Album fuit disputaturum*," NL 16135, 12vb–14vb (49–50): "Sometimes the verb 'is' is predicated as a third element, sometimes as a second element, in which case it is an extreme and predicates what is in itself. But sometimes it predicates what is in another, and then it is a third element, in which case it is a copula and posits its content concerning the other thing, and then the extreme and the copula are measured by the same *differentia* of time. For example, 'Socrates was running,' where it is clear that the sense is 'Socrates ran' [Hoc verbum 'est' quandoque praedicatur tertio adiacens, quandoque secundo adiacens, et tunc est extremum et praedicat quod in se est; quandoque vero praedicat quod in alio est, et tunc est tertio adiacens, et tunc est copula et ponit rem suam circa alteram et tunc eadem differentia temporis mensurantur extremum et copula, ut 'Sor fuit currens'; et patet quod sensus est: 'Sor cucurrit']." Ibid.: "In the proposition 'a white thing was [going to argue]' one thing is enunciated of another; therefore, the time measuring a composition of this sort will be one; therefore, the time will be either present, past, or future. But whether one time or another it is always false, which is clear of itself; therefore, the first proposition is false [In hac: 'Album fuit etc.,' enuntiatur unum de uno; quare tempus mensurans huiusmodi compositionem erit unum; ergo vel praesens, vel praeteritum, vel futurum; sed sive sic sive sic semper est falsa, quod patet de se; ergo prima falsa]." Ibid.: "Certain persons suppose that it is false *simpliciter*, and this is because when an enunciation enunciates one thing of another, it has to be that the time measuring the composition of the predicate with the subject is similarly one; but whether it is present, past, or future, it is false simpliciter [quidam ponunt ipsam simpliciter esse falsam, et hoc, quia, cum sit enuntiatio unum de uno enuntians, oportet quod tempus mensurans compositionem praedicati cum subiecto sit unum similiter; sed sive sit praesens, vel praeteritum, vel futurum, falsa est simpliciter]."

137. See Nicholas of Paris, "*De modo significandi tempus in verbis, utrum significetur communiter aut discrete*" in *Syncategoremata*, 2:28. Cf. also his question on whether the common term is restricted by the time co-signified (ibid., 2:30): "That a verb co-signifies time is commonly held, because a verb does not co-signify time unless because it is a measure of composition. But it is impossible for something divisible to be measured by something indivisible, as is proved in the sixth book of the *Physics*. Therefore, since every composition brought about by the verb 'is' is divisible, it is clear that every time measuring verbal composition will be a divisible time [Quod verbum consignificet tempus communiter videtur, quia verbum non consignificat tempus nisi quod est mensura compositionis; sed divisibile ab indivisibili mensurari est impossibile, ut probatur in sexto Phisicorum; ergo, cum omnis compositio importata per hoc verbum 'est' sit divisibilis, manifestum est quod omne tempus mensurans compositionem verbalem erit tempus divisibile]."

terms themselves are present at the same time, for we can compose what exists in the future at the present time. This is fundamental to his argument about the sea-battle: a proposition can signify now that something will happen in the future without having to signify that reality is now such that it will happen. For to signify its being the case now that something will happen, signifies more than simply that something will happen. See also n. 17 of the reply to q. 7 of *Opus II.I* below.

See also n. 33 in q. 4 of Scotus's *Categories* commentary,[138] where he likewise rejects the principle. According to Scotus, signification does not follow understanding as effect necessarily follows cause; instead, 'signifying follows understanding' means that understanding is a *sine qua non* of signifying: something cannot be signified unless it is understood.[139]

[n. 3] The second reply contends that what is on the side of the predicate does not restrict the subject. For if we make the contrary assumption that the predicate 'white' restricts the supposition of 'man' to white men in 'a man is white,' we get the absurd conclusion that 'every man is white' is true because in that case 'man' would supposit only for white men. This would be tantamount to treating 'a man is white' as if it were a universal and indefinite proposition, which it is not. For more on the subject not being restricted by what is on the side of the predicate, see n. 2 of q. 9 above.

[n. 4] The third reply invokes a principle, 'time is an unqualified accident of a verb,' which is due to Priscian, who says, "time accrues to the verb for the signification of different acts appropriate [to it]" (*Institutiones Grammaticae* VIII.38). But if time is proper to the signification of the verb, it cannot also be proper to the subject, that is, as something that restricts it.

[n. 5] Like n. 3, the fourth reply is another effort to reduce the view of n. 1 to absurdity: if the subject is restricted to presently-existing things in the proposition '*b* can be *a*,' then the proposition is false because no things that are presently *b* are also presently *a*, even though they may become so in the future.

[n. 6] The argument of the unnamed others, "that the cause of restriction is taken on the side of the purpose of speech," seems to be motivated by the kind of semantic holism we see in Pseudo-Kilwardby, who holds that concepts and

---

138. Duns Scotus, *Praedic.*, q. 5, n. 33 (*OPh* I, 283, ll. 5–13).
139. This is yet another reason for supposing that *Opus I* and *Opus II.I* are not different versions of the same work, but rather different sections (or possibly different versions of different sections of the same work).

words are joined according to the relation of the end and what is related to it, or according to the relation between a sign and what is signified.[140] Thus, if Albert the Great is right that words were invented "so that what we conceive, we can express to others" (which is the passage quoted by Scotus here), then any restriction in my conception of a thing must find expression in the subject term of the corresponding proposition, completing the link between sign and signified. As it is in concept, so it must also be in word.

Interestingly, Scotus uses the same premise to reach precisely the opposite conclusion in n. 10 of q. 9 above.

[n. 7] The next three sections reply to the argument in n. 6. Against the opinion advanced in n. 6, Scotus argues that if the purpose of a word is its signification, it is question-begging to say we find the reason for the restriction in the purpose of a word, that is, in its signifying a 'this' that is present to me, for this does not explain why the signification is restricted in the first place. If the signification of a word is what is restricted, then we will not find the reason for the restriction in the word's signification, since its signification would be logically prior to its restriction.

[n. 8] In the same way, if a subject term with a present-tense verb fails to signify that the predicate inheres in the subject with regard to presently-existing things (for example, 'a man runs' when no man is presently running), the purpose of that word is not frustrated because I can still understand the subject, 'man,' and am able to signify it by another word (for example, 'walking' or 'sitting'). Therefore, there is no need to restrict the signification of a common term to the time of the verb.

Scotus likens this to arguing that it is useless to make axes because this particular axe cannot chop. Of course, the poor performance of one axe is no obstacle to other axes doing what they were made to do; moreover, I also understand that the purpose of the bad axe was to chop, and this understanding is how I judge it to be bad.

[n. 9] Scotus points out that we can understand a term as abstracted from any

---

140. Ps.-Kilwardby, *Commentary on Priscian Major*, 61: "But the mode of union is according to a relative disposition, which is the end, and [holds] of what is related to that end, or according to the relative disposition of what is signified to its sign generally [Modus autem unionis est secundum relativam habitudinem, quae est finis et eius quod est ad finem vel secundum relativam habitudinem significati generaliter ad suum signum]."

time. However, he seems to be saying, if the signification of that term is already restricted to presently-existing individuals, then my intention to signify something inhering in the subject of that term at present would be pointless, since the only possible subjects would be presently-existing individuals.

Scotus also says that if the term is restricted to those presently-existing individuals that I understand, I would fail to signify them because my understanding of them is in fact established by the significate of any of them. This appears to beg the question against the other side, because it assumes that my understanding of those individuals is unrestricted by any time, which is precisely the point at issue.

[n. 10] Here Scotus states, again in a somewhat question-begging manner, that what is signified by a noun does not concern any *differentia* of time. In more modern terminology, we might say that common terms signify their subjects timelessly.

[n. 11] The third argument is simply that a term is restricted because a term only supposits for its *supposita*. But only presently existing *supposita* are 'under' the term. Therefore the term is restricted to presently existing *supposita*.

There is no explanation of the inference from 'a term only supposits for its *supposita*' to 'a term only supposits for its presently existing *supposita*.' The critical edition says that no reference for the argument has been found, but Scotus may have had in mind the sort of argument advanced by anonymous author of "*Omnis homo de necessitate est animal*," who says that a 'present *suppositum*' is that which can at present be the subject of a common term, or which can receive its predication.[141] In other words, the present tense of 'supposits' automatically restricts the range of supposition to presently existing individuals.

[n. 12] The next two sections reply to the argument in n. 11. The first reply is that what the *suppositum* is a *suppositum* of, presumably the common term, abstracts from being and therefore does not include being. Thus, Socrates is a *suppositum* of the common term 'man,' which abstracts from being. Therefore, it cannot be by virtue of his presently existing that Socrates is a *suppositum* of 'man,'

---

141. "*Omnis homo de necessitate est animal*," NL 16135, ff. 52vb–62vb (201): "But now we must say that all individuals, whether entities or non-entities, are present *supposita*, because I mean by 'present *suppositum*' that it can presently be the subject of a common term, or be the recipient of its predication [Nunc autem dicamus quod omnia individua sive entia sive non entia sunt praesentia supposita, quia intendo per 'suppositum praesens' ita quod praesentialiter potest subici termino communi vel recipiendo eius praedicationem]." Roger Bacon also holds that "should the term be common to something present, past, and future, its supposition can in no way be ampliated; therefore, it will not thus be common. Therefore, it will only be the name of present things" (*Summulae*, part 2, §247).

because 'man' does not include being, and the suppositum must not "include more than that of which it is the *suppositum*."

[n. 13] The second reply is that the existent and the non-existent fall under the same logical aspect or concept (*ratio*), and this concept is undivided because it is abstracted from both existing and non-existing individuals. Therefore, the term corresponding to this concept signifies something common to Socrates and Plato univocally, even if Socrates exists and Plato does not.

It is not clear why Scotus concludes, "therefore, through one and the same aspect [*ratio*] there will be a *suppositum*, and a remainder [*reliquum*]." Given that he is replying here to the argument that a common term is restricted to presently existing *supposita*, one would expect past, present, and future individuals to be among the *supposita* of the term, not that Socrates, say, would be a *suppositum* of 'man' because he presently exists, but not of Plato because he does not presently exist (making him a *reliquum* or a kind of semantic leftover).

The critical edition notes that there is an additional sentence here not found in all manuscripts. This is the somewhat tangential remark that unlike the case of things existing now and that once existed in the past, there is no proper undivided concept to be abstracted from a being and a non-being, for "there does not appear to be anyone who would abstract the nature of an animal from a donkey and a chimera," that is, the goat-stag mentioned by Aristotle.

Scotus's Determination

[n. 14] Scotus resolves the question in nn. 14–28: the main determination is given in nn. 14–15, followed by three arguments (nn. 16–18) against this determination, and their replies (nn. 19–21). A further argument against the determination is given in n. 22, followed by three replies (nn. 23–25).

Scotus argues (n. 14) that a term suppositing with a present-tense verb is restricted. This is practically the opposite of his reply to q. 9 above (at n. 24), where he concludes that a common term in any proposition, including present-tense propositions, supposits for any of its *supposita*, whether existing or non-existing.

His reasoning is based on a complex analogy between heating, inhering, and being 'terminated [*terminatur*],'[142] which becomes clearer if we step back from

---

142. Scotus seems to be playing here on the natural ambiguity in Latin between *terminus* in the sense of 'term,' i.e., the subject or predicate understood as the limit or 'end' of a proposition, and the terminus or end-point of a process.

the text. Recall that the question to be resolved is whether the subject term in a proposition is restricted to suppositing only for things existing in the present, given that the term consists of a name whose semantics appear to be unrestricted by tense or modality: for example, it does not appear to be part of the meaning of the name 'man' that a man has to exist in the present; a man has existed in the past, will exist in the future, and may possibly exist. Scotus argues that when a proposition involves 'actual inherence' (meaning presumably that the proposition is present-tense assertoric) the supposition of the subject is restricted by the predicate. This is where the analogy in n. 14 comes in: supposition is to be compared to heat.[143] Just as heat radiates out from a hot body, striking bodies 'capable of being heated,' and being 'terminated' by the heating and warming them up, so a term emits (as it were) quantifying radiation that is terminated by its *supposita*. If the heat is actual, the only bodies that can terminate it are actual bodies. Similarly, if the proposition asserts actual inherence, the only *supposita* that can terminate the quantifying rays are actually existing *supposita*. Hence, the supposition of the subject term is restricted.

In the second half of n. 14, Scotus explains why it is the predicate that restricts the subject: the quantifying radiation of actual inherence begins at the predicate, and ends at, or is 'terminated by' the subject. Thus, if we consider the subject term 'under the aspect' of what is terminated by it, viz., the actual inherence, then under this aspect it cannot supposit only for actually existing things.

[n. 15] Here Scotus explains Aristotle's claim in the *Prior Analytics* that when the major is assertoric, it cannot be subsumed with a minor proposition about contingency (*de contingenti*). This is because the major involves actual inherence, and so the subject of the major supposits only for actually existing things, whereas the minor involves possible inherence, and so its subject is not required to supposit only for things that actually exist, and it cannot 'terminate inherence' indifferently for actually and contingently existing things. That is why '*b* can be *a*' has two senses. See also our comments on nn. 46–47 of q. 11 above.

We have translated *sumere sub* and *accipere sub* as compound verbs rather than

---

143. For the metaphysical analysis, see Aristotle, *Metaph.* V.15.1021a15–18 (trans. Ross in Barnes, *Works of Aristotle*, 2:1612): "The active and the passive imply an active and a passive capacity and the actualization of the capacities, e.g., that which is capable of heating is related to that which is capable of being heated, because it *can* heat it, and, again, that which is heating is related to that which is being heated and that which is cutting to that which is being cut, because they are actually doing these things."

as verb-plus-preposition constructions. This form is frequently used by Ockham in his discussion of the *dici de omni* in *Summa logicae* III.1. 'Supposition under' or 'taking under' or 'accepting under' seems to mean reading a term or proposition with a certain range or domain that is set by another term or proposition. Here, we have to read or interpret the domain of the subject as including only those individuals in which the predicate can inhere.

The same point is referenced in Aristotle (*Prior Analytics* I.13.34a2–b19) as mentioned in q. 10, n. 17 (see also q. 6, n. 50), from which it is clear that b6–b19 is the relevant section. Aristotle says that we must read the universal assertoric proposition *simpliciter* or the syllogism will not be valid: for example, 'every moving thing is now a man,' or 'possibly every horse is moving.' Both of these may be true if nothing else is moving apart from men, but 'possibly every horse is a man' is false. The major must be taken *de inesse simpliciter*.

"Therefore, '*b* can be *a*' is said in two ways" is a clear reference to Aristotle (*Prior Analytics* I.13.32b23-37). In Latin, as in English, 'a man can be white' can mean that, of presently existing men, one of them can possibly be white, or it can mean that in the future, there can exist a white man not identical to any existing man.

Objections to Scotus's Determination

[n. 16] Against this determination, it is objected that an inherent actuality (*actus inhaerens*) cannot restrict actual inherence (*actualis inhaerentia*). Using the heating analogy of n. 14, we might say that actual inherence is analogous to the type of radiant power emitted by a term, whereas the actually inhering thing is analogous to the termination of this radiation at the boundaries (*termini*) of the objects it strikes.

Perhaps the distinction here is between the timeless understanding of *a* inhering in *b* and the actual inherence of *a* in *b* in the present (actuality in these discussions is usually connected with the present time). This fits the heating analogy as long as the termination of the radiation is an act that occurs in the present time.

[n. 17] The second objection is that if in the proposition 'an animal talks' the inherence of 'talking' in the animal restricts 'animal' to talking animals only, 'every animal talks' would be true, even though it is obviously false. In terms of the heating analogy of n. 14, if the radiant power were emitted by the predicate, the range of 'animal' in 'an animal speaks' would be restricted to speaking animals. Thus, 'every animal speaks' would be true, even though it is obviously false (giraffes do not speak).

Nicholas of Paris mentions a similar objection: if in the proposition 'a man runs' the predicate 'runs' restricted 'man' only to men who run, it is obvious that 'man' would supposit only for running men, and 'every man runs' would be true, even if some men were not running.[144]

[n. 18] The third objection is that the actual composition of the terms does not restrict them; therefore, by parity of reasoning, neither does actual inherence. This follows on the assumption that the composition is based on the actual inherence.

Scotus's Replies to These Objections

[n. 19] To the objection at n. 16 above, Scotus replies by drawing a distinction between the actual and present act (heating, in the above example) and the actual inherence (being hot). Both must be present for the supposition of the subject term to be restricted, even though it is "more immediately" restricted by what actually inheres in it, just as the property of being hot is more proximate to the subject than the heating action which causes it to be hot.

Another way of making the point: if the heat is actual, the only bodies that can terminate it are actual bodies. Similarly, if the proposition asserts actual inherence, the only *supposita* that can terminate the quantifying rays are actually existing *supposita*. Hence, the supposition of the subject term is restricted. It is not clear to us how the inherence of paternity in the son restricts the son.

[n. 20] To the objection at n. 17 above, Scotus replies that the actual inherence of anything in an animal requires the existence of actual animals, but actual animals are indifferent with respect to talking and non-talking. So the subject "is not

---

144. See Nicholas of Paris, *Syncategoremata*, 2:31. In response to the question, "whether a common term is restricted by the time co-signified by the verb to suppositing for things existing in the present," Nicholas says that "when we utter 'a man runs,' if the predicate 'runs' restricts the subject 'man,' it is manifest that the term 'man' only supposits for those that are running, but if the restricted term is distributed, it is distributed only for those for which it is restricted, therefore given that only three men are running, 'every man runs' would be true—which is false, therefore the time of the predicate does not restrict the subject [Item, cum dicitur: 'homo currit,' si hoc praedicatum 'currit' restringit hoc subiectum 'homo,' manifestum quod iste terminus 'homo' non supponit nisi pro currentibus; sed si terminus restrictus distribuatur, pro eis solum distribuetur pro quibus restringitur; posito ergo quod tantum tres homines currant, haec erit vera 'omnis homo currit.' Hoc autem falsum: ergo tempus praedicati non restringit subiectum]."

more restricted with respect to talking than with respect to non-talking," from which it follows that 'every animal talks' is not true but false.

[n. 21] To the third argument at n. 18 above, Scotus replies with a point he will make later in his discussion of the sea-battle problem (*Opus II.I*, qq. 7–9 below): we must distinguish the time at which the linguistic or logical composition of the terms occurs (that is, now) from the time at which the action signified by the proposition occurs. The present existence of the composition refers only to the composition, and not to the extremes of the proposition, which will exist at a future time. Only when the proposition involves actual inherence do the things denoted actually have to exist in the present.

[n. 22] Scotus now considers an objection to his determination (nn. 14–15): a term may supposit for non-existing things because a term supposits for whatever follows from it (that is, whatever the subject of the consequent supposits for, the subject of the antecedent supposits for). Since 'the Antichrist runs; therefore, a man runs' is a valid consequence, and since 'man' supposits for a man, therefore 'Antichrist' supposits for something even though the Antichrist will only exist in the future.

[n. 23] Scotus replies to the objection in n. 22 that the consequence is valid only if the Antichrist is a man. The consequence mentioned in the objection has a missing premise, which becomes obvious when we analyze it into proper syllogistic form. The missing premise is 'the Antichrist is a being,' which (Scotus implies) is clearly false.

Scotus has already considered a similar argument in n. 21 of qq. 5–8 and n. 7 of qq. 9–11 above. In the former, he argues that the implicit premise, 'Caesar is a man,' is necessary because the understanding of 'Caesar' involves the understanding of 'man.' Later, in n. 7, he argues (and appears to accept) that the same principle also applies to the Antichrist. This appears to be another example of the positions Scotus takes in qq. 12–13 going against what he defends in qq. 5–11.

[n. 24] Scotus elaborates on n. 23 above: the assumption that some *a* exists is additional to the assumption that *a* is something or other (say, a man). Thus, the consequence does not follow without the additional premise that *a* exists.

[n. 25] In nn. 25–26, Scotus considers the objection that some propositions, such as 'Homer is a poet,' can be true without implying that Homer exists, even though this appears to contradict the previous suggestion that this involves a missing premise of the form 'Homer is a being' or something similar.

[n. 26] Scotus replies that we must distinguish between propositions where the subject has being "of itself [*de se*]" and propositions where the subject inherits being from something else. Thus, it is not necessary for the truth of the proposition, 'the father lives in the son,' that the father be alive. Likewise, 'Homer is a poet' means that Homer exists, but in his poetry, for the truth of which it is sufficient that his poetry exists, just as it is sufficient that a son exists in order for the father to 'live in him.'

[n. 27] Though the edition does not mention it, n. 27 appears to refer back to n. 9, where it is argued that we can understand the subject term in a tenseless way, and so if the term is restricted to those presently-existing *supposita* that I understand, I would fail to signify because my understanding of them is in fact established by the significate of any of them.

He replies, quoting n. 9: when it is said that I "signify something presently inhering in something," this not mean that the subject of inherence has to be present. Thus, when I presently say, 'a man is going to run,' the composition of predicate and subject occurs in the present, but what is signified by that present composition can occur in the future, such as when 'is running' is true of the Antichrist, who will exist at some time, but not at present. This reiterates the point made at n. 21 above, that we must distinguish the time at which the linguistic or logical composition of the terms occurs (that is, now) from the time for which it occurs.

As we will see below, this is substantially Scotus's solution to Aristotle's sea-battle problem: the proposition about the sea-battle is made today, but what makes it true or false, its truth-maker, does not have to exist today.

[n. 28] Scotus continues with the point he makes at n. 27: there is a difference between actual inherence and actual composition, because something can actually be composed with something, yet not actually inhere in it.

Some Noteworthy Points

In nn. 29–33, Scotus makes some commonplace observations about supposition theory that do not appear to be directly related to the subject of the present question.

[n. 29] Here it is noted that common terms can be taken for (i) the nature signified by a common term in relation to its nature (*ratio*), abstracting from the individuals of which it is truly predicated (for example, 'man is a species'); (ii) the nature as it is found in the individuals of which it is truly predicated (for example, 'pepper is sold here and in Rome,' where we mean pepper in general and not the species of pepper); and (iii) the individuals of which it is truly predicated (for example, 'a man runs,' which is true when Socrates, an individual man, is running).

The difference between (ii) and (iii) becomes clearer if we reflect on the difference between the sentences, 'no pepper is sold here and in Rome' and 'pepper is sold here and in Rome': the former would be true only if the common term 'pepper' is taken in sense (iii), that is, only if no particular sacks of pepper are sold either here or in Rome, whereas the latter would be true only if pepper, as opposed to salt or coriander (and in a sense that does not pick out this or that particular sack of pepper), is sold both here and in Rome.

[n. 30] In the case of 'pepper is sold here and in Rome' we have to be careful, however. If 'pepper' supposits personally, for particular sacks of pepper, and the conjunctive phrase in the predicate 'is sold here and in Rome' is taken copulatively, that is, as jointly attributed to the subject, then the proposition is false because it means that the same particular sacks of pepper are being sold here and in Rome at the same time, which is impossible (we assume here that selling something requires that it be physically present to buyers in the marketplace). To make the proposition true when 'pepper' is in personal supposition, the subject term must be taken twice: 'pepper is sold here and pepper is sold in Rome.'

[n. 31] Scotus notes that strictly speaking, only the subject term of a proposition supposits because supposition' is said in relation to individual things. The right term for what the predicate term has is copulation, rather than supposition.

[n. 32] Here Scotus notes that when a common term supposits, this can be understood in relation to (i) the predicate for which it supposits; (ii) the particular things contained under it, for which it also supposits; and (iii) the predicate's belonging to the things contained under it. Thus, the common term 'man' supposits for the predicate 'is a man' and for the particular men (Socrates, Plato, etc.) of which it is truly predicated. The latter usage is more strictly called 'appellation,' where we might say that in addition to standing for the predicate, the common term also connotes those individuals of which it is truly predicated. Finally, there is a relation between the things contained under a common term and the predicate, because that predicate is truly said of all those things by virtue of the common term.

[n. 33] Scotus here provides an illustration of the ways in which we can understand the supposition of a common term mentioned in n. 32 above. He adds that there is a "twofold status" under which a common term can supposit: (i) such that "it follows upon anything for which it supposits," as in the indefinite proposition, 'a man runs,' which implies that if any of its supposits (Socrates, Plato, etc.) is running, then that individual is a man (although it implies "nothing" in the sense that of no particular man does it imply that he is actually running); or (ii) such that "anything follows upon it," as in the universal proposition, 'every man is running,' which implies that every *suppositum* of the term 'man' (Socrates, Plato, etc.) is running.

OPUS II ❦ QUESTIONS ON THE TWO BOOKS OF *PERIHERMENIAS:* ON BOOK I

[Prologue]

Summary

The *Perihermenias* concerns things falling under the second activity or operation of the understanding, which is the activity of composing and dividing. Composing and dividing is the process by which the understanding "makes an assertion [*format enuntiationem*]" or complex expression from simple expressions or words (*dictiones*). The *Perihermenias* is about the product of that process rather than the process itself, which is what *De anima* addresses.

Discussion

The prologue to *Opus II* parallels the first question of *Opus I*: "What is the Subject of *On Interpretation*?" As noted in the summary to the latter question above, the prologue to *Opus II* appears to be a précis of the introduction to Thomas Aquinas's *De interpretatione* commentary. Scotus's version is shorter, and the terminology varies somewhat, but the points made in both texts are largely the same.

Commentary

[n. 1] Scotus distinguishes the three operations of the understanding, viz., the "thinking of indivisibles" (simple apprehension); composition and division; and discursive reasoning.

[n. 2] Scotus links the *Perihermenias* to the second activity of composition and division, or rather, to its product, stressing that the book is about the proposition or assertion (*enuntiatio*), which "is not an act of understanding itself, but is more what is done by the understanding." Investigating the process or act of understanding is a matter for psychology. This principle, based on *De anima* I.1.402b23–25, became a standard topic in fourteenth-century *De anima* commentaries.

In a remark that is not from the text of Thomas Aquinas, Scotus notes that "the books of the new logic concern what falls under the third activity of the understanding, however, in which it is taught when one should proceed from what is known to possessing a cognition of what is unknown." This is a reference to the *logica nova* or corpus of Aristotelian logical writings recovered in the twelfth century, that is, *Prior Analytics*, *Posterior Analytics*, *Topics*, and *Sophistical Refutations*.[1] By contrast, the 'old logic' (*logica vetus* or *ars vetus*) usually meant five or six works: Aristotle's *Categories* and the *Perihermenias* (along with Boethius's commentaries on them), Porphyry's *Isagoge*, and (somewhat later) the *Liber sex principiorum* associated with Gilbert of Poitiers.

[n. 3] Scotus picks up from Thomas the idea that assertion involves not only forming statements, as opposed to simple expressions or words, but also "expressing 'something being the case or not being the case,' that is, as regards simple assertion; for other statements do not expound being or not being."

Thomas associates only Aristotle's *Prior Analytics* with the third activity of the understanding in the corresponding passage of his commentary. But Scotus thinks that the *Posterior Analytics*, *Topics*, and *Sophistical Refutations* also find their subjects in the third activity of the understanding (discursive reasoning), though he is careful to add that it is related "primarily to the *Prior Analytics* and indirectly to the others, because a syllogism is [made] from propositions."

[n. 4] The order of Aristotle's books of logic has a pedagogical purpose, to convey "the art of the syllogism." In the minds of most medieval thinkers, the *Perihermenias* is part of a systematic account of rational discourse, the practice of which holds the key to knowledge in all the arts and sciences.

---

1. The phrase *logica nova* was current when Scotus was writing. Likewise, Scotus uses the term *syncategoremata* where Thomas has "conjunctions and prepositions and other words of this kind" (n. 3).

[Question 1. Does a Name Signify a Thing or an Affection?]

Summary

This question closely corresponds to q. 2 in *Opus I*. Both are based on *De interpretatione* I.1.16a3–4, which is taken as raising the question of whether names signify (i) things outside the mind, or (ii) species, affections, or likenesses of things inside the mind.

The question begins with five arguments (nn. 1–5) that names signify species, opposed by three arguments (nn. 6–8) that a thing is signified. We then have an objection to these arguments (n. 9), followed by four replies to this objection (nn. 10–13). Like the corresponding question in *Opus I*, there are two determinations, both holding that names signify species as well as things, both of which are substantially similar to the determinations in *Opus I*, though occuring in a different order. The first (nn. 14–15) is that a name primarily signifies a thing as it is conceived, according as our cognitive power is brought to the essence (*quod quid est esse*) of a thing. This corresponds to the second view stated in *Opus I*, q. 2, n. 39. There follow (nn. 16–20) replies to or discussions of all the initial arguments (nn. 1–13). To the authorities, Scotus says that Aristotle and Boethius mean by 'affection' a thing as it is considered by the mind. To the arguments that a thing is signified, he says that these are consistent with the view that 'thing *as* signified' is meant. In n. 21 he introduces the view that a name primarily signifies a likeness or species. In his replies to the main arguments according to this view (nn. 22–29), he argues that the species is itself a sign or representation of a thing, and so the name signifying the species also signifies the thing. This second view closely corresponds to the first view of *Opus I*, q. 2. As with the earlier question, he indicates doubts about both views (n. 30).

Commentary

Arguments That Names Signify Species

[n. 1] Here Scotus repeats the argument of n. 2 in *Opus I*, appealing to Aristotle's remark in *De interpretatione* I.1 that "spoken sounds are signs of those affections in the soul." These arguments closely follow the corresponding sections in *Opus I*, though the arguments of n. 4 and nn. 7–8 are omitted here.

[n. 2] The authority of Aristotle is invoked again: these affections "are the likenesses of things."

[n. 3] Scotus appeals to the authority of Boethius, who says in the second version of his commentary on *De interpretatione* that utterances signify a kind of mental speech. This argument is not found in *Opus I*.

[n. 4] Boethius is cited again, this time his remark that affections are likenesses of things. This section corresponds to *Opus I*, q. 2, n. 5.

[n. 5] This is an appeal to Priscian, corresponding to *Opus I*, q. 2, n. 6.

Arguments That Names Signify Things

[n. 6] Scotus begins by citing Aristotle's argument that what a name signifies is the proper concept or nature (*ratio*) expressed by the definition. But the nature belongs to a thing, rather than to a concept in the mind. This corresponds to *Opus I*, q. 2, n. 12, where he adds that the definition expresses the "true essence of a thing."[2] This reference is not given in the edition.

[n. 7] The second argument is that a name signifies what we *primarily* mean to signify by it, so when we say 'a man runs,' we primarily mean to predicate running of a man, not of something in the mind.

[n. 8] The third argument invokes the Modist principle that signifying follows (or presupposes: cf. *Opus I*, q. 3, n. 4) understanding. Since we primarily signify things and not affections, it follows that things are what are primarily understood.

[n. 9] Scotus mentions a view that is held "on account of these arguments." This is the view that a name signifies both an affection and a thing, but it signifies an affection "through what comes earlier," that is, directly, but a thing "through what comes later," that is, by means of an effect. It is not clear who holds this view, but the edition cites Thomas Aquinas, Albert the Great, and the anonymous author of a commentary on William of Sherwood's *Introduction to Logic*. Thomas says that, according to Aristotle, utterances signify affections directly and things indirectly. Albert says that signs are of affections or concepts in the soul, and thus are not primarily signs of things, but of likenesses in the soul. The anonymous author says that an utterance presents an affection directly, but a thing indirectly.

[n. 10] The objection to the argument in n. 9 is that if names primarily signified affections, the primary meaning of 'a man is an animal' would entail that

---

2. Aristotle, *Metaph.* IV.7.1012a24–25.

some affection (of a man) was some other affection (of an animal). But this is false because the two affections are not the same, whereas this man and this animal are the same. The edition cites Radulphus Brito, who says in q. 3 of his *De interpretatione* commentary that if utterances signified affections, every proposition would be false.³

This argument and most of those that follow correspond (though in a slightly different order) to *Opus I*, q. 2, nn. 13–19, where it is argued that names do not signify species. The argument in n. 10 here corresponds to n. 15 in *Opus I*, q. 2: a name does not signify a species; otherwise, every proposition would be false (for example, 'a man is an animal' would falsely say that the species of a man is the species of an animal).

[n. 11] The next argument corresponds to *Opus I*, q. 2, n. 19: just as the image or species of a tree is not what we see (for it is the tree that we see), but rather, the medium by which we see, so (by implication) it is not an intelligible species that we understand, but the thing; the species is a medium.

[n. 12] The next argument corresponds to *Opus I*, q. 2, n. 16: a stone is not in the soul, for otherwise the sentence 'a stone is not in the soul' would be false (cf. Aristotle, *De anima* III.8.431b29–432a1). The edition also mentions here (though not in the corresponding section of *Opus I*) an argument by from the *De interpretatione* commentary of Simon of Faversham, who mentions Aristotle and provides an argument very similar to this one—"If 'stone' did not signify a thing outside the soul but only the species of stone, then a stone would be in the soul."

[n. 13] The final argument, corresponding to *Opus I*, q. 2, n. 17, is that if a name were to signify an affection primarily, 'Socrates exists' would be true even though the actual Socrates did not exist, since it refers to something that has being in the mind, such as a species or affection.

Determination

[n. 14] According to the edition, nn. 14–15 are an exposition of the 'first way' or view on the question. However, these sections are introduced by the non-neutral *dicendum* ('it must be said') and the view presented seems closer to Scotus's own Modist position, which is discussed in the commentary on *Opus I*, q. 2, n. 39 above, where he says that a name signifies primarily the essence of a

---

3. Radulphus Brito, *Quaestiones super arte veteri* (ed. Vercellensis & Vercellensis; Venice: 1499).

thing, or [signifies] the thing as it is understood, or under the aspect of understood being.

Scotus says that three things must be distinguished: (i) the intelligible species, which, according to Averroes (*De anima* III, com. 5), exists in the understanding in the way individual forms exist in prime matter; (ii) the essence or "what it is [*quod quid est*]" of a thing, which is the object of the understanding; and (iii) the individual thing itself.

[n. 15] As for the first, Scotus argues that we do not primarily understand the intelligible species except by reflecting on it. The understanding grasps that it understands by reflecting or 'turning back' on its cognition of something else, such as when I become aware that I am revising this commentary on Scotus at my desk.[4] Compare *Opus I*, q. 2, n. 36, where Scotus denies the analogy, arguing that sense is not reflexive because it is material. But the understanding is immaterial, and so can reflect upon itself and go beyond what it immediately cognizes.

Likewise, we do not understand the third thing (the individual) because the understanding does not understand the singular primarily.

Therefore what we understand is the second, that is, the essence of a thing, or a thing as it is conceived. Once again, Scotus disparagingly mentions the view of Plato, who, it is said, held that a thing exists as it is understood, against Aristotle's view. Compare Scotus's reply in *Opus I*, q. 7, n. 43, where he says that to assume that any (individual) thing exists under the aspect of the common nature is to assume Platonic ideas.[5]

Reply to the Main Arguments

Reply to the Arguments That Names Signify Species

[n. 16] In nn. 16–20, we get replies to the arguments of nn. 1–5 above. Scotus defends a view that is somewhere between 'names signifying concepts' and 'names signifying things,' which in some ways awkwardly encompasses both. Thus, he addresses both sides of the argument. As for the authorities, he says that they understand 'affection' to mean a thing as it is considered by the soul.[6]

[n. 17] The remaining replies address the arguments for the other view, start-

---

4. Like Hume, most medieval authors do not distinguish between the intellect's awareness of its own operations and its self-awareness, but those two acts are not necessarily about the same object.
5. Cf. also the closely corresponding passage in *Opus I*, q. 2, n. 39 and commentary.
6. Cf. *Opus I*, q. 2, n. 40.

ing with n. 7 above, which was the argument that 'a man runs' asserts running of a thing and not of a species. Scotus replies that the proposition makes an assertion about the thing as signified, although the proposition is verified for the singular thing.

[n. 18] According to the edition, the next reply is to nn. 12–13, but it may be a reply (corresponding to *Opus I*, q. 2, n. 36) to the argument by analogy with sense perception in n. 11. We are not aware of the visible species by means of which we see; rather, we are aware of the visible thing. In the same way, we are not aware of the intelligible species.

[n. 19] The next reply is to n. 10, where it was objected that if names primarily signify affections, the primary meaning of 'a man is an animal' would be that some affection (of a man) was some other affection (of an animal), which is false, and so every sentence would be false. Scotus replies that what we primarily understand by a name is predicated of what is primarily understood through an intermediary, that is, a species. Thus, in 'a man is an animal,' we primarily understand 'man' as what we primarily understand by means of the concept of a man, viz., a man, and so we are not predicating a species of another species. See the reply to the corresponding question in *Opus I* (q. 2, nn. 27–30), where Scotus argues that a proposition asserts the identity not of the primary significates (the species) but of the ultimate significates (things), and invokes an argument by analogy with written letters and spoken sounds (the written sentence 'a man is an animal' is not false even though the utterance 'man' is not the utterance 'animal').

The topic is treated in greater detail and with greater complexity in *Opus I* than in *Opus II*. It is not clear whether this is because *Opus I* is a development of ideas in *Opus II*, and hence written later (as *Principia Mathematica* is a development of Russell's *The Principles of Mathematics*), or whether *Opus I* is being summarized in *Opus II*, and hence written earlier (as Hume's *Enquiries* essentially summarize his earlier *Treatise*).

[n. 20] According to the edition, the next reply is to n. 11, but it is more likely a reply to n. 13, where it was argued that if a name were to signify an affection primarily, 'Socrates exists' would be true even though the actual Socrates did not exist, since 'Socrates' refers to something that has being in the mind (a species or affection). Scotus replies that 'Socrates exists' is not affirmed of our idea of Socrates, but what is understood by means of that idea, that is, Socrates himself. This reply corresponds to the one given in *Opus I*, q. 2, n. 28, where Scotus argues that all questions about truth and falsity are questions involving the ultimate significates of propositions, which are things.

Reply to the Arguments That Names Signify Things

[n. 21] Scotus now considers a second view about signifying alluded to in n. 9 above: a name immediately signifies the species that is in the soul primarily, and only indirectly signifies the thing.

[n. 22] Replying to n. 7, which argues that running is asserted of a man rather than the idea of a man, Scotus says that the likeness of a thing is natural to a thing, and signifies the thing; consequently, the name signifying the species signifies the thing. This is the 'transitivity argument' we mentioned in *Opus I*: a sign of a sign of thing is itself a sign of the thing.[7]

[n. 23] Scotus invokes what we called the 'representation argument' in *Opus I*; a statue of Hercules can be considered in two ways: as a likeness, or as a thing with a certain shape. In the first way, the name signifying the species is also a sign of the thing. The analogy with Hercules's statue recalls Thomas Aquinas's argument in his *De interpretatione* commentary that the image of Hercules according to itself is called an image, and is bronze, but insofar as it is a likeness of Hercules, it is called a man.[8] Scotus also uses the analogy with writing: just as writing is a sign of a sign, so are utterances.

[n. 24] He adds, however, that we must understand the arguments given above—the edition refers to nn. 7–8, but Scotus probably has nn. 10–12 in mind, where he discusses the problem of what are the primary significates that the proposition composes or divides, and refers specifically to the signification of 'a man is an animal'—in terms of the analogy with writing: just as the written sentence 'a man is an animal' does not say that one utterance is another, so the utterance is not saying that one species is another.

[n. 25] Scotus replies (probably to the first argument in n. 10) that the truth of a sentence depends on the ultimate significates, that is, the things, because the terms are signs of signs. In 'a man is an animal,' the term 'man' is a sign of what

---

7. Scotus's reference to *De interpretatione*, "names are like thoughts," is slightly inaccurate, as the quoted passage is from chapter 1; chapter 2, 'On Names,' begins at 16a19.

8. Thomas Aquinas, *In Perihermenias* I. lect. 3, n. 4. Cf. *Summa Contra Gentiles* IV.26, where Thomas compares the divine similitude in man to the similitude of Hercules in stone, quoting Genesis 1:26: "let us make man in our image and likeness [faciamus hominem ad imaginem et similitudinem nostrum]."

is a sign of a man in reality; thus, the sentence is true. Therefore, the inscription is not said to be false, even though the written term 'man' is not the same as the utterance that it signifies. Similarly, 'a man is an animal' is not false even though one species is not the other.

[n. 26] Replying to the argument from analogy (the edition refers to n. 12, but n. 11 may be intended), Scotus says that there is no objection from the priority and posteriority of a thing and its concept as long as we distinguish between what is signified primarily or per se (the concept) and what is signified through what is signified per se (the thing). Thus, even though the thing outside the mind is prior in its nature to the concept of that thing, both are signified by the corresponding utterance: the concept primarily and the thing through the concept.

[n. 27] Scotus replies to the argument in n. 13 that when the understanding of a sentence signifies what is true in reality, what is true in the understanding depends on what is true in reality, "because the thing itself is the measure of the understanding." Therefore, insofar as the sentence 'Socrates is' signifies that Socrates really exists, it is false, given that Socrates no longer exists.

[n. 28] Scotus returns to "a certain argument" from 'a stone is not in the soul,' that is, the argument in n. 12 above. The reply again makes use of the distinction between what is signified primarily and what is signified through a primary or per se significate. Thus, 'a stone is not in the soul' primarily signifies the understanding (*intellectum*) that is the "natural sign" of it being the case that a stone is not in the soul (*esse*). Its being the case is "outside the soul [*extra animam*]," of course, although the understanding through which it is signified is inside the soul. And so the concept of stone is in the soul, but not the stone itself.

[n. 29] Here Scotus points out that utterances can be imposed to signify an inscription, or marks on a page, as well as the likeness that is the sign of a thing in the soul, which is how "a name can signify a thing as it is understood."

[n. 30] The edition treats n. 30 as "the view of Scotus," but it is probable that the first determination beginning at n. 14 is his actual view. Scotus does, however, concede that "neither way is particularly necessary," adding that "it is completely absurd to say that a thing is signified absolutely."

The edition mentions the view of Simon of Faversham as though it were opposed to Scotus. Simon says that by names we signify things and not the species of things, although they signify things not as they have being outside the soul, nor as they have being in the soul, but "absolutely [*absolute*]," that is, "as that which exists absolutely, by leaving out any accident, as is apparent in connection with the name 'man.'"[9] But see n. 14 of q. 2 below, where Scotus expresses a view similar to Simon's—"what is strictly speaking signified by the utterance is the thing, not as it exists [*exsistens est*] or does not exist, but as it abstracts from them [that is, from existing and non-existing] absolutely and is extraneous to any one of them"—though, as the editors note, the latter passage may be an interpolation by Scotus's editor, Antonius Andreas.

[Question 2. Does a Name Signify a Thing Univocally When the Thing Is Existing and When It Is Not?]

Summary

The question begins with four arguments (nn. 1–4) that a name does not signify univocally, followed by two arguments (nn. 5–6) on the opposing side. Scotus gives his determination in nn. 7–8. The replies to the initial arguments are in n. 9 (to the first argument), n. 10 (to the second), and n. 11 (to the fourth).[10]

Discussion

The question corresponds partly to *Opus I*, q. 3, which asks whether a change occurs in the signification of an utterance when a change occurs in the thing it signifies, and partly to *Opus I*, q. 5, which asks whether a common term is predicated univocally of existing and non-existing things. However, few of the arguments overlap.

Commentary

Negative Arguments

[n. 1] The first argument is that an affection or idea signifies a thing under its proper aspect or nature (*sub propria ratione*). Once a thing has been transformed, however, it loses its proper nature. Therefore, the signification of the name corresponding to the idea is also altered.

The view that the understanding apprehends a thing under its proper nature

---

9. Simon of Faversham, *Periherm.*, q. 5 (155).
10. The edition erroneously indicates that n. 11 replies to n. 3, the third argument that a dead animal only has a foot or a hand equivocally.

is endorsed by Thomas Aquinas in his *De interpretatione* commentary, based on Aristotle's remark in *De anima* III.4 that the proper object of the understanding is the quiddity (*quod quid est*) of a thing.[11]

[n. 2] The second argument invokes Averroes, who says that in a substantial transformation a thing loses its name and definition. This argument corresponds to the one in *Opus I*, q. 3, n. 2.

[n. 3] The third argument is that, according to Aristotle (*De partibus animalium* I.1.640b33–641a5), a dead animal only has a foot or a hand equivocally. This argument is not found in the corresponding q. 3 in *Opus I*.

[n. 4] The fourth argument is that there is nothing univocally common to what exists and what does not exist. The same argument is given in *Opus I*, q. 5, n. 3. See the commentary there for notes and references.

Affirmative Arguments

[n. 5] The arguments on the opposing side (nn. 5–6) reflect *Opus I* more closely.

Scotus argues first that the nature (*ratio*) of a thing in the soul is the same whether the thing exists or not, and hence the same as the signification of an utterance (which, according to those who hold this view, is the same as the understanding of it). This view is consistent with *Opus I*, q. 1, nn. 5–9 above.

This is clear, he says, in the case of states of affairs that frequently come into and out of existence. Thus, regardless of someone's running or not running, we understand the same by 'an animal runs' (the example given in *Opus I*, q. 3, n. 5 was of Socrates sitting or not sitting). Scotus mentions the possibility of demonstration from non-existent things (compare *Opus I*, q. 3, n. 10 *et passim*).

[n. 6] The second argument cites Aristotle's view in *Categories* c. 5 that statements and beliefs "remain completely unchangeable in every way," so it must be due to changes in the actual thing that they come to have the contrary truth-value.[12]

Determination

[n. 7] Scotus replies that a name signifies a thing univocally whether the thing exists or not, although the reasons he gives here do not correspond closely to either q. 3 or q. 5 of *Opus I*.

---

11. Thomas Aquinas, *In Perihermenias* I. lect. 10, n. 5 (citing Aristotle, *De an.* III.4.429b10).
12. See Aristotle, *Categories* 5.4a36–b2.

The first reason is that the likeness of Socrates in the soul is Socrates's form as he actually is; therefore, the name signifies him as he actually is.

[n. 8] The second reason is that the likeness of a thing in the soul is a sign of the thing univocally. Thus, a name equally signifies a thing whether the thing exists or not.

[n. 9] To the first argument (n. 1 above, regarding the idea of a thing signifying it under its proper aspect or nature), Scotus replies that a name signifies a thing indirectly via the mediation of the likeness in the sign, which signifies the thing directly. This likeness signifies the thing whether the thing exists or not.

[n. 10] To the second argument (n. 2 above) Scotus replies that in a substantial change, the substance of the thing that is corrupted does not remain. But the name of the substance (for example, 'Socrates') still signifies the same even when Socrates does not exist. Apart from saying that this is the view of the authorities, however, Scotus gives no further argument here.

The reply to the second argument in q. 3 of *Opus I* (n. 12, replying to n. 2) is more comprehensive. There Scotus says that the name continues to signify the same because it does not signify an individual *suppositum* (such as Socrates).

[n. 11] To the third argument (n. 4 above; the edition mistakenly refers to n. 3), Scotus replies that while there is no concept common to the concepts of Socrates existing and of Socrates not existing, there can be a common concept of Socrates who does not exist (though not *as* he does not exist) and of someone else who does exist now.

Remarks on the Signification of a Name

[n. 12] Scotus comments that a likeness of a thing in the soul is a likeness indifferently of what exists or does not exist.

He argues that Caesar does not share the name 'man' according to the being he has now. For a name signifies a thing by means of a likeness in the mind that is shared equally by what exists and what does not exist (that is, not as it exists, or as it does not exist). Nor does the Antichrist share the name 'man' under the aspect of potential being (*sub esse potentiali*). In other words, Scotus distinguishes between the per se understanding of a common name (which is indifferent to what exists now, or in the past, or in the future) and understanding that name under the aspect of 'existing' or 'possibly existing.'

[n. 13] Further, Scotus argues that the per se understanding or concept corresponding to a common name is indifferent to the aspects of past, present, and future, or of possible or actual existence. Thus any aspect under which we conceive the name (for example, conceiving of Caesar as existing, or of the Antichrist as possibly existing in the future) is beyond the per se understanding of that name, and hence this 'aspectual' way of conceiving or understanding the name will not cause any equivocation in the name.

[n. 14] A further determination is found here in some manuscripts. We do not know whether the author was Scotus. It is argued that an utterance signifies a thing not as existing or as non-existing, but "as it abstracts from them absolutely and is extraneous to any one of them." Compare *Opus I*, q. 2, nn. 40–41, where Scotus says that a name signifies a thing not as it exists, but as it is conceived or understood.[13] Here, however, the writer does not talk about a thing as it is understood, but rather "as it abstracts from them" (presumably from the concepts of existence and non-existence) absolutely and as it is "extraneous" to any one of those concepts.

The writer then appeals to the transitivity argument (that the sign of a sign of a thing is also indirectly a sign of the thing) using the analogy with writing signifying speech, as well as an analogy with the sun's power to lighten: the sun illuminates many parts of a medium, each of which is illuminated by the sun immediately, but in a certain order, because the more remote parts are illuminated by mediation of the parts that are more proximate.

The edition notes that this section bears many similarities to the *Ordinatio* of Scotus, as well as to the question, "Whether a name signifies a thing or an affection in the soul," from the *Perihermenias* commentary of his editor, Antonius Andreas.[14] Antonius's version is an amalgam of material from *Opus I*, q. 2 and this section. It is the only place where Antonius uses material from the duplicated qq. 1–2 here.[15]

Andrews states that the paragraph appears verbatim in Antonius's *Quaestiones*, and that the absence of the text in some manuscripts "suggests that it might be an

---

13. See also *Opus I*, q. 3, n. 10; qq. 5–8, nn. 43, 64, 71; and q. 1, n. 15.

14. Duns Scotus, *Ordinatio* I, d. 27, qq. 1–3, n. 83 (VI, 97). See also *Lectura* (*Opera Omnia* XVII, 357); *Reportata Parisiensia* (Vivès XXII, 334b), mentioned in Robert Andrews, "The Modistae and John Duns Scotus's *Quaestiones super Perihermenias*," in *Aristotle's* Peri Hermeneias *in the Latin Middle Ages: Essays on the Commentary Tradition*, eds. H. A. G. Braakhuis and C. H. Kneepkens (Groningen-Haren: Ingenium, 2003), 73; and Antonius Andreas, "*Utrum nomen significet rem vel passionem in anima*," in *Periherm.*, f. 66va.

15. With the exception of the introduction to *Opus II*, which Antonius amalgamates with the *Opus I*, q. 1.

appended note, but it may indeed have been added by Scotus himself." He says, "in many central phrases both are identical to the summary account in Scotus's later theological works."[16]

Actually it is not verbatim, but contains an important and interesting variation from our version. For example, where our version has "what is strictly speaking signified by the utterance is a thing," Antonius adds, "not a thing as it is understood." Scotus, by contrast, is insistent that a word does signify a thing as it is understood—an idea, as we noted in the commentary above, that is central to many parts of the work.

This amendment is consistent with other changes that Antonius makes in his version of Scotus's *Quaestiones*. For example, in *Opus I*, q. 3, n. 10, Scotus says that "a thing is not signified as it exists, but as it is understood," to which Antonius adds "according to one opinion," stating further that according to another opinion, an intelligible species is signified, and according to yet another, a thing is signified absolutely, as it abstracts from being or non-being.[17]

In n. 11 of the same question, Scotus says that 'thing' is understood not only as applying to existing things but also to a thing as it is understood, to which Antonius adds "or [a thing] taken absolutely, as it abstracts from both [existence and non-existence]." Note again the addition of the idea of 'abstraction.' In n. 19, Scotus says that an existing thing was not signified by the utterance before, nor is a non-existing thing signified now, but rather what is signified is the thing as it is understood. Antonius deletes 'as it is understood.' In *Opus I*, q. 6, n. 10, Scotus says that both the *suppositum* and the common nature are related in the same way to existence and non-existence, to which Antonius adds "because the significate of a name abstracts from both [existence and non-existence]; therefore, a name signifies without time."[18] Note the use of *abstrahit*, which indicates that these amendments almost certainly reflect the mind of Antonius; Scotus rarely uses *abstrahitur* in this context.[19]

16. Andrews, "Scotus's *Quaestiones super Perihermenias*," 73.
17. Antonius Andreas, *Periherm.*, q. 6 (68ra).
18. Ibid., q. 7 (69ra).
19. However, Timothy Noone notes (private communication): "Scotus does often use *abstrahere* both in the active and passive voices; a quick electronic search of *Lectura* I [*Opera Omnia* XVI] reveals that he uses it seventeen times there alone. Most of the occurrences have to do with abstracting a notion from things, but also isolating one notion from another. In the univocity discussion, for example, he argues that *sapientia*, when it is abstracted from creatures, has to have some overlap with that same notion when applied to God, or else there is no warrant for attributing wisdom to God at all.

This suggests the passage is not by Antonius, unless he was perhaps editing an earlier work of his, after he had changed his mind about *ut intelligitur*. Whether it is actually by Scotus is difficult to say.

[Question 3. Do Truth and Falsity Only Concern Composition and Division?]

Summary

The main negative arguments are in nn. 1–5, followed by a single affirmative argument in n. 6. Scotus's determination of the question (nn. 7–11) contends that truth and falsity concern composition and division of the understanding only. The replies to all the arguments of nn. 1–5 are in n. 12.

Discussion

The edition notes the similarity between Scotus's discussion and that of Thomas Aquinas in his commentary on *De interpretatione* I.3. Both authors agree with Aristotle that truth and falsity reside in the intellect's act of composition and division. The problem is how to treat cases where single concepts or things are called 'true' or 'false,' such as 'true' gold versus 'false' gold, or where an artifact such as a chair is 'true' because it conforms to the idea in the mind of the person who made it. The latter sense underlies certain English expressions, such as 'my aim is true.'[20]

Commentary

Negative Arguments

[n. 1] The first argument is that division—the denial that one thing is another, such as 'Socrates is not a donkey'—is "terminated" in simple elements, that is, denial can involve nothing more than the existence of simple terms. Thom-

---

[There are also] many occasions upon which Scotus uses *abstrahit* to speak, in reference to the mode of *cognitio abstractiva*, of how that mode of cognition contains objects that are indifferent to or bear no relation to existing things. This latter usage, though in psychological contexts, may be somewhat parallel with the cases at stake in your texts."

20. Simon of Faversham takes substantially the same position on this question as Thomas (and later, Scotus); see his *Perihermermias* (second recension), q. 2. See also Elvis Costello, *My Aim Is True* (New York: Columbia Records, 1978).

as mentions a similar argument, saying that "division comes about by resolution into indivisibles or simples, so that just as there is not truth and falsity in simples, so neither in division."[21] Thomas illustrates this using an analogy of the statue of Hercules similar to the analogy mentioned by Scotus earlier (see *Opus II.I*, q. 1, n. 23), arguing that just as the statue can be called both 'bronze' (as the staute is in itself) and 'a man' (as it refers to reality), so our thoughts always involve composition in themselves—even those involving denial, for this still requires comparison of simple concepts—but both composition and division when they refer to reality. Denial, or negation, is a comparison of ideas signifying a separation of things. Scotus makes the same argument, but in less detail.

[n. 2] The second argument is that we call gold 'true' gold, and brass 'false' gold; cf. Thomas Aquinas: "a [simple] thing is called true or false, just as we call gold true or false."[22]

[n. 3] The third argument is that being, or something's being the case, and truth are convertible, offering Aristotle's epigrammatic remark from *Metaphysics* II.1.993b30–31 to this effect.

[n. 4] The fourth argument is that a sense [*sensus*]—referring here to the cognitive power of sensation, not to a Fregean thought—is said by Aristotle to be true of its proper object (*De anima* II.6.418a11–15). See Thomas Aquinas, on the same passage: "The philosopher says in the book *De anima* that the sensing of proper sensibles is always true; but sense does not compose or divide; therefore, truth is not only in composition or division."[23]

[n. 5] The fifth argument again cites Aristotle, who says in *De anima* III that when the understanding grasps the what-it-is or essence of a thing, it is a true understanding and never deceived. The edition refers here to the commentary of Averroes on *De anima* III (com. 36), but the corresponding discussion in Aristotle is *De anima* III.6.430b26–30.

Affirmative Argument

[n. 6] On the opposing side, Scotus cites Aristotle's remark that the true and false are not in things, as if good things are true and bad things false; rath-

---

21. Thomas Aquinas, *In Perihermenias* I. 1ect. 3, n. 4.
22. Ibid., n. 5.
23. Ibid. The reference to Aristotle's *De anima* is erroneously given as III.4.428b18–20 in the edition.

er, true and false exist in the mind, or "in thought [*in mente*]" (*Metaphysics* VI.4.1027b26–27).

Determination

[n. 7] Truth and falsity relate to the operation of the faculty of understanding in composing and dividing. Likewise, a thing is said to be true because it is "equal to its measure," meaning that it is true in comparison to its conception in the understanding, which provides "the measure of each thing."

[n. 8] However, there are two senses in which the understanding is compared to reality. In the first way, our understanding is measured by reality, as when we make judgments about naturally occurring things. In the second, it is the opposite: artifacts like tables and houses have forms which are said to be 'true' insofar as they 'measure up' to the design in the mind of the craftsman or architect. But naturally occurring things are also said to be true in the second way in relation to the divine understanding, for each imitates, according to its form, a species in the divine mind. In this sense, every being is a true being, just as brass, even though it is said to be false gold, is nevertheless true brass. The argument of n. 8 closely follows the corresponding sections in the commentary of Thomas Aquinas.[24] It is also the only section of the whole work that mentions God.

[n. 9] The argument continues: the sensation of simple objects cannot be called true in the proper sense because something is true primarily in comparison to its measure. But simple sensation cannot be true in this way (nor can simple understanding) because the relation between it and what it senses is not itself something it can sense, nor can it sense itself 'conforming' with its object. The argument here and in n. 10 also corresponds to the commentary of Thomas Aquinas.[25]

[n. 10] Further, Scotus says that in composing, our understanding can recognize its conformity to reality. For it judges that it is so in reality, and it does this by composing or dividing. Composing and dividing is nothing other than the understanding judging that things are, or are not, as reality conforms to the understanding.

We might ask here how the understanding is to measure the correspondence between the composition it sets up in itself and the corresponding composition

---

24. Thomas Aquinas, *In Perihermenias* I. lect. 3, nn. 7–8.
25. Ibid., nn. 9–10.

in reality without having to occupy a position outside itself to measure the correspondence, and so on *ad infinitum*. Alternatively, if there is no composition in reality, how would the understanding ever be in a position to grasp that there is not?

[n. 11] Perhaps recognizing the difficulty here (see n. 10), Scotus again mentions Aristotle's remark in *Metaphysics* VI that the true and the false are in the mind only, or in the person cognizing (see n. 6 above). A simple understanding of gold expresses no judgment; rather, it simply corresponds to its intelligible object. Otherwise, there would be no understanding of gold at all. Likewise, a sensation of gold that misses the mark fails to be a sensation of gold, since 'false gold' does not correspond to anything real.

Reply to the Main Arguments

[n. 12] Scotus replies to all the arguments (nn. 1–5), and particularly to the first, by distinguishing between concepts as they are related just to one another, and as they are related to reality. The same distinction is invoked by Thomas Aquinas (see n. 1 above). In the first sense, even denial involves composition, for it involves comparison, and comparison is a form of composition. In the second sense, denial involves distinction (and hence division) because we are comparing concepts as representing or signifying different things. As Scotus says, when I say 'a man is not a donkey,' I am expressing the concepts 'man' and 'donkey' in relation to reality, that is, as signifying different or distinct things.

The edition mentions Antonius Andreas, who makes substantially the same point in his *De interpretatione* commentary, in the question, "whether truth or falsity only involve composition and division."[26] Note, however, that this is the only question where Antonius differs substantially from Scotus. Antonius's determination and discussion is somewhat different from both Scotus and Thomas, agreeing only in the initial arguments and final reply, as here.

---

26. Antonius Andreas, *Periherm.*, q. 3 (f. 64va).

[Question 4. Does an Indefinite Name Posit Something, Such That the Predication of the Being of That Thing Is Required?]

Summary

The question begins with the four main arguments (nn. 1–6) on behalf of the view that an indefinite term posits something, followed by the four main arguments against (nn. 7–11). The replies of others follow (nn. 12–14), along with objections to those replies (nn. 15–16). Scotus then gives his determination (nn. 17–18), which is that indefinite terms posit 'signifiable being' but not 'being according to nature.' Finally, he replies to the main affirmative arguments (nn. 19–24).

Discussion

This question is logically and historically connected with *Opus II.I*, qq. 2–5, which concern the validity of the inference, 'this is not just; therefore, this is non-just [*hoc non est iustum, ergo hoc est non-iustum*].' If an indefinite term posits something—that is, if it asserts or presupposes or predicates the existence of something—then the affirmative proposition 'this is non-just' posits the existence of something (a non-just thing). But on the other hand, a negative proposition, such as 'it is not the case that this is just,' does not posit the existence of anything since it is merely a negation that removes what is affirmed by the corresponding affirmative proposition, including the existence of what 'this' refers to. Thus, if an indefinite term posits something, the inference 'this is not just; therefore, this is non-just' is not valid, since the consequent posits more than the antecedent.

Commentary

Affirmative Arguments

[n. 1] The first main argument appeals to Aristotle, who says in *Prior Analytics* I.46.51b25–28 that being non-equal and not being equal are not the same because something underlies the one, that is, what is non-equal, but not the other. The unequal (*inaequale*) underlies what is non-equal.[27]

---

27. The argument is mentioned by a number of other writers from the late thirteenth century, e.g., Peter of Auvergne, *Quaestiones super librum Perihermeneias*, q. 12, and Radulphus Brito, *Quaestiones super arte veteri*, q. 4 (ed. Vercellensis & Vercellensis; Venice: 1499): "whether an indefinite name pos-

Commentary: On Book I   293

[n. 2] The second argument is that negation (that is, predicate negation) removes something from something. But in that case, something must be left behind, which is not the same as the removal of the entire thing (that is, sentential negation).

[n. 3] The third argument is that if the indefinite term posited nothing, then 'it is not the case that a is b,' which posits nothing, would imply 'a is not-b,' a consequence Aristotle denies in *De interpretatione* II.10.19b20–20a3.[28]

[n. 4] An objection: the consequence is only invalid in the case of complex predicates. For example, "a is not a white log; therefore, a is a non-white log" is not valid (following Aristotle in *Prior Analytics* I.46.51b29–31). The consequent asserts the existence of a log, whereas the antecedent does not.

[n. 5] Here we get two replies to the objection in n. 4. The first cites Aristotle, who says that the verb 'is' is conjoined with 'just' or 'non-just,' that is, he is not speaking only of composite predicates (*De interpretatione* II.10.19b25–26).

The second reply is that the syllogism: 'every non-animal is a non-man; a stone is a non-animal; therefore, a stone is a non-man' is valid. If 'a stone is not an animal' were to imply the minor premise 'a stone is a non-animal,' as assumed, it would also imply the conclusion, 'a stone is a non-man.' Therefore, 'a stone is not an animal' would imply 'a stone is a non-man.' But the argument is not complete as it stands. Simon of Faversham, who also mentions it, clarifies the argument as follows: if 'non-man' posited something, the conclusion 'a stone is a non-man' would imply 'a stone exists'; therefore 'if every man is an animal, a stone exists' would be valid, which it clearly is not.[29] See n. 10 below.

[n. 6] The fourth main argument appeals to Boethius: an indefinite name is a privation of the species that is present, although it leaves behind other indefinites. Presumably, referring to a as a non-man leaves it open as to whether a is a non-donkey, a non-ox, and so on.

---

its anything, so that from its being predicated of any thing, the predication of existence of that thing follows."

28. Peter of Auvergne and Radulphus Brito mention the same argument. See also Sten Ebbesen, "*Termini accidentales concreti*: Texts from the late thirteenth century," *Cahiers de l'Institut du Moyen-Age grec et latin* 53 (1986): 75.

29. As John Longeway comments, the argument would be clearer still if the example were not stone, but a rose (in midwinter, when there are none), or a chimera. See Simon of Faversham, *Perihermenias*, 151–70.

Negative Arguments

[n. 7] Scotus now moves to the main arguments in opposition (nn. 7–11). The first is that we can predicate an indefinite term of a non-existent object, for example, 'a chimera is a non-man.'[30]

[n. 8] The second argument is that just as the inference '*a* is a man; therefore, *a* is something' follows, so does '*a* is a non-something; therefore, *a* is a non-man.' But if the indefinite term 'non-man' posits something, then the consequent '*a* is a non-man' posits something. But the antecedent '*a* is a non-something' denies that *a* is anything by denying that *a* posits anything. But that is contradictory.

[n. 9] An objection to the argument in n. 8 is that the noun 'something' cannot be made indefinite, that is, there cannot be a 'non-something.' Every thing is something. The edition mentions Albert the Great's remark in his commentary on *De interpretatione* that transcendental names cannot be infinitized.[31]

Scotus replies to the objection by saying that 'being' clearly can be infinitized, and 'being' is no less general than 'something [*aliquid*].' He appeals to the authority of Aristotle in *Physics* V.1.225a16–17.

As noted below, Albert is probably the source for Scotus and other writers on this point. However, Peter of Ireland (Petrus de Hibernia), who taught in Naples around 1240, and who, at least according to early fourteenth-century biographies of Thomas Aquinas, taught the young Thomas Aquinas at the University of Naples circa 1239–44,[32] discusses this subject in his commentary on *De interpretatione*, where he says that 'non-man [*non homo*]' is equivalent to 'something having the privation-of-man [*aliquid habens privationem hominis*]' and that transcendental names cannot be infinitized.[33]

[n. 10] The third argument repeats the counter-argument given in n. 5 above:

---

30. See also Radulphus Brito in Ebbesen, "*Termini accidentales concreti*," who says that what can be verified of a non-being posits nothing. But we can say that a chimera is a non-man, and so an indefinite term posits nothing.

31. *Perihermenias* I.2; ed. Borgnet, I.393a–393b.

32. Karen Dalgaard, "Peter of Ireland's *Commentary on Aristotle's* 'Peri Hermeneias,'" *Cahiers de l'Institut du Moyen-Age grec et latin* 43 (1982): 7.

33. See Ebbesen, "*Termini accidentales concreti*," 127–28, and Sten Ebbesen, "Concrete Accidental Terms: Late Thirteenth-Century Debates about Problems Relating to such Terms as 'Album,'" in *Meaning and Inference in Medieval Philosophy: Studies in Memory of Jan Pinborg*, ed. Norman Kretzmann (Dordrecht: Reidel, 1988), 146.

if an indefinite name posited something, 'every man is an animal' would imply 'a stone is something.'[34]

[n. 11] The fourth argument is that an indefinite term is imposed by denying a form (that is, the term 'non-man' denies the form of 'man'). But with the privation of that form, nothing remains deriving its being from that form. Therefore, an indefinite term posits nothing.[35]

Replies of Others

[n. 12] The question now shifts in nn. 12–16 to consider the opinion of others, together with Scotus's reply. According to this opinion, there are two kinds of indefinite term: substantial and accidental. A substantial indefinite term posits nothing because (as suggested above) when things are deprived of a quality, whatever has being through that quality is also deprived. By contrast, an indefinite accidental term must posit something, because with the privation of a quality such as 'white,' what exists by that quality need not suffer privation.

As indicated in the edition, the distinction between substantial and accidental terms, and its use in the context of this question, comes from Albert the Great (*Perihermenias* I.2; ed. Borgnet, I.393a). It is probable that Duns Scotus, Peter of Auvergne, and Radulphus Brito all had Albert in mind when they raised the issue. Brito even mentions Albert by name, quoting Albert's view about a difference between privative and indefinite negation.[36]

[n. 13] According to this opinion, a 'substantial' term is one like 'man' or 'whiteness.' But an indefinite accidental term like 'white' must posit the existence of whatever it is predicated of, because the privation of an accidental quality does not require the privation of the thing of which the quality is predicated.

---

34. This version of the argument is also close to Simon of Faversham's version, even repeating the scholastic formula about transitivity (*a primo ad ultimum*). John Longeway renders this as 'by transitivity' in his translation of Walter Burley's *Scriptum* on the *Posterior Analytics*, c. 13; http://uwp.edu/~longeway/interpre.htm

35. This argument is again close to Simon of Faversham, who says in *Periherm.*: "An indefinite name is imposed by negation of a form, hence, because it is imposed by negation of a form, since the negation of a form is equally said of a being and a non-being, since someone denying a form denies every determination, therefore an indefinite name is equally said of a being and a non-being" (translated by John Longeway; http://uwp.edu/~longeway/interpre.htm).

36. Radulphus Brito, *Quaestiones super arte veteri* (ed. Vercellensis & Vercellensis; Venice: 1499): "Again, this seems to be the intention of Albert, who posits a difference in negation between privative and infinitizing negation [Item hoc videtur de intentione alberti, qui ponit differentiam inter negationem negatione privative et infinite]."

[n. 14] In support of this argument, Scotus mentions Aristotle's view that something must be the subject of an indefinite accidental term (see also the passages from Aristotle cited in n. 1 and n. 3 above).

[n. 15] Scotus replies: a substantial term signifies the composition of matter and (substantial) form. Thus, with the privation of substantial form, the matter would still remain. Since the matter counts as something, it follows, by parity of reasoning, that a substantial indefinite term would posit something.

[n. 16] Also, Scotus continues, an accidental term signifies a quality rather than a subject, and it is only this that the indefinite term negates. The argument is obscure, but the idea seems to be that unlike a privative term, an indefinite term does not signify the removal of some form from a determinate subject because it does not determine a subject in the way that a privative term does. Thus, the privative term 'blind' determines the subject of which it is predicated by saying that it positively lacks the form of sightedness, which it is naturally suited to have. But 'not-seeing' does not say anything about the inherent qualities of the subject of which it is predicated, but rather only that there is a failure of the act of seeing.

Determination

[n. 17] In his two-part determination (nn. 17–18), Scotus qualifies two senses in which an indefinite term can posit something: the 'something' can signify a thing and a nature that exists, or else it can be taken for anything whatsoever that can be signified by an utterance.

[n. 18] In the sense that 'something' signifies a nature or essential being, an indefinite term posits nothing. But in the sense that it signifies anything whatsoever—for example, whatever can be understood under the negation of 'man'—it signifies something. Here Scotus cites Boethius, who says that being is predicated indifferently whether the subject exists or does not exist.[37] Boethius actually says that 'non-man' signifies a 'something,' that which is not a man, but which could be a dog or a horse or a stone or whatever is not a man, and is predicated 'equally' respecting what exists and does not exist.[38]

---

37. *De interpr.* I.2 (62; PL 64:424D).

38. Likewise, according to Thomas Aquinas, 'non-man' can be predicated indifferently of what does not exist in reality, such as a chimera, or what does, such as a horse. Therefore, "'non-man' can be said indifferently both of what does not exist in reality, as when we say 'a chimera is a non-man,' and of what exists in reality, such as when we say 'a horse is a non-man.' But if it were imposed from privation, it would require a subject that at least existed. But because it is imposed by negation, it can be said of

Robert Kilwardby advances a similar thesis in his commentary on the *Prior Analytics*, where he says that the predication of an indefinite term presupposes the being of reason or understanding only. Like earlier Parisian authors, he concedes that 'non-man [*non homo*]' is equivalent to 'being that is not a man [*ens quod non est homo*],' but holds that *ens* refers not to real being but to the being of reason or understanding. Thus 'being [*ens*]' and 'something [*aliquid*]' can be infinitized.[39]

This is also why, according to Scotus, the name 'something' cannot be made indefinite, at least in the second sense mentioned above. In the sense that it means anything signifiable, it cannot be made not to signify (that is, we cannot signify a 'not-something' in the sense of something not signifiable, for we would have signified it by that very act). And if an indefinite name meant something non-signifiable, the hearer would no more comprehend it than a nonsense expression such as '*bers bars*.' Thus, it is clear that an indefinite name posits something as 'signifiable being.'

Replies to the Main Arguments

[n. 19] Scotus next replies to the main arguments (nn. 1–6), which held that an indefinite name does posit something. His reply to the first main argument (n. 1 above) is that there is something underlying what is not equal in the sense of 'that of which it is predicated' (presumably he means 'signifiable being' here), but not in the sense that something unequal is posited in the privative sense.

[n. 20] He replies to the second argument (n. 2 above) by conceding that ne-

---

a being and a non-being, as Boethius and Ammonius say [non-homo potest dici indifferenter et de eo quod non est in rerum natura, ut si dicamus, chimaera est non homo, et de eo quod est in rerum natura, sicut cum dicitur, equus est non homo. Si autem imponeretur a privatione, requireret subiectum ad minus existens, sed quia imponitur a negatione, potest dici de ente et de non ente, ut Boethius et Ammonius dicunt]" (*In Perihermenias* [Aristotle, *De interpr.* I.1.16a30] I.4, n. 13).

39. Robert Kilwardby: "I say that 'non-man' expounded in this way [is] 'a being which is not a man,' but the term 'being' in this exposition does not mean some being according to nature, but it is accepted commonly as 'being according to nature' and as 'being according to reason or understanding,' and in saying 'being' in this way does not mean 'something' without qualification [dico quod sic exponitur 'non homo': "ens quod non est homo," sed hoc quod dico "ens" in hac expositione non dicit 'aliquid' [?] ens secundum naturam, sed accipitur communiter ad ens secundum naturam et ad ens secundum rationem vel intellectum, et sic ponendo 'ens' non ponit aliquid simpliciter]" (*Commentary on the 'Prior Analytics,'* ms. Cambridge Peterhouse 205: 116va; Ebbesen, "*Termini accidentales concreti*," 127–28). This leads Tabarroni, "Tenth Thesis in Logic," 350, to suggest that the theory of the existential import of indefinite terms loses general support before the middle of the thirteenth century. See also the commentary on *Opus II.I*, q. 2, nn. 2–5 above.

gation is the removal of 'something from something,' but that the 'something' left behind is the "intelligible and signifiable being" he defined in the determination; there is nothing left of the 'nature' that was there before.

[n. 21] To the third argument (n. 3 above), he replies that the verb 'is' is not just a way of uniting the subject and predicate of a proposition, but is composed of two things, namely the composition and a certain content joined to the predicate. Hence, 'this is not just; therefore, this is non-just' is not valid, essentially for the same reason (it seems) that 'this is not a white log; therefore, this is a non-white log' is not valid. The predicate of 'this is just' is composite, being made up of 'just' and the content of the verb 'is.'

The sense in which 'is' is more than just a copula is explained in nn. 20-25 of *Opus II.I*, q. 5 below.

[n. 22] Scotus mentions an alternative reply. It is not entirely clear, however, because the expression "yields to its content on the side of the extreme [*pro re sua cedat in partem extremi*]" is difficult to understand. A possible interpretation of the argument might run as follows. Perhaps 'some *a* is *b*' really means 'some *a* is an *a* that is *b*,' so that "the predicate has the power of the two extremes or terms [*praedicatum habet virtutem duorum extremorum vel terminorum*]." Thus, any proposition is really equivalent to the case of '*a* is not a white log,' and thus the negation of the definite predicate does not imply the affirmation of the indefinite. That is, just as 'it is not the case that *a* is a white log' does not imply '*a* is a non-white log,' so 'it is not the case that *a* is an *a* that is *b*' does not imply '*a* is an *a* that is non-*b*.'

[n. 23] To the argument of n. 4 above (which objects to n. 3 that the consequence is only invalid in the case of complex predicates), Scotus concedes that Aristotle's remark is to be understood only as it applies to composite predicates.

[n. 24] Finally, Scotus replies to the argument of n. 6, which was that an indefinite name 'leaves behind' other indefinites. He says that when a negative is applied to a finite term such as 'man,' it removes the form corresponding to the term (presumably the form of man). Thus, it does not remove the form of donkey or horse. But Boethius does not mean that it actually posits those forms in the process.

[Question 5. Is the Verb 'Is' Only a Copula of the Predicate with the Subject?]

Summary

The question begins with five arguments (nn. 1–5) that the verb 'is [*est*]' is not only a copula, followed by four arguments (nn. 6–9) on the opposing side. After an interlude (nn. 10–19) for q. 6, q. 5 resumes at n. 20 with a determination arguing that the verb is not merely a copula, and that it is part of the predicate as the aspect under which the predication occurs, that is, the aspect of being actual (*sub ratione actus*). Thus Scotus replies (nn. 21–25) to the arguments on the opposing side (nn. 6–9). In n. 26, he notes another opinion, followed by a discussion (nn. 27–28).

Scotus then argues (nn. 29–32) that the copula and predicate do not form a composition in the strong sense of a 'verbal mode of signifying.' Thus he replies to the first set of arguments (n. 1). His reply to the first argument of n. 1 is at n. 33, to the second at n. 34. At n. 34, he offers a generic reply to the other arguments.

Discussion

This question is concerned with the discussion at the end of *De interpretatione* I.3 on verbs, where Aristotle says that 'to be' or 'not to be' does not signify any reality, unless something is added: "for by itself it is nothing, but it additionally signifies some combination, which cannot be thought of without the components."[40] It has no obvious connection with the discussion in q. 6, which it contains, except for the possible location in an earlier part of *De interpretatione* I.3.16b8–10, where Aristotle says that a verb (in the present tense, at least) indicates the present existence of the state in question. In his commentary, Antonius Andreas splits these questions up so that the first is his q. 5 ('Is the verb only the copula of the predicate with the subject or the predicate or part of the predicate?'), which he locates at 16b23, but the second is his q. 15 ('Is a present-tense verb a copula for the present 'now,' or indifferently, for anything present?'—the same wording as Scotus's q. 6), which he locates far away in *De interpretatione* I.10.20b1ff, where Aristotle says that converting the position of subject and predicate in a sentence does not

---

40. Aristotle, *De interpr.* I.3.16b23–25.

produce a difference in meaning, that is, such that 'a man is white' and 'a white thing is a man' are semantically equivalent.[41] There is no clear connection with the passage, although it is possible that Antonius sees a connection with an earlier claim in *De interpretatione* I.10.20a16, where Aristotle says that the propositions 'every animal is just' and 'no animal is just' will never be true in the same subject at the same time (*neque verae simul neque in eodem ipso*).

Commentary

Arguments for

[n. 1] The first main argument is that the verb 'is' has the same significate when predicated as a second element as when a predicate is added; that is, the 'is' in 'Socrates is' (that is, exists) and the 'is' in 'Socrates is white' have the same meaning.

[n. 2] The second argument also concludes that there is no difference between predication as a second or third element. In 'a man is,' the mode of signifying of the verb 'is' is that the *suppositum* of some man is united with the content of the verb 'is.' In 'a man is white,' the added 'white' does not change the mode of signifying of the first proposition, because the addition "does not change per se modes of signifying."

Note there is a similar assumption in modern predicate logic, which effectively assigns the same meaning to the existential quantifier in 'a man is' and 'a man is white':

$(\exists x)\ \text{man}(x)$

$(\exists x)\ (\text{man}(x)\ \&\ \text{white}(x))$

[n. 3] The third argument appeals to Boethius, who says that predicative and categorical propositions consist of two simple terms only.[42] If so, then 'is' belongs to the predicate 'is white,' because it is more reasonable to hold that the composition signified by 'is' belongs to the predicate. This is also similar to the assumptions of modern predicate logic, which postulates a twofold division of the proposition into a subject or argument A, and a propositional function $f(x)$. The proposition $f(A)$ signifies that the propositional function is satisfied for A.

---

41. Antonius Andreas, *Periherm.*, q. 5: "Utrum verbum sit tantum copula praedicati cum subiecto vel praedicatum vel pars praedicati" (f. 67va); q. 15: "Utrum verbum de praesenti copulet nunc quod instat vel indifferenter quodlibet praesens" (f. 80vb).

42. Boethius, *De interpr.* IV.10 (251; PL 64:519D).

Scotus follows the older terminology of Boethius's Latin translation of *De interpretatione* at I.10.19b19–20, which renders Aristotle's *triton proskategorethe* or as a 'third element,' *tertium adiacens* (literally 'being adjacent or next to'), rather than the newer (and more accurate) translation of William of Moerbeke, *tertium adpraedicatum* (literally 'additionally predicated' or 'adpredicated').[43]

[n. 4] The fourth argument is that when someone says, 'a man is an animal [*homo est animal*],' what is designated is that a man is actually an animal, and so as well, not only 'animal,' but 'animal in actuality.' Scotus presumably means that since the proposition designates something actual, its function is more than just to unite subject and predicate.

[n. 5] The fifth argument is that since Aristotle speaks of 'is' being predicated as a third element, it cannot be only a copula.

Arguments against

[n. 6] The first argument on the opposing side relies on the convertibility of subject and predicate that is fundamental to syllogistic logic: for example, our ability to convert 'some a is a b' into 'some b is an a.' If the copula were part of the predicate, however, no proposition could be converted absolutely. If the content of the verb 'is' in 'some a is a b' were part of the predicate b, then if we converted it to 'some b is an a,' the content would be part of the subject. But this is impossible, since otherwise every syllogism in the first figure would consist of four terms, as the middle term in the major premise would be understood such that 'being' is not part of it.

[n. 7] The second argument is that if 'being' is predicated by the proposition 'a man is,' then so is 'animal'; but being is also understood in 'animal.' Therefore, the same thing would be said twice, as in 'a man is is an animal,' which is nonsense.

[n. 8] The third argument invokes Boethius, who says that the third element 'is' is predicated with respect to the whole proposition, not as a part, but in order to demonstrate its quality (that is, the fact that it is an affirmative proposition). Thus it is only a copula.

[n. 9] The fourth argument appeals to the common view that when 'is' is predicated as a third element, it predicates what is in another such that it does not

---

43. For discussion, see Gabriel Nuchelmans, '*Secundum/Tertium Adiacens*': *Vicissitudes of a Logical Distinction* (Amsterdam: Royal Netherlands Academy of Arts and Sciences, 1992); and L. M. de Rijk, *Aristotle: Semantics and Ontology*, vol. 1 (Leiden: Brill, 2002), 306–14.

predicate its content as it is in itself, but as it is in another. The edition mentions William Arnauld as a possible source for this view, but another possible and more proximate source may have been Peter of Cornwall, who remarks in his commentary on Boethius's *De interpretatione*, "Boethius would have it the same way—the verb 'is' is sometimes a copula, such that it is an extreme, as when it is given per se, and then it predicates what is in itself; and sometimes a copula such that it is not an extreme, and then it predicates what is in another."[44]

He also appeals to Boethius, who says in his second commentary on *De interpretatione* that in 'a man is just,' the verb 'is' is not predicated as such, but as a third element, that is, in the second position and adjoining 'just.'

[Question 6. Is a Present-Tense Verb a Copula for the Present 'Now,' or Indifferently, for Anything Present?]

Summary

This question begins with three arguments (nn. 10, 11, 15) against the proposition that the copula represents the 'now' at this moment, including a more detailed discussion (nn. 12–14) of one view. Two arguments follow for the proposition (nn. 16–19). Scotus's determination, in favor of the proposition, is given at nn. 36–38. Then there are replies (nn. 39–42) to the four main arguments against, with an extra section (n. 43) discussing the arguments for (nn. 17–19).

Discussion

In q. 6, Scotus asks whether a present-tense verb joins subject and predicate for the 'now' at this moment, which he later calls the 'determinate present' (n. 14) and the 'discrete present' (nn. 36, 38), or indifferently for any present.

The origins of the idea of 'confused' and 'determinate' time are obscure. It is not found in William of Sherwood, or in Lambert of Lagny. However, something similar is mentioned in the anonymous late twelfth-century text, '*Cum sit nostra*':

The first rule of copulation is that a verb having the force of ampliation can signify time in two ways, viz., confusedly and determinately. The second rule is this: a verb

---

44. Peter of Cornwall, "*Omnis homo est*." For the Latin text and references, see the commentary on *Opus I*, q. 8, n. 42 above.

of the future tense can act as copula confusedly and determinately. And it should be known that when a common term acts as copula for the present, past, or future time confusedly, it signifies being such-and-such (*quale quid*); but when it acts determinately, it signifies a particular something (*hoc aliquid*).[45]

In his *Summae Metenses*, Nicholas of Paris says that the term 'present' has a twofold sense: present under the aspect of discrete time, and present under the aspect of the present. Thus:

'Present' in the former sense restricts [its associated categorematic term] to suppositing for things existing in the present. The rule just given was as regards this present. But there is another present related through indifference to all presents, and in this sense [propositions] are true according to [common] use. In this way, the sense of 'Easter is a beautiful time,' is, viz., 'when it exists.' And this sense is called the 'confused' present.[46]

Likewise, in his *Syncategoremata*, Nicholas argues that the time co-signified by the verb must be common and not discrete. "This is clear," he says, "because everything that has its existence from something else exists in the manner of [its] cause, and not in its own manner, and so, since time is a measure, it must be taken

---

45. *Logica 'Cum sit nostra'* V: 'De terminis' (Rijk, *Logica Modernorum*, II.ii:450); see also ibid., 451, ll. 23–24: " The first rule of predication is this: a verb having ampliative force can signify time in two ways, viz., confused and determinate. The second rule is this: a future-tense verb can be predicated confusedly and determinately. And it should be known that when a common term predicates with [a verb in] the present, past, or future tense confusedly, it signifies what kind of thing; but when it is joined determinately, it signifies a particular thing [Prima regula de copulatione est: verbum habens vim ampliandi potest significare tempus dupliciter, scilicet confusum et determinatum. Secunda regula est talis: verbum futuri temporis potest copulari confuse et determinate. Et sciendum quod quando terminus communis copulat praesens tempus vel praeteritum vel futurum confuse, significat quale quid; cum autem determinate, significat hoc aliquid]."

46. Nicholas of Paris, *De appellationibus*, NL 11412, f. 26v (Rijk, *Logica Modernorum*, II.i:460): "It should be said that the meaning of the term 'present' is twofold: present in the sense of discrete time or present in the sense of what is present. And such a 'present' is restricted to suppositing for things that are present. The aforementioned rule applies to such [a present] as this. And the other sense of 'present' is related indifferently to all present times, and of such a present truly are these [sentences such as 'Easter is a beautiful time' and "A rose is a beautiful flower'] according to use. Hence the sense is 'Easter is a beautiful time,' viz., when it is [Easter]. In such a case the present is said to be confused [Dicendum quod duplex est 'praesentis' sensus: praesens in ratione temporis discreti vel in ratione praesentis. Et tale praesens restringit ad supponendum pro praesentibus. Et de tali datur regula praedicta. Et est aliud praesens quod se habet per indifferentiam ad omnia praesentia et de tali vere sunt iste secundum usum. Unde sensus est 'Pascha est pulchrum tempus,' scilicet quando est. Et de tali dicitur praesens confusum]." See Roger Bacon, *Summulae*, 287 for an almost identical discussion; Roger also notes that the rule about restriction is invalid for the confused use of the present tense.

according to the nature of what is measured."[47] He adds (against the objection that it signifies the present 'now') that the 'present' has two senses: "viz., one of time, in which sense it is discrete and indivisible, and is called 'the present instant,' through whose continuation time flows into times; and of action, which receives quantity from action." He mentions the author of the *Book of Six Principles*, who says that time is long when the action is long, short when the action is short: in this sense, the present is common.[48]

Later in the thirteenth century, the anonymous Parisian author of *Album fuit disputaturum* explains the distinction by noting that there are two kinds of 'indifference,' viz., of *supposita* and of times. The first is removed by adding a sign (by which he means a quantifier, such as 'every' or 'some'); the second by adding 'necessarily.' Thus, where 'a man runs' is indifferent to any time, 'a man necessarily runs' removes this indifference. Likewise, in 'a man runs,' the copula joins the content of the verb in the 'confused' present. In the same way, if the copula joined the content in the discrete (*distinctum*) present, it would be the same to say 'a man runs' and 'a man runs now.'[49]

---

47. Nicholas of Paris, *Syncategoremata*, 2:29: "It must be said that the time consignified in a verb is common and not discrete time. This is clear, because everything that exists from another exists by way of a cause and not by way of itself, and thus, since time is a measure, it must be taken in keeping with the nature of what is measured [Dicendum quod tempus consignificatum in verbo est tempus commune et non discrete. Quod patet, quia omne quod est ab alio est secundum modum causae et non secundum modum suum, et ita, cum tempus sit mensura, secundum rationem mensurati oportet ipsum accipi]." See also John le Page, *Appellationes* III.17 (252).

48. Nicholas of Paris, *Syncategoremata*, 2:29-30: "To the objection that the present signifies the now, it must be said that the present is twofold: viz., [the present] of time, and in this way it is discrete and indivisible, [or] what is called an instant, through the continuation of which time flows into times; and the present of actions, which receives quantity from action. That is why the author of the *Liber Sex Principiorum* [says that] time is long because an action is long and short because an action is short. Likewise as well, the now is common [Quod obicitur quod significat praesens nunc, dicendum quod duplex est praesens: scilicet temporis, et ita est discretum et indivisibile, quod dicitur instans, per cuius continuationem fluit tempus in tempora; et est praesens actionis, quod recipit quantitatem ab actione; unde auctor Sex principiorum: tempus longum, quia actio longa, et breve, quia actio brevis. Similiter et nunc commune est]."

49. "*Album fuit disputarum*," q. 6 (NL 16135, 14va [76–77]): "Because indifference is twofold: viz., of individuals and times. The first is removed by the application of a sign; the second is removed by the fact that it is 'by necessity'; thus, since the indifference of times would be removed in saying 'A man runs by necessity,' it must be that it was initially related to all times through indifference. This would not be unless it joined its content to the present confusedly ... If it were joined to the distinct present, it would then be the same to say 'A man runs' and 'A man runs now'; but running now cannot be not running in the time that is now; therefore it will be the same to say 'A man runs now by necessity' and 'A man runs by necessity.' But this is false; therefore, the first [mode of indifference

John Styckborn also distinguishes between a common present and a confused present. He says the verb 'is' joins for a common and not a confused time, for if it were to signify the now at this moment, when that became past, sometimes it would co-signify its past, although it always joins for the present. According to him, 'confused' is what can be verified for many; 'common' is what can be preserved in many successively. Since it is repugnant to the present to be understood in many things at the same time, the verb 'is' joins for a common time.[50]

Against this background, Scotus offers his first set of arguments that the copula is in some sense a part of the predicate. The opposing arguments are that it is not. Scotus argues that both of these positions are wrong because the copula can be part of the predicate in two senses. In the first sense, it can be part of the predicate in just the way 'white' is part of 'white man'; this sort of composition is what Scotus calls a 'verbal mode of signifying.' In this sense, however, the copula is not part of the predicate, since 'being' and 'man' do not form a composite in the way 'white' and 'man' do. Thus Scotus replies to the first set of arguments (nn. 1–5).

In the second sense, it is part of the predicate as the aspect (*ratio*) under which predication occurs, that is, the aspect of being actual. This form of composition is not a 'verbal mode of signifying,' although it is still a form of composition, and the copula is in this sense part of the predicate. Thus Scotus replies (in nn. 21–25) to the arguments on the opposing side (nn. 6–9).

The edition incorrectly states that the position expressed in n. 20 is the expo-

---

applies] [Quia duplex est indifferentia: suppositorum, scilicet, et temporum. Prima tollitur per adventum signi, secunda per hoc quod est 'necessario'; quare, dicendo 'homo currit necessario' cum tollatur indifferentia temporum, oportet quod prius se haberet per indifferentiam ad omne tempus. Hoc non esset, nisi copularet rem suam pro praesenti confuse.... Si copularet praesens distinctum, idem esset dicere tunc 'homo currit' et 'homo currit nunc'; sed nunc currens non potest non currere pro tempore quod nunc est; idem igitur erit dicere 'homo currit nunc necessario 'et 'homo currit necessario' Hoc autem falsum, ergo primum]." The same author continues, "Peter Helias, in his *Summa super Priscianum maior*, in the chapter on *Time*, says that the verb 'is' can act as copula for any differentia of time, for example 'is present,' 'is past,' 'is future'; but when it is placed in an assertion, it joins subject and predicate for the time for which the assertion was made ... thus, when we assert 'a man runs,' since running is only in him in the present, the verb only joins its content to men existing in the present [Petrus Helie supra "Maius volumen," capitulo de tempore, dicit quod hoc verbum 'est' potest copulare pro qualibet differentia temporis, ut 'est praesens' 'est praeteritus,' 'est futurus,' sed, quando ponitur in enuntiatione, copulat extrema pro tempore pro quo fit enuntiatio, et hoc secundum exigentiam extremorum; quare, cum dicitur 'homo currit,' cum cursus non insit nisi pro praesenti, non copulat rem suam nisi pro praesenti]."

50. John Styckborn, *Questiones super librum Peryarmenias* (Caius 344/540, 210vb; cited in Lewry, "Oxford Condemnations," 276).

sition of the position of others, and that nn. 21–25 are replies to the arguments in nn. 1–4 according to this opinion. In fact, nn. 20–25 do express Scotus's view, insofar as he holds that the copula is part of the predicate in the second sense explained above, and so he disagrees with the arguments in nn. 6–9, according to which it is not a part of the predicate in any sense. The arguments in nn. 29–35 express Scotus's own view insofar as he holds that the copula is not part of the predicate in the first, 'verbal mode of signifying' sense, and so disagrees with nn. 1–2 explicitly and nn. 3–5 implicitly.

The edition also incorrectly states that sections nn. 20–25 are the exposition of some 'First Opinion.' It is in fact Scotus's opinion, as noted above.

Commentary

Arguments against

[n. 10] The first argument is that if 'running' supposited only for 'now' at the present moment, the proposition 'I run, if I run' would be false. The reason is that the consequent, 'I run,' is false if the present tense of the verb 'run' is joined to the present moment, because it happens that I am sitting at the present moment.

[n. 11] The second argument is that if the copula were joined to the 'now' of the present moment, 'Socrates always exists [*est*]' would involve a contradiction. That is, 'Socrates always exists' implies 'Socrates exists in the future,' which would be self-contradictory if the verb 'exists'/'is' were a copula only for the present time, as though Socrates's future existence were one and the same as his present existence.

[n. 12] The structure of nn. 12–14 is confusing. It begins with *dicitur*, which usually signals a discussion of the opinion of others. Here, however, it appears to be Scotus's own view, or a view very close to it, as evidenced by the repetition of the phrase, "but because it does not serve as a copula in this way, but for any 'now' when it was present [*sed quia non sic copulat, sed pro quolibet nunc cum institerit*]" in n. 42 below. He says that the verb serves as copula for the present time that was the present moment (*quod instat*) when it was the present moment, for example, 'now' for that moment which is 'now,' and otherwise for another when it was the present moment.

He gives an example of "the gate" which was so narrow that only one person could pass through, the analogy being to the present serving as a gate through which successive times pass: future moments have yet to pass through, whereas past moments have passed through already.[51] Let anyone who is in the gate be called *a* (that is, *a* is 'now'); then *a* will stand always for some person in the gate, viz., now for John, now for Robert. Thus, different moments (the analogues of John, Robert, etc.) can be 'now.'

Then Scotus argues that a present-tense verb acts as a copula for anything present, and not for the instant designated. What he means by 'the instant designated' is not quite clear, but presumably he means that the word 'now' cannot designate a specific time (for example, twelve o'clock on March 12, 1295); otherwise, a 'now' sentence would only be true for what was the case at twelve o'clock on March 12, 1295, which is clearly absurd.

The edition mentions Simon of Faversham as being among those who held this view. This claim is not entirely supported by the text. Certainly, Simon says that "a present-tense verb signifies the present time by, as it were, excluding what is past and future," but that is not what is said in n. 16 (although Scotus does say something like it in n. 43, replying to n. 18). Simon also says that if the present moment is called *a* and a present-tense verb co-signifies *a* and that moment becomes past, then a present-tense verb will co-signify a time that has past, which is the same as the argument given later in n. 12.

[n. 13] The format of the edition suggests that n. 13 argues against the view proposed in n. 12. However, it is not clear what *contra hoc* is replying to. The most plausible interpretation is that it is a reply to the last part of n. 12, where it is suggested that the present-tense verb 'is' has a new imposition for each moment it is uttered.

Scotus's own view, as expressed in his reply in n. 41, seems to be expressed in the sentence, "but now the aspect of this, i.e., the present time, no more respects the 'now' than the 'then,' but rather it is said of the present insofar as it possesses the aspect [*ratio*] of the present."

The added qualification at the end of the first sentence, "at least not with regard to anything [*aliquid*] except what is white," seems odd. Given the argument in n. 12 is that 'is' restricts the reference of the subject to the present 'now,' that is, to when the sentence is actually uttered, the objection seems to be saying that determination of a subject cannot go beyond the 'form' of the determining attribute. Presumably, the objector assumes that a present-tense copula does not restrict

---

51. Perhaps a reference to Mt 7:13–14.

the reference of the subject term to things that exist now, that is, at the present moment.

[n. 14] Here we have a further objection to the point made in n. 12: if a verb in the present tense were not acting as a copula for the determinate present, the proposition 'a man runs' could be true for a man running tomorrow, because the literal sense [*virtus sermonis*] would not constrain it to this present more than that. This also clearly reflects Scotus's view, as expressed in n. 41 below.[52]

[n. 15] Scotus now returns to the main arguments. The copula cannot act for the discrete present; otherwise, any present-tense proposition would be absolutely necessary: what exists or does not exist at the present instant necessarily exists or does not exist at the present instant.

Arguments for

[n. 16] The next three sections appear to offer arguments on the opposing side, that is, arguments for the copula acting for the present 'now,' rather than indifferently or confusedly for any 'present.' In actuality, there is only one opposing argument (n. 16), together with an objection (n. 17), and two replies to the objection (nn. 18–19).

The argument is that otherwise, 'everything that is, is at this instant' would be false, in which case something would be and not be in this instant.

"Everything that is, is at this instant [*omne quod est, est in hoc instanti*]" was actually a popular sophism among later medieval logicians. Versions of it were discussed by, among others, William of Sherwood, Henry of Ghent, and Walter Burley.

[n. 17] Scotus considers an objection to this argument: 'everything that is, is at this instant' would be true as long as it is governed by the copula, though its truth would be *per accidens*, since it consignifies only the present, as the actual past and the actual future do not yet exist. The objection looks close to the passage from Simon of Faversham quoted in the edition.

---

52. "*Album fuit disputarum*," q. 6 (NL 16135, 14va [76]) likewise argues for a discrete rather than a confused present: "if composition extended to any time, then [it would also extend] to the extremes, and so, with no man running now, let there be someone running in the future, and so 'a man runs' is true—but this is false [si compositio se extendat ad quodlibet tempus, et extrema similiter; et ita, nullo homine nunc currente de modo, aliquis currat in futuro, haec est vera: 'Homo currit.' Hoc autem falsum]."

[n. 18] Scotus replies to this objection by quoting Priscian to the effect that the present tense is said of a present that is divisible, just like time itself. Accordingly, "there are many partial presents [existing] at the same time, just as there are many pasts."

[n. 19] This objection adds to the previous reply by noting that the sophism mentioned in n. 17 need not be true if it is said of many partial presents (except that in this version, the phrase, 'in this instant [*in hoc instanti*]' is replaced 'in this "now" [*in hoc nunc*]').

Determination of Question 5
Argument That the Verb Is Not Merely a Copula

[n. 20] As noted above, the critical edition states incorrectly that n. 20 is the first opinion on the determination of the question. Scotus's actual opinion is given at nn. 29–32. In fact, nn. 20–25 also give Scotus's opinion: he is arguing here against the view that the verb 'to be' is merely a copula; rather, it is part of the predicate as the aspect under which predication occurs, that is, the aspect of being actual.

Scotus says, somewhat obscurely, that being is 'the actuality of being.' The meaning becomes clearer in n. 22 below, where he says that the verb 'to be' is not added to the predicate as if it were a content (*res*), that is, in the way that 'rational' is added to 'animal,' but rather as the potentiality inherent in the predicate 'animal' is joined to the actuality expressed by 'to be.' In other words, the predicate involves potentiality whose actuality is signified by its juxtaposition with 'is.' Thus, when we say 'Socrates is white,' Socrates being under the predicate 'white' is signified as being under the actuality of white. In this sense, being is part of what is predicated, because 'white' of itself does not signify the actuality of the subject.

The edition mentions Thomas Aquinas and William of Sherwood as among those holding the view that the copula is part of the extreme, and that 'to be' signifies the actuality of being.[53] It is not clear how their views are connected with the view expressed here. Thomas simply distinguishes between the use of 'is' as a

---

53. However, a reviewer for this book noted that what is said in the edition here about the copula in Aquinas deviates from the view of Gyula Klima, "Aquinas' Theory of the Copula and the Analogy of Being," *Logical Analysis and the History of Philosophy* 5 (2002): 159–76, and Giorgio Pini, "Scotus on Assertion and the Copula: A Comparison with Aquinas," in *Medieval Theories on Assertive and Non-Assertive Language. Acts of the 14th European Symposium on Medieval Logic and Semantics, Rome, June 11–15, 2002*, eds. Alfonso Maierù and Luisa Valenti (Rome: L. S. Olschki, 2004), 314–16. Pini also comments on Scotus's view of the copula in his commentaries on *Perihermenias* (ibid., 320–22).

second word in a proposition expressing Socrates's real existence, as in 'Socrates is/exists,' and its use as a third word or element. The passage in William of Sherwood is brief and confused and does not compare in scope with the longer treatment in his *Syncategoremata*, where he distinguishes, like Thomas, between these two uses of the verb.[54] Neither Thomas nor William explicitly mentions the view that the copula is 'part of the extreme,' nor do they say that it is or that it signifies the actuality of being.[55]

Antonius Andreas, who does not distinguish any differing opinions on the matter, makes this section part of his determination, consisting of Scotus's nn. 6–9, 20, and 23.[56]

Reply to the Main Arguments of Question 5 according to This Opinion

[n. 21] The footnotes to the edition incorrectly state that nn. 21–25 are replies to arguments nn. 1–5. As noted above, they are replies to the arguments of nn. 6–9.

The reply to n. 6 is found at n. 21. Scotus distinguishes two components of the predicate, viz., what is predicated, and the aspect (*ratio*) under which it is predicated. Thus, the copula can be part of the predicate in two senses. In the first sense, the copula is part of the predicate exactly in the way that 'white' is a part of 'white man.' In the second sense, it is part of the predicate as the aspect under which predication occurs, that is, the aspect of being actual. In the latter sense the copula does not form a composite with the predicate as 'man' and 'white' do, for the actuality of something does not form a composite of that of which it is the actuality. Therefore, the initial assumption of the argument in n. 6, viz., that the content of the copula is part of the predicate, is false, for it is not part of the predicate in the sense required by the argument.

[n. 22] Here Scotus replies to n. 7 (not to n. 4). The objection was that it would be nugatory or pointless for being or actuality to be predicated by the verb 'is' in 'a man is an animal,' for 'animal' just means 'existing animal' and so being would be predicated twice. Scotus replies that it is not nugatory because 'animal' on its own is taken as a possible animal; what is conveyed by the verb 'to be' is the actu-

---

54. William of Sherwood, *Syncategoremata* (ed. O'Donnell, 70–71). William also mentions a third use that does not seem relevant here.
55. See also Thomas Aquinas, *Quodlibet* IX, q. 2, a. 2, co.; *Quodlibet* XII, q. 1, ad 1.
56. Antonius Andreas, *Periherm.*, 67vb.

ality of being an animal. Accordingly, the verb 'to be' is not added to the predicate as if it were part of its content (*res*), that is, in the way that 'rational' is added to 'animal,' but rather it should be understood as the joining of the potentiality inherent in the predicate being with the actuality expressed by 'to be.'

[n. 23] Here Scotus replies to the argument of n. 8 (not n. 3), which was that, as stated by Boethius, the copula is a third element not as part of the proposition, but as "the demonstration of a quality in a proposition," and so it is only a copula. Scotus replies by granting what Boethius says, though he contends that it is still in some sense part of the proposition because of the composition it conveys (*importat*). And he concedes that it demonstrates the quality of the proposition because of the kind of composition it conveys. The "essential understanding" of a verb is what it makes known in the mind of the hearer, for example, running in the case of 'Socrates is running'; the 'is' conveys the actuality of the predicate inhering in the subject, that is, running inhering in Socrates.

[n. 24] Finally, Scotus replies to the argument of n. 9 (not n. 5). There, it was argued that when the copula is a third element, it does not predicate its own content, but the content of another term (or "as" it is in the other term), and so it "adjoins" the predicate. Scotus replies that when it adjoins another term, it predicates the being of what it adjoins. For example, in 'Homer is a poet,' the being-a-poet of Homer is predicated.[57] Thus "being a third" element of the proposition means being the aspect under which the predicate is predicated. It is part of the predicate in this sense only, although not (he adds) part of it in the sense that the concept 'predicable' belongs to it.

[n. 25] Here the argument of n. 24 is continued: the copula is not part of the predicate in the sense that it is part of what is predicated, nor is it part of the *intentio* or concept or mental state corresponding to the predicate, but rather it is "the thing as informed by such an intention," meaning the actual inherence of the predicate in the subject. Thus, the composition of subject and predicate is rather like the composite of matter (which is potentiality) and form (which is actuality) in that the predicate is made out of the subject, rather as (our example) the sphere is made out of bronze. The verb 'is' signifies that the subject as potentiality is combined under the aspect of form and actuality represented by the predicate.

---

57. Scotus's remark that in saying 'Homer is a poet,' we predicate being-a-poet of Homer, not the being of Homer of Homer, corresponds to n. 31 below, where he says that the same sentence signifies that a poet in his actuality is the same as Homer.

Exposition of Another Opinion

[n. 26] We learn of another opinion at nn. 26–28. This is stated in n. 26, which has it that the copula enters into the composition of the entire predicate as a verbal mode of signifying, which is to say that it 'inclines' the content of the verb to being predicated of another. Thus, the copula 'is' in 'Socrates is running' inclines the content of the verb, running, to being predicated of the subject, Socrates, and establishes the dependency of the former on the latter.

The edition states that the source of the opinion is not known, but one possibility is the treatise on syncategorematic words attributed to Henry of Ghent, which remarks at one point: "since the composition only has being through the inclination of one extreme to the other, the composition [understood] without the extremes is nothing."[58]

Against the Other Opinion

[n. 27] Scotus argues against this view, questioning whether it is really a verbal mode of signifying that is being assumed here. For the composition in which the copula signifies something to be the case or not to be the case, and which involves truth or falsity, is not a 'verbal mode of signifying' because it is the same in an affirmative or negative proposition, just as the nominative case of a noun is the same whether the proposition is affirmative or negative. Therefore, the reply is irrelevant.

[n. 28] He objects further that it is false that composition, the content of the verb, and the predicate make the predicate into a whole. This is not true because the mode—presumably the mode of signifying—of a proposition is neither the extreme, nor any part of it.

Further Determination of Question 5
The Composition of Copula and Predicate Is Not a 'Verbal Mode of Signifying'

[n. 29] According to the edition, Scotus's opinion alone is given in nn. 29–35. As we have argued above, however, nn. 20–25 also express Scotus's view, but with

---

58. Henrici de Gandavo, *Syncategoremata*, in *Opera Omnia* XXXVII, ed. Gordon A. Wilson (Leuven: Leuven University Press, 2010), 2:356: "Unde cum compositio non habet esse nisi per inclinationem unius extremi ad alterum, compositio sine extremis nihil est."

a different objective. The objective in nn. 29–35 is to argue that the composition of copula and predicate is not a verbal mode of signifying, and so the copula does not form part of the predicate in the way that 'white' and 'man' do. He says first that when 'to be' is predicated third, it is neither part of the subject nor the predicate. Rather, it signifies that the predicate and subject are the same in actuality.

[n. 30] Scotus here explains that every concept is understood through the mode of actuality, adding that in some sense a potentiality can be in actuality because the proper nature of a potentiality is to be distinguished from non-potentiality, just as a privation exists in actuality. The mode of actuality, signifying the actual inherence of the predicate in the subject, is what is relevant to the truth of a proposition, not the fact that the predicate is 'inclined' to be in a subject, as in n. 27 above.

[n. 31] Scotus repeats what he said in n. 21 above, viz., that the verb 'to be' signifies actual being such that the actuality of something does not form a composite with that of which it is the actuality; likewise, the aspect of the being of a thing and the thing itself do not form a composite.

[n. 32] Scotus repeats the arguments above (n. 27) that there are two types of composition, viz., the verbal mode of signifying, which does not make a proposition affirmative or negative, and the composition signified by the copula, which signifies that something is the case or not the case.

When Scotus says, "the composition generally in every personal verb ... is called by some 'personation [*personatio*],'" the edition states that it is not known to what or whom he is referring.[59]

Reply to the Main Arguments of Question 5

[n. 33] In nn. 33–34, Scotus replies to the main arguments in nn. 1–2 above, which he takes to support the view that the composition of copula and predicate is a verbal mode of signifying.

In reply to first argument (n. 1), he says that if the composition of copula and predicate were like the composition of 'white' and 'man' that makes 'white man,' then the consequence would hold. The consequence in question is that "the verb 'is' predicates the same as a second and as a third element; therefore, the specified content of the verb is predicated by means of another [term]." He says that the

---

59. But see Duns Scotus, *Opus Oxoniense* III, d. 2, q. 1, n. 13 (*Opera Omnia* XIV, 122b–123a).

consequence would be valid because the verb 'is' would be part of the predicate just as 'man' is part of 'white man.' This of course depends on the assumption that the term 'man' means the same in 'white man' as it does on its own. But this is not so, because when 'is' is predicated on its own it is predicated absolutely, but when it is adjoined to a predicate it is predicated secondarily, and the predicate is predicated primarily. Presumably, Scotus means that this is unlike the case of 'man,' which is predicated absolutely and primarily even when conjoined with 'white.'

[n. 34] In reply to the second argument (n. 2)—that in 'a man is [that is, exists],' the content of 'is' is united by a verbal mode of signifying—Scotus concedes that when the verb 'is' is predicated on its own, the composition of subject and verb is a verbal mode of signifying, but (according to what was argued in n. 29 above) this mode of composition does not signify the true or the false and so is relevant only to the grammarian, and not the logician.

[n. 35] According to the edition, this remark relates to n. 26 above, but it is not clear why. Why does Scotus not resolve the remaining three arguments (nn. 3–5)? Nor is it clear what is meant by the "final position [*ultimae positionis*]."

Determination of Question 6

[n. 36] Scotus's determination of q. 6 is given in nn. 36–38: the copula acts for the discrete present rather than the common or confused present. Two considerations in support of this follow at nn. 37–38.

[n. 37] The first consideration is that a verb signifies the present as present and 'under the mode of present being.' This is somewhat similar to the way Scotus resolved the question of whether a name signifies a thing or an idea by claiming that it signifies a thing as conceived or understood, that is, it signifies something suspiciously like an idea, but which is a thing in name (at the very least).

Therefore, what is signified by 'now' is in one sense similar to what is signified by a common term like 'man.' It is similar (he says) in that 'man' signifies an actual man rather than a man in potentiality, but it is dissimilar in that 'man' can be understood as applying to a number of different men at once, whereas 'now' cannot apply to many different times at once. The present tense always signifies under the mode of present being, and (by implication) there can only be one such mode.

For a parallel treatment, see our anonymous Parisian commentator, who argues that by the 'distinct present' of a verb we should understand the exclusion only of the aspect (*ratio*) of past and present, so that it is imposed to signify a distinct present that is common to any distinct present under the aspect by which it is present, which includes the past and the future. Likewise, the word 'man' is imposed to signify a single form which is common to present, past, and future things, but not under the aspect by which they are past or future.[60]

[n. 38] The second consideration is that a verb in the present tense co-signifies for the discrete present, and so acts as a copula under (that is, under the aspect of) the discrete present. Thus, it cannot serve as copula for the actual or designated 'now,' for when this 'now' has passed (as the man mentioned in n. 12 above has passed through the door), it cannot be signified by a present-tense verb because it is in the immediate past, and hence past, and therefore not 'now' any more.

Scotus again emphasizes that a "common present" cannot be signified in the way that a common name signifies many things that fall under the name, noting also that if that were the case, 'you will be white' could verify 'you are white.' Accordingly, it serves as a copula for any present time, when it was (or will be) actually present.

Reply to the Main Arguments of Question 6

[n. 39] Scotus first considers the first main argument (n. 10), which was that if 'running' supposited only for the present moment—the edition notes that the exclusive 'only [tantum]' should be read after 'supposited'—the conditional statement 'I run, if I run' would be false.

Scotus replies that in a conditional, the present is not predicated absolutely or of anything present absolutely, but the present of one statement (the antecedent) is posited under the relation of one to another (the consequent), signifying that when one is in the present, so is the other. In the case of the conditional, the present is 'confused,' but otherwise we are talking about a verb acting as a copula absolutely.

[n. 40] Next, Scotus replies to the second main argument (n. 11): if the copula represented the 'now' of the present moment, 'Socrates always exists [est]' would be self-contradictory.

There is no contradiction, says Scotus, for in this case the predicate is joined to the subject under the aspect of the present, rather than under the aspect of the

---

60. "*Album fuit disputaturum,*" q. 6 (NL 16135, 14va [75]): "Utrum verbum praesentis temporis copulet rem suam pro praesenti distincto vel confuse."

past or future. Thus, in the proposition 'Socrates always exists,' the verb 'exists' acts for any time as distinguished from the past and future.

[n. 41] The edition says that n. 41 replies to n. 14 above, but it seems more likely that it is in reply to nn. 13–14, which are not the main arguments, but a discussion of the 'narrow gate' argument of n. 12. Scotus's remark, "and for that reason, it restricts the content of the verb by its form," clearly echoes "no determination under which a determinable is understood restricts the determinable beyond the form of the determination" of n. 13. Likewise, "for the present that will be or was, is not present" echoes Simon of Faversham's treatment of the question, when he says, "a present-tense verb signifies the present time by, as it were, excluding what is past and future" (see commentary on n. 13 above).

Even so, Scotus denies that in this sense there is a 'common' present. The word 'now' does not signify different presents in the way that the name 'man' signifies many men under its proper aspect. Thus, the content of a present-tense verb, under its proper aspect, is not understood indifferently. And thus (clearly replying to the point made in n. 14) 'a man runs' is not true because some man will run tomorrow.

[n. 42] Here Scotus considers the argument of n. 15, that if the verb were a copula for any present indifferently, any present-tense proposition would be necessary without qualification.

He replies that this would be true if it were a copula for this present necessarily, for then 'the Antichrist exists' and 'the Antichrist exists at *a* [*Antichristus est in a*]' would be impossible, as the argument claims. However, it is not a copula for the present necessarily, but for any 'now' when present, and the proposition 'the Antichrist exists' uttered today is no different from one uttered tomorrow. Hence, it is not an impossible proposition, although it cannot be verified now. It only follows that it is impossible now, not that it is impossible for all time.[61]

[n. 43] According to the edition, n. 43 is a reply to nn. 17–19 above, but it is more likely to be a reply to the objection given in n. 18 to the argument made in n. 17 that the verb is a copula for the present that exists at this moment. The objection is that this shows there are many presents at the same time, citing the

---

61. There is a similar argument in "*Album fuit disputaturum*" (NL 16135, 14va–vb [75–76]): "if the predicate is joined to the subject for any *differentia* of time, then in 'a man is an animal,' there would be a distribution for present, past, and future times, and so 'therefore, Caesar is an animal' and 'therefore, the Antichrist is an animal would follow [i.e., necessarily follow]."

saying of Priscian that "the present is that of which part is past, part is future." The reply here is that the whole time that is distinct from the past and the future is called 'the present,' whose quantity is taken with respect to action, as when we say a house 'is' built in a week, which is why Priscian says this. Thus, although the present has many parts, none has the aspect of the present that could be called 'many presents at the same time.'

[Questions 7–9. Future Propositions and Truth]

Summary

Questions 7–9 concern whether a future proposition is determinately true or false (q. 7); whether '*a* will be [the case]' is determinately true (q. 8); and whether it is possible for neither of a contradictory pair of propositions to be true (q. 9).

Discussion

The doctrine proposed here has been taken as evidence by some that Scotus was not the author of these *Questions*. This is because it seems to contradict Scotus's mature doctrine, which Calvin Normore has called 'the contingency of the present.' It is set out in Book I, d. 39 of the *Lectura* (the first of his two Oxford commentaries on the *Sentences* of Peter Lombard), where Scotus claims that although God knows the future, it is nevertheless contingent, and while the past is necessary, there is no necessity in the present. Even if it is now the case that p, it might not now be the case that p. It is thought that Scotus was the first person in the Middle Ages to allow for alternative possibilities at a given time.[62]

This view contrasts sharply with tradition, where it was taken for granted that while the future is contingent, the past and present are necessary. For example, in a treatise ascribed to William of Sherwood (c. 1190–1249),[63] it is argued that if it

---

62. Despite this, Calvin Normore and others have argued that Henry of Ghent adopts a similar position in his *Quodlibeta* and that there are related suggestions in Peter John Olivi's *Sentences* Commentary (Normore, "Scotus' Moral Theory," 157–58n5). Moreover, Henrik Lagerlund has argued that Richard Campsall also rejects the necessity of the present in his *Quaestiones* on Aristotle's *Prior Analytics*, written before 1308; see Henrik Lagerlund, *Modal Syllogistics in the Middle Ages* (Leiden: Brill, 2000), 58–90.

63. William of Sherwood[?], *Obligationes* (Paris, NL 16617, f. 56v), cited in Calvin Normore, "Duns Scotus' Modal Theory," in *The Cambridge Companion to Duns Scotus*, ed. Thomas Williams (Cambridge: Cambridge University Press, 2002), 158n6.

is false that you are in Rome now, at time t1, it is necessarily false that you are in Rome at t1. The reason is that if you are actually not in Rome now, the proposition 'you are in Rome now' cannot be made true except by a motion or sudden change, either of which would have to take place in time. But then your being in Rome could only be realized at some time later than t1, after the present instant. Since it is impossible for the proposition to be made true at t1, it is necessarily false at t1.

Scotus appears to accept the traditional doctrine in the present work, arguing that a future proposition can be understood in two ways: either as signifying that it is true now in reality that something will be the case, or that it signifies now that you will be white in the future (see n. 17 of q. 7 below). The first sense is stronger than the second, for to signify it to be true now that you will be white at t1 signifies more than merely that you will be white at t1, for it commits us to the present existence of a state of affairs that is (in contemporary terminology) a 'truth-maker' for the future event. The second sense commits us to no such present state of affairs, only to a future one.

Scotus argues that the first, stronger reading is determinately false because 'this will be the case [*hoc erit*],' being determinately true now, is inconsistent with 'this will possibly not be the case [*hoc potest non fore*],' and for the same reason, the present-tense propositions, 'you are white now [*tu es albus nunc*]' and 'you are now able not to be white [*tu potes nunc non esse albus*],' are inconsistent (see n. 27 of q. 8 below). Scotus's analogy with present-tense propositions is not in keeping with his mature doctrine of the contingency of the present, which asserts the compatibility of such propositions.[64]

This seems to have been a hot topic in late thirteenth-century Oxford. John of Seccheville (d. before 1292), an Oxford master, discusses the question of whether future contingent propositions are determinately true.[65] The different question of whether they are necessarily true must have been actively discussed in the 1270s, as the eighth proposition condemned by Robert Kilwardby (c. 1215–79) was that every (true) proposition about the future is necessary.[66] Kilwardby had already

---

64. As Normore notes ("Scotus' Modal Theory," 130), there is no hint of the later doctrine in this early work, although he takes a weaker stand against the authenticity of Scotus's *Octo Quaestiones* than he did in an earlier paper.

65. John de Seccheville, *In Physicam Aristotelis Quaestiones* (Gonville and Caius 509/386, f. 124ra–206vb; cited in Lewry, "Oxford Condemnations," 249–50).

66. See Lewry, "Oxford Condemnations," 248; and Lewry, "Grammar, Logic and Rhetoric 1220–

rejected the proposition in his own discussion of *De interpretatione* I.9,[67] arguing that it is only in the disjunction of contradictory statements about the future ("there will be a sea-battle tomorrow or there will not be") that there is necessity: "as Aristotle understands it, there is a kind of necessity in a contradictory pair of statements, but not taken dividedly," that is, necessarily p or not-p, but not necessarily p or necessarily not-p.[68] Kilwardby's position is similar to that of William of Montoriel, who says that it is necessary that there will (or will not) be a Welsh war this year, taken disjunctively, but this is not determinately necessary, since either can happen indifferently.[69]

There are similarities between Scotus here and Radulphus Brito's treatment of the question, "whether all future events happen by necessity."[70] Scotus mentions in n. 30 below the argument that a proposition about the future is determinately true because "the future is future; therefore, the future is [*futurum est futurum, igitur futurum est*]" is a valid consequence. This is the first main argument of Brito's question. The similarity of structure between the commentaries of Brito and Scotus on *De interpretatione* has already been noted. However, Brito has other arguments about God's infallible knowledge of the future that Scotus does not mention here.[71]

1320," in *The History of the University of Oxford, Vol. 1: The Early Oxford Schools*, eds. J. I. Catto and Ralph Evans (Oxford: Clarendon Press, 1984), 401–34.

67. See Jean Isaac, *Le Peri Hermeneias en Occident de Boèce à saint Thomas* (Paris: J. Vrin, 1953), 121–25 and 176. See also R. Hisette, *Enquête sur les 219 articles condamnés à Paris le 7 mars 1277* (Louvain-Paris: Peeters, 1977), 160–77.

68. Robert Kilwardby, *Scriptum super librum Peryhermeneias* (Madrid, Bibl. Univ. 73, 44r–66v; cited in Lewry, "Oxford Condemnations," 273): "At tamen intellige, sicut intelligit Aristoteles <19a29>, quod in ipsa contradictione quae est de futuro est veritas determinata et quaedam necessitas, non tamen dividentem dicere."

69. William of Montoriel, in his *Summa* on the *Perihermenias* (Digby 2, 92r; cited in Lewry, "Oxford Condemnations," 249): "It is necessary under disjunction that there is going to be a war in Wales, or not be a war, and it is not determinately necessary that it is going to be, or not to be this year, because one or the other could contingently be the case. For if they are obedient to the kind, there is no war, otherwise there will be one. Hence there is truth or falsity in future contingents, namely indeterminately [Necesse <est> enim futurum esse bellum Walense in hoc anno vel non esse futurum sub disiunctione, et non est necesse determinate esse futurum hoc anno vel determinate non esse, quia indifferenter alterum potest contingere. Si enim oboedierint regi, non est bellum: sin autem, erit. Quare sic erit veritas et falsitas in contingentibus de futuro, scilicet indeterminate]." There are also discussions contemporary with Scotus by John Styckborn, who was probably writing in the early 1290s. William Dallying, who seems to have been a Cambridge master writing around the same period, discusses the same sophism (Gonville and Caius 512, 10va–12vb; cited in Lewry, "Oxford Condemnations," 249).

70. Radulphus Brito, *Quaestiones super arte veteri* (ed. Vercellensis & Vercellensis; Venice: 1499).

71. Also related to this question (and to earlier questions about whether a term is restricted and

[Question 7. Is a Proposition about the Future Determinately True or False?]

Summary

Three arguments (nn. 1–3) for the view that a proposition about the future is determinately false are followed by one argument (n. 4) on behalf of Aristotle's view that "where there are real alternatives [*in his quae sunt ad utrumlibet*, literally 'in those things that exist either way'], a sentence is no more true than false." After a short interlude for qq. 8–9, we have the determination of q. 7 that a singular proposition about a future contingent is neither true nor false without qualification nor determinately true nor false (nn. 14–20). Finally, nn. 21–24 reply to the initial arguments.

Commentary

[n. 1] The first argument invokes Aristotle's remark (in *De interpretatione* I.9.19a33) that, to the extent that a proposition is true, so things stand in reality. But a future-tense proposition signifies being otherwise than in reality. So (according to the argument) any such proposition is determinately false.

[n. 2] The second argument invokes Boethius, who says in a comment on Aristotle's second argument (in *De interpretatione* I.9.18b9–16) that a future-tense proposition such as 'tomorrow there will be a sea-battle' is uttered as if it were necessary. Thus, it is false "in the mode of prediction," meaning that someone predicting a sea-battle will happen contingently would not be saying what is true. Instead of 'prediction,' the edition has 'predication [*praedicatio*],' which is an alternative reading in the apparatus of Meiser's edition of Boethius. On this reading,

---

whether a proposition is true for this instant), is Robert Kilwardby, *Scriptum super librum Peryhermeneias*, lib. I, lect. 9 (Madrid, Bibl. Univ. 73, 54va; cited in Lewry, "Oxford Condemnations," 275): "We say that the content of the proposition, 'Caesar was,' truly is, and the 'is' is the pastness of Caesar, as established by the words of Augustine in *Confessions* <possibly XI.18.23, though he does not say there exactly what Augustine says, nor does there seem to be anywhere that Augustine says that 'was' = 'is past'> for this is to resolve every verb of the past and future into the present, such as when I say 'Caesar was,' Caesar is past and this belongs to Caesar in the past or is the memory of him [Dicimus quod res huius propositionis, Caesar fuit, vere est, et hoc 'est' praeteritio Caesaris est; secundum praehabitum verbum Augustini in libro de Confessionibus, est enim resolvere omne verbum de praeterito et futuro in praesens, ut cum dico, Caesar fuit, Caesar est praeteritus, et haec est praeteritio Caesaris sive memoria est]."

the argument would be that a sea-battle could not be said to happen contingently if it is uttered as if it were necessary.

[n. 3] The third argument is similar to the first. Every proposition "signifies itself to be true." But what the future-tense 'you will run at time a [*tu curres in a*]' signifies is that 'you are going to run at time a' is true—that is, the truth of a future-tense proposition amounts to the truth of a proposition that combines the present tense of the verb 'is' with a future participle. But the present-tense proposition signifies a truth that exists now, and no such truth exists.

[n. 4] The argument on the opposing side appeals to Aristotle (*De interpretatione* I.9.19a37–39). Propositions which are 'bilateral,' or which present real alternatives (*ad utrumlibet*), concern states of affairs whose existence or non-existence is equally possible, and so their associated propositions are no more true than false.[72]

[Question 8. Is 'A will be' Now Determinately True?]

Summary

This question asks whether, assuming a will happen later, 'a will be' is now determinately true. There are two affirmative arguments (nn. 5–6) plus a counter-argument and reply (nn. 7–8), and one argument (n. 9) against. Scotus's determination of the question is at n. 25, followed by his replies (nn. 26–27) to the two main arguments.

Discussion

This question may have been aimed at the aforementioned English commentator, Geoffrey of Aspall, who discusses future contingents in connection with Book II of his commentary on the *Physics*. Geoffrey argues that 'to happen determinately' has two senses. First, it can mean that an event is naturally determined to happen, and not otherwise; in this sense, a proposition about a future

---

72. Mark Thakkar, "Gregory of Rimini and the Logic of the Future," D.Phil. Thesis (University of Oxford, 2010), says that the 'bilateral' is one of a set of cases discussed by Aristotle in *Prior Analytics* I.13.32b4-18, which include the contingent *ut in pluribus* (occurring more often than not) and *ut in paucioribus* (less often than not). Thus, the bilateral is equally likely to occur as not.

contingent cannot be determinately true. But it can also be understood according to the truth or falsity of what is asserted coming about; in this second sense, a future-tense proposition can be determinately asserted, while the future event is still contingent or accidental.[73]

Commentary

Arguments for

[n. 5] The first argument is that the truth or falsity of a proposition is not determined by what is the case now, but by what is the case for the time signified by the proposition. Thus, in 'you will be white at time *a*' nothing is signified to be the case in reality now, but rather something is signified to be the case at time *a*. Thus a future-tense proposition signifies now that something will be the case, but if it truly will be the case in the future, the proposition must be determinately true now.

[n. 6] The second argument curiously invokes the synchronic conception of modality, which allows for alternative possibilities at a given time. Scotus rejects this idea at n. 27 below, although he later came to accept it. Here, it is argued that the truth of a future-tense proposition is consistent with the falsity of the corresponding counterfactual. For example, to say that you will be white tomorrow is consistent with saying that you could (in the future) not be white. But if the fact and counterfactual are consistent tomorrow, why could they not be consistent today?

[n. 7] Scotus considers an objection: if '*a* will be' is determinately true now, it is not consistent with the reality, *a*, being able not to be tomorrow.

[n. 8] The reply to the objection is that 'this will necessarily be' does not follow from 'this will be' because the modality applies to the future proposition, that is, *posset res non fore cras* means 'tomorrow possibly not-p' and not 'possibly tomorrow not-p,' though this is difficult to express in English. Thus, 'this will possibly not be' is consistent with 'this will be.'[74]

---

73. Geoffrey of Aspall, *In librum Physicam Aristotelis* (Gonville and Caius 509/386, f. 147a; cited in Lewry, "Oxford Condemnations," 249–50).

74. In his commentary on the *Perihermenias*, John Styckborn mentions a similar argument, that 'this will necessarily be' *does* follow from 'this will be' (with which Scotus agrees below). See Styckborn, *Questiones super librum Peryarmenias* (Caius 344/540, 212va; cited in Lewry, "Oxford Condemnations," 274).

Argument against

[n. 9] On the opposing side, Scotus cites the same passage from Aristotle concerning the bilateral (*ad utrumlibet*), that is, a type of proposition that is no more true than false because it concerns what is equally likely to occur as not.

[Question 9. Is It Possible That Neither Part of a Contradiction Is True?]

Summary

Picking up on the argument in n. 9 about bilateral propositions, q. 9 asks whether it is possible that neither part of a contradiction is true. The affirmative argument is given in n. 11, followed by opposing arguments in nn. 11–12. Aristotle's negative answer to the question is noted in n. 13.

Scotus's determination of q. 9 begins at n. 28, followed his reply to the main argument at n. 29 and further counterexamples and replies (nn. 30–35).

Commentary

[n. 10] The first argument is based on a *reductio* of the conclusion of n. 5 above: if a future-tense proposition signifies now that something will be the case, and if it truly will be the case in the future, that proposition must be determinately true now. Therefore, each member of a pair of contradictories about the future signifies itself to be determinately true. But since neither is determinately true, both must be false.

The *dictum* of a proposition is what the proposition says, usually rendered by the 'accusative and infinitive' construction in medieval Latin. Thus, the *dictum* of 'you will not be white,' or what that proposition asserts, is literally 'you not going to be white [*te non fore album*].' English expresses the same idea with a 'that' clause: 'you will not be white' says that you are not going to be white.

[n. 11] In opposition to the argument in n. 10, there is the principle of excluded middle: "of any [subject] the affirmation or negation is truly predicated [*de quolibet dicitur affirmatio vel negatio vera*]," that is, either the affirmation or the denial of a predicate is true. Thus, 'you will be white at *a*' and 'you will not be white at *a*' cannot both be false.

[n. 12] Again, in opposition to n. 10, we have the principle of non-contradiction. If neither of the contradictories is true, and on the implicit assumption that not being true means 'determinately false,' a contradiction results. For if 'you will be white at a' is determinately false, 'you will not be white at a' is true. And if its contradictory, 'you will not be white at a', is determinately false, then 'you will be white at a' is true.[75] And so at time a, both 'you are not white' and 'you are white' will be true, and so two contradictories will be true.

[n. 13] Here the text says that Aristotle is "on the opposing side," invoking the principle of non-contradiction stated at *De interpretatione* I.9.18a29–30. Although this suggests that n. 13 begins the arguments on the opposing side of q. 9, they clearly begin at n. 11 above.

Replies to Questions 7–9
Determination of Question 7

[n. 14] Scotus replies to q. 7 that a singular future contingent proposition is neither true nor false without qualification, nor is it determinately true or false.

First, Scotus repeats the Aristotelian formula about the relation between truth and being (or rather, being-the-case), noting that we are not concerned with being-the-case, but rather, with going-to-be-the-case. That which is going to exist does not have present existence or being in itself but only in relation to a present cause. This can happen, he says, in three ways:[76] (i) an effect can be related to a cause such that the effect necessarily follows from it, where presumably Scotus has in mind a relation of natural necessity between something happening now and an event in the future, for example, applying fire to ice, which eventually causes the ice to melt; (ii) an effect can tend to be produced by the cause, although it can be prevented, for example, eating sugary foods tends to produce dental cavities, although it can be prevented if I brush regularly and drink fluoridated water; and (iii) an effect can be genuinely indifferent to the cause(s) which precede it, for example, my finding money in the pocket of an old coat (as opposed to my not finding it, or someone else finding it).

[n. 15] Second, Scotus says that a sentence asserting the being of a thing is true "in keeping with the way it [that is, the thing or reality it is asserting] is relat-

---

75. Omitting the 'not' of the Latin, as seems required in order to make sense of the argument.
76. Cf. Thomas Aquinas, *In Perihermenias* I. lect. 13, n. 11.

ed to being." Here he is anticipating his own reply (n. 21 below) to the first main argument (n. 1 above), where he says that if a sentence about the future signifies that it is now the case that some future event will happen, then it is false, because its 'mode of assertion' is not in keeping with the way it is related to being. A future-tense statement must signify that it will be the case that it happens, that is, the reality it asserts must correspond to the future existence of a state of affairs.

[n. 16] Third, Scotus points out that it is not the future proposition's mode of signifying that is at issue here, since the meaning of a proposition about the future is the same regardless of whether the things designated by it exist or not. Thus, 'you are white' and 'you will be white' both signify the same things; what differs is their mode of assertion.

[n. 17] Fourth, Scotus argues that a future-tense proposition may signify something 'in the future' in two senses: either (i) such that it is true now that something will happen; or (ii) such that it signifies now that something will happen. For to signify that it is now the case that a is going to happen, signifies more than to signify (now) that a will happen. This builds on the point made at n. 15 above about the way that a proposition must be related to being. A proposition which signifies a state of affairs to be the case now is related differently to being than one which signifies (albeit signifies now) a state of affairs to exist in the future.

[n. 18] Here Scotus emphasizes that the proposition 'you will be white at a' is determinately false if it signifies that a thing is related to being in such a way that you must be white at a because (in keeping with n. 15 above) "sentences are true as things [that are asserted] are related to being." But when a thing of this sort is asserted, it is not now related in its cause in such a way that it must have future being; otherwise, what is asserted will of necessity be the case now, and the proposition would be determinately true now.

[n. 19] However, if a proposition about the future only signifies a future state of affairs as if it were present, then it is indeterminately true or false.[77] For if what our future proposition asserts is the present disposition of the thing rather than the present existence 'in its causes' of some future state of affairs, then it is indeterminately true or false. For example, 'this flame will melt this ice cube' (assuming the flame is not yet applied to the ice cube?) is not determinately true,

---

77. But is an indeterminately true proposition true? Perhaps we should read 'indeterminately' (*indeterminate*) as '*not* determinately.'

because what is asserted is not the actual future melting of the ice cube, but its present disposition to melt if the flame is applied to it. The determinate existence of the truth-maker (the flame melting the ice cube) is the only thing that could make the proposition determinately true.

[n. 20] Finally, Scotus notes that his reply fits what Aristotle says of propositions about 'bilateral' events, viz., that their affirmations are no truer than their negations. But if someone does assert a future proposition determinately, saying that things are now such that some future state of affairs will exist, that proposition would be false.

Reply to the Main Arguments of Question 7

[n. 21] Here Scotus replies to the first main argument (n. 1 above). If a future-tense proposition is understood in the first of the two ways defined at n. 17 above, it is false, for it signifies that it is now the case that something will happen, thereby signifying a reality that is other than actual reality and so employing the wrong mode of assertion. But if it understood in the second way, the proposition is now neither true nor false, because it is now indeterminate which of the contradictory states of affairs will be the case at that future time.

[n. 22] Scotus briefly notes that the second main argument (n. 2 above) depends on a particular reading (that is, the wrong one) of a future-tense proposition.

[n. 23] His reply to the third main argument (n. 3) is that the proposition 'it is true that you will be white' has two senses, one of composition and one of division. In the sense of composition, the subject is the *dictum* 'that you will be white.' As noted in the remarks on n. 10 above, the *dictum* is literally 'what is said' by the proposition. It corresponds roughly to what we would now call the 'content' of the proposition, or what it expresses in the indicative mood or following a 'that' clause. Understood in this way, the predicate 'is true' is a present-tense predication of truth of a presently existing *dictum*, and, as Scotus puts it, 'you going-to-be-white is true' (or 'that you are going to be white is true') signifies that truth "inheres" in the *dictum* at the present time. In this sense it is false for the reasons given above.

In the sense of division, however, the proposition signifies only that it is true that you will be white, which is indeterminately true for the reasons already given.

[n. 24] Scotus considers another reply: even in the sense of composition, the proposition 'it is true that you will be white' or 'you going-to-be-white is true' does not signify how reality is disposed now, but is rather "a sort of true assertion about the thing conveyed by the *dictum* for the time for which the extremes of the dictum are denoted to be united." That is, the extremes of the *dictum*, 'you' and 'white,' will be united at some future time if the proposition is true, and to say it is true that they will be so united means that it will be true that they will be so united at that time, and so the proposition says nothing about the present.

This reply requires that the present tense of 'is true,' when properly understood, means the same as 'the future will be true,' although Scotus does not consider the oddness of this reading worthy of comment.

Determination of Question 8

[n. 25] Scotus next replies to q. 8 (nn. 5–9 above), which asked whether a future-tense proposition is determinately true. Since he indicated at n. 18 above that future propositions are not true in the sense of 'determinate' required here, viz., that there is something existing in reality now that determines the truth of the proposition, he briefly replies to the question in the negative.

[n. 26] Scotus replies to the first main argument (n. 5 above): a future-tense proposition does not assert a present disposition towards something that is going to be the case or a disposition towards not being the case. It simply asserts now that something will have determinate being at some future time, which is why it is neither determinately true nor determinately false now.

[n. 27] In his reply to the second main argument (n. 6 above), Scotus effectively denies the synchronic conception of modality that allows for alternative possibilities at a given time. If a future-tense proposition were determinately true now—that is, if there were some presently existing truth-maker for a future-tense proposition—then 'a will be the case' and 'it could possibly be that a is not the case' would be inconsistent. This is because (as Scotus sees it) the determinate truth of these future-tense propositions would have to involve the truth of some present-tense propositions. For example, let a be the presently existing truth-maker for 'b will be the case.' Thus if b will be the case, 'a exists' is now true. And if it were possible that b could not be the case in the future, it is possible that a does not now exist, even though a actually does exist.

But Scotus denies this because he does not allow for alternative possibilities at a given time, from which it follows that he does not allow for alternative possibilities at the present time. The future-tense modal proposition is inconsistent with the future-tense assertoric proposition for the same reason that the present-tense modal proposition, 'you are now able not to be white,' is inconsistent with the present-tense assertoric proposition 'you are now white.'

Determination of Question 9

[n. 28] Scotus replies to the ninth question (nn. 10–13 above), which asked whether neither of a pair of contradictory statements is true, that is, whether the principle of the excluded middle is false. He says that if future-tense propositions are determinate assertions, that is, if they assert the existence of some presently existing truth-maker, then neither the statement nor its contradictory is true in this way, since the one asserts the determinate future existence of *a*, the other the determinate future non-existence of *a*, and so both assertions are false. But if the assertions are indeterminate, as Scotus maintains they usually are, then one or the other is indeterminately true.

Replies to the Main Arguments of Question 9

[n. 29] To the first main argument (n. 10 above) Scotus basically repeats what he has said earlier: the argument depends on the assumption that a proposition must be determinately true now in order to signify now that something will be the case, but this is not necessarily so. A future-tense proposition can be indeterminately true now, meaning that it has no presently existing truth-maker, but also determinately true in the future, meaning that its truth-maker has yet to come into existence.

Some Counterexamples and Replies

[n. 30] Scotus considers some counterexamples or objections to his position. The first is that a future-tense proposition is determinately true because 'the future is future, therefore the future is [*est*]' is a valid consequence. The antecedent is determinately true, for the same reason that any proposition of the form '*a* is *a*' is determinately and necessarily true. See *Opus I*, qq. 5–8, n. 33 above, where Scotus mentions, with apparent approval, Boethius's maxim that 'no proposition is truer than one in which the same thing is predicated of itself.'

[n. 31] The second objection concedes that a future-tense proposition does not assert anything to be determinately the case now (but only in the future). However, a proposition of contingency—that is, one which itself asserts a contingency, such as 'it is contingently true that Socrates will be white'—is determinately true now. So why could not a proposition about the future assert the future occurrence of something determinately?

[n. 32] To the first of these objections, Scotus replies that the argument commits the fallacy of *quid in quale*.[78] The fallacy occurs when there is an apparent likeness between two expressions having diverse modes of signifying. In this case, something in the category of substance (*quid*) has been changed into something in the category of quality (*quale mutatur quid in quale*). Scotus provides the following syllogism as an example:

P1—Every future [event] will be [*erit*];
P2—'You will be a bishop' is futural;
C—'You will be a bishop' will be.

In the major premise, the term 'future event' distributes over events or states of affairs, which are substances. In the minor premise, however, 'future' is predicated as though it were a quality. Therefore, the argument is invalid.

There is a semantic relationship between the concepts of existence and the future (or something futural, like an event) in Latin that is not evident in English, as *futurum* is the future participle of the Latin verb *esse* (to be). Not so in English, where the adjective 'future' has lost its connection with the English verb 'to be,' or 'will be ⌊*erit*⌋,' even though it is derived directly from the Latin.

[n. 33] To the second objection, Scotus replies that propositions about contingency do assert something determinately true now, viz., they signify in the present that something will occur contingently in the future. Propositions about the future, however, do not assert anything about what exists in the present. Thus, 'it is contingently true that Socrates will be white' says something definite about Socrates at the present moment, but 'Socrates will be white' does not, because nothing that presently exists would make that proposition true (or false).

[n. 34] Scotus here considers an objection to his reply, which notes that when we say 'this will be,' it is the same as saying 'and this is future.' But the latter proposition is determinately true or false; therefore, so is the former. The objection uses the same strategy as n. 31 above of assimilating future-tense propositions to present-tense propositions about the future.

---

78. For discussion of this fallacy, see the remarks on *Opus I*, qq. 9–11, n. 28 above.

[n. 35] Scotus replies to the objection in n. 34 by saying that both propositions ('this will be' and 'this is future') are indeterminately true or false, at least if the latter is treated as the *analysans* of the former. For in that case, the present tense of the verb in 'this is future' does not fully capture the meaning of the proposition; rather, an "actuality measured under a future time is understood to be joined to a subject for the present time," and this actuality may be consignified by the predicate with a present-tense verb because the present serves as the "initial boundary" of the future. But this is enough to make the proposition indeterminately true or false. The same reasoning applies to the propositions 'a man will be' and 'a man is going to be,' that is, the future actuality signified by the predicate is joined to the subject in the present time as adjacent to it.

OPUS II ❧ QUESTIONS ON THE TWO BOOKS OF *PERIHERMENIAS:* ON BOOK II

[Question 1. Does an Indefinite Verb Remain Indefinite in a Sentence?]

Summary

After giving five arguments (nn. 1–5) for the proposition that an indefinite verb does remain indefinite, Scotus presents three arguments (nn. 6–8) on the opposing side. His determination in nn. 9–11 is against the proposition, followed by replies to the five affirmative arguments (nn. 12–16).

Discussion

The starting point of q. 1 is Aristotle's brief remark (in *De interpretatione* I.3.16b15) that expressions such as 'is not-healthy' and 'is not-ill' are not verbs, although they do signify time; rather, they are indefinite verbs.

The question here is whether the verb remains indefinite when it is part of a sentence, that is, should 'he is not healthy' be parsed as the affirmative 'he is non-healthy' or split into two parts, the verb and the negative particle, to form the negative 'he is not healthy,' that is, 'it is not the case that he is healthy.'[1] Scotus says that they are predicated equally of what exists and what does not exist.

---

[1]. Radulphus Brito discusses the same question in his commentary on the *Perihermenias*: "Consequenter quaeritur utrum verbum infinitum manens infinitum possit ingredi enunciationem." See Radulphus Brito, *Quaestiones super arte veteri* (ed. Vercellensis & Vercellensis; Venice: 1499).

Commentary

Arguments for

[n. 1] The first argument appeals to Aristotle (*De interpretatione* I.3.16b15–16), who says that an indefinite verb is predicated in the same way of what exists and what does not exist, and that it is only predicated of something in a sentence. Therefore, it remains indefinite in both cases.

[n. 2] The second argument goes again to Aristotle (*De interpretatione* I.3.16b10–11), who says that verbs are always signs of something said of some subject, and that this is only possible in a sentence.

[n. 3] The third argument is that an indefinite verb is an expression that has "modes of signifying" or principles by which it is ordered or construed together with other expression(s) in a sentence. Moreover, since it possesses these principles per se, that is, prior to its being so ordered, the mode determining its construal will remain when it is placed in a sentence. The edition mentions Scotus's contemporary Simon of Faversham (c. 1260–1306) here, who has a similar argument.

[n. 4] The fourth argument is that it is absurd for an expression to lose its definition or associated concept (*ratio*) simply because of where it occurs in a sentence, and that it should lose its signification to two expressions (that is, the negative particle and the verb). And it is likewise absurd that two expressions with different meanings should be produced—for example, 'not healthy,' where before there was one ('non-healthy')—given that words should not change their meaning depending on how sentences begin or end, or because of the order of words in the sentence.

[n. 5] The fifth argument appeals to a remark by Boethius in his *Second Commentary* on *De interpretatione*, viz., that if the verb did not remain indefinite, then a syllogism mentioned by Plato would be negative. This is a reference to *Theaetetus* 186d-e, where Plato argues:

P1—The senses do not reach the nature of substance;
P2—What does not reach [something] does not reach the notion of truth;[2]
C—Therefore, sense does not reach the notion of truth.

---

2. The edition here reads *nec ipsius veritas contingit notionem*, but clearly this should be *nec ipsius veritatis contingit notionem*, as confirmed by Meiser in his edition of Boethius, *De interpr.*, 251.

Boethius comments that Plato appears to have produced a syllogism entirely from negatives, something which cannot be done, since there is no valid, standard form of syllogism with two negative premises (the 'fallacy of exclusive premises').

Arguments against

[n. 6] The first argument on the opposing side appeals to the same work of Boethius, where he says that an indefinite verb does not retain its semantic force in the sentence, but is purely negative. Thus the sentence 'a man is not running' does not attribute anything to a man, but rather removes something from him.

[n. 7] The second argument is that if the verb remained indefinite, 'a man is not running' and 'a man is non-running' would be equivalent, from which 'a non-running thing is a man' follows. This is incorrect, for when no man exists, the antecedent 'a man is not running' could be true but the consequent false.

Scotus will say more about the inference from the negation of the finite predicate to the affirmation of the indefinite in *Opus II.II*, q. 2 below.[3]

[n. 8] The third argument is that according to Aristotle (*De interpretatione* II.10.19b11–12), there is no affirmation or negation apart from the verb. But if there were affirmation or negation by an indefinite verb, it would follow that when 'is' is predicated as a second element, different opposing propositions [*oppositiones*] could be generated in as many ways as when it is predicated as a third element.

The point here is obscure, but it might involve the idea that affirmation or negation by an indefinite verb would violate Aristotle's principle that each affirmation has one and only one negation, or proposition opposed to it.

Determination

[n. 9] Scotus replies to the question that in a sentence, an indefinite verb does not differ from a purely negative verb. Citing Boethius again, he says that verbs are indefinite when they are by themselves, but definite when joined with a noun. But nothing is affirmed of a man by 'a man is not running,' which is why such verbs are understood with negation applying to the entire proposition (that is, with sentential rather than predicate negation).

[n. 10] Elaborating on his reply, Scotus echoes both Thomas Aquinas and Simon of Faversham, claiming that a verb is composed of two parts: the content

---

3. See also *Opus II.I*, q. 4 above.

and the composition of subject and predicate that it signifies. But because an indefinite verb includes the negative particle ('not' or 'non-'), which has the effect of 'removing' the verb 'in itself' ('not running' cancels the activity signified by 'running'), adding an indefinite verb to a noun signifies the removal of what corresponds in reality to the content of the verb, from what is signified by the noun. An indefinite verb is thus "a verb understood with negation."

[n. 11] Continuing his reply, Scotus allows that if an infinitizing negation is related to the content of the verb, the indefinite verb would remain indefinite in a sentence, as in the case of 'he is blinded,' where the composition (of the person, and his being blinded) is affirmed and only the privation of something (sight) is understood.

Reply to the Main Arguments

[n. 12] To the first argument (n. 1) that an indefinite verb is predicated in the same way of what exists and what does not exist, Scotus replies that the content of the verb is equally suited to what exists and what does not exist. Thus, an indefinite verb does not signify any determinate concept, just as an indefinite name does not.[4] But it does not follow from this that an indefinite verb, *qua* indefinite, is said of anything.

[n. 13] To the second argument (n. 2) that a verb is always a sign of what is predicated of something else, which is only possible in a sentence, Scotus says that an indefinite verb is 'a sign of what must be predicated of something,' since it is taken per se. But when the verb is adjoined with something else (that is, with a noun), it denotes that something is to be removed from something. Negation does not relate to the content of the verb but to the composition of subject and predicate.

[n. 14] To the third argument (n. 3) that an indefinite verb has "modes of signifying" which it possesses per se, Scotus replies that these modes are not such as to cause the concept associated with the indefinite verb to remain when the verb is ordered with another expression in a sentence. For if it did, the verb would not signify that the being of something is removed from something, but that the negation of something is in something. Thus, 'a man is not running' signifies the removal of the being (or reality or actuality) of running from a man; it does not positively assert the activity of not-running of a man.

---

4. See his remarks about this in *Opus II.I*, q. 4 above.

[n. 15] To the fourth argument (n. 4) that it is absurd for an expression to lose its associated concept because of where it occurs in a sentence, and that it should lose its signification to the negative particle and the verb, Scotus replies (effectively repeating the point above) that indefinite verbs must generate two expressions in a sentence because the negative particle signifies the removal of something from something.

[n. 16] To the fifth argument (n. 5) that if the verb did not remain indefinite, then Plato's syllogism would be negative, Scotus offers an obscure reply which does not have anything to do with "the syllogism posited by Plato." Scotus talks about Socrates running or not running (a common example in the Boethius text and elsewhere), whereas Plato's syllogism concerns what the senses can or cannot reach. That aside, he does understand Boethius's position, which is that a negative syllogism can be avoided only if the indefinite verb remains indefinite, for then "the composition is affirmative" in the premises, presumably because they affirmatively predicate 'not-reaching' or 'not-running' of their subjects. But Scotus disagrees with Boethius, as he holds that "the negative particle added to the verb 'is [*est*]' immediately makes the proposition negative," which would make Plato's syllogism fallacious.

It is possible that Scotus held Plato's syllogism to be fallacious, quite apart from his position on indefinite verbs, but it is more likely that something has been lost in the transmission of this part of the text.

[Questions 2–5. On Inferential Relations between Propositions Containing Definite versus Indefinite Terms]

Summary

In qq. 2–5, Scotus explores some of the inferential relations between propositions containing definite versus indefinite terms, specifically whether 'this is non-just' follows from 'this is not just' (q. 2, nn. 1–10); whether it holds for 'respective terms' (q. 3, nn. 11–12); whether it holds for past-tense verbs (q. 4, nn. 13–14); and finally, whether it holds assuming the constancy of the subject (q. 5, nn. 15–16).

In the determination (nn. 17–21), Scotus argues that whenever two predicates *a* and non-*a* are 'said of anything' (*dicuntur de quolibet*), that is, whenever the principle of the excluded middle[5] applies to the definite and indefinite predicate such that either *a* or non-*a* applies to any subject, then if it is not the case that something is *a*, it is the case that it is non-*a*, and the consequence is valid; otherwise, the consequence is not valid. But composite predicates are not 'said of anything.' For example, neither 'white log' nor 'non-white log' is true of anything that is not a log. This means that if a predicate like 'man' means 'existing man,' it is composite, and so is not 'true of anything.' For example, 'existing man' and 'existing non-man' are not true of non-existent men. If, on the other hand, existence is not part of a predicate, then 'man' and 'non-man' are 'said of anything,' and the consequence is valid.

Following his analysis of the question, Scotus gives two sets of replies to the arguments. To the affirmative arguments he replies (nn. 22–24) that the consequence will not be valid when the indefinite and definite predicate are not 'true of anything.' To the negative arguments he replies (nn. 25–29) that the consequence will be valid when the verb 'is' is predicated as a third element in such a way that being is not predicated *simpliciter*, and so the indefinite and definite predicates are 'true of anything.'

Discussion

This series of questions is closely connected with *Opus II.I*, q. 4, on whether an indefinite term posits the existence of a subject. If it does, then the inference from 'it is not the case that *a* is *b*'—which is negative and which does not (in the view of medieval philosophers) posit the existence of a subject—to '*a* is non-*b*' is not valid.

Andrea Tabarroni has given a brief history of the question in which he argues that in the first half of the thirteenth century, the consequence from the negative definite to the affirmative indefinite proposition was "unanimously rejected by commentators on the *Perihermenias*" unless the condition of the *constantia subiecti* or constancy of the subject was supplied.[6] For example, Nicholas of Paris says that 'non-man' means 'a thing other than a man [*aliud ab homine*],' that 'Caesar is something that is not a man' follows from 'Caesar is a non-man.'[7] Robert Bacon,

---

5. Here, we use the principle of the excluded middle, which usually applies to sentential negation, to predicate negation.

6. Tabarroni, "Tenth Thesis in Logic," 349.

7. See A. Tabarroni, "Lo Pseudo Egidio (Gugliemo Arnaldi) e un' inedita continuazione del com-

probably writing in the first half of the thirteenth century, says that a negative name (that is, a name in a negative proposition such as 'it is not the case that *a* is *b*') posits nothing, since it can be predicated equally of a being and a non-being. But an indefinite name posits being, for 'nonjust' means a being that does not possess justness.⁸ Likewise, John le Page contends that an indefinite name is only predicated of existing things.⁹ Tabarroni notes that all three authors subscribe to the theory of restriction, according to which a verb in the present tense restricts the subject to presently existing things.

Closer to Scotus in the 1290s, Roger Bacon rejects the inference, saying that there are two reasons it is not valid. In one way, because the subject of a negative proposition is "common to a being and a non-being," but this reasoning is fallacious, he says; in another way, because the subject term can signify a being and a non-being equivocally.¹⁰

---

mento di Tommaso al Peryermenias," *Medioevo* 14 (1988): 371–427, where he discusses Nicholas's question, "Whether an indefinite name could equally be predicated of a being and a non-being." According to Nicholas, "'Non-man' causes privation in one way and 'dead man' in another because 'dead' causes privation of form either in the substance or the matter in which the form is naturally suited to be made, and in which it is not possible for the opposing forms to be; but 'non-man' causes privation of the form of the term and leaves behind a general substance in which it is possible for opposing forms to inhere, a substance which is signified by the name 'something' or 'being' [Aliter privat 'non homo' et aliter 'mortuus homo,' quia 'mortuum' privat formam vel a substantia vel a materia in qua est nata forma fieri et in qua non est possibile formas oppositas esse; sed 'non homo' privat formam termini et relinquit substantiam generalem in qua est possibile inesse formas oppositas, quae significatur per hoc nomen 'aliquid' vel 'ens']" (Nicholas of Paris, "Utrum haec sit vera: 'Caesar est non-homo,'" in *Syncategoremata*, "*de adverbio 'non'*"; 2:44–45).

8. Robert Bacon: "Negative, indefinite, and privative names differ in this way: a negative name posits nothing, but can be equally said of being and non-being. An indefinite name posits being, for a 'non-just' is a being not having justice [Differunt nomen negatum et nomen infinitum et nomen privatum hoc modo: nomen negatum nihil ponat, sed equaliter potest dici de ente et non ente. Nomen infinitum ponit ens, nam 'non iustum' est ens non habens iustititiam]" (Robert Bacon, "*De verbo 'est*,'" in *Syncategoremata*, 1:144).

9. John le Page: "An indefinite name is predicated only of what exists [Nomen infinitum non dicitur nisi de eo quod est]" (*Syncategoremata*, 2:224–25).

10. "Therefore, it should be said that there is a twofold reason why it can be understood that an indefinite or privative [proposition] does not follow from a negative predicate: either because the term which is the subject to such a negative predicate is understood as common to being and non-being univocally, and this is false; or that the subject term can signify a being and a non-being equivocally, or that the subject can be a being or non-being [Dicendum est igitur quod duplici de causa potest intelligi quod non sequitur a negativo praedicato ad infinitum vel privativum: aut quia terminus subiectus tali praedicato negativo sumitur commune enti et non enti univoce, et hoc est falsum, vel quod subiectus {terminus} potest aequivoce significare ens et non ens, sive quod subiectum potest esse ens vel non ens]" (*Compendium studii theologii*, c. 4, n. 106 [98]); see also Roger Bacon, *Summulae*, cap. "*De appellatione*" (285).

Tabarroni claims that the theory of restriction lost support in Paris before the middle of the thirteenth century, and thus support for the consequence is evident in the work of Peter of Auvergne and Hervaeus Brito: "from this time on this feature is shared by most Parisian commentaries on the *Perihermenias*."[11]

Peter of Auvergne's position is close to the one argued by Scotus in qq. 2–5. Peter distinguishes between the use of 'is' as a second element, where being *simpliciter* is predicated, and its use as a third element, where being something (such as being-a-man) is predicated. In the latter case, an affirmative proposition with an indefinite predicate can be true of a non-existent thing, since actual being is not predicated.[12]

P. Osmund Lewry mentions a number of Oxford masters who discussed this question in the middle half of the thirteenth century: John of Seccheville, writing about 1265; William of Bonkes, teaching at Oxford in the 1290s; John Styckborn, also teaching in the 1290s; and William of Montoriel, whose dates are unknown, but who was probably a contemporary of the others.[13] William of Montoriel denies the consequence, saying that the affirmative indefinite proposition implies the negative definite, but not conversely.[14] Bonkes says that it is customary to say that a negative proposition posits nothing, but an affirmative does, and so the consequence depends on the constancy of the subject. Styckborn discusses this in his second question on Book II of his commentary on the *Perihermenias*,[15]

11. See Tabarroni, "Tenth Thesis in Logic," 350. Tabarroni names *Ps.*-Peter of Auvergne, Peter of St. Amour, Simon of Faversham, Durandus of Auvergne, the supposed Henry of Brussels, Gerard of Nogent, Siger of Courtrai and Radulphus Brito. For Brito, see "*Utrum ad negativam de praedicato finito sequatur affirmativa de praedicato infinito*," in *Quaestiones super arte veteri* (ed. Vercellensis & Vercellensis; Venice: 1499). See also Tabarroni, "Lo Pseudo Egidio," and Siger of Courtrai, "*Quomodo terminus infinitus differat a termino finito negate*," Ars Priorium, in *Les Oeuvres de Siger de Courtrai: Etude critique et textes inédits*, ed. G. Wallerand (Louvain: Institut supérieur de philosophie de l'Université, 1913).

12. Peter of Auvergne, *Questiones super librum Peryermenias*, q. 42: "Utrum ad negativam de praedicato finito sequatur affirmativa de praedicato infinito" (ms. Madrid, Biblioteca Nacional 1565, f. 10rava; cited in Tabarroni, "Tenth Thesis in Logic," 353).

13. See Lewry, "Oxford Condemnations," 251–53. For Seccheville, Bonkes, and Styckborn, see *In Perihermenias Aristotelis* I-II (ms. Caius 344/540, ff. 173–218). For Montoriel, see his *Summa in Perihermenias* (ms. Oxford Bodl., Digby 2, ff. 85r–94v; cited in Lewry, "Oxford Condemnations").

14. William of Montoriel, *Summa in Perihermenias*: "Est quinta oppositio de enuntiationibus (93v) in quibus sunt praedicata privativa, verbi gratia, 'homo est iniustus,' 'homo non est iniustus.' Praedic[a?]ta autem affirmativa quae est de praedicato infinito est antecedens ad negativum de praedicato infinito et non e converso" (ms. Oxford Bodl., Digby 2, 93r–v; quoted in Lewry, "Oxford Condemnations," 277n150).

15. John Styckborn, *Periherm.* (ms. Cambridge, Gonville and Caius College, 344–540), quoted in Lewry, "Oxford Condemnations," 252.

likewise appealing to the principle that a negative proposition posits nothing, as well as to the view that a negative has two truth conditions (*causae verititatis*), whereas the affirmative has only one. Whether these masters influenced Scotus is not known, but the question was clearly topical in late thirteenth-century Oxford.

As discussed in the commentary to *Opus II.I*, q. 4 above, Robert Kilwardby does not think that the being implied by the predicate 'being a non-man' is real being alone, but also the being of reason or understanding, such as when we say that a chimera is a non-man. His opposition to the consequence, expressed in his 1277 Oxford ban of the proposition that it follows without the 'constancy of the subject' (the tenth thesis), is therefore surprising. As we have argued, the position that the indefinite name does not posit anything is difficult to reconcile with the position that the consequence does not hold without qualification. Tabarroni explains it by the influence of John of Seccheville, who, like many writers of the period, opposes the consequence on grounds of restriction.[16] Generally, those who opposed the consequence were committed to the classical theory of restriction, according to which an affirmative (but not a negative) present tense verb in a proposition restricts the range of the subject term to presently existing *supposita*. As we have seen, Scotus opposes this in qq. 5–11 of *Opus I*. The anonymous author of "*Omnis Phoenix est*" explains that the consequence does not follow because the affirmative indefinite, being affirmative, posits more than the negative definite, for the term in the negative can stand for a non-being; otherwise, it would always posit something just like the affirmative.[17] In the same way, the anonymous author of "*Album fuit disputaturum*" cites Aristotle, saying that the consequence does not follow without the constancy of the subject (*De interpretatione* II.10.19b23–32); therefore, it is clear that the term in the negative can supposit for a non-being, for otherwise it would be pointless to add the qualification about 'constancy.'[18]

Scotus does not mention the difficulties with this view. One is that a term supposits in the same way in an affirmative proposition and in the negative contradicting it,[19] but then the term *a* must supposit for exactly the same things in '*a* is non-*b*' and 'not: *a* is *b*.' If it supposits for non-entities in the negative proposition,

---

16. Tabarroni, "Tenth Thesis in Logic," 351.
17. "*Omnis Phoenix est*," NL 16135, ff.62vb–67vb (211–17).
18. "*Album fuit disputaturum*," NL 16135, ff.12vb–14vb (49–81).
19. Ibid., NL 16135, f. 13vb (65). Cf. Aristotle, *De interpr.* I.7.17b38–39 (AL II.1–2).

it must supposit for non-entities in the affirmative, and a non-existent *a* is non-*b*, just as it is not the case that it is *b*. One reply is that *b* is not denied in the negative proposition because of *a*'s non-existence, but because it is not present. But in the affirmative, '*a* is non-*b*,' the presence of *a* is asserted, and so it is false.[20]

[Question 2. Does 'This is not just; therefore, this is non-just' Follow?]

Arguments against

[n. 1] Scotus begins with five arguments (nn. 1–7) that the consequence is not valid. The first simply appeals to Aristotle, who says (*De interpretatione* II.10.19b22–25) that of the four propositions: (i) man is just, (ii) man is not just, (iii) man is non-just, and (iv) man is not non-just, (iv) follows from (i), and (ii) follows from (iii). But the converse does not follow, that is, the inference from the negative to the affirmative indefinite does not hold.

[n. 2] To n. 1 it is objected that Aristotle is speaking in this passage of composite terms. Note that precisely the same argument is made in *Opus II.I*, q. 4, n. 4, viz., that the consequence is invalid or not a "good consequence [*bona consequentia*]" in the case of complex predicates. Thus, '*a* is not a white log; therefore, *a* is a non-white log' is not valid, since the consequent asserts the existence of a log whereas the antecedent does not.

[n. 3] The reply to n. 2 is the same as in q. 4 of Book I: Aristotle remarks that the verb 'is' is conjoined with 'just' or 'non-just' (*De interpretatione* II.10.19b26–30), so it is not true that he is speaking only of composite predicates here.

[n. 4] The second argument appeals to Aristotle again, who says (in *Prior Analytics* I.46.51b5–6) that 'being not-this' and 'not being this' are different, and also (51b7–10) that an affirmative proposition with an indefinite predicate does not follow from a negative proposition with a definite predicate. This is because 'to be non-white' and 'not to be white' are related in the same way as 'to be able to not-walk' and 'not to be able to walk,' that is, the indefinite term is in some way

---

20. "*Album fuit disputaturum*," NL 16135, f. 14ra (67). See also "*Omnis Phoenix est*," NL 16135, f. 67ra (215–16) and the sophism attributed to Robert Kilwardby, "*Omnis Phoenix est*" (ms. Erfurt Q 328, f. 20va–vb; cited in Braakhuis, "Kilwardby versus Bacon," 131). For further discussion, see Lewry, "Oxford Condemnations."

privative. Clearly, being deprived of something does not follow from merely not having something.[21]

[n. 5] The third argument is that the predicate 'non-white' is in effect composite, as it means 'a being which is not white,' and so it predicates both existence and whiteness. Thus, the negation 'is not an existing white thing' denies both existence and whiteness, whereas the affirmation 'is an existing non-white thing' denies only the whiteness. Accordingly, the affirmation does not follow from the negation because something is posited in the affirmation (existence) that is not posited in the second.

[n. 6] The fourth argument is that a negative proposition "has two causes of truth [*habere duas causas veritatis*]." As Scotus's contemporary on Peter of Auvergne notes, 'a is not b' may be true either because there is no such thing as *a* (and so it is not the case that *a* is *b*, which Peter calls the "sense of non-being [*sensus non entis*]") or because *a* exists but is not *b*. But an affirmative proposition, '*a* is non-*b*,' has only one cause of truth, viz., when *a* exists but is not *b*, which is the "sense of being [*sensus entis*]."[22] As noted in the edition, the English scholastic

---

21. Siger of Courtrai also mentions the analogy with the modal proposition in discussing the difference between definite and indefinite terms: see "*Quomodo terminus infinitus differat a termino finito negato*," in *Ars Priorium*.

22. Peter of Auvergne, *Questiones super librum Peryermenias*, q. 42: "Utrum ad negativam de praedicato finito sequatur affirmativa de praedicato infinito" (ms. Madrid, Biblioteca Nacional 1565, f.10ra–va; quoted in Tabarroni, "Tenth Thesis in Logic," 354): "To that, certain persons have said that the affirmation of the indefinite predicate does not follow from the negation of the finite predicate. Certain persons have said that the negation of the finite predicate has two causes of truth, because the negation precedes the verb 'is' and the finite predicate. And so they proposed a sense of being, and a sense of not being. For example, 'a man is not just' can have two senses, either because the man does not exist, and so is not just, and this is the 'sense of not being,' or because the man exists, but is not just, and this is the 'sense of being.' They have said also that the affirmative of the indefinite predicate only has the 'sense of being,' for they have said that the indefinite term posits some being of itself. And furthermore, they have said that the verb 'is' posits a sort of being, if not preceded by negation. And therefore they have proposed that the affirmation of the indefinite predicate does not follow from the negation of the finite predicate, because [otherwise] there would be a passage from two causes of truth to one, and thus there would be the 'figure of speech' fallacy [*Ad istud dixerunt quidam quod ad negativam de praedicato finito non sequitur affirmativa de praedicato infinito. Quidam dixerunt negativam de praedicato finito habere duas causas veritatis, eo quod negatio praecedat hoc verbum 'est' et praedicatum finitum. Et ideo posuerunt habere sensum entis et sensum non entis. Ut verbi gratia, 'homo non est iustus' potest habere suos sensus; aut quia homo non est, et sic non est iustus, et sic est sensus non entis; aut quia homo est, et tamen non est iustus, et sic est sensus entis. Dixerunt etiam affirmativam de praedicato infinito habere solum unum sensum entis; dixerunt enim terminum infinitum ponere aliquod ens de se. Et ulterius dixerunt hoc verbum 'est' ponere aliquod ens, si negatio ipsum non praecederet. Et ideo posuerunt negativam de praedicato finito non sequi affirmativam de*

John Styckborn also refers to the two causes of truth, as does his contemporary William of Bonkes. The view is clearly an old one, as both Bonkes and Styckborn call it "customary."[23] Radulphus Brito also mentions "causes of truth" in his question on the *Perihermenias*.[24]

[n. 7] Finally, the fifth argument once again appeals to Aristotle (*Prior Analytics* I.46.51b25–28). The very same argument is mentioned in *Opus II.I*, q. 4, n. 1.

Arguments for

[n. 8] There are three arguments on the opposing side (nn. 8–10). The first is that either 'just' or 'not just' is "said of anything [*dicuntur de quolibet*]." This is a reference to the principle of the excluded middle: "of any [subject], the affirmation or negation is truly predicated [*de quolibet dicitur affirmatio vel negatio vera*]."[25] Thus, if it is not true to say that *a* is *b*, it must be true to say that it is not the case that *a* is *b*.

---

praedicato infinito, quoniam ibi esset processus a duabus causis veritatis ad unam, et sic esset fallacia figurae dictionis]."

23. John Styckborn: "To the question it must be said that the consequence is not good. The reason is that a negative [proposition] posits nothing, but the affirmative—from the fact it is affirmative—posits something. Therefore it was customarily said that any negative proposition has two causes [of truth], but the affirmative only one. Therefore the consequence is not valid as regards the negative form in these three terms: 'is not a man; therefore, is a non-man' [Ad quaestionem dicendum est quod consequentia non est bona. Cuius ratio est, negativa nihil ponit; affirmativa eo ipso quod est affirmativa aliquid ponit. Ideo solebat dici quod negativa propositio quaelibet habet duas causas; affirmativa tantum unam. Ideo consequentia non valet de forma negativa in istis terminis tribus, 'non est homo, igitur est non homo]" (ms. Gonville and Caius 344/540, f. 213rb). William of Bonkes: "It is customarily said that a negative [proposition], in virtue of its form, posits nothing, and that the affirmative posits something. And therefore I say that in "a man is non-just," in virtue of its form—since here the verb is affirmative in the understanding and in the utterance, and since affirmation in the understanding is a sort of positing, and not only negation; therefore, from the form of the affirmative by every affirmation, etc., something is posited that is not [posited] by the negative ['affirmative' in ms.], and because it posits something in virtue of its form, it does not follow from [a proposition which?] posits nothing. Since the consequent ought to involve less, and not more, I say that an affirmative does not follow from every negative [Solebat dici quod negativa de sua forma nihil [ponit, et quod affirmativa] de sua forma aliquid ponit, etc. [189rb] ... Et ideo dico quod in ista, 'homo est non iustus,' de sua forma, cum hic sit verbum affirmativum apud intellectum et vocem, et affirmatio apud intellectum est aliqualiter positio, et non solum negatio, ideo ex forma affirmativae per omnem affirmationem, etc., aliquid ponitur quod non per negativam [affirmativam ms.]; et quia aliquid ponit ex sua forma, non sequitur ad nihil ponit. Cum consequens debet esse in minus, et non in plus, dico quod non ad omnem negativam sequitur affirmativam]" (ms. Gonville and Caius 344/540, f. 189ra–rb; quoted in Lewry, "Oxford Condemnations," 278).

24. Radulphus Brito, "*Utrum ad negativam de praedicato finito sequatur affirmativa de praedicato infinito*," *Quaestiones in Perihermenias*, in *Quaestiones super arte veteri* (ed. Vercellensis & Vercellensis; Venice: 1499). Cf. also Aristotle, *Prior Analytics*, I.13.32b25–30; Roger Bacon, *Summulae* II, n. 587.

25. Applied to predicate negation, as noted above.

[n. 9] The second argument appeals to Aristotle (*De interpretatione* II.10, 20a24–26): if we ask a question such as 'is Socrates wise?', and the reply is 'no,' then it seems to follow that Socrates is non-wise.

[n. 10] The third argument also invokes Aristotle (*De interpretatione* II.10.20a21–23), who says that the affirmative statement 'some man is just' follows from the negative 'not every man is non just,' and likewise the affirmative 'every man is non-just' follows from the negative 'no man is just.' By parity of reasoning, then, the affirmative 'this is non-just' follows from the negative 'it is not the case that this is just.'[26]

[Question 3. Does a Consequence of This Sort Hold for Relational Terms?]

Argument against

[n. 11] By 'relational terms,' Scotus appears to mean terms that refer to the same substance, but in different respects or under different descriptions. If this is right, then there is potential for fallacious reasoning whenever relational terms are employed of a subject, since the same term can be double and not double at the same time (the 'double' example is from Aristotle, *Categories* 7.6a36). Thus, a geranium can be twice as big as it was a month ago without being twice as big as itself. Presumably, the point is that the 'not *a* to non-*a*' consequence at issue in qq. 2–5 is blocked because the respects or descriptions under which *a* is related to its subject are different in each case.

[n. 12] Aristotle says (in *Categories* 6.6a26) that it is "most distinctive" of quantity to be called both equal and unequal, for example, body, number, and time—unlike quality, for which he reserves the term 'similar.' If so, then no inference from being unequal to being non-equal will follow, since only non-quantitative terms can be non-equal. Likewise, if a quantity is said to be unequal (rather than equal), then what follows is that it is not the case that it is equal, not that it is 'not equal,' where the negation is applied to the term rather than the proposition.

---

26. Tabarroni, "Tenth Thesis in Logic," 345, discusses *De interpr.* I.10.20a21–23 in the context of the same inference. The passage seems to assert an equivalence between 'not: S is P' and 'S is not P,' and for universal and particular propositions. Boethius also accepts the equivalence, at least for definite propositions (see Boethius, *De interpr.*, 327). However, the matter is complicated because of textual ambiguity in Aristotle.

[Question 4. [Does a Consequence of This Sort] Hold with Past-Tense Verbs: First, Would 'It was non-white; therefore, it was not white' Follow?]

Summary

Questions 4–5 (nn. 13–16) both involve propositions with verbs in the past tense. Where q. 4 (nn. 13–14) discusses whether the consequence from the indefinite affirmative to the definite negative is valid, q. 5 (nn. 15–16) asks whether the consequence from the definite negative to the indefinite affirmative is valid. There is one argument on each side.

Argument for

[n. 13] The first argument is that the consequence 'it was non-white; therefore, it was not white' is valid because "time does not change the disposition" of a proposition when the proposition is taken *simpliciter*, because then it is true independent of time whenever the subject exists. The assumption seems to be that whatever time is supposed in the antecedent proposition is the same as the time supposed in the consequent, that is, we must read the consequence as 'it was non-white at t_1; therefore, it was not white at t_1.' This is clearly valid: nothing can be non-*a* and *a* at any given time.

Argument against

[n. 14] The assumption that the same time is implied in antecedent and consequent is dropped in the opposing argument, however. 'You have been non-white' is true if there was any past time that you were non-white (t_1). But 'you have not been white' (that is, it is not the case that you were white) is false if at any time apart from t_1 (such as t_2) you were white. Since falsehood cannot follow from truth, the consequence is invalid.

[Question 5. Conversely, [Does a Consequence of This Sort] Follow, Assuming the Constant Existence of the Subject?]

Argument for

[n. 15] This question asks whether the converse holds, that is, 'it was not white; therefore, it was non-white,' given the constancy or constant existence of the subject. In n. 15 it is argued that it does: if you existed in the past, and if it is not the case that you were white (either at some particular time, or any time), then it follows that you were non-white, since at any point in your past existence you were either white or non-white, and so if it was not the case that you were white, you were then non-white. This assumes that 'constancy of existence' is constancy of past existence.

Arguments against

[n. 16] On the opposing side, it is argued that the consequence does not hold. For the past-tense proposition 'you were white' is equivalent to the present-tense proposition 'you are previously white.' But as a predicate, 'previously white' is analogous to 'white log,' and since 'you are not a white log, and you are; therefore, you are a non-white log' is not valid, then neither is 'you are not previously white, and you are; therefore, you are previously non-white.' For not being a white log can be false if you are not a log, and not being previously white can be false if you did not previously exist. Thus, the assumption here (unlike the argument in n. 15) is that 'constancy of existence' is constancy of present existence.

Determination

[n. 17] Scotus begins his resolution of the question by saying that whenever two predicates *a* and non-*a* are "said of anything"—that is, whenever the principle of the excluded middle applies to the definite and indefinite predicate such that either *a* or non-*a* applies to any subject—then if it is not the case that something is *a*, it is the case that it is non-*a*, and the consequence is valid; otherwise, the consequence is not valid.

[n. 18] He then argues for the conclusion of n. 17 by means of a *reductio*:

(i) Assume that the consequence is not valid;
(ii) Assume that the principle of the excluded middle applies to definite and indefinite predicates;
(iii) If the consequence is not valid, then for some *a* (say 'good'), Socrates is not *a* and Socrates is not non-*a*;
(iv) If Socrates is not non-*a*, then by the principle of the excluded middle, Socrates is *a*;
(v) Therefore, Socrates is *a* (from iv) and Socrates is not *a* (from iii);
(vi) This (from v) violates the principle of non-contradiction; and
(vii) Thus (from i, ii, *reductio*), if the principle of the excluded middle applies to predicates, the consequence is valid.

[n. 19] Here Scotus proves that the converse holds, that is, if excluded middle does not apply to predicates, the consequence is not valid. For if excluded middle does not apply—he gives the example of 'being a white log' and 'being a non-white log,' neither of which are true of Socrates—then it is clear the consequence does not hold, since 'Socrates is not a white log' is true (and so the antecedent is true) and 'Socrates is a non-white log' is false (and so the consequent is false). But a falsehood does not follow from a truth, and so in this case the consequence is not valid; this applies generally for any composite predicate.

[n. 20] This leads Scotus to consider whether an apparently simple predicate such as 'is non-good' is really complex, involving the predication of both 'being' and 'non-good.' This would make the consequence '*a* is not good; therefore, *a* is non-good' invalid, assuming 'it is not the case that *a* is good' is true when *a* is non-existent, whereas '*a* is existent and non-good' is false.

[n. 21] Finally, Scotus returns to a thesis he established earlier (in *Opus I*, q. 3, n. 11, and qq. 5–8, n. 67): when 'is' is predicated as a third element, it is only a copula, and then only the predicate is predicated, not being or existence; thus, 'a man is good' predicates 'being good,' and not 'being' *simpliciter*. Accordingly, 'being non-good' does not require existence *simpliciter*, and the consequence is valid. But if, on the other hand, being is part of the predicate, then 'being non-good' implies the existence of something that is not good, and so 'being non-white' and 'being white' may both fail to be true of something. There is no excluded middle, and the consequence will not be valid.[27]

27. Peter of Auvergne argues for a similar position in q. 42 of his commentary on the *Perihermе-*

[Reply to the Main Arguments of Question 2]
Replies to the Positive Arguments

[n. 22] Scotus now replies to both the positive arguments (nn. 22–24) and the negative arguments (nn. 26–29) from q. 2 above.

To the positive argument (n. 8 above) where it was assumed that 'just' and 'non-just' are "predicated of anything," that is, that the principle of the excluded middle holds for predicates, he replies that it is obvious that the principle does not hold when existence is part of the understanding of the predicate. In other words, 'being a man' and 'being a non-man' may both fail to be true of *a* if *a* is a non-entity.

[n. 23] To the second positive argument (n. 9 above), Scotus replies that in a question, the existence of the subject is presupposed. Thus, if we reply 'no' to the question 'is Socrates wise?' we presuppose the existence of Socrates, which means that a negative reply implies the existence of an unwise Socrates.

[n. 24] To the third positive argument (n. 10 above), which claimed that according to Aristotle, 'not every man is non-just' implies 'some man is just,' Scotus replies that Aristotle assumes the existence of man in this inference.

Replies to the Negative Arguments

[n. 25] Scotus now considers the negative arguments. These will not hold when 'being' is predicated as a third element, for then 'is *a*' and 'is non-*a*' would be predicated of anything. In other words, the principle of the excluded middle applies to the predicate.

Note that we adopt here the variant addition *non* in the margin of ms. R, which would place the beginning of Scotus's reply to the negative arguments just above n. 25, as these are the arguments which assume that the consequence, 'this is not just; therefore, this is non-just,' does not hold.

[n. 26] To the first negative argument (n. 1 above), Scotus replies that Aristotle means the affirmatives are not implied by the negatives unless the positive and

---

nias, citing the commentator Ammonius (*Quaestiones super librum Perihermenias*): "when the verb 'is' is predicated as a second element, it predicates 'absolute being' of the subject. But when it is predicated third, it does not: when I say 'a man is not just' the verb 'is' posits nothing "of itself." Therefore, it is false to say that the negation of the indefinite predicate does not imply the affirmation of the indefinite predicate" (Tabarroni, "Tenth Thesis in Logic," 354).

negative predicates are "said of anything," that is, if the principle of the excluded middle holds.

[n. 27] To the objection (n. 3 above) that Aristotle does not think the consequence holds even for simple terms (where, according to Scotus, the excluded middle holds), it is replied that Aristotle does not mention the distinction between simple and complex terms, which occurs "incidentally" on his part. Rather, Aristotle is distinguishing between definite and indefinite predicates.

[n. 28] To the second negative argument (n. 4 above), which cited Aristotle's *Prior Analytics* to the effect that 'not being *a*' is different from 'being not-*a*,' Scotus replies that how a proposition asserts what it says (its "mode of assertion") determines its inferential relations with other propositions where the same terms occur. Thus, we can affirm that Socrates is non-running (or among the non-runners) or deny that Socrates is running, but only the latter proposition would directly contradict another.

[n. 29] To the third argument (n. 5 above, mistakenly cited in the edition as n. 6), which says that 'this is non-white' affirms the existence of 'this,' whereas 'this is not white' (that is, 'it is not the case that this is white'), does not affirm the existence of 'this,' Scotus replies that 'being non-human' posits no more than 'not being human' unless being or existence is affirmed *simpliciter*, that is, as a second element.[28]

---

28. As noted above, Peter of Auvergne takes a similar view in his commentary on the *Perihermenias*, citing Ammonius's claim that when 'is' is predicated as a third element, it does not predicate the "absolute" being of the subject, and so in 'a man is not just,' the verb 'is' does not posit anything of itself: "But against what is said further on—that the verb 'is' posits some being, unless negation precedes it—is the commentator Ammonius on that book saying that the verb 'is,' when predicated as a second element, means the unqualified being of its subject; but when it is predicated as a third element, or with some other [term] adjoined, then it does not predicate the unqualified being of its subject, but rather predicates the being of that which has the subject by means of the third element. For example, when I say, "a man is not just," here the verb 'is' posits nothing of itself [Sed quod dicitur ulterius quod hoc verbum 'est' ponit aliquod ens, nisi ipsum praecedat negatio, contra hoc est commentator Amonyus super librum istum dicens quod hoc verbum 'est,' quando praedicatur secundo adiacens, dicit esse absolutum ipsius subiecti; quando autem praedicatur tertio adiacens, aut cum aliquo alio adiuncto, tunc non praedicat esse absolutum ipsius subiecti, sed praedicat esse ipsius quod habet illud subiectum per illud tertium adiacens. Ut verbi gratia, cum dico sic 'homo est non iustus,' hic hoc verbum 'est' de se nihil ponit']" (ms. Madrid, Biblioteca Nacional 1565, f. 10ra-va, quoted in Tabarroni, "Tenth Thesis in Logic," 354; the reference is to Ammonius, *De interpr.*, ad 10, 20a20–23; ad 12, 21a25–33). Kilwardby uses similar language, saying that that the word 'a being' (*ens*) does not posit being *simpliciter*: "I say that 'non-man' is expounded as 'a being which is not a man,' but when I say 'being' in this exposition, it does not mean some being according to nature, but it is commonly understood for being according to nature and for being according to reason or understanding, and so

[Questions 6–9. The Unity and Complexity of Propositions]

Summary

Questions 6–9 of *Opus II.II* focus on what makes a proposition simple as opposed to complex or composite. Each question asks whether a given proposition is "one [*una*]": 'A white man runs' (q. 6); 'A white thing is musical' (q. 7); 'A white man is a musical man' (q. 8); and 'A man, who is white, runs' (q. 9). These are traditional examples, all drawn from *De interpretatione* II.11.

After presenting the arguments on both sides of each question (nn. 1–36), Scotus gives his determination of each, replying to the main arguments on the opposing side (nn. 37–46 for q. 6; nn. 47–49 for q. 7; nn. 50–51 for q. 8; and nn. 52–59 for q. 9).

Discussion

In qq. 6–9, Scotus addresses himself to *De interpretatione* I.11, where Aristotle distinguishes between propositions that are simple, that is, where one thing is predicated of another such that they "make up some one thing" (20b14–19), and those that are complex, that is, where the predication (sometimes despite its grammatical simplicity) does not make up one thing. The key here is Aristotle's understanding of the relation between truths and truth-makers: if what makes the proposition true is something one, then the proposition is also one. He argues that there is no unity where one thing is predicated of several subjects unless the several things are one thing in reality, so that being an animal, bipedal, and domesticated combine to form a unity, whereas 'white,' 'man,' and 'walking' do not. Thus, predicates that are accidental to the same subject or to one another do not combine to form a unity: for example, 'a white man is musical' is not a single proposition, for being white and being musical do not, according to Aristotle, form a unity. It is only incidental that someone musical is white.

---

in saying 'being,' something is not posited absolutely [Dico quod sic exponitur 'non homo': "ens quod non est homo," sed hoc quod dico "ens" in hac expositione non dicit 'aliquid' ens secundum naturam, sed accipitur communiter ad ens secundum naturam et ad ens secundum rationem vel intellectum, et sic ponendo 'ens' non ponit aliquid simpliciter"]" (cited in Ebbesen, "Termini accidentales concreti," 127–28).

Note that in modern predicate logic, all general propositions are composite; only singular propositions are single. Thus 'a man is white,' which according to Aristotle is a single proposition, is on the modern view a composite of 'some x is a man' and 'x is white.' Likewise, the Aristotelian unitary proposition 'every man is an animal' is composite: '(x)(x is a man ⊃ x is an animal),' that is, 'for all x, if x is a man, then x is an animal.'

[Question 6. Is 'A white man runs' One?]

Summary

There are three main arguments followed by a discussion on behalf of the view that the proposition is not one (nn. 1–11) and three arguments (nn. 12–14) on the opposing side. The view of unnamed others is given later, at nn. 37–38. Scotus's reply is at n. 39, and his replies to the main arguments (and to some of the arguments in the discussion) are at nn. 40–46.

Commentary

Arguments against

[n. 1] The first argument appeals to Boethius, who says that if the elements making up the subject or predicate of a proposition do not form something one, then the proposition is not one. But 'man' and 'white' do not form something one. Since Boethius suggests in the next sentence (quoted at n. 2 below) that the combination of 'animate,' 'sensible,' and 'substance' do make something one, his point must be that something one is made only if the elements in question combine into one substantial form. 'Man' and 'white' cannot combine in this way, however, because 'white' is an accidental attribute of a man.

[n. 2] The second argument repeats the appeal to Boethius, this time mentioning the remark about animate sensible substance.

[n. 3] Here Scotus considers the view of those who say that where the sense of the term, or that "under which [*sub quo*]" the term is taken is one, the proposition is one, and that a white thing satisfies this criterion. Conversely, where the sense of the term is not one (for example, one species) the proposition will not be one. The claim is that a white thing is one in this way.

[n. 4] There follow three objections to this argument. The first (n. 4) is that in the proposition 'a white man runs' we attribute running to a man who is white *per accidens*, and so 'man' is not understood in relation to running under the aspect of white.

[n. 5] The second objection is that, by the same reasoning, 'a walking white man runs' would be one, because the subject, 'white man,' could be understood to be walking, which Scotus claims both Aristotle and Boethius deny (although where they deny it is not found in the sources). Presumably, they would deny it because nothing understood to be walking can also be said to be running.

[n. 6] The third objection is what Aristotle says (in *De interpretatione* I.11.21a17–33): predicates that are accidental to the same subject or to one another do not combine to form a unity.

[n. 7] Scotus now returns to his presentation of the arguments for the thesis that 'a white man runs is one' with the third main argument: if an affirmation of a proposition is one, then so is its negation. But there is not one negation of 'every white man runs,' for if there were, it would be 'a white man does not run,' which is inconsistent because both are false when no man is white.

Scotus suggests that there is an intermediary between 'man' and 'white,' just as there is between what needs completion (*exigens*) and what is needed for completion (*exactum*). He may be referring to the grammatical concept *exigens-exactum* explained in Pseudo-Jordan of Saxony's *Notulae super Priscianum Minorem*. The *exigens* is an expression requiring completion by another, in order to complete a phrase: because of its lack of power (*inpotentia*), it requires something else to create a complete (*perfectum*) understanding.[29] In the present case, there is an implied composition that some man is white, and so the proposition is not one. See n. 44 below, where Scotus says that the middle is 'being' or 'who is,' so that 'a white man runs' can be analyzed as 'a man, who is white, runs' or 'a man-being-white runs.'

[n. 8] The next three sections concern the argument of n. 7, beginning with two objections (nn. 8–9). The first (n. 8) is that in the universal affirmative 'every white man runs,' the predicate is universally affirmed of the subject 'white man'; therefore, the denial of the same predicate by means of the particular proposition 'some white man does not run' is its proper contradictory.

[n. 9] The second objection is that 'every rational animal runs' is one, and its

---

29. Cf. Joke Spruyt, "The Semantics of Complex Expressions in John Duns Scotus, Peter Abelard and John Buridan," in *Aristotle's* Peri Hermeneias *in the Latin Middle Ages: Essays on the Commentary Tradition*, eds. H. A. G. Braakhuis and C. H. Kneepkens (Groningen-Haren: Ingenium, 2003), 274–303.

contradictory is 'some rational animal does not run.' But if that is one, then by parity of reasoning, 'every white man runs' and 'some white man does not run' are contradictories. The 'notwithstanding' clause says that this is true independent of the logical relation between the elements that make up the subject of the proposition: 'rational' and 'animal' in the first case; 'man' and 'white' in the second.

[n. 10] In reply to the second objection (n. 9), the 'notwithstanding' clause is rejected: the cases are not the same because an accident does not relate to a substance in the way that a *differentia* relates to a genus.

[n. 11] In reply to this objection (n. 10) to the original objection (n. 9): just as 'man' and 'white' need completion by an intermediary, so do 'animal' and 'rational.' In other words, the cases really are the same, and we cannot say that one requires an intermediary but not the other.

Arguments for

[n. 12] The next three sections give arguments on the opposing side, viz., on behalf of the view that the proposition 'a white man runs' is one.

The first is that the proposition 'every white man runs' expresses one truth (*una veritas*). It is not the same as the composite proposition 'every man is white and every man runs,' as is shown by the fact that 'every man runs' follows from the composite but not from 'every white man runs.'

[n. 13] The second argument is that Aristotle (*De interpretatione* I.11.20b31–37) says that we can unite the predicates in the proposition 'Socrates is a man and white' into a single predicate (actually, he says that we can take them separately, or as one).

[n. 14] The third argument cites the authority of Ammonius, who says in chapter 11 of his *De interpretatione* commentary that some things are appropriately compounded into a unitary predicate, such as 'animal' and 'two-footed,' which are not predicated as divided, but together. (On Aristotle's view, they can be predicated either separately or together.)

[Question 7. Is 'A white thing is musical' One?]

Summary

Scotus offers two arguments against the proposition (nn. 15–16), followed by one argument for (n. 17).

Commentary

Arguments against

[n. 15] The first argument repeats the argument of Aristotle mentioned in n. 6 above, that is, predicates accidental to the same subject or to one another do not combine to form a unity.

[n. 16] The second argument is that 'a white thing is musical' is equivalent to 'there is a white musical thing'; but 'Socrates is a white musical thing' is composite, for there are really two propositions here, just as there are in 'Socrates is white, who is musical,' which is the same composition found in 'Socrates is a white musical thing.' Therefore, 'a white thing is musical' is also composite.

Argument for

[n. 17] The opposing argument notes that a proposition is said to be one in which "one is predicated of one." But this works for subjects and predicates alike, which makes unity transitive. Thus, 'Socrates is a musical thing' is one, as is 'Socrates is white'; therefore, 'a white thing is musical' must also be one.

[Question 8: Is 'A white man is a musical man' One?]

Summary

Scotus offers three arguments on behalf of the proposition (nn. 18–20), followed by one argument against (n. 21).

Commentary

Arguments for

[n. 18] The first argument appeals to the unity of extremes argument in n. 17 above: since the proposition 'a white man runs' is one, as was shown in nn. 12–14 above, and since the unity of the white man suffices for the unity of the extreme (and likewise with 'a musical man'), therefore in a proposition of the form, 'a white man is a musical man,' either extreme is one, and does not stand in need of completion by anything else.

[n. 19] The second argument is that 'man' and 'white' form one thing, just like actuality and potentiality.

[n. 20] The third argument is that by parity of reasoning, one thing is made from man and musical (though this looks to be merely an extension of the arguments in nn. 18–20).

Argument against

[n. 21] The opposing argument invokes the same argument of Aristotle given at n. 15 above: predicates that are accidental to the same subject or to one another do not combine to form a unity.

[Question 9. Is 'A man, who is white, runs' One?]

Summary

In the ninth and final question on the unity and complexity of propositions, Scotus offers five arguments that the proposition is one (nn. 22–26), followed by six arguments on the opposing side (nn. 27–36).

Commentary

Arguments for

[n. 22] The first argument is that the pronoun 'who' implicitly has the nature of an article because it restricts what precedes it. Thus, in the proposition 'a man runs,' the term 'man' ranges over all existing men. But in 'a man *who is white* runs,' the pronoun phrase implicitly restricts the subject to range over men who are white. Therefore, it is understood under the aspect of the relative clause, and so it is one proposition.

[n. 23] The second argument is that we can construct the following syllogism: every man who is white runs; this is a man who is white; therefore, this runs. The middle term is 'man who is white,' and since the middle term is by definition all of what (*totum illud*) is taken in both the major and minor premises, the whole expression ('man who is white') is the subject of distribution.

[n. 24] The third argument is that if the unity of 'a man, who is white' is sufficient for the unity of the middle, as was argued in n. 23 above, then it is sufficient for the extremes (that is, the major and minor terms) because valid syllogisms can only be constructed from propositions that are one.

[n. 25] The fourth argument is that the unity of a name and of its quality is the same. With propositions, this would mean their being affirmative or negative, so perhaps this is a reference to term-negation (and term-affirmation). But the example is adverbial: saying that something runs fast (*velociter*) does not make the resulting proposition several (*plures*).

[n. 26] The fifth argument is that when a proposition is several (or not-one), the extremes must also be several (or not-one). But if the word 'man' is not restricted by the word 'white' in 'every man who is white runs,' then it would imply 'every man runs.' In other words, we would have to read it as 'every man runs and every man is white,' but this is not the natural reading and therefore not the natural implication. Thus, the proposition is one.

Arguments against

[n. 27] The first argument against the proposition that 'a man, who is white, runs' is not one is that a 'relative of substance' refers in the same number as its antecedent. According to William of Ockham, a relative of substance is a grammatical concept, that is, a term like 'this' or 'that' or 'the same' which relates individual substances. A 'relative of accident' is derived from several accidents, like 'such' or 'so much' or 'so many.' Ockham mentions the rule that a relative of substance always supposits for what its antecedent supposits for, and is verified in respect of the same *supposita*, for example, 'Socrates runs and he argues.'[30]

30. William of Ockham, *Summa Logicae* I.76 (236): "But first, you should know that according to the way grammarians use the term, some relatives are called 'relatives of substance'; others are called 'relatives of accident.' A word like 'this,' 'that,' or 'the same' is called a relative of substance. Words imposed in some way or derived from multiple accidents are called relatives of accident, e.g., 'such,' 'so much,' 'so many,' and words of this sort. Some relatives of substance are relatives of identity; others are relatives of diversity. Of relatives of identity, some are reciprocal, others non-reciprocal. The non-reciprocal relatives are those like 'that,' 'the same,' and so on. And concerning them, the following rules are given: that they always supposit for that for which their antecedents supposit, such that if they are verified, they are verified of the same thing, as is clear in the case of 'Socrates runs and he disputes': to the fact that this copulative proposition is true, it is required that the second part be verified of the same thing of which the first part is verified, and likewise in the case of 'man is a species and that <species> is predicated of many' [Est autem primo sciendum quod 'relativum,' secundum quod grammatici utuntur relativo, quoddam vocatur relativum substantiae, quoddam vocatur relativum accidentis. Relativum substantiae vocatur sicut 'iste,' 'ille,' 'idem.' Relativa accidentis vocantur illa quae imponuntur aliquo modo vel derivantur a pluribus accidentibus, sicut 'talis,' 'tantus,' 'tot' et huiusmodi. Relativa substantiae quaedam sunt relativa identitatis, quaedam diversitatis. Relativorum identitatis quaedam sunt non reciproca, quaedam sunt reciproca. Non reciproca sunt sicut 'ille,' 'idem' et sic de aliis. Et de istis dantur regulae: quod semper supponunt pro illo pro quo supponunt sua antecedentia, ita quod pro eodem verificantur, si verificentur. Sicut patet hic 'Sortes currit et ille disputat': ad hoc quod ista copulativa sit vera requiritur quod secunda pars verificetur pro illo eodem pro quo prima pars verificatur. Similiter hic 'homo est species et ille praedicatur de pluribus']." See also Ockham, *Summa Logicae* II.4 (265): "For example, by 'every animal is healthy' it is literally de-

This is clearly what Scotus has in mind here: the expression 'who' in 'a man who is white runs' refers back to or supposits for whatever 'a man' stands for, and so it must refer 'in the same number'; thus, any expression referring back to the original subject, such as a pronoun, must have the same grammatical number as its antecedent.

The claim is that if the term 'man' is repeated in such a way that a man is first the subject of 'running,' and then the subject of 'being white,' there cannot be a single subject of the proposition, for "there cannot be one subject of a proposition from 'man' taken again with respect to diverse things."

[n. 28] The second argument makes the same point with regard to the number of compositions in the proposition. There are at least two: 'man' and 'runs,' and 'man' and 'white'; therefore, the proposition cannot be one.

[n. 29] An objection: one composition is said to be material or the 'matter' with respect to another if it supplies its content (that is, its subject and/or predicate), as opposed to its form or mode of composition. But 'a man is white' supplies part of the content of 'a man, who is white, runs'; therefore, etc.

[n. 30] First reply to the objection in n. 29: the composition in question is formal rather than material because the expression 'who' in 'who is white' combines 'man' and 'white' in the same way that 'a man is white' does: both compositions say that a man is white (the *dictum*). Since the composition is not material, the proposition cannot be one.

[n. 31] Second reply to the objection in n. 29: a composition is material when the elements of the composite are related as one matter to another. Yet the composition conveyed by 'is' is formal *simpliciter*, not material.

[n. 32] Returning to the main arguments, the third and final argument is a parallel to n. 7 of q. 6 above, where it was objected that 'every white man runs' and 'some white man does not run' are not contradictories because both are false when no man is white. Similarly, 'every man, who is white, runs' cannot be one or single because if it were, it would have a single contradictory, viz., 'a man, who

---

noted that every man is healthy and that every cow is healthy and so on for others, because otherwise the syllogism in the first [mode] of the first figure, governed by the rule, 'being said of all,' would not be valid: 'every animal is healthy; every man is an animal; therefore, every man is healthy,' which is nevertheless perfectly good [Sicut per istam 'omne animal est sanum' de virtute sermonis denotatur quod omnis homo sit sanus et quod omnis bos sit sanus, et sic de aliis, quia aliter iste syllogismus in primo primae [figurae] regulatus per dici de omni, non valeret 'omne animal est sanum; omnis homo est animal; ergo omnis homo est sanus,' qui tamen est optimus]."

is white, does not run.' But we could also contradict it if no man is white (Scotus does not mention this case here, but presumably that is what is meant).

Note that while Scotus does not endorse the argument of n. 7 above because according to him, 'a white man does not run' does not posit that a man is white, he apparently does endorse the argument here because he accepts in his reply to the question (n. 53 below) that the proposition 'a man, who is white, runs' is non-unitary, unlike 'a white man runs.' Presumably he thinks that 'a man, who is white, does not run' does posit that some man is white because of the relative 'who.'

[n. 33] It is objected that the true contradictory is 'a man, not one who is white, runs [*homo, non qui est albus, non currit*].'

[n. 34] The next three sections (nn. 34–36) reply to the objection in n. 33 above.

The first reply points out that if (as in the traditional square of opposition) the particular negative (some *a* are not *b*) contradicts the universal affirmative (all *a* are *b*), then 'a man, who is white, does not run' contradicts 'every man, who is white, runs,' as in n. 32 above.

[n. 35] The second reply is that a categorical proposition is composed of simple terms whose understanding does not involve truth or falsity, as discussed in *Opus II.I*, q. 3 above and elsewhere. Thus, 'man' on its own does not involve truth or falsity, and there is no composition. But 'a man, who is white' does involve truth and falsity because it signifies that a man is white; upon hearing the word 'man,' the mind of the hearer is suspended until something is added to it, and when the relative clause 'who is white' is added, truth or falsity is involved. Therefore, 'a man, who is white, does not run' asserts that a man is white (unlike 'a white man runs,' which Scotus discusses in n. 43 below), and thus it cannot be the contradictory of 'every man who is white runs,' since both are false when no man is white.

[n. 36] The third reply is that when a categorical, unitary proposition is negated, the composition is negated. But if 'a man, who is white, does not run' is unitary, the negation 'not every man, who is white, runs' relates to one composition only. Scotus says this is not possible, presumably because the composition 'a man who is white' is also involved. Given that no man is white, both propositions are false, and thus they cannot be contradictories.

Determination of Question 6
The Opinion of Others and an Objection

[n. 37] Responding to q. 6, which asked whether 'a white man runs' is one, Scotus first mentions another view, according to which the proposition is non-single (or 'several') because it contains two compositions: the explicit composition of 'white man' and 'runs,' and the implicit composition of 'white' and 'man.' The latter elements are related as requiring and required for completion, respectively (for which, see n. 7 above); their composition is made explicit by the addition of the relative pronoun-and-copula 'who is,' as in 'a man, who is white, runs.'

[n. 38] An objection: by the same reasoning, 'a rational animal runs' would be non-single, since 'animal' and 'rational' are related just like 'white' and 'man,' that is, as elements requiring and required for completion. The composition involved can be made explicit in the same way by the addition of 'who is,' as in 'an animal, who is rational, runs.'

The problem is that Boethius does not think that a proposition is several when its elements combine to make one substantial form. Thus, 'a rational animal runs' is not like 'a white man runs' in this regard.

Scotus's Reply to the Sixth Question

[n. 39] Scotus argues that 'a white man runs' is one, although it is not one *simpliciter*, or without qualification. He says that the unity of propositions is proportionate to the unity of things, and that the latter are said to be one either absolutely or in a qualified sense, such as when an accident is predicated of a substance as opposed to its species or genus or difference. In cases of qualified unity, the resulting proposition is one provided it satisfies the other criteria for unity, that is, that in its logical relations with other propositions—"opposition, contradictories, contraries, being divided by affirmation and negation, and syllogism-making [*syllogizatio*]"—it functions like a proposition that is one without qualification.

Reply to the Main Arguments of Question 6

[n. 40] Scotus replies to the first main argument (n. 1 above), which appealed to Boethius's statement that if a single thing is not formed from the elements that make up the subject or predicate, the proposition is not single, and that you cannot make a single thing from 'man' and 'white.' Scotus says that Boethius understands an extreme to represent a 'single thing' in the sense that a single species is a single thing; in other words, Boethius was talking about what makes a proposition one *simpliciter*.

[n. 41] Continuing his reply, Scotus concedes that the extreme 'a white man' does not represent a single species. However, the proposition 'a white man runs' can still in some sense be single even though one of its extremes is not because a single thing is formed from actuality and potentiality, and the man's being white is in a sense the actuality of a man, although not absolutely. He appeals to Ammonius's claim that this is a "superficial actuality," that is, being made one in a certain way. Ammonius says that a man's being white is naturally suited to be joined to the man, and that it signifies a quality that is superficial (*superficialis*) compared to the quality that is asserted absolutely (*simpliciter*).

[n. 42] The second argument (n. 2 above) was essentially a repetition of the first. Accordingly, Scotus says the reply will be clear from the reply to the first.

[n. 43] The third argument (n. 7 above) was that there is no single negation of 'every white man runs' when no man is white, and so the proposition must be composite. Scotus replies that the contradictory of 'every white man runs' is 'some white man does not run,' arguing that it is a mistake to claim that both are false when no man is white because 'a white man does not run' does not 'posit' or assume that a man is white. That is, 'a white man does not run' may be true even when no man is white. This may seem strange. Modern predicate logic analyzes the proposition 'a white man does not run' as 'some x is a man, x is white, and it is not the case that x runs,' which implies that some man is white. But this begs the question, since modern logic analyzes all such categorical propositions as composite. It is difficult to say exactly how Scotus thinks we should understand the proposition. He probably has in mind his answer to *Opus II.II*, qq. 2–5 above, where he suggests that a predicate like 'is not a runner' can be understood in two ways: as 'is an existing non-runner' (in which case it does posit the existence of any subject to which it truly applies) or as 'is not an existing runner,' which does not posit anything existing, although it arguably posits things which do not have existence or being (a non-existent man, for example). See also *Opus I*, q. 9, n. 37 above, where Scotus mentions, with apparent approval, the view that a negative proposition like 'some man does not exist' can be true of some man (namely, a non-existent man), and that we should not read it as the contradictory and false proposition 'some man who exists does not exist.'

[n. 44] Here Scotus elaborates on his remark about there being an intermediary between 'man' and 'white' in 'a white man runs.' The adjective ('white') is united to the substantive ('man') as actuality to potentiality. But the potentiality thus related is a sort of actuality, as when we say 'the Antichrist is actually now in potentiality': the potentiality is actual insofar as it expresses a nature (*ratio*). Thus, in 'a white man,' 'man' has the nature of potentiality with respect to 'white,' meaning that man is naturally suited to be actualized into a white thing. To indicate this actuality of potentiality, Scotus interposes the expressions 'being' or 'who is,' as in 'a man who is white runs.' But (and here is the important point for the resolution of q. 6) Scotus says that this mode of expression does not signify that anything is or is not the case, that is, 'being' or 'who is' does not assert that being white is the case or not the case with respect to the man, but is rather a "simple concept" that does not involve truth or falsity.[31] Thus 'a white man runs' does not posit that a man is white, just as 'rational animal' does not posit that an animal is rational.

But this does not seem right. As noted above, '(∃x)(x is a man & x is white & x does not run)' involves or implies the assertion that some man is white as well as asserting that some man runs. Likewise, Scotus's reasoning here about the actuality of potentiality seems to involve the truism that there is an implicit 'actual' operator in any statement. For example, we could write 'actually-p' to say that it is actually the case that p, and this would be equivalent to the ordinary 'p.' Any statement that something is the case would therefore be equivalent to the statement that it is actually the case, and so 'possibly-p' is equivalent to 'possibly-actually-p.' In other words, if it is possibly the case that p, it is possibly the case that it is actually the case that p. This is similarly equivalent to 'actually-possibly-p' and 'actually-possibly-actually-p.' None of this supports the conclusion that 'some man who is white runs' does not imply that some man is white, of course. At the very least, Scotus's reasoning here seems muddled.

[n. 45] Next is a reply to the second objection to the second argument of q. 6, which is that by the same reasoning, 'a walking white man runs' (n. 5). Scotus replies that the reasoning is not the same, since 'walking' and 'white' are accidents of each other, and neither is an act or a potentiality with respect to the other in the way that 'a white man' is taken as a single subject with respect to the predicate. Therefore, from man and white and walking one thing is not made, although one thing is made from man and white and walking dividedly.

---

31. Cf. the earlier discussion of truth and composition in *Opus II.I*, q. 3.

Note that his position here is not that the subject of the proposition 'a white man runs' is non-composite, but that the proposition is non-composite.

[n. 46] Finally there is a reply to the third objection to the second argument of q. 6, which is that predicates that are accidental to the same subject, or to one another, do not combine to form a unity (n. 6). Scotus agrees with this point: in such a case, the proposition is not one. In the present case of 'a white man runs,' however, 'man' and 'white' are not accidents of a third thing (Socrates), although white is an accident of man.

Determination of Question 7

[n. 47] To q. 7 (nn. 15–17 above), Scotus replies that 'a white thing is musical' is one or non-composite since "the white thing makes itself the subject *per accidens*." The point is somewhat obscure, but it appears to be that the proposition effects a *per accidens* unity between the subject and predicate, each of which is one when taken separately (that is, one white thing and one musical thing) but they become one in the proposition 'a white thing is musical.'

Reply to the Main Arguments of Question 7

[n. 48] To the first argument of n. 15 above, which repeated Aristotle's argument (mentioned in n. 6) that predicates that are accidental to the same subject or to one another do not combine to form a unity, Scotus replies that although the extreme of the proposition is not one *simpliciter*, it is one to a degree sufficient for the proposition to be the subject of truth and falsity, to be affirmed or denied, and to enter into syllogistic relations with other propositions (see n. 39 above).

[n. 49] To the second argument, at n. 16 above—that 'a white thing is musical' is equivalent to 'there is a white musical thing' and that just as 'Socrates is a white musical thing' is composite, so is 'a white thing is musical'—Scotus replies that the composition implied in the subject ('white' and 'thing' or 'person') is the composition of actuality and potentiality, and similarly in the predicate. This is different from 'a man is a musical white thing,' as 'white' and 'musical' are two things, neither of which is in potentiality with respect to the other, but both of which are actualities, meaning that they cannot be predicated of the same thing as if to make something one. Thus, a proposition is several where two accidents are predicated or made into the subject.

Determination of Question 8

[n. 50] To q. 8, which asked whether 'a white man is a musical man' is one (nn. 18–21), Scotus replies that it is, for the reason already given (see nn. 47 and 49), viz., that 'white' is related to 'man' as actuality to potentiality, and similarly 'musical.' One extreme is made from man and white, another extreme is made from man and musical, and one thing is predicated of one thing. He repeats the argument made in n. 7 above that the medium or middle, that is, the implied being between an adjective like 'white' and a noun like 'man,' does not posit anything being the case or not. It is more a "mode of understanding" than a copula expressing a state of affairs.

Reply to the Opposing Argument in Question 8

[n. 51] To the opposing argument of q. 8—Aristotle's remark that multiple predicates that are accidental to the same subject or to one another do not combine to form a unity (n. 21 above)—Scotus replies that the proposition is not composite unless two things are predicated as actualities of some third thing in which they inhere. The idea seems to be that more than one *per accidens* actuality is sufficient to render the proposition composite. The problem is that Scotus simply denies that this is what is happening in 'a white man is a musical man.' The only clue he gives us is when he says that the objection in n. 21 is not sufficient to refute his position "because it leaves out the ultimate particle." But what is "the ultimate particle'? Presumably, this is the term 'musical,' which is "left out" in the proposition mentioned in the final sentence of n. 21 ('Socrates is a white man'). The claim there was that 'a white man is a musical man' is one, just as 'Socrates is a white man' is not. Based on his determination of qq. 6–7, Scotus has grounds for saying that the latter proposition is one, so the propositions are not analogous. But why should this be a reason for thinking that 'a white man is a musical man' is one?

Determination of Question 9

[n. 52] To q. 9, which asked whether 'a man, who is white, runs' is one, Scotus offers an equivocal reply. "It is said," he states, that the proposition is one because it can be part of a syllogism and because it has contradictories and so on. But then he mentions the difficulty about its contradictory: is 'some man, who is white, does not run' true when there are no men (see nn. 32–36 above)? The problem is that it does not seem to be true because it seems to assert the existence of a white man via the 'is' in 'who is white,' which suggests that the proposition is composite.

[n. 53] However (repeating his reasoning at n. 50 above) if the 'who' is interpreted as a mode of understanding between the adjective ('white') and the noun ('man'), then the proposition is one, just like 'a white man runs,' and its contradictory is 'a man, who is white, does not run.' The proposition remains one because nothing is posited by this mode of understanding.

Reply to the Main Arguments of Question 9

[n. 54] To the first argument (n. 22 above), which was that the pronoun 'who' implicitly has the nature of an article because it causes what follows it to restrict what precedes it, he replies that the extreme of the proposition ('a man') is not one absolutely, but the proposition does not thereby become several because the effect of the pronoun is to restrict the subject term so that it is understood under the aspect of the relative clause. But it remains one *per accidens* and to a degree sufficient for the unity of truth and falsity as well as the unity of affirmation and negation, and is sufficient to appear in a syllogistic argument.

[n. 55] In reply to the second argument (n. 23 above), which was that the unity of the subject of distribution (for example, the expression 'a man, who is white') suffices for the unity of the syllogistic middle, Scotus explains that there is no distribution of that subject absolutely (*absolute*), although 'man' as restricted by 'who is white' is distributed. For some reason he calls the latter distribution 'per se,' even though he has been at pains to defend the unity of the proposition *per accidens* via the oneness of its truth or falsity, its affirmation or negation, and its role in syllogistic argument.

[n. 56] The third argument (n. 24 above) was that if the unity of 'a man, who is white' is sufficient for the unity of the middle (as was argued in n. 23 above), then it is sufficient for the extremes (that is, the major and minor terms) because syllogisms can only be constructed from propositions that are one. Scotus replies that the expression 'who is white' does not belong to the syllogistic middle per se and so presumably belongs to it *per accidens*, though Scotus does not say this explicitly. Perhaps his point is that the determination 'who is white' is superfluous in the minor premise of the syllogism he gives as an example here:

P1—Every man, who is white, runs;
P2—This is a man;
C—Therefore, this man, who is white, runs.

The reason is that we do not need to add a determination to the man referred to by the middle term as long as the conclusion makes it clear that 'this man' is the one 'who is white.'

[n. 57] Here Scotus appears to concede that 'every man, who is white, runs' could also be interpreted as not-one, or several, in which case he grants the further consequence that it cannot be made into a syllogism *simpliciter*. He also recognizes that in such a case we must deny that 'white man' is one as a distributable term.

[n. 58] According to the edition, this is the reply to the fourth argument of q. 9 at n. 25, but it does not appear to be related to the argument given in n. 25, which claims that the unity of a proposition is not impeded by the plurality involved in the composition of act and quality, as in an adverbial modification: 'this runs fast.'

[n. 59] In reply to the fifth argument of q. 9 at n. 26, which says that when a proposition is not-one or "several [*plures*]" its extremes must also be several, Scotus says that in the proposition 'every man, who is white, runs; therefore, every man runs,' there are four extremes: 'man,' 'running,' 'man related,' and 'white,' which are "denoted to inhere in the same place." It follows from this that the proposition is several. What is not clear is why this follows or how it fits with his other replies to the main arguments of q. 9. It is possible that this reply is actually not to the argument in n. 26, which does not mention the term 'man related (*homo relatus*)'?

BIBLIOGRAPHY

Primary Sources

Adam of Wodeham. *Adam de Wodeham, Lectura secunda in primum librum Sententiarum.* Edited by Rega Wood and Gedeon Gál. 3 vols. St. Bonaventure, N.Y.: The Franciscan Institute, 1990.

Albert the Great. *Alberti Magni Opera Omnia.* Edited by A. Borgnet and A. Borgnet. 38 vols. Paris: 1890–99; Köln: Institutum Alberti Magni, 1951–.

Al-Ghazali. *Algazels's Metaphysics: A Medieval Translation.* Translated by J. T. Muckle. Toronto: St. Michael's College, 1933.

Ammonius. *Ammonius, Commentaire sur le Peri hermenias d'Aristote (opus a Guillelmo de Moerbeke translatum).* Edited by G. Verbeke. Corpus latinum commentariorum in Aristotelem graecorum 2. Louvain: Institut supérieur de philosophie, 1961.

———. *Ammonius, in Aristotelis De Interpretatione Commentarius.* Edited by Adolf Busse. Commentaria in Aristotelem Graeca 4.5. Berlin: Reimer, 1897.

Anonymous. *César et le Phénix: Distinctiones et sophismata parisiens du XIIIe siècle.* Edited by Alain de Libera. Centro di cultura medievale 4. Pisa: Scuola Normale Superiore, 1991.

———. "Thirteenth-Century Notes on William of Sherwood's Treatise on Properties of Terms. An Edition of *Anonymi Dubitationes et Notabilia circa Guilelmi de Shyreswode 'Introductionum logicalium Tractatum V'* from ms. Worcester Cath. Q.13." Edited by Jan Pinborg and Sten Ebbesen. *Cahiers de l'Institut du Moyen-Age grec et latin* 47 (1984): 103–41.

Antonius Andreas. *Scriptum Antonii Andreae in Perihermenias Aristotelis.* In *Scriptum Antonii Andreae in arte veteri*, 63r–88r. Venice: 1508.

Aristotle. *Aristoteles Latinus.* Corpus philosophorum medii aevi. Academiarum consociatarum auspiciis et consilio editum. 1939–. (II^1 5 = *De interpretatio vel Periermenias translatio Boethiii, specimina translationum recentiorum*, edited by Laurentius Minio-Paluello. Bruges: Desclée de Brouwer, 1965.)

———. *Aristotelis opera cum Averrois commentariis, latine.* Venice: apud Iunctas. 11 vols. Venice: 1562–74.

———. *Aristotle's 'Metaphysics,' Books G, D, E*. Translation and commentary by Christopher Kirwan. Oxford: Clarendon Press, 1971.

———. *The Complete Works of Aristotle: The Revised Oxford Translation*. Edited by Jonathan Barnes. 2 vols. Princeton, N.J.: Princeton University Press, 1984.

Averroes. *Averrois Cordubensis, Commentarium Magnum in Aristotelis De Anima Libros*. Edited by F. Stuart Crawford. Corpus Commentatorium Averrois in Aristotelem, Versionum Latinarum, 6.1. Cambridge, Mass.: Medieval Academy of America, 1953.

———. *Averrois Cordubensis, Metaphysica V*. Edited by R. Ponzalli. Berne: Edizioni Francke, 1971.

Avicenna. *Avicenna, Liber de philosophia prima sive scientia divina, V–X*. Edited by Simone van Riet. Leiden: Brill, 1980.

Boethius. *Anicii Manlii Severini Boethii Commentaria in Librum Aristotelis Peri Hermenias*. Edited by C. Meiser. Leipzig: Teubner, 1877 and 1880 (= *Patrologiae cursus completus*, series latina, accurante J. P. Migne [Paris 1844, sqq.], vol. 64.)

———. *Anicii Manlii Severini Boethii De divisione liber: Critical Edition, Translation, Prolegomena, and Commentary*. Translated and edited by John Magee. Philosophia Antiqua 77. Leiden: Brill, 1998.

———. *Anicii Manlii Severini Boethii De hebdomadibus*. Edited by R. Peiper. Leipzig: Teubner, 1871.

———. *Anicii Manlii Severini Boethii In Isagogen Porphyrii commenta*. Edited by Samuel Brandt. Corpus Scriptorum Ecclesiasticorum Latinorum 48. Vienna: F. Tempsky, 1906.

———. *Boethius, 'De topicis differentiis.'* Edited by Eleonore Stump. Ithaca, N.Y.: Cornell University Press, 1978.

Boethius of Dacia. *Boethii Dacii Modi Significandi sive Quaestiones super Priscianum Maiorem*. Edited by Jan Pinborg, Heinrich Roos, and P. J. Jensen. Corpus Philosophorum Danicorum Medii Aevi 4. Copenhagen: G. E. C. Gad, 1969.

———. "Des 12 und 13 Jahrhunderts mit Textausgabe eines Sophisma des Boethius von Dacien." Edited by Martin Grabmann. *Beiträge zur Geschichte der Philosophie und Theologie des Mittelalters* 36, no. 1 (1940): 77–95.

———. "Studies in the Logical Writings Attributed to Boethius of Dacia." Edited by Jan Pinborg and Sten Ebbesen. *Cahiers de l'Institut du Moyen-Age grec et latin* 3 (1970): 1–54.

Gerardus Odonis. *Giraldus Odonis, Opera Philosophica. Vol. 1: Logica*. Edited by L. M. de Rijk. Studien und Texte zur Geistesgeschichte des Mittelalters 60. Leiden: Brill, 1997.

Godfrey of Fontaines. *Les quatres premiers Quodlibets de Godefroid de Fontaines*. Edited by M. De Wulf and A. Pelzer. Les Philosophes Belges 2. Louvain: Institut Supérieur de Philosophie de l'Université, 1904.

Henry of Ghent (Henrici de Gandavo). *Syncategoremata*. In *Opera Omnia* XXXVII, Ancient and Medieval Philosophy, De Wulf-Mansion Centre, Series 2, edited by Gordon A. Wilson. Leuven: Leuven University Press, 2010.

Isidore of Seville. *Isadori Hispalensis Episcopi Etymologiarum sive Originum libri XX*. Edited by W. M. Lindsay. 2 vols. Oxford Classical Texts. Oxford: Oxford University Press, 1985.

Johannes de Fonte, ed. *Les Auctoritates Aristotelis*. Philosophes Médiévaux 17. Louvain-Paris: Publications Universitaires-Béatrice Nauwelaerts, 1974.

Johannes Rubeus Vercellensis and Albertinus Vercellensis, eds. *Questiones subtilissimae Magistri Rodulphi Britonis super arte veteri*. Venice: Rubeus, 1499. http://diglib.hab.de/inkunabeln/3-8-log-1/start.htm?image=00005.

John Buridan. *John Buridan, 'Summulae de dialectica.'* Translated by Gyula Klima. Yale Library of Medieval Philosophy. New Haven, Conn.: Yale University Press, 2001.

John Duns Scotus. *B. Ioannis Duns Scoti, 'Quaestiones in librum Porphyrii Isagoge' et 'Quaestiones super Praedicamenta Aristotelis' (Opera Philosophica, vol. 1)*. Edited by R. Andrews, G. Etzkorn, G. Gál, R. Green, T. Noone, and R. Wood. St. Bonaventure, N.Y.: Franciscan Institute Publications-St. Bonaventure University, 1999.

———. *B. Ioannis Duns Scoti, 'Quaestiones in libros Perihermenias Aristoteli,' op. prim. et sec. (Opera Philosophica, vol. 2)*. Edited by R. Andrews, G. Etzkorn, G. Gál, R. Green, T. Noone, R. Plevano, A. Traver, and R. Wood. St. Bonaventure, N.Y. and Washington, D.C.: The Franciscan Institute and The Catholic University of America Press, 2004.

———. *B. Ioannis Duns Scoti, 'Quaestiones super libros Metaphysicorum Aristotelis' (Opera Philosophica, vols. 3–4)*. Edited by R. Andrews, G. Etzkorn, G. Gál, R. Green, F. Kelley, T. Noone, and R. Wood. St. Bonaventure, N.Y.: Franciscan Institute Publications-St. Bonaventure University, 1997–98.

———. *Commentaria Oxoniensa ad. IV Libros Magistri Sententiarum*. Edited by M. Fernandez Garcia. Quaracchi: Ex Typographia collegii S. Bonaventura, 1914.

———. *Duns Scotus, Metaphysician*. Translated and edited by William A. Frank and Allan B. Wolter. West Lafayette, Ind.: Purdue University Press, 1995.

———. *Ioannis Duns Scoti Doctoris Subtilis Ordinis Minorum Opera Omnia*. Edited by L. Vivès. (Reprint, with corrections, of Wadding's edition of 1639). Paris: 1891–95.

———. *Ioannis Duns Scoti Doctoris Subtilis Ordinis Minorum Opera Omnia*. Edited by L. Wadding. 12 vols. Lyon: 1639.

———. *John Duns Scotus, Contingency and Freedom*: Lectura I 39. Translated by A. Jaczn, H. Vos, A. A. Veldhuis, E. Looman-Graaskamp, E. Dekker, and N. W. Den Bok. New Synthese Historical Library 42. Dordrecht: Kluwer, 1994.

———. *John Duns Scotus, The Examined Report of the Paris Lecture (Reportatio I-A)*, vol. 1. Translated and edited by Oleg V. Bychkov and Allan B. Wolter. St. Bonaventure, N.Y.: The Franciscan Institute, 2004.

———. *John Duns Scotus, The Quodlibetal Questions: God and Creatures*. Translated and edited by Felix Alluntis and Allan B. Wolter. Princeton, N.J.: Princeton University Press, 1975.

———. *Opera Omnia* ("The Vatican edition"). Civitas Vaticana: Typis Polyglottis Vaticanis, 1950–.

Lambert of Lagny. *Logica (Summa Lamberti)*. Edited by Franco Alessio. Pubblicazioni della facoltà di lettere di filosofia dell'università di Milano 59. Firenze: La Nuova Italia Editrice, 1971.

———. "Le traité *De appellatione* de Lambert de Lagny (Lambert d'Auxerre)." Translated by Alain de Libera. *Archives d'histoire doctrinale et littéraire du Moyen Age* 48 (1982): 227–85.

Martin of Dacia. *Die Modi significandi des Martinus de Dacia*. Edited by Heinrich Roos. Beiträge zur Geschichte der Philosophie und Theologie des Mittelalters 37.2. København-Münster-Westfalen: A. Frost-Hansen-Aschendorffsche Verlagsbuchhandlung, 1952.

———. *Martini de Dacia Opera*. Edited by Heinrich Roos. Corpus philosophorum Danicorum Medii Aevii 2. Copenhagen: G. E. C. Gad, 1961.

Peter Helias. *Petrus Helias, Summa super Priscianum*. Edited by Leo A. Reilly. 2 vols. Studies and Texts 113. Toronto: Pontifical Institute of Mediaeval Studies, 1993.

Peter of Auvergne. *Peter of Auvergne's Commentary on Aristotle's 'Categories': Edition, Translation, and Analysis*. Translated and edited by Robert Andrews. PhD diss., Cornell University, 1988.

Peter of Spain. *Petrus Hispanus, Tractatus, called afterwards Summule logicales*. Edited by L. M. de Rijk. Assen: Van Gorcum, 1972.

Porphyry. *Porphyry, Isagoge et in Aristotelis Categorias Commentarias*. Edited by Adolf Busse. Commentaria in Aristotelem Graeca 4.1. Berlin: Reimer, 1887.

Pricianus. *Prisciani Caesarensis Grammatici institutionum grammaticarum libri XVIII*. Edited by M. Hertz. Leipzig: 1855–60.

Robert Grosseteste. *Robertus Grossatesta Lincolniensis, Commentarius in Posteriorum analyticorum libros*. Edited by P. Rossi. Corpus philosophorum medii aevi. Testi e studi 2. Firenze: Unione accademica nazionale, 1981.

Robert Kilwardby. "The Commentary on *Priscian Maior* ascribed to Robert Kilwardby." Edited by Karin Margareta Fredborg. *Cahiers de l'Institut du Moyen-Age grec et latin* 15 (1975): 21–146.

———. *Robert Kilwardby O.P.: On Time and Imagination*. Edited by P. Osmund Lewry. Oxford: Oxford University Press for the British Academy, 1987.

Roger Bacon. "Les *Summulae dialectices* de Roger Bacon. 1–2: *De termino, De enuntiatione*. 3: *De argumentatione*." Edited by Alain de Libera. *Archives d'histoire doctrinale et littéraire du Moyen Age* 53 (1986): 139–289; 54 (1987): 171–278.

———. *Roger Bacon, Compendium of the Study of Theology*. Translated and edited by Thomas S. Maloney. Studien und Texte zur Geistesgeschichte des Mittelalters 20. Leiden: Brill, 1988.

———. *Roger Bacon, The Art and Science of Logic*. Translated and edited by Thomas S. Mahoney. Medieval Sources in Translation 47. Toronto: Pontifical Institute of Mediaeval Studies, 2009.

———. *Opera hactenus inedita Rogeri Bacon*. Edited by Robert Steele. 16 vols. Oxford: Clarendon Press, 1909–40.

———. "An Unedited Part of Roger Bacon's *Opus maius: 'De signis.'*" Edited by Karin Margareta Fredborg, Lauge Nielsen, and Jan Pinborg. *Traditio* 34 (1978): 75–136.

Siger of Brabant. "*Quaestio utrum haec sit vera: Homo est animal, nullo homine existente.*" In *Siger de Brabant, Écrits de logique, de morale et de physique*, edited by B. C. Bazán, 53–59. Philosophes Médiévaux 14. Louvain-Paris: Publications Universitaires-Éditions Béatrice-Nauwelaerts, 1974.

———. *Siger de Brabant, Questions sur la Métaphysique*. Edited by Cornelio Andrea Graiff. Philosophes Médiévaux 1. Louvain: Éditions de l'Institut Supérieur de Philosophie, 1948.

Siger of Courtrai. *Les Oeuvres de Siger de Courtrai: Etude critique et textes inédits*. Edited by G. Wallerand. Les Philosophes Belges 8. Louvain: Institut supérieur de philosophie de l'Université, 1913.

———. *Zeger van Kortrijk, Commentator van 'Perihermeneias.'* Edited by C. Verhaak. Brussels: Paleis der Academiën, 1964.

Simon of Faversham. *Magistri Simonis Anglici sive de Faverisham Opera Omnia*. Vol. 1: *Opera logica, tomus prior*. (1) *Quaestiones super libro Porphyrii*. (2) *Quaestiones super libro Praedicamentorum*. (3) *Quaestiones super libro Perihermeneias*. Edited by Pasquale Mazarella. Pubblicazioni dell'Istituto universitario di magistero di Catania, serie filosofica, testi critici 1. Padua: Cedam, 1957.

———. *Simon of Faversham*, Quaestiones super libro Elenchorum. Edited by Sten Ebbesen, Thomas Izbicki, John Longeway, Francesco del Punta, Eileen Serene, and Eleonore Stump. Toronto: Pontifical Institute of Mediaeval Studies, 1984.

Thomas Aquinas (Sancti Thomae Aquinatis, Doctoris Angelici). *Opera omnia / iussu impensaque Leonis XIII P. M. edita*. Rome: 1882–.

——— (Thomas von Aquin). *Quaestio disputata 'De unione Verbi incarnate' (Über die Union des fleischgewordenen Wortes)*. Edited by Klaus Obenauer, Walter Senner, and Barbara Bartocci. Stuttgart-Bad Cannstatt: Frommann-Holzboog, 2011.

Walter Burley. "Walter Burley, *Questions on the* Perhermenias." Edited by Stephen Brown. *Franciscan Studies* 34 (1974): 202–95.

William Arnauld (Guillelmus Arnaldi). *Liber Peryermenias (opus Aedigio Romano attributum)*, in *Expositio domini Aegidii Romani in Artem veterem*. Venice: 1507.

William of Ockham. *William of Ockham, 'Quodlibetal Questions' Vol. 1–2, Quodlibets 1–7*. Translated by Alfred J. Freddoso and Francis E. Kelly. Yale Library of Medieval Philosophy. New Haven, Conn.: Yale University Press, 1991.

———. *William of Ockham, 'Summa Logicae.' (Opera Philosophica, vol. 1)*. Edited by P. Boehner, G. Gál, and S. Brown. St. Bonaventure, N.Y.: The Franciscan Institute, 1974.

William of Sherwood. "William of Sherwood, *Introductiones in logicam*." Edited by Charles H. Lohr, P. Kunze, and B. Mussler. *Traditio* 39 (1983): 219–99.

———. *William of Sherwood's* Introduction to Logic. Translated by Norman Kretzmann. Minneapolis: University of Minnesota Press, 1966.

———. "William of Sherwood's *Syncategoremata*." Edited by J. R. O'Donnell. *Mediaeval Studies* 3 (1941): 46–93.

Secondary Sources

Andrews, Robert. "Andrew of Cornwall and the Reception of Modism in England." In *Medieval Analyses in Language and Cognition*, edited by Sten Ebbesen and Russell L. Friedman, 105–16. Historisk-filosofiske Meddelelser 77. Copenhagen: Royal Danish Academy of Sciences and Letters, 1996.

———. "The Modistae and John Duns Scotus's *Quaestiones super Perihermenias*." In *Aristotle's* Peri Hermeneias *in the Latin Middle Ages: Essays on the Commentary Tradition*, edited by H. A. G. Braakhuis and C. H. Kneepkens, 67–83. Artistarium Supplementa 10. Groningen-Haren: Ingenium, 2003.

Ashworth, E. J. "Jacobus Naveros (fl. ca. 1533) on the Question, 'Do Spoken Words Signify Concepts or Things?'" In *Logos and Pragma. Essays on the Philosophy of Language in Honour of Professor Gabriel Nuchelmans*, edited by L. M. de Rijk and H. A. G. Braakhuis, 189–214. Artistarium Supplementa 3. Nijmegen: Ingenium, 1987.

———. "Some Notes on Syllogistic in the Sixteenth and Seventeenth Centuries." *Notre Dame Journal of Formal Logic* 11, no. 1 (1970): 17–33.

Bäck, Allan. *On Reduplication*. Studien und Texte zur Geistesgeschichte des Mittelalters 49. Leiden: Brill, 1996.

Bendiek, Johannes. "Die Lehre von den Konsequenzen bei Pseudo-Scotus." *Franziskanische Studien* 34 (1952): 205–34.

Biard, Joël. "La signification d'objets imaginaires dans quelques texts anglais du XIVe siècle (Guillaume Heytesbury, Henry Hopton)." In *The Rise of British Logic: Acts of the Sixth European Symposium on Medieval Logic and Semantics, Balliol College, Oxford, 19–24 June 1983*, edited by P. Osmund Lewry, 265–84. Papers in Mediaeval Studies 7. Toronto: Pontifical Institute of Mediaeval Studies, 1983.

Bos, E. P. *Medieval Semantics and Metaphysics. Studies Dedicated to L. M. De Rijk*. Artistarium Supplementa 2. Nijmegen: Ingenium, 1985.

———, ed. *John Duns Scotus, 1265/6–1308: Renewal of Philosophy*. Acts of the Third Symposium Organized by the Dutch Society for Medieval Philosophy, Medium Aevum (May 23 & 24, 1996). Amsterdam: Rodopi, 1998.

———, ed. "The Theory of the Proposition According to John Duns Scotus: Two Commentaries on Aristotle's *Perihermenias*." In *Logos and Pragma. Essays on the Philosophy of Language in Honour of Professor Gabriel Nuchelmans*, edited by L. M. de Rijk and H. A. G. Braakhuis, 121–39. Artistarium Supplementa 3. Nijmegen: Ingenium, 1987.

Bos, E. P. and P. A. Meijer, eds. *On Proclus and his Influence in Medieval Philosophy*. Philosophia antiqua 53. Leiden: Brill, 1992.

Bott, Alan. *Merton College: A Short History of the Buildings*. Oxford: Merton College, 1993.

Braakhuis, H. A. G. *De 13de eeuwse Tractaten over syncategorematische Termen: Uitgave van Nicolaas van Parijs' sincategoreumata*. 2 vols. Inleidende Studie 1. Meppel: Krips Repro, 1979.

———. "Kilwardby versus Bacon? The Contribution to the Discussion on Univocal Signification of Beings and Non-Beings Found in a *Sophisma* attributed to Rober Kilwardby." In *Medieval Semantics and Metaphysics. Studies dedicated to L. M. De Rijk*, edited by E. P. Bos, 112–42. Artistarium Supplementa 2. Nijmegen: Ingenium, 1985.

———. "The Views of William of Sherwood on Some Semantical Topics and Their Relation to Those of Roger Bacon." *Vivarium* 15 (1977): 111–42.

Braakhuis, H. A. G. and C. H. Kneepkens, eds. *Aristotle's Peri Hermeneias in the Latin Middle Ages: Essays on the Commentary Tradition.* Artistarium Supplementa 10. Groningen-Haren: Ingenium, 2003.

Braakhuis, H. A. G., C. H. Kneepkens, and L. M. de Rijk, eds. *English Logic and Semantics from the End of the Twelfth Century to the Time of Ockham and Burleigh, Acts of the Fourth European Symposium on Mediaeval Logic and Semantics, Leiden/Nijmegen 23–27 April 1979.* Artistarium Supplementa 1. Nijmegen: Ingenium, 1981.

Brampton, C. K. "Duns Scotus at Oxford, 1288–1301." *Franciscan Studies* 24 (1946): 1–20.

Brentano, Franz. *Psychologie vom empirischen Standpunkt.* Leipzig: Duncker & Humblot, 1874 and 1911.

Callebaut, A. "Le bx. Duns Scot a Cambridge vers 1297–1300." *Archivum Franciscanum Historicum* 21 (1928): 608–11.

Costello, Elvis. *My Aim Is True.* New York: Columbia Records, 1978.

Cross, Richard. "Divisibility, Communicability, and Predicability in Duns Scotus's Theories of the Common Nature." *Medieval Philosophy and Theology* 11, no. 1 (2003): 43–63.

Dalgaard, Karen Elisabeth. "Peter of Ireland's *Commentary on Aristotle's 'Peri Hermeneias.'*" *Cahiers de l'Institut du Moyen-Age grec et latin* 43 (1982): 3–44.

Dumont, Stephen D. "Duns Scotus's Parisian Question on the Formal Distinction." *Vivarium* 43, no. 1 (2005): 7–62.

Ebbesen, Sten. "The Chimera's Diary." In *The Logic of Being*, edited Simo Knuuttila and Jaakko Hintikka, 115–43. Dordrecht: Reidel 1986.

———. "Concrete Accidental Terms: Late Thirteenth-Century Debates about Problems Relating to such Terms as 'Album.'" In *Meaning and Inference in Medieval Philosophy. Studies in Memory of Jan Pinborg*, edited by Norman Kretzmann, 107–74. Synthese Historical Library 32. Dordrecht: Reidel, 1988.

———. "The Copenhagen School of Medieval Philosophy." In *Medieval Analyses in Language and Cognition*, edited by Sten Ebbesen and Russell L. Friedman, 7–13. Historisk-filosofiske Meddelelser 77. Copenhagen: Royal Danish Academy of Sciences and Letters, 1996.

———. "The Dead Man Is Alive." *Synthese* 40 (1979): 42–70.

———. "Talking about What Is No More: Texts by Peter of Cornwall (?), Richard of Clive, Simon of Faversham, and Radulphus Brito." *Cahiers de l'Institut du Moyen-Age grec et latin* 55 (1987): 135–68.

———. "*Termini accidentales concreti:* Texts from the late thirteenth century." *Cahiers de l'Institut du Moyen-Age grec et latin* 53 (1986): 37–150.

———. "The Tradition of Ancient Logic-cum-Grammar in the Middle Ages—What's the Problem?" *Vivarium* 45 (2007): 136–52.

Ebbesen, Sten, and Russell L. Friedman, eds. *Medieval Analyses in Language and Cognition*. Historisk-filosofiske Meddelelser 77. Copenhagen: Royal Danish Academy of Sciences and Letters, 1996.

Emden, A. B. *A Biographical Register of the University of Oxford to A.D. 1500*. 3 vols. Oxford: Clarendon Press, 1957–59.

Fredborg, Karin Margareta. "Roger Bacon on *Impositio vocis ad significandum*." In *English Logic and Semantics from the End of the Twelfth Century to the Time of Ockham and Burleigh, Acts of the Fourth European Symposium on Mediaeval Logic and Semantics, Leiden/Nijmegen 23–27 April 1979*, edited by H. A. G. Braakhuis, C. H. Kneepkens, and L. M. de Rijk, 167–92. Artistarium Supplementa 1. Nijmegen: Ingenium, 1981.

Frege, Gottlob. "On Concept and Object." In *Translations from the Philosophical Writings of Gottlob Frege*, translated and edited by Peter Geach and Max Black, 42–55. Oxford: Blackwell, 1952.

Gál, Gedeon. "Adam of Wodeham's Question on the *Complexe significabile* as the Immediate Object of Scientific Knowledge." *Franciscan Studies* 37 (1977): 66@102.

Gaskin, Richard. *The Unity of the Proposition*. Oxford: Oxford University Press, 2008.

Gilson, E. "Avicenne et le point de départ de Duns Scot." *Archives d'histoire doctrinale et littéraire du Moyen Age* 2 (1927): 89–149.

———. "Les sources gréco-arabes de l'augustinisme avicennisant." *Archives d'histoire doctrinale et littéraire du Moyen Age* 4 (1929): 5–149.

Gölz, B. "Die echten und unechten Werke des Duns Scotus nach dem gegenwärtigen Stand der Forschung." *Lektorenkonferenz der deutschen Franziskaner für Philosophie und Theologie* 6–7 (1931–33): 53–60.

Grabmann, M. "De Thomas Erfordiensi auctore Grammaticae quae Ioanni Duns Scoto adscribitur speculativae." *Archivum Franciscanum Historicum* 15 (1922): 273–77.

Gracia, Jorge J. E., ed. *Individuation in Scholasticism: The Later Middle Ages and the Counter-Reformation, 1150–1650*. Albany, N.Y.: State University of New York Press, 1994.

Gracia, Jorge J. E. and Timothy Noone, eds.. *A Companion to Philosophy in the Middle Ages*. Oxford: Blackwell, 2003.

Harris, C. R. S. *Duns Scotus*. 2 vols. Oxford: Clarendon Press, 1927.

Hisette, R. *Enquête sur les 219 articles condamnés à Paris le 7 mars 1277*. Philosophes Médiévaux 22. Louvain-Paris: Peeters, 1977.

Isaac, Jean. *Le Peri Hermeneias en Occident de Boèce à saint Thomas*. Paris: J. Vrin, 1953.

Joseph, H. W. B. *An Introduction to Logic*. Oxford: Clarendon Press, 1906.

Kelly, L. G. *The Mirror of Grammar: Theology, Philosophy, and the Modistae*. Amsterdam Studies in the Theory and History of Linguistic Science, Series 3: Studies in the History of the Language Sciences 101. Philadelphia: John Benjamins, 2002.

King, Peter. "The Problem of Individuation in the Middle Ages." *Theoria* 66 (2000): 159–84.

Klima, Gyula. "Aquinas' Theory of the Copula and the Analogy of Being." *Logical Analysis and the History of Philosophy* 5 (2002): 159–76.

Kneale, William C. and Martha Kneale. *The Development of Logic*. Oxford: Clarendon Press, 1962.

Kretzmann, Norman, and Eleonore Stump, trans. *The Cambridge Translations of Medieval Philosophical Texts, Volume 1: Logic and the Philosophy of Language*. Cambridge, Mass.: Cambridge University Press, 1988.

Kretzmann, Norman, Anthony Kenny, and Jan Pinborg, eds. *The Cambridge History of Later Medieval Philosophy: From the Rediscovery of Aristotle to the Disintegration of Scholasticism, 1100-1600*. Cambridge, Mass.: Cambridge University Press, 1982.

Kripke, Saul. *Naming and Necessity*. Cambridge, Mass.: Harvard University Press, 1980.

Lagerlund, Henrik. *Modal Syllogistics in the Middle Ages*. Studien und Texte zur Geistesgeschichte des Mittelalters 70. Leiden: Brill, 2000.

Landgraf, A. M. "Das Problem *Utrum Christus fuerit homo in triduo mortis* in der Frühscholastik." In *Études d'histoire littéraire et doctrinale de la scolastique médiévale offertes à Mgr Auguste Pelzer, scriptor de la bibliothèque Vaticane, à l'occasion de son soixante-dixième anniversaire*, 109-58. Recueil de travaux d'histoire et de philologie, 3ᵉ série, 26ᵉ fascicule. Louvain: éditions de l'Institut supérieur de philosophie, 1947.

Latham, R. E. *Revised Medieval Latin Word-List from British and Irish Sources*. London: The British Academy, 1965.

Lewry, P. Osmund. "Grammar, Logic and Rhetoric 1220–1320." In *The History of the University of Oxford, Vol. 1: The Early Oxford Schools*, edited by J. I. Catto and Ralph Evans, 401–34. Oxford: Clarendon Press, 1984.

———. "The Oxford Condemnations of 1277 in Grammar and Logic." In *English Logic and Semantics from the End of the Twelfth Century to the Time of Ockham and Burleigh, Acts of the Fourth European Symposium on Mediaeval Logic and Semantics, Leiden/Nijmegen 23–27 April 1979*, edited by H. A. G. Braakhuis, C. H. Kneepkens, and L. M. de Rijk, 235–78. Artistarium Supplementa 1. Nijmegen: Ingenium, 1981.

———. "Oxford Logic 1250–1275: Nicholas and Peter of Cornwall on Past and Future Realities." In *The Rise of British Logic: Acts of the Sixth European Symposium on Medieval Logic and Semantics, Balliol College, Oxford, 19–24 June 1983*, edited by P. Osmund Lewry, 19–62. Papers in Mediaeval Studies 7. Toronto: Pontifical Institute of Mediaeval Studies, 1983.

———, ed. *The Rise of British Logic: Acts of the Sixth European Symposium on Medieval Logic and Semantics, Balliol College, Oxford, 19–24 June 1983*. Papers in Mediaeval Studies 7. Toronto: Pontifical Institute of Mediaeval Studies, 1983.

———. "Robert Kilwardby on Meaning: A Parisian Course on the *Logica Vetus*." In *Sprache und Erkenntnis im Mittelalter*, edited by J. P. Beckmann, et al., 376–83. Miscellanea Medievalia 13. Berlin: De Gruyter, 1981.

———. *Robert Kilwardby's Writings on the* Logica Vetus *Studied with Regard to Their Teaching and Method*. D.Phil. Thesis, University of Oxford, 1978.

———. "Two Continuators of Aquinas: Robertus de Vulgarbia and Thomas Sutton on the *Perihermenias* of Aristotle." *Mediaeval Studies* 43 (1981): 58–130.

Libera, Alain de. "La littérature des *Abstractiones* et la tradition logique d'Oxford." In *The Rise of British Logic: Acts of the Sixth European Symposium on Medieval Logic and Semantics, Balliol College, Oxford, 19–24 June 1983*, edited by P. Osmund Lewry, 63–114. Papers in Mediaeval Studies 7. Toronto: Pontifical Institute of Mediaeval Studies, 1983.

———. "Les *Appellationes* de Jean le Page." *Archives d'histoire doctrinale et littéraire du Moyen Age* 51 (1984): 193–255.

———. "The Oxford and Paris Traditions in Logic." In *The Cambridge History of Later Medieval Philosophy: From the Rediscovery of Aristotle to the Disintegration of Scholasticism, 1100–1600*, edited by Norman Kretzmann, Anthony Kenny, and Jan Pinborg, 174–87. Cambridge, Mass.: Cambridge University Press, 1982.

Little, A. G. "Chronological Notes on the Life of Duns Scotus." *English Historical Review* 47 (1932): 568–82.

———. *The Grey Friars in Oxford. Part 1: A History of Convent. Part 2: Biographical Notices of the Friars, Together with Appendices of Original Documents*. Oxford: Clarendon Press, 1892.

Lohr, Charles H. *Commentateurs d'Aristote au Moyen-Age latin. Bibliographie de la littérature secondaire récente*. Vestigia 2. Paris: Éditions Universitaires-Éditions du Cerf, 1988.

———. "Medieval Latin Aristotle Commentaries." *Traditio* 28 (1972): 281–396.

Marmo, Costantino. "The Semantics of the *Modistae*." In *Medieval Analyses in Language and Cognition*, edited by Sten Ebbesen and Russell L. Friedman, 83–104. Historisk-filosofiske Meddelelser 77. Copenhagen: Royal Danish Academy of Sciences and Letters, 1996.

McDermott, A. C. S. "Notes on the Assertoric and Modal Propositional Logic of the Pseudo-Scotus." *Journal of the History of Philosophy* 10 (1972): 273–306.

Minges, P. Parthenius. *Ioannis Duns Scoti doctrina philosophica et theologica*. 2 vols. Quaracchi: 1930.

Minio-Paluello, L. "Les traductions et les commentaires Aristoteliciens de Boece." *Studia Patristica* 2 (1957): 358–65.

———. "Note sull'Aristotele latino medievale." *Rivista di filosofia neo-scolastico* 44 (1952): 398–401.

Noone, T. "Universals and Individuation." In *The Cambridge Companion to Duns Scotus*, edited by Thomas Williams, 100–128. Cambridge: Cambridge University Press, 2002.

Normore, Calvin. "Duns Scotus' Modal Theory." In *The Cambridge Companion to Duns Scotus*, edited by Thomas Williams, 129–62. Cambridge: Cambridge University Press, 2002.

———. "Petrus Aureoli and His Contemporaries on Future Contingents and Excluded Middle." *Synthese* 96 (1993): 83–92.

Nuchelmans, Gabriel. *'Secundum/Tertium Adiacens': Vicissitudes of a Logical Distinction*. Amsterdam: Royal Netherlands Academy of Arts and Sciences, 1992.

Pinborg, Jan. "Der Logik der Modistae." *Studia Mediewistyczne* 16 (1975): 39–97.

———. "The English Contribution to Logic before Ockham." *Synthese* 40 (1979): 19–42.

———. "Speculative Grammar." In *The Cambridge History of Later Medieval Philosophy: From the Rediscovery of Aristotle to the Disintegration of Scholasticism, 1100–1600*, edited by Norman Kretzmann, Anthony Kenny, and Jan Pinborg, 254–69. Cambridge, Mass.: Cambridge University Press, 1982.

Pini, Giorgio. *Categories and Logic in Duns Scotus: An Interpretation of Aristotle's Categories in the Late Thirteenth Century*. Studien und Texte zur Geistesgeschichte des Mittelalters 77. Leiden: Brill, 2002.

———. "Critical Study: Duns Scotus's Metaphysics." *Recherches de théologie et philosophie médiévale* 65 (1998): 353–68.

———. "Scotus on Assertion and the Copula: A Comparison with Aquinas." In *Medieval Theories on Assertive and Non-Assertive Language. Acts of the 14th European Symposium on Medieval Logic and Semantics, Rome, June 11–15, 2002*, edited by Alfonso Maierù and Luisa Valenti, 307–31. Rome: L. S. Olschki, 2004.

———. "Species, Concept, and Thing: Theories of Signification in the Second Half of the Thirteenth Century." *Medieval Philosophy and Theology* 8, no. 1 (1999): 21@52.

Read, Stephen. "Formal and Material Consequence, Disjunctive Syllogism and Gamma." In *Argumentationstheorie: Scholastische Forschungen zu den logischen und semantischen Regeln korrekten Folgerns*, edited by Klaus Jacobi, 233–59. Studien und Texte zur Geistesgeschichte des Mittelalters 38. Leiden: Brill, 1993.

———. "Self-reference and Validity Revisited." In *Medieval Formal Logic. Obligations, Insolubles and Consequences*, edited by Mikko Yrjönsuuri, 183–96. New Synthese Historical Library 49. Dordrecht: Kluwer, 2001.

Rijk, L. M. de. *Aristotle: Semantics and Ontology*, vol. 1. Leiden: Brill, 2002.

———. *Logica Modernorum: A Contribution to the History of Early Terminist Logic*. 2 vols. Assen: Van Gorcum, 1962 and 1967.

Rijk, L. M. de and H. A. G. Braakhuis, eds. *Logos and Pragma: Essays on the Philosophy of Language in Honour of Professor Gabriel Nuchelmans*. Artistarium Supplementa 3. Nijmegen: Ingenium, 1987.

Roest, Bert. *A History of Franciscan Education (c. 1210–1517)*. Leiden: Brill, 2000.

Rosier-Catach, Irène. "Modisme, pre-modisme, proto-modisme: vers une definition modulaire." In *Medieval Analyses in Language and Cognition*, edited by Sten Ebbesen and Russell L. Friedman, 45–81. Historisk-filosofiske Meddelelser 77. Copenhagen: Royal Danish Academy of Sciences and Letters, 1996.

———. "Roger Bacon and Grammar." In *Roger Bacon and the Sciences: Commemorative Essays*, edited by Jeremiah Hackett, 67–102. Leiden: Brill, 1997.

Sagüés-Azcona, Pius. "Apuntes para la historia del escotismo en España en el siglo XIV." In *De doctrina Ioannis Duns Scoti*, edited by Camille Berubé, Vol. 4: *Scotismus decursu saeculorum*, 3–19. Rome: Societas Internationalis Scotistica, 1968.

Sainsbury, Mark. *Reference without Referents*. Oxford: Clarendon Press, 2005.

Salmon, Nathan and Scott Soames, eds. *Propositions and Attitudes*. Oxford: Oxford University Press, 1988.

Seel, Gerhard. *Ammonius and the Seabattle: Texts, Commentary, and Essays*. Peripatoi, Bd. 18. Berlin: De Gruyter, 2000.

Smeets, Uriël. *Lineamenta Bibliographiae Scotisticae*. Rome: Commissio Scotistica, 1942.

Spade, Paul Vincent. "The Semantics of Terms." In *The Cambridge History of Later Medieval Philosophy: From the Rediscovery of Aristotle to the Disintegration of Scholasticism, 1100–1600*, edited by Norman Kretzmann, Anthony Kenny, and Jan Pinborg, 188–96. Cambridge, Mass.: Cambridge University Press, 1982.

Spruyt, Joke. "The Semantics of Complex Expressions in John Duns Scotus, Peter Abelard and John Buridan." In *Aristotle's Peri Hermeneias in the Latin Middle Ages: Essays on the Commentary Tradition*, edited by H. A. G. Braakhuis and C. H. Kneepkens, 274–303. Artistarium Supplementa 10. Groningen-Haren: Ingenium, 2003.

Tabarroni, A. "Lo Pseudo Egidio (Gugliemo Arnaldi) e un' inedita continuazione del commento di Tommaso al Peryermenias." *Medioevo* 14 (1988): 371–427.

———. "The Tenth Thesis in Logic Condemned at Oxford in 1277." In *Aristotle's Peri Hermeneias in the Latin Middle Ages: Essays on the Commentary Tradition*, edited by H. A. G. Braakhuis and C. H. Kneepkens, 339–61. Artistarium Supplementa 10. Groningen-Haren: Ingenium, 2003.

Thakkar, Mark. "Gregory of Rimini and the Logic of the Future." D.Phil. Thesis, University of Oxford, 2010.

Van Steenberghen, F. *La philosophie au XIIIe siècle*. 2e édition. Philosophes Médiévaux 28. Louvain-Paris: Éditions de l'Institut supérieur de philosophie-Éditions Peeters, 1991.

———. *Maître Siger de Brabant*. Philosophes Médiévaux 21. Louvain-Paris: Publications universitaires-Vander Oyez, 1977.

Vaux, R. de. *Notes et textes sur l'avicennisme latin aux confins des XIIe–XIIIe siècles* Bibliothèque thomiste 20. Paris: J. Vrin, 1934.

Vos, Antonie. *The Philosophy of John Duns Scotus*. Edinburgh: Edinburgh University Press, 2006.

Williams, Thomas, ed. *The Cambridge Companion to Duns Scotus*. Cambridge: Cambridge University Press, 2002.

Wippel, John F. *The Metaphysical Thought of Godfrey of Fontaines*. Washington, D.C.: The Catholic University of America Press, 1981.

Zupko, Jack. "How It Played in the *rue de Fouarre*: The Reception of Adam Wodeham's Theory of the *Complexe Significabile* in the Arts Faculty at Paris in the Mid-Fourteenth Century." *Franciscan Studies* 54 (1994–97): 211–25.

———. "Thomas of Erfurt." *The Stanford Encyclopedia of Philosophy (Spring 2011 Edition)*, edited by Edward N. Zalta. http://plato.stanford.edu/archives/spr2011/entries/erfurt/.

INDEX OF NAMES

Adam Wodeham, 8, 10, 34n39, 36n49
Albert the Great, 12, 20, 32n28, 52n103, 70n199, 83n144, 88n263, 99n11, 115n68, 115n70, 178, 179n15, 215, 264, 277, 294–95
Alcuin, 12
Ammonius Hermiae, 12, 32n28, 155n52, 160n59, 178, 296n38, 346n27, 348n28, 352
Andrews, Robert, 9n25, 286–87
Antichrist, 16–17, 31, 50, 55, 66, 69, 85n253, 92–93, 108–9, 131, 161, 177, 210–11, 225, 236–37, 242–43, 270–71, 285–86, 316, 360
Antonius Andreas, 4, 5, 10–11, 47n84, 74n216, 109n51, 110n52, 112n60, 145n12, 259–60, 283, 286–88, 291, 299–300, 310
Aquinas. *See* Thomas Aquinas
Ashworth, E. J., 7n16, 250n122
Augustine, 232, 319n71
Averroes, 20, 29n19, 39n57, 44n73, 50n93, 86n255, 90, 100, 106, 110n56, 175n7, 184–85, 187–88, 210, 225, 259, 279, 284
Avicenna, 96n3

Bäck, Alan, 8
Bland, David, 12n33
Boethius, 12, 25, 27–29, 31, 32n28, 39, 41, 52n103, 61n152, 83n144, 86n258, 97–98, 101, 105, 114, 117, 119–21, 124–25, 132, 143–44, 146, 153–54, 159–60, 169–72, 174, 177–78, 188, 199, 214, 217n83, 222, 225, 276–77, 293, 296, 298, 300, 302, 311, 320, 328, 332–33, 335, 343n26, 350–51, 358
Boethius of Dacia, 15, 84n247, 191, 214–15, 220n88, 256n126

Boniface VIII, Pope, 2
Braakhuis, H. A. G., 198nn40–41
Brampton, C. K., 4
Brentano, Franz, 173
Bychkov, Oleg, 3n5

Cajetan, Thomas 12n35
Charlemagne, 12
Costello, Elvis, 288n20
Cross, Richard, 218

Dalgaard, Karen, 294n32
Dumont, Stephen, 238n111
Durand of St. Pourçain, 174
Durandus of Auvergne, 338n11

Ebbesen, Sten, 19, 21n60, 226n91, 293n28, 294n30, 294n33

Fredborg, Karin, 175n6
Frege, Gottlob, 173

Gál, Gedeon, 8n19
Geoffrey of Aspall, 201, 321–22
Gerard of Nogent, 338n11
al-Ghazali, 206
Gilbert of Poitiers, 11, 275, 304
Gölz, B., 8n18
Grabmann, Martin, 8
Grosseteste. *See* Robert Grosseteste

Hackett, Jeremiah, 229n5
Hamesse, Jacqueline, 26n5

Heidegger, Martin, 4n7, 8
Henry of Brussels, 338n11
Henry of Ghent, 224n91, 308, 312, 317n62
Hervaeus Brito, 338
Hissette, Roland, 319n67
Hume, David, 279n4, 280

Isaac, Jean, 319n67
Isidore of Seville, 51n100

John Buridan, 15, 199, 205, 256
John de Seccheville, 318, 338–39
John le Page, 203n53, 232n98, 242n114, 337
John of Aston, 19
John of Cornwall, 8
John Styckborn, 148n27, 305, 319n69, 322n74, 342
Joseph, H. W. B., 234n105

Kant, Immanuel, 6
Klima, Gyula, 309n53
Kneale, William C. and Martha, 11
Kripke, Saul, 173

Lagerlund, Henrik, 317n62
Lambert of Lagny. See Ps.-Lambert of Auxerre
Landgraf, A. M., 197
Lewry, P. Osmund, 19n56
Little, A. G., 2n3
Locke, John, 15
Longeway, John, 293n29, 295nn34–35

Marsh, Adam, 19
Marsh, Richard, 19
Martin of Dacia, 178
Master of Abstractions (*Magister Abstractionum*). See Ricardus Sophista
McDermott, A. C. S., 8
Minges, P. Parthenius, 8n21
Minio-Paluello, L., 12n32

Naveros, Jacobus, 7
Nicholas of Paris, 200, 252n123, 262, 269, 303–4, 336
Noone, Timothy, 287n19
Normore, Calvin, 9n26, 317–18
Nuchelmans, Gabriel, 301n43

Peirce, Charles Sanders, 6
Peter Abelard, 12
Peter Aureol, 5
Peter Helias, 128n105, 304n49
Peter John Olivi, 224n91, 317n62
Peter Lombard, 2, 208
Peter of Auvergne, 235n106, 292–93nn27–28, 295, 338, 341, 346n27, 348n28
Peter of Cornwall, 65n181, 85n253, 182–83, 212n77, 217n83, 220n88, 252n123, 258, 302
Peter of Ireland, 294
Peter of Spain, 20, 58n137, 221n90, 226
Peter of St. Amour, 338n11
Philip of Bridlington, 2
Philip the Fair, king of France, 2
Pinborg, Jan, 19n58, 21n60
Pini, Giorgio, 4, 309n53
Plato, 55, 101, 143, 279, 332–33, 335
Porphyry, 4, 11, 20, 171, 184–85, 198n41
Priscian, 29, 88n261, 98, 123n92, 128n105, 131, 174–75, 263, 277, 309, 317
Ps.–Boethius of Dacia, 84n247, 85n254, 257–58
Ps.–Jordan of Saxony, 351
Ps.–Kilwardby, 263
Ps.–Lambert of Auxerre (Lambert of Lagny), 16n48, 179n15, 201n47, 203n53, 207, 229, 232n98, 235–36, 248, 261, 302
Ps.–Peter of Auvergne, 338n11

Quine, W. V. O., 236

Radulphus Brito, 99n12, 174, 188, 190–91, 199n43, 256n128, 278, 292–93nn27–28, 294n30, 295, 319, 331n1, 338n11, 342
Read, Stephen, 9
Ricardus Sophista, 20
Richard Campsall, 317n62
Richard Clive, 19, 208n69, 224n91
Richard Rufus of Cornwall, 20, 197, 208
Richard the Sophister. See Ricardus Sophista
Rijk, L. M. de, 301n43
Robert Bacon, 336–37
Robert Grosseteste, 51n100
Robert Kilwardby, 14n39, 175n6, 178, 198n41, 201n49, 232, 255, 297, 318–19, 339, 340n20, 348n28

Index of Names 379

Roger Bacon, 15, 19, 68n191, 84n247, 94n275, 175n6, 197–98, 207n63, 208–9, 228, 232n99, 236, 257, 265n141, 303n46, 337
Rosier-Catach, Irène, 19n57
Russell, Bertrand, 173, 214n80, 280

Sagüés-Azcona, Pius, 4n10
Salmon, Nathan, 13n17
Siger of Brabant, 191, 199n43, 224n91
Siger of Courtrai, 178, 338n11, 341n21
Simon of Faversham, 85n253, 100n13, 105n39, 121n89, 122n90, 123n91, 142n3, 144n9, 174, 238n111, 278, 282, 288n20, 293, 295n34, 307–8, 316, 332–33, 338n11
Smeets, Uriel, 8n21
Spade, Paul Vincent, 179n15
Spruyt, Joke, 351n29

Tabarroni, Andrea, 297n39, 336–38, 343n26
Thakkar, Mark, 321n72
Thomas Aquinas, 6, 9–10, 12, 20–21, 26nn5–6, 32n28, 43n71, 44n74, 45n80, 96n1, 96n2, 96n3, 98n8, 99n11, 103n30, 110n53, 117n74, 144n11, 169, 175n7, 176n10, 178, 179nn14–15, 201n50, 202n51, 214n80, 245, 255n124, 275, 277, 281, 284, 288–91, 294, 296n38, 309–10, 324n76, 333
Thomas of Erfurt, 4n7, 8, 175n6
Twyne, John, 19

Vincent Ferrer, 16n47
Vos, Antonie, 1n1, 1n2, 4, 5, 18n53

Walter Burley, 15, 237, 244n117, 308
William Arnauld, 121n86, 179n16, 302
William Dallying, 319n69
William of Alnwick, 3, 5
William of Bonkes, 338, 342
William of Moerbeke, 12
William of Montoriel, 319, 338
William of Ockham, 6, 12, 15, 18n52, 188, 214n80, 215, 220n89, 221, 233, 242, 250n122, 255n124, 268, 355
William of Sherwood, 19–20, 66n182, 94n274, 123n93, 198n40, 232n99, 236n109, 277, 302, 308, 309–10, 317
Williams, Thomas, 1n1
Wolter, Allan B., 2n4, 3n5, 4

Zupko, Jack, 4n7, 8n17, 8n19, 175n6

GENERAL INDEX

abstraction, 89–90, 99n11, 109, 264–65, 271, 283, 286–87
accidents, 31–33, 36, 49, 52n103, 58n137, 59–60, 65, 74, 82–83, 86n255, 88, 103, 105–6, 116, 118, 155, 161–63, 177, 180, 201, 214, 218n86, 222, 228, 263, 283, 349–55, 358, 360–62. *See also* change; fallacy; terms
actuality: vs. aptitude, 60–61, 223; complete or terminated, 48, 50, 90–91, 110, 223, 239, 266–69, 288; future, 141, 239–40, 330; joined to the subject, 141; as mode of understanding, 127, 129, 313; particularized, 108–9; of a potentiality, 161, 359–60; superficial, 160, 359; of what is present, 129, 131. *See also* being
affections of the soul. *See* concepts
alternatives (bilateral), 321, 323, 326; real, 132, 136, 139, 320–21
ampliation, 16, 200, 202, 208, 232, 236, 265n141, 302–3. *See also* restriction; supposition; *suppositum*
appellation, 66–67, 94–95, 208, 229–30, 232, 236, 272
aptitude. *See* actuality
argument from analogy, 101, 177, 179–81, 259, 282. *See also* signification
Aristotelianism, 3, 6, 9, 14, 170, 185–86, 232n102, 275, 324, 350
Aristotle's works: *Categories*, 25–26, 32, 39, 46n83, 50, 78, 96, 97, 107n44, 169, 179, 189, 210, 248, 284, 343; *De anima*, 26n5, 29, 31, 44, 61, 96, 100n13, 110n55, 175, 184, 192, 196, 274–75, 278, 284, 289; *De partibus animalium*, 106n42, 284; *De sophisticis elenchis*, 30, 58n137, 68n190, 140n148, 149, 176, 209, 233; *Metaphysics*, 30, 36, 44, 47, 50, 51n98, 53, 56, 64n171, 83, 84n251, 98, 104n35, 110n54, 111, 113n62, 135n129, 150n36, 176, 196, 201, 204, 211, 215, 230, 255, 257–58, 267n143, 289; *Physics*, 69n194, 115n69, 236, 262n137, 294; *Politics*, 43n71; *Posterior Analytics*, 30, 40, 41, 42, 51, 55, 57, 59, 73n209, 107n43, 150n36, 190, 193, 212–13, 222, 226, 243; *Prior Analytics*, 25, 54, 57, 72, 91, 113, 114n64, 115, 116, 147, 148n28, 150, 153, 169, 178, 220, 241–42, 267–68, 275, 292–93, 340, 342; *Topics*, 61, 150n36, 234, 245
assertion: mental, 26–27, 70, 169–72, 237–38, 249, 277, 311; modes of, 135, 137, 153, 325–26, 348; as proper subject of *On Interpretation*, 26–27, 97–99, 169–72, 274–75; spoken, 26–29, 33, 35, 40, 43n70, 45, 98–99, 102, 169–72, 174, 180–81, 194–95, 198, 205, 261, 276, 280; written, 28nn13–14, 33–35, 43n70, 98n5, 98n7, 103, 140, 169–72, 174, 179–81, 194–95, 261, 280–82. *See also* proposition
Augustinianism, 6

being (*ens, esse*): actuality of, 123–25, 127–28, 300, 305, 309–14; aggregate, 46, 201; cause in, 42, 193; essential (*esse essentiae*), 117–18, 224, 296; existential (*esse existere*), 60–61, 224; future, 135, 139, 243, 325; imaginary, 38, 186; in its cause, 136, 138–39, 325; modes of, 26, 129, 134, 170–71, 314; as participle vs. as name or noun, 61–62, 64, 208, 223–24, 227; *per accidens* vs. *per se*, 36, 222; predicated incidentally, 58, 68; predicated as second element, 31, 59, 61, 76,

381

being (*ens, esse*) (*cont.*)
119, 144, 191, 209, 223, 226, 247, 262n136, 300, 309–14, 333, 338, 346n27, 348; predicated as third element, 54, 60, 76, 119–20, 124, 125, 127–28, 144, 151–52, 191, 216–17, 223, 226–27, 246–47, 261–62, 300–302, 309–14, 333, 336, 338, 346, 348n28; present (*esse praesentiale*), 85n253, 129–30, 314; signifiable, 17, 117–18, 292, 296–98; true, 49, 56, 59, 111, 209, 219, 222, 290; univocity of, 3, 9, 64–67, 287n19. *See also* existence; non-being

change, 62: accidental (incidental), 86, 187, 222, 259; substantial, 13, 39, 41, 50, 62, 86, 106–10, 187–94, 210, 215, 225, 259, 283–88
completion, 154–55, 159, 358
composition: and division, 105, 110–13, 169–72, 174, 184, 209, 233–34, 274–75, 281, 288–91; formal, 164, 247; implicit, 156, 159, 358; mode of, 81–82, 92–93, 127–28, 158–59, 248, 305, 311, 314, 356; in reality, 52, 87, 105, 181, 214, 227, 261–62, 291; sense of, 67–68, 74, 137, 220–22, 233–34, 244, 246, 326; of subject and predicate, 106, 125, 145, 311–12, 334; time (actuality) of, 68, 77, 87–95, 105, 127, 130, 150, 230, 235, 239–40, 247, 260–73, 308n52; in the understanding, 16, 105, 181, 185–86, 214, 220. *See also* division; negation; terms; unity
concepts, 26, 28, 29, 30, 32n28, 36, 43–45, 78, 89, 98–106, 108, 145, 161, 194, 214, 217, 237, 249–50, 263–64, 266, 277, 279–80, 282, 285–91, 311, 313, 329, 332, 334–35, 355, 360
consignification, 84n246, 121n89, 122n90, 123n91, 141, 212n77, 235, 261–62, 269n144, 304, 308, 330
constancy: of existence, 345; of subject, 150–53, 335–39
contingency: accidental to a per se *suppositum*, 81; modes of, 50, 81, 250–53; synchronic, 3, 9, 133, 251–52, 317–18, 322, 328. *See also* proposition
contradiction, 31, 53–54, 58, 64–65, 69–71, 77–78, 114, 133–41, 148, 151, 153–55, 158–60, 163–64, 177, 215–16, 218, 225, 228, 235–36, 238, 248–49, 256, 270, 294, 306, 315, 317, 319, 323–30, 348, 351–52, 356–59, 362–63
conversion, 53, 87, 120, 151, 234, 246, 260, 299, 301

copula. *See* verb, 'is'
copulation, 94, 272, 302–3
correlatives, 39, 188–89

deception, 44, 196
demonstration, 41, 51, 55, 63, 107, 120, 124, 190, 213, 284, 311
denomination, 46, 92
determination: adverbial, 234; conflicting, 50; contracting, 69–74, 79–82, 122, 238, 241–53; and determinable, 122, 316; diminishing, 51, 60, 70, 184, 212, 226, 238, 249; pre–, 82, 253; real, 82, 253; by the word 'who [*qui*],' 157–59, 164–65, 354–58, 360, 362–64
Dialectica Monacensis (anon.; ed. de Rijk), 207, 232n98
dici de omni (being said of all), 49, 57, 63, 72–73, 79, 91, 177, 205, 220, 243, 250, 253, 268, 355n30
dictum, 133, 137, 158, 233, 254, 323, 326–27, 356
differentia, 46, 60–61, 155, 223, 352
differentia of time, 46, 66–67, 72–73, 80, 85n253, 89, 200–202, 223, 229–30, 232, 242, 252n123, 261, 262n136, 265, 304n49, 316n61
discourse, 69–70, 82, 135, 175n6, 194, 238, 275
distribution, 49, 56, 66n182, 71–82, 95, 140, 157, 165, 177, 205, 230, 232, 241–53, 260, 269n144, 316n61, 329, 354, 363–64
division, 74, 75, 76, 110, 136–37, 155, 220–22, 233–34, 244, 288–89, 319, 360. *See also* composition
Dominican Order, 6
Dubitationes et Notabilia circa Guilelmi de Shyreswode 'Introductionum logicalium Tractatum V' (anon.; Worcester Cath. Q.13), 19, 99n11, 277
Duns Scotus's works: Aristotle commentaries, 3–4; authentic, 2–5; *Categories* commentary, 26n7, 62, 209n72, 225, 263; *De sophisticis elenchis* commentary, 73n209, 108n48, 140n149, 243; *Isagoge* of Porphyry commentary, 27n11, 37, 171, 184–85; *Lectura*, 3, 5, 9, 218, 286n14, 287n19, 317; *Metaphysics* commentary, 111n58, 112, 218; *Ordinatio*, 2–3, 109n51, 179n15, 204, 218, 286n14; *Reportatio*, 2–3, 151n37, 218, 286n14; Scotus Commission, 5; Wadding-Vivès edition, 4–5

General Index 383

essence (what-something-is = *quod quid est*), 35, 38, 41, 44, 59–60, 100–101, 140, 176, 182, 196, 205, 212–13, 222–23, 279, 284, 299, 296
essentialist theory of predication, 14–16, 191
exigens-exactum, 154, 351
existence: extraneous to understanding, 48, 58, 85, 109, 222, 283, 286; extrinsic cause of, 192, 303; individuated, 14, 100, 218, 224n91; posited by proposition, 143–64, 349–64; presupposed by the verb 'is [*est*],' 54, 113–21, 152, 216–19, 292–302; in reality vs. in understanding, 13–18, 182–83, 204, 208, 221, 225, 278–79, 285, 297; 'that-something-is (*quia est*),' 213; 'whether-something-is (*si est*),' 59, 60, 73–74, 222–23. *See also* constancy

fallacy: of accident, 38, 58, 65, 187, 221; of affirming the consequent, 148; of division, 209; of exclusive premises, 333; of figure of speech, 68, 234, 245, 246, 341n22; of *quid in quale*, 75, 245, 329
first principle. *See* principle
form, 26, 31n27, 38, 48, 62, 68, 74, 75, 79, 80, 111, 115, 117, 122, 125, 130, 158, 164, 235, 242, 247, 249, 311, 315–16, 356; and matter, 29, 37n51, 56n120, 85n253, 100, 111, 116, 175, 184, 259; propositional, 328, 342n23, 353; substantial, 41, 62, 82, 107, 109, 116–17, 129, 252–53, 279, 285, 290, 295–96, 298, 336n7, 350, 358; syllogistic, 62, 65, 77, 92, 170, 215–16, 225, 270, 333
formal cause, 185
formal distinction, 238
Franciscan Order, 1–2, 5–6, 18–19
future contingents, 17, 136–37, 318–21, 324. *See also* proposition about a future contingent

grammar, 1
grammarian, 128, 175, 314, 355n30
Greyfriars, 18–19

ideas: Platonic, 55, 99n11, 101, 218n86, 279
imposition: 33, 35, 38, 42, 45, 47, 101, 104–5, 115, 117n74, 122, 173–76, 190, 192–93, 196, 201, 243, 258n133, 282, 295, 296n38, 307, 314–15, 355n30
infinite regress, 79, 177, 181–82, 250, 291

inherence: actuality of, 90–93, 268–71; of predicate in subject, 49, 164, 84n247, 217n83
intellect. *See* understanding

logic: Aristotelian, 11; medieval English, 18–21; modern philosophical, 173; modern predicate, 300, 350, 359; 'old' vs. 'new,' 11, 15, 97, 257, 275; syllogistic, 301
Logica (anon; Venice 1506), 206
Logica 'Cum sit nostra' (anon.; ed. de Rijk), 208n66, 232n98, 302–3
logician, 17, 22, 128, 173, 190, 199, 220, 308, 314

measure, 68, 70, 87, 104, 111–12, 131, 141, 183n19, 235, 239, 249, 260–62, 282, 290, 303–4, 330
Merton College, Oxford, 19
Modism, 13, 21n60, 175n6, 178, 182, 184, 235n106, 238, 262, 277–78

names. *See* terms
nature: common, 14, 47–49, 55–58, 93–95, 186, 202–6, 217–19, 221, 228, 271–72, 279, 287; conceived as a 'this' (*haec*), 55, 218–19, 221; individual, 14, 204, 228; *per se*, 56, 72; signification of, 28–38, 172–87; of the *suppositum*, 48, 54–55, 62, 89, 244n117; true, 45, 47–49, 202–6, 219
negation: and/or affirmation, 11, 65, 103, 134, 136, 143, 147, 150n36, 153n48, 154, 156–57, 160, 162, 323, 326, 333, 342, 351, 358, 363; of form, 115–16, 295n35; indefinite, 142–53, 295–96, 298, 331–50; infinitizing, 145, 147–53, 295n36, 334; perfect, 143n5; and privation, 113n62, 114, 116–18, 145, 147n23, 293–94, 295–96, 334, 336n7; predicate, 113–19, 144, 147–53, 293–98, 333, 336n5, 341–43, 346n27, 348n28, 355; propositional (sentential), 113–19, 144–53, 159, 216, 292–98, 333, 336n5, 351, 357, 359; relation to composition, 145, 159, 289, 334; remotive effect, 113–19, 133–34, 143–46, 215, 226, 292–99, 332–34; universal, 87, 260
non-being, 14, 39, 40, 42, 45–67, 68–69, 83, 85–86, 90, 92, 105–7, 108, 115, 117, 122, 135–36, 139, 144–45, 164, 173, 176n9, 189–94, 197–230, 234, 236, 241, 244, 248–49, 254–60, 266, 270, 278, 283–84, 286–87, 294–95, 297, 321, 328, 336–37, 339–41, 346, 359

non-existence. *See* non-being
noun, 25, 27–28, 56, 61–62, 83n246, 89, 97–98, 120, 144, 161, 163, 169–71, 200, 208, 218, 224n91, 265, 294, 312, 333–34, 362–63
'now' (= the present moment), 121–33, 302–17

personation (*personatio*), 127, 313
prime matter, 100, 279
principle: of excluded middle, 134, 138, 323, 328, 336, 342, 345–48; of non-contradiction (first principle), 84, 134, 150n36, 211–12, 257, 324, 346
privation, 114–18, 127, 293–94, 313, 334, 336n7. *See also* negation
predication: copulated, 94, 113–21, 292–302; definite vs. indefinite, 153, 333; denominative, 46; first mode, 48, 84n247, 160n59, 204–6, 257; future mode, 139, 140n146; incidental (*per accidens*), 14, 52, 58–59, 128, 156, 221–22, 235, 314; intentional vs. real, 38; mode of, 122, 125, 132; nature of, 126; the same thing of itself, 52–54, 68, 83, 214–17, 255–56; univocal (per se, essential), 45–48, 128, 197–230, 287n19, 314, 337n10. *See also* being; negation
presentism, 17
pronoun, 202, 218, 354, 356, 358, 363
proposition (*enuntiatio*), 11; as-of-now (*ut nunc*), 49, 72, 79–80, 206, 221, 256; assertoric (*de inesse*), 11, 49, 57, 72, 79–82, 91, 205–6, 211, 214, 219–21, 241–43, 250–51, 267–68; conditional, 130, 173, 315; about contingency (*de contingenti*), 49, 50, 62, 72, 79–80, 82, 91, 139–40, 206, 210, 225, 241–43, 250–52, 267, 328–29; about the future, 18, 131–41, 318–20, 325, 329; about a future contingent, 17, 134, 136–37, 317–30; impossible, 49, 54, 62, 63, 131, 206, 210, 216, 225, 242, 243, 248, 251–52, 256, 316; indefinite, 95, 273; modes of, 10, 126, 233–34; about necessity (*de necessario*), 50, 57, 72, 82, 210, 220–21, 225, 243–44, 251; signification of, 57, 132–33, 321; unity of, 153–65, 349–64. *See also* assertion; negation; verb, *entries on* tense

Quaestiones super logicam veterem (anon; Paris: Bib. Nat. Mazarine 3523), 224n91

quantity, 10, 72, 86, 131, 235, 259, 304, 317, 343
quiddity. *See* essence

reflection, 35–38, 101, 181–82, 184–86, 279
remainder, 90, 266
replication, 158
representation, 16, 22, 32, 43–5, 107, 176n8, 179–81, 195–96, 201, 224n91, 276, 281, 291, 302, 311, 315, 359
restriction, 16–17, 68–70, 77–79, 87–95, 122, 130, 164–65, 200, 202–3, 208, 231–40, 244, 248–49, 257, 260–73, 303, 308, 337, 339, 355. *See also* ampliation; supposition; *suppositum*

science (*scientia*), 6, 26–27, 170–71, 275
sea-battle example of Aristotle, 7, 17–18, 132, 235, 247, 262–63, 270–71, 319–21
significate: immediate, 32, 38, 102, 108, 110, 178–79, 186, 281; loss of, 192, 208; per se (primary), 34, 47, 51, 99–100, 104, 106–7, 116, 122, 180–81, 237, 280–88; proper, 41, 143; ultimate, 33–35, 179n15, 180–81, 186, 280–82. *See also* signification; *suppositum*
signification (meaning): analogical, 101, 104, 345, 362; change in, 39–42; conventional, 35, 45, 70n199, 88n263, 105, 194–95, 198; equivocal, 9, 32–33, 47, 51n81, 58, 101, 103, 104, 106, 108, 109, 179–80, 201–2, 227, 243, 245, 284, 286, 337; hypothetical, 164; modes of, 119, 122–28, 135, 142, 145, 161, 175, 243, 245, 299–300, 305–6, 309–14, 325–26, 329, 332, 334; of names, 13, 25, 28–43, 98–110, 172–94, 208, 226, 274–88, 276–83; presupposes understanding, 37, 186, 192–93, 217; vs. representation, 196; transitivity of, 179, 281; univocal, 47–49, 106–10, 202–6, 227, 229, 283–88. *See also* significate
singulars, 38, 51n81, 99n11, 186, 213. *See also suppositum*
sophisma (anon; Caius 611/341), 65n181, 183n19, 188
sophismata, 7, 14n38, 231
sophismata (anon. [multiple]; Paris: Bib. Nat. Lat. 16135), 176nn8–9, 188–89, 192, 200n44, 202nn51–52, 203n53, 205–6, 207, 210n73, 211, 224n91, 231n97, 232, 236nn108–9, 242,

General Index   385

248n121, 252n123, 255n125, 258n133, 261, 265, 304, 308n52, 314–16, 339, 340n20
species: intelligible, 28–38, 40, 42, 98–106, 172–87, 276–83; visible (intention), 31, 100, 280
speech: abuse of, 61n152; figure of, 68, 75, 139, 140, 234, 245, 246, 341n22; genus of assertion, 26; parts of, 29, 98n7, 98n9, 120, 175; power of (*virtus sermonis*), 122; purpose of, 88, 89, 249, 261, 263–64; significant, 169, 171. *See also* fallacy
statement. *See* proposition
substance: relative of, 157–58, 355–56; secondary, 50; as significate, 32–33
subsumption, 91
Summa Metenses (anon.; ed. de Rijk), 207
supposition (*suppositio*): accidental, 15–16, 252n123; of a common term, 45–49, 52–82, 87–95, 197–206, 213–53, 260–73; natural, 14–17, 200, 203, 241–53, 248, 252; personal, 94, 237, 272–73; simple, 237; theory of, 15. *See also* ampliation; restriction
suppositum (pl. *supposita*), 31, 35, 41, 45–49, 50, 54–57, 62, 65–67, 69, 72–75, 192, 202–6; accidental, 16, 82, 242, 252–53; contingent, 82, 253; distinct from subject, 74–75, 244; future, 70–82, 238–53, 263, 268; non-existing, 45–67, 197–253; past, 70–82, 237–53; per se, 241–53; present, 67–82, 89, 121–31, 202–3, 210, 231–53, 261–73, 302–17, 339; of time, 46, 75, 77, 78, 79–80, 200. *See also* singulars
syllogism: art of, 98, 275; first figure, 114, 120, 143, 220, 301, 355n30; not made from composite proposition, 157, 165, 354, 363; from opposites, 53–54, 62–63, 83, 86, 215–16, 225–26, 256, 259; perfect, 31, 35, 82, 177, 181, 253; second figure, 63n163, 216; subject of *Prior Analytics*, 170, 275

terms: accidental, 116–17, 236, 295–96; common, 45–49, 55, 67–82, 87–95, 129, 192 197–206, 231–53, 260–73; concrete, 74, 118, 162; definite (finite), 147–53, 335–48; empty, 7, 13, 173, 197–230; indefinite (infinite), 113–19, 145, 147–53, 292–98, 335–48; middle, 31, 35, 38, 50; relational, 147, 149, 343; substantial,

97, 115–16, 142–46, 236, 295–96; syncategorematic, 97, 170, 260. *See also* distribution; negation, and privation; signification, equivocal
'thisness' (*haecceitas*), 3
'tomorrow' (= future time), 17, 85, 122, 131–33, 138, 259, 308, 316, 322
topic: 'from the greater' (*a maiori*), 59; 'from the superior to the inferior in negating,' 61
topic (*locus*), 59, 61, 199
Tower of Babel, 194–95
Tractatus de Univocatione Monacensis (anon.; ed. de Rijk), 229
Triduum, 197
truth: causes of, 17–18, 148, 183, 215, 318, 325–28, 338, 341–42, 349; conditions, 54, 57, 63–64, 83–87, 104, 111, 132–33, 135, 174, 180–82, 186, 212, 216, 220, 226–27, 254–60, 271, 281–82, 284, 324–27, 338; determinate, 131–41, 317–30; and falsity, 33–34, 104, 110–13, 131–41, 288–91, 317–30; indeterminate, 136–41, 325–26, 328, 330; theories of, 14–15. *See also* measure

understanding: composition/division in, 11, 16, 29, 34–36, 64, 96–99, 110–13, 274–75; does not depend on existence of things, 63, 89, 100, 172–94, 226, 283–88; essential, 125, 311; vs. imagination, 38; implicit, 157, 161, 164; modes of, 77, 81, 122, 161, 163–64, 210, 216, 225, 355n30; operations of, 11, 25–27, 63, 96–97, 274–75, 279, 290; primary, 21, 99, 101–2, 105, 122, 184, 193, 277, 280; reflection of, 35–36, 37, 101, 181–82; simple, 29, 36, 110–13, 158, 291; *sine qua non* of signifying, 37, 39, 42, 185–86, 189, 192–93, 263
unity: absolute, 159; criteria of, 159–60, 358; less-than-numerical, 3; metaphysical, 184; of name and quality, 157, 354–55; of a science (*scientia*), 170–71; of the subject of distribution, 157, 165, 354, 363. *See also* proposition; distribution
univocity: of being, 3, 9, 64–65; of cause, 37, 185; of common terms, 45–49, 72, 197–206
utterance: complex vs. incomplex, 25, 97; and inscription, 35, 43–45, 103–4, 194–96;

utterance (*cont.*)
  naturally formed by throat and lungs, 45, 196; as *suppositum*, 48; unspoken, 28, 169–72. *See also* signification, of names

verb: composition of, 118, 125–31, 144–46; content of (*res*), 54, 68, 76, 118, 119, 120, 125–31, 144–46, 309–11, 333; future tense, 17, 70–71, 131–41, 149, 238–40, 317–30; indefinite, 142–46, 331–35; 'is,' 31, 34, 46, 54, 56, 59n139, 64, 66–67, 73–75, 93, 107, 114, 118–20, 147, 152, 158, 163–64, 177, 199, 204, 216–17, 219, 220n88, 224n91, 228–30, 231–38, 246, 293, 298, 299–317, 321, 329–30, 335–36, 340, 341n22, 346n27, 348n28; measure of composition, 262; past tense, 70–71, 149, 210, 238–43, 344; present tense, 17, 67, 69, 71–72, 88, 90, 121–31, 149, 210, 231–43, 302–18; significate of, 122, 303. *See also* existence

verification, 47–48, 84n247, 101, 130–31, 153, 203, 234, 280, 294n30, 305, 315–16, 355

will: autonomy of, 6

'yesterday' (= past time), 75, 245

Duns Scotus on Time & Existence was designed in Arno and composed by Kachergis Book Design of Pittsboro, North Carolina. It was printed on 50-pound Nature's Book Natural and bound by Thomson-Shore of Dexter, Michigan.

www.ingramcontent.com/pod-product-compliance
Lightning Source LLC
Chambersburg PA
CBHW020313010526
44107CB00054B/1826